Photoshop®
Elements 2022

by Barbara Obermeier
and Ted Padova

for

dummies®
A Wiley Brand

Photoshop® Elements 2022 For Dummies®

Published by: **John Wiley & Sons, Inc.,** 111 River Street, Hoboken, NJ 07030-5774, www.wiley.com

Copyright © 2022 by John Wiley & Sons, Inc., Hoboken, New Jersey

Published simultaneously in Canada

For general information on our other products and services, please contact our Customer Care Department within the U.S. at 877-762-2974, outside the U.S. at 317-572-3993, or fax 317-572-4002. For technical support, please visit https://hub.wiley.com/community/support/dummies.

Wiley publishes in a variety of print and electronic formats and by print-on-demand. Some material included with standard print versions of this book may not be included in e-books or in print-on-demand. If this book refers to media such as a CD or DVD that is not included in the version you purchased, you may download this material at http://booksupport.wiley.com. For more information about Wiley products, visit www.wiley.com.

Library of Congress Control Number: 2021947192

ISBN: 978-1-119-83721-3

ISBN 978-1-119-83723-7 (ebk); ISBN 978-1-119-83722-0 (ebk)

SKY10029802_101421

Table of Contents

INTRODUCTION 1

About This Book. 1

Icons Used in This Book 2

Beyond the Book 3

Where to Go from Here 3

**PART 1: GETTING STARTED WITH PHOTOSHOP
ELEMENTS 2022** 5

CHAPTER 1: **Getting Started with Image Editing** 7

Getting Familiar with the Home Screen 7

Launching the Photo Editor 9

Making Basic Edits in Quick Mode 10

Sharing a Photo 12

Retracing Your Steps. 14

Using the History panel 14

Reverting to the last save 15

Getting a Helping Hand 16

Saving Files with Purpose. 17

Using the Save/Save As dialog box 17

Saving files for the web. 19

CHAPTER 2: **Basic Image-Editing Concepts** 21

Grappling with the Ubiquitous Pixels. 22

Understanding resolution 22

Understanding image dimensions 25

The Art of Resampling 25

Choosing a Resolution for Print or Onscreen 28

Working with File Formats 29

JPEG (*.jpg, *.jpeg, *.jpe). 29

PNG (*.png). 30

TIFF (*.tif, *.tiff). 30

Getting Familiar with Color 31

Getting Color Right 33

Color the easy way 33

Calibrating your monitor 33

Choosing a color workspace 34

Understanding how profiles work 35

CHAPTER 3: **Exploring the Photo Editor** 37

Examining the Photo Editor 37
    Examining the image window 41
    Uncovering the contextual menus 45
    Selecting the tools 45
    Selecting from the Tool Options 48
    Playing with panels 48
Using the Photo Bin 51
    Creating different views of an image 51
    Viewing filenames 52
    Using Photo Bin Actions 52
Using Some Creative Features 52
    Using Guided Edits 53
    Moving Objects and Moving Photos 54
Controlling the Editing Environment 55
    Launching and navigating Preferences 55
    Checking out all the Preferences panes 57
    Perusing preset libraries 59

PART 2: MANAGING MEDIA 61

CHAPTER 4: **Navigating the Organizer** 63

Organizing Photos and Media on a Hard Drive 64
Adding Images to the Organizer 66
    Adding files from folders and removable media 66
    Downloading camera images with the Elements Downloader 68
    Importing additional photos from folders 70
Navigating the Media Browser 71
Using a Scanner 73
    Understanding image requirements 73
    Using scanner plug-ins (Windows) 74
    Scanning on the Mac 75
    Scanning many photos at a time 76
Phoning in Your Images 77
Setting Organizer Preferences 79

CHAPTER 5: **Organizing Your Pictures** 81

Touring the Organizer 81
Organizing Groups of Images with Tags 84
    Creating and viewing a tag 85
    Adding icons to tags 87
    Working with custom tags 88
    Working with default tags 89
    Working with sub-categories 90
    Sorting photos according to tags 91

Auto Generating Tags 91
    Working with Auto Creations. 91
    Adding new Events 92
Rating Images with Stars 93
Adding Images to an Album. 94
    Creating an album. 94
    Using albums for temporary work 96
    Editing an album 96
    Finding out more about sharing your albums 97
Adding People in the Media Browser. 97
Placing Pictures on Maps 99
Working with Events 101

CHAPTER 6: **Viewing and Finding Your Images** 103
Cataloging Files 103
    Using the Catalog Manager 104
    Working with catalogs. 105
    Backing up your catalog 106
    Backing up photos and files. 107
Switching to a Different View. 108
Viewing Photos in Memories (Slideshow) 109
Searching for Photos. 111
    Using Search. 111
    Searching for untagged items 113
    Searching captions and notes 113
    Searching by history 114
    Searching metadata 114
    Searching similarities 116
Grouping Files That Get in the Way 117
    Marking files as hidden. 117
    Stackin' 'em up 118
    Creating versions. 119

PART 3: SELECTING AND CORRECTING PHOTOS 121

CHAPTER 7: **Editing Camera Raw Images** 123
Launching the Camera Raw Editor 124
Understanding Camera Raw 125
    Learning Raw file format attributes .126
    Opening images in the Camera Raw Editor. 127
Getting Familiar with the Raw Editor 128
Getting Familiar with the Panels. 132
    Using the Basic panel 132
    Sharpening and reducing noise. 135
    Using the Calibration panel 138

Working with Filmstrips 138
Working with Profiles 140
    Looking at the Adobe Camera Raw profiles 140
    Managing profiles 141
    Creating a Favorites list 142
Opening Non-Raw Images in the Camera Raw Editor 143
Changing Image Defaults 143
Working with XML Files and Preferences 144
    Changing program defaults 144
    Using Save Options 146
    Using sidecar files 146

CHAPTER 8: **Making and Modifying Selections** .149
Defining Selections 149
Creating Rectangular and Elliptical Selections 150
    Perfecting squares and circles with Shift and Alt
    (Option on the Mac) 151
    Applying Marquee options 152
Making Freeform Selections with the Lasso Tools 154
    Selecting with the Lasso tool 155
    Getting straight with the Polygonal Lasso tool 157
    Snapping with the Magnetic Lasso tool 157
Working Wizardry with the Magic Wand 160
    Talking about Tolerance 161
    Wielding the Wand to select 161
Modifying Your Selections 164
    Adding to, subtracting from, and intersecting a selection 164
    Avoiding key collisions 165
Painting with the Selection Brush 165
Painting with the Quick Selection Tool 167
Selecting with the Auto Selection Tool 169
Selecting Your Subject 171
Fine-Tuning with the Refine Selection Brush 172
Working with the Cookie Cutter Tool 174
Eliminating with the Eraser Tools 176
    The Eraser tool 176
    The Background Eraser tool 177
    The Magic Eraser tool 179
Using the Select Menu 179
    Selecting all or nothing 179
    Reselecting a selection 180
    Inversing a selection 180
    Feathering a selection 180
    Refining the edges of a selection 181

Using the Modify commands. 182
Applying the Grow and Similar commands. 183
Saving and loading selections 183

CHAPTER 9: **Working with Layers** 185
Getting to Know Layers. 185
Converting a background to a layer 186
Anatomy of the Layers panel. 187
Using the Layer and Select menus 190
Working with Different Layer Types 192
Image layers. 192
Adjustment layers 193
Fill layers. 195
Shape layers. 196
Type layers 197
Tackling Layer Basics. 197
Creating a new layer from scratch 198
Using Layer via Copy and Layer via Cut .199
Duplicating layers 199
Dragging and dropping layers. 200
Using the Paste into Selection command 201
Moving a Layer's Content. 202
Transforming Layers. 203
Adding Layer Masks 204
Flattening and Merging Layers 206
Flattening layers. 206
Merging layers 207

CHAPTER 10: **Simple Image Makeovers** 209
Cropping and Straightening Images. 209
Cutting away with the Crop tool 210
Fixing distortion with the Perspective Crop tool. 212
Cropping with a selection border 214
Straightening images 214
Recomposing Images 215
Employing One-Step Auto Fixes 218
Auto Smart Fix 218
Auto Smart Tone 218
Auto Levels 220
Auto Contrast. 221
Auto Haze Removal. 221
Auto Color Correction. 221
Auto Shake Reduction. 222
Auto Sharpen 223
Auto Red Eye Fix 223

Editing in Quick Mode. 225
Fixing Small Imperfections with Tools 229
    Cloning with the Clone Stamp tool 229
    Retouching with the Healing Brush 231
    Zeroing in with the Spot Healing Brush .234
    Repositioning with the Content-Aware Move tool 236
    Lightening and darkening with Dodge and Burn tools 238
    Smudging away rough spots 239
    Softening with the Blur tool 241
    Focusing with the Sharpen tool. 242
    Sponging color on and off 243
    Replacing one color with another 244

CHAPTER 11: **Correcting Contrast, Color, and Clarity** 247
Editing Your Photos Using a Logical Workflow 248
Adjusting Lighting 249
    Fixing lighting with Shadows/Highlights. 249
    Using Brightness/Contrast. 250
    Pinpointing proper contrast with Levels 251
Adjusting Color 254
    Removing color casts automatically 254
    Adjusting with Hue/Saturation 255
    Eliminating color with Remove Color 257
    Switching colors with Replace Color 258
    Correcting with Color Curves. 259
    Adjusting skin tones 261
    Defringing layers 263
    Eliminating haze. 264
    Adjusting color temperature with photo filters 265
    Mapping your colors 266
Adjusting Clarity. 267
    Removing noise, artifacts, dust, and scratches. 268
    Blurring when you need to. 269
    Sharpening for better focus. 272
    Opening closed eyes. 275
    Colorizing a photo 276
    Smoothing skin 277
    Adjusting facial features. 278
    Reducing shake 279
    Moving Overlays 281
    Moving Photos. 282
Working Intelligently with the Smart Brush Tools 283

PART 4: EXPLORING YOUR INNER ARTIST.................287

CHAPTER 12: **Playing with Filters, Effects, Styles, and More**.....289

   Having Fun with Filters 289
      Applying filters...290
      Corrective or destructive filters...........................291
      One-step or multistep filters 291
      Fading a filter 292
      Selectively applying a filter...............................292
      Working in the Filter Gallery 293
      Distorting with the Liquify filter..........................295
   Correcting Camera Distortion 297
   Exploring Elements' Unique Filters 298
      Creating a comic 299
      Getting graphic 300
      Using the Pen and Ink filter 301
   Dressing Up with Photo and Text Effects......................302
   Adding Shadows, Glows, and More 305
      Applying styles..305
      Working with styles....................................307
      Using the Graphics panel................................308
   Mixing It Up with Blend Modes 309
      General blend modes....................................309
      Darken blend modes....................................310
      Lighten blend modes 310
      Lighting blend modes...................................312
      Inverter blend modes...................................313
      HSL blend modes.......................................315
   Using Photomerge...316
      Photomerge Panorama 316
      Photomerge Group Shot 319
      Photomerge Scene Cleaner 320
      Photomerge Exposure 322
      Photomerge Compose 324

CHAPTER 13: **Drawing and Painting**...............................327

   Choosing Color..327
      Working with the Color Picker............................328
      Dipping into the Color Swatches panel 329
      Sampling with the Eyedropper tool 331

Getting Artsy with the Pencil and Brush Tools 332
    Drawing with the Pencil tool 332
    Painting with the Brush tool 334
    Using the Impressionist Brush 336
    Creating your own brush 337
Filling and Outlining Selections 339
    Fill 'er up 339
    Outlining with the Stroke command. 341
Splashing on Color with the Paint Bucket Tool 342
Working with Multicolored Gradients 343
    Applying a preset gradient. 343
    Customizing gradients 345
Working with Patterns 348
    Applying a preset pattern. 348
    Creating a new pattern. 349
Creating Shapes of All Sorts. 349
    Drawing a shape 350
    Drawing multiple shapes 352
    Specifying Geometry options. 352
    Editing shapes 354

CHAPTER 14: **Working with Type** 355
Understanding Type Basics 355
    Tools 356
    Modes 357
    Formats. 357
Creating Point Type. 358
Creating Paragraph Type 359
Creating Path Type 360
    Using the Text On Selection tool. 360
    Using the Text On Shape tool 362
    Using the Text On Custom Path tool 363
Specifying Type Options. 364
Editing Text. 366
Simplifying Type. 367
Masking with Type. 368
Stylizing and Warping Type 371
    Adjusting type opacity. 371
    Applying filters to your type. 372
    Painting your type with color and gradients 373
    Warping your type. 374

PART 5: PRINTING, CREATING, AND SHARING 377

CHAPTER 15: **Getting It on Paper** 379

    Getting Pictures Ready for Printing. 380

    Working with Color Printer Profiles 381

        Printing a photo with the printer managing color 383

        Printing a photo with Elements managing color. 385

        Printing a picture package or contact sheet 386

    Getting Familiar with the Print Dialog Box. .386

        Using the Prints options. 386

        Creating transfers, borders, and more with More Options. 388

    Outsourcing Printing. 389

CHAPTER 16: **Sharing Your Work** 391

    Getting Familiar with the Elements Sharing Options. 391

        Planning ahead 392

        Understanding photo sharing in Elements 393

    Using the Share Panel. 394

        Emailing photos. 395

        Working with Adobe Premiere Elements. 397

        Sharing your photos on social networks 397

CHAPTER 17: **Making Creations** 401

    Checking Out the Create Panel 401

    Grasping Creation-Assembly Basics 402

    Creating a Quote Graphic. 406

    Creating a Memories Video 408

    Creating a PDF Slideshow. 409

    Making Additional Creations 410

PART 6: THE PART OF TENS. 411

CHAPTER 18: **The Ten Best Guided Edits** 413

    Correct Skin Tone 413

    Sharpen. 415

    Object Removal 416

    Perfect Portrait. 418

    Replace Background 421

    Remove a Color Cast. 423

    Levels. 424

    Resize Your Photo 426

    Recompose. 428

    Move & Scale Object 430

CHAPTER 19: **Ten (or So) More Project Ideas** 433

    Screen Savers. 433
    Flyers, Ads, and Online Auctions 434
    Clothes, Hats, and More 436
    Posters 437
    Household and Business Inventories 437
    Project Documentation. 438
    School Reports and Projects 438
    Blogs 438
    Wait — There's More. 438

INDEX 439

Introduction

We are now in version 20 (Photoshop Elements 2022) of Photoshop Elements. Time to celebrate Elements' 20th anniversary. As with previous updates, this version has some fascinating additions as well as performance improvements.

About This Book

This book is an effort to provide as much of a comprehensive view of a wildly feature-rich program as we can. Additionally, this book is written for a cross-platform audience. If you're a Mac user, you'll find all you need to work in Elements 2022 for the Mac, exactly the same as when we refer to using Elements on Windows.

In Photoshop Elements 2022, you won't find a huge number of new features. However, some of the new features that are added can wow you. Of particular interest to us is the addition of two menu commands in the Enhance menu. There you find Moving Objects and Moving Photos. These commands add some animation to your photos, and you can save the result either as an animated GIF image or a movie file. This is truly a spectacular addition to help you provide some content to your social media accounts. You find an introduction to the commands in Chapter 3 and an expanded explanation in Chapter 11.

We also see a wonderful addition that has long been requested by users. The Warp tool is a new feature in this release. When transforming objects you can now warp the images in a variety of ways.

When it comes to effects, Elements has a new feature labeled Artistic Effects. You'll find a number of different effects as stylized presets that you can transfer to images on your photos. We've long featured "Exploring Your Inner Artist" as a chapter in this book, and the new feature just adds more capability for you to express your artsy side.

Adobe has also provided support for exporting video in the MP4 file format. MP4 is better quality than animated GIF, plus it results in smaller file sizes.

If you're an Adobe Premier Elements user, there are also several new features added to Premiere Elements. For information on those additions, see the help files for Premiere Elements.

Throughout this book, especially in step lists, we point you to menus for keyboard commands. For accessing a menu command, you may see something like this:

Choose File ⇨ Get Photos ⇨ From Files and Folders.

In this case, this means to click the File menu to open its drop-down menu, click the menu command labeled Get Photos, and then choose the command From Files and Folders from the submenu that appears. It's that simple.

We also refer to *context menus,* which jump up at your cursor position and show you a menu of options related to whatever you're doing at the time. To open a context menu, just right-click the mouse, or Control-click on a Mac if you don't have a two-button mouse.

When we mention that keys need to be pressed on your keyboard, the text looks like this:

Press Alt+Shift+Ctrl+S (Option+Shift+⌘ +S on the Mac).

In this case, you hold down the Alt key on Windows or the Option key on the Mac, then the Shift key, then the Control key on Windows or the ⌘ key on the Mac, and then press the S key. Then, release all the keys at the same time.

Icons Used in This Book

In the margins throughout this book, you see icons indicating that something is important.

NEW

This icon informs you that this item is a new feature in Photoshop Elements 2022.

WARNING

Pay particular attention when you see the Warning icon. This icon indicates possible side-effects or damage to your image that you might encounter when performing certain operations in Elements.

REMEMBER

This icon is a heads-up for something you may want to commit to memory. Usually, it tells you about a shortcut for a repetitive task that can save you time.

TIP

A Tip tells you about an alternative method for a procedure, giving you a shortcut, a work-around, or some other type of helpful information.

TECHNICAL STUFF

Elements is a computer program, after all. No matter how hard we try to simplify our explanation of features, we can't entirely avoid some technical information. If a topic is a little on the technical side, we use this icon to alert you that we're moving into a complex subject. You won't see many of these icons in the book because we try our best to give you the details in nontechnical terms.

Beyond the Book

In addition to what you're reading right now, this product also comes with a free, online Cheat Sheet that includes a detailed look at the Elements photo-editing workspace, Tool Panel shortcuts, tricks for selecting objects, and more. To get this Cheat Sheet, simply go to www.dummies.com and type **Photoshop Elements 2022 For Dummies Cheat Sheet** in the Search box.

Where to Go from Here

Try to spend a little time reading through the chapters in Part 1. After you know how to edit and save photos, feel free to jump around and pay special attention to the cross-referenced chapters, in case you get stuck on a concept. After exploring the Elements Photo Editor, look over Part 2, where we talk about organizing and searching photos. When it comes to editing photos, look over Chapter 7 carefully. Everything begins with adjusting photos for brightness, contrast, and color. In Chapter 7, you learn that using the Camera Raw Editor is your first stop when editing a photo for any kind of output. If you're ready to jump into more advanced tasks, check out Parts 3 and 4, where you learn how to make selections; layer images and effects together; add filters and type; and much, much more.

We hope you have much success and enjoyment in using Adobe Photoshop Elements 2022, and it's our sincere wish that the pages ahead provide you with an informative and helpful view of the program.

1

Getting Started with Photoshop Elements 2022

Open the Photo Editor and make quick and easy edits to one of your photos in Quick mode.

Select the best file format when you save your image.

Tour the Photo Editor interface so that you know how to switch among images and navigate the many panels and options.

IN THIS CHAPTER

» **Opening the Home screen**

» **Starting the Photo Editor**

» **Opening, editing, sharing, and saving a photo**

» **Using Undo History**

» **Finding help**

» **Saving your files**

Chapter **1**

Getting Started with Image Editing

I mage editing is incredibly fun, especially with a tool like Photoshop Elements, which enables you to modify, combine, and even draw your own images to your imagination's content. To get the most out of Elements, you need to understand some basic technical concepts, but like most people, you probably want to jump in, play around, and basically just get started right away.

You're in luck: In Quick mode, Elements helps you make basic edits to your photos, like revealing your child's face darkened by a baseball cap's shadow or cropping out the gigantic trash can on the left edge of your otherwise perfect landscape shot. In this chapter, we help you jump-start your image-editing skills by guiding you through Quick mode and how to share photos online, retrace your steps, save your edits, and more.

Getting Familiar with the Home Screen

After installing Elements, launch the Elements application, and you arrive at the Home screen (or Hub, as Adobe calls it), shown in Figure 1-1.

FIGURE 1-1:
The Photoshop
Elements Home
screen.

NEW

From the Home screen, you have the following options:

>> **Search (What would you like to do today?):** At the top of the window, you can search for a task and have help returned to you (see the text at the top of the window where it reads: "What would you like to do today?").

>> **Instagram, Facebook, Twitter, and Help:** At the top right, click one of the three respective buttons to share files on Instagram, Facebook, and Twitter. Click the fourth icon to get some help using Elements. Clicking Help takes you to a web link.

>> **Try This/What's New/Guided Edits/Make Creations:** The individual cards appearing at the top of the Home screen offer options for trying different tasks, exploring features, performing a Guided Edit (Guided Edit is a step-by-step set of instructions to perform an edit), and a quick launch to make a new creation. When you mouse over a card, a link is shown where you perform the task in question.

>> **Application Launcher:** Click one of the three icons to launch the Elements Photo Editor, the Organizer, or Video Editor (Adobe Premier Elements must be installed to launch this item).

>> **Recent Files:** Click an image in the Recent Files list, and the file opens in the Photo Editor.

Launching the Photo Editor

Photoshop Elements has two separate components:

>> **The Organizer** is where you manage photos. It's full of tools for tagging, rating, sorting, and finding your images. Part 2 of this book helps you start using the Organizer.

>> **The Photo Editor** is where you correct photos for brightness and color, add effects, repair images, and so on.

In this chapter, you work in the Photo Editor to make basic edits to a photo.

Here's how to start Elements and open the Photo Editor:

1. **Double-click the Photoshop Elements shortcut on your desktop or in your Applications folder (Mac) to launch the Home screen.**

2. **Click the Photo Editor button shown in the Home screen (refer to Figure 1-1).**

   The Photo Editor workspace loads and appears, as shown in Figure 1-2. By default, you see the Quick tab selected at the top of the Photo Editor workspace, which means you're in Quick mode (or right where you want to be for the purposes of this chapter). Quick mode offers a limited number of tools for adjusting brightness, contrast, color, and sharpness.

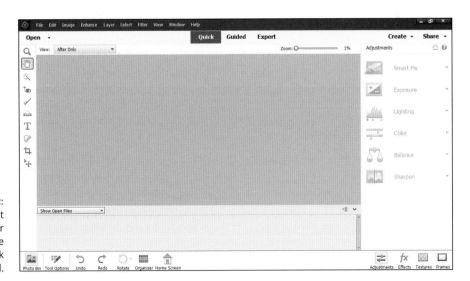

FIGURE 1-2:
The default Photo Editor workspace with the Quick tab selected.

On the right side of the workspace, you see the Adjustments panel docked in an area dubbed the Panel Bin. When in any one of the three editing modes (Quick, Guided, Expert), you find different panels, always on the right side of the window. On the left side of the workspace, you see a Tools panel. Interacting with the items in the Panel Bin and using tools in the Tools panel provide you with an enormous number of options for editing, improving, and stylizing your pictures.

Making Basic Edits in Quick Mode

For beginning users, the Quick mode in the Photo Editor is both powerful and easy to use. Follow these steps to make some simple changes to an image:

1. **Open the Photo Editor and make sure the Quick tab is selected at the top.**

2. **Choose File ⇨ Open or click the Open button at the top left of the Photo Editor.**

   If Elements is your default editing application, you can also double-click your photo file in Windows Explorer or the Mac Finder, and the file opens in Elements.

3. **In the Open dialog box that appears, navigate your hard drive to locate the file you want to open, select the file, and click Open.**

4. **From the View drop-down list (in the upper left of the image window), choose Before & After – Horizontal, as shown in Figure 1-3.**

5. **Make edits to your photo.**

   Here's an introduction to two simple edits you can make in Quick mode:

   - **Apply a Smart Fix:** Click Smart Fix in the Panel Bin to see the options. To begin with, click Auto at the bottom of the Smart Fix panel. At the top left of the window, you find options for viewing by opening the drop-down menu. Choose After Only or choose Before & After (Horizontal or Vertical) to see before and after views.

     Several items are listed in the Panel Bin below the Smart Fix option. Click an item to expand it, and move the sliders or click the thumbnail images to tweak the overall brightness, contrast, and color. In many cases, there isn't a right or wrong adjustment. Play with the options to bring it close to your overall vision for the picture. For a more in-depth look at correcting photos in Quick mode, flip to Chapter 10.

FIGURE 1-3:
The before and
after views in
Quick mode.

TIP

Each of the Quick Fix options provides you with thumbnail previews showing you the result of a given edit. For a quick preview of an editing task, mouse over a Smart Fix thumbnail to see what the edit will look like when it is applied.

- **Crop the photo:** In the Tools panel on the left side of the window, click the Crop tool. You immediately see a rectangle on top of the photo. Drag the sides to crop the image to your liking. When finished, click the green check mark, as shown in Figure 1-4, to accept your edit.

REMEMBER

When making any one of a huge number of edits to your pictures, you often see icons on top of the image, similar to what's shown in Figure 1-4. The green check mark accepts the edit you're making at the time the icons appear. The circle with a diagonal line is the Cancel button. Click this button when you don't want to apply the recent edit.

TIP

At the bottom of the Editor window, you see some hints that Elements gives you for crop suggestions. Click one of the options to employ the respective crop.

6. **Choose File ⇨ Save As and, in the Save As dialog box that opens, provide a new name for the photo. Click Save.**

   Note: When you use Save As and give your image a new name, you don't destroy your original image. You save a copy of the original with the new edits applied. For more on saving files, see the section "Saving Files with Purpose," later in this chapter.

Sharing a Photo

After you edit your photo, you can print the photo to share with family and friends or post the photo on a social network site.

In earlier versions of Elements, you could upload directly from within Facebook. In more recent versions, you need to edit the file, save it, and then open your Facebook account to upload the file. Here's how to do it:

1. **Prepare the photo you want to upload to Facebook.**

   Typically, digital cameras take photos sized very large — too large for an image that your friends and family will want to download quickly and view via Facebook on a computer screen or mobile device. To adjust your image so that it's the right size and resolution for viewing online, follow these steps:

   (a) **Choose Image ⇨ Resize ⇨ Image Size.**

   (b) **In the Image Size dialog box that appears, enter your desired width (or height).**

Either Width or Height is fine because the image will maintain correct proportions by choosing either. A width of 720 pixels, 960 pixels, or 2,048 pixels works well.

REMEMBER

Facebook recommends that supported sizes for regular photos are widths of 720 pixels, 960 pixels, and 2,048 pixels, with file sizes no more than 100KB — especially if you have text in the cover photo. When you save as JPEG, the files are compressed, and you'll find the larger size to be within Facebook recommendations. However, you don't have to be too concerned about staying within Facebook recommendations. You can upload images much larger than 100KB, but the uploads and screen refreshes will take longer. Just be certain to stay within 100 KB if you have text on a cover photo.

(c) **Select the Resample Image check box if for some reason the box is not selected.**

(d) **Type either** 72 **or** 144 **in the Resolution box.**

For screen viewing only, 72 ppi is fine. However, if you want your friends to print the image, 144 is a better choice. You can use either resolution. Be sure the file size is no larger than 100KB.

The image is sized to a workable size for Facebook. Click OK when finished editing in the Image Size dialog box.

2. **Choose File ⇨ Save As ⇨ JPEG to save the file as a JPEG.**

Note the location where you save the file on your hard drive. (JPEG is one of many file formats that Elements supports.)

3. **Log in to your Facebook account.**

4. **Click Photo/Video.**

Locate the saved file and upload it to Facebook.

Your photo is added to your Facebook account, as shown in Figure 1-5.

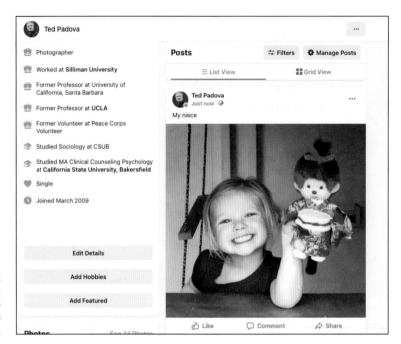

FIGURE 1-5:
An edited
photo
uploaded to
Facebook.

Retracing Your Steps

In Elements, Undo is a favorite command for both beginners and experienced users alike. If you don't like a change to your image, you simply choose Edit ⇨ Undo or press the keyboard shortcut Ctrl+Z (⌘ +Z on the Mac).

Because the process of trial and error (and thus the ability to undo your work) is so important to making your image look just right, Elements also offers ways to undo that are much more sophisticated than simply reverting to the last view. In the following sections, we introduce you to these more sophisticated tools.

Using the History panel

On the History panel, you see a record of your changes in an editing session. And from this record, you can undo your changes from any step in an editing sequence. To work with the History panel, you must be in Expert mode. After you click Expert at the top of the Photo Editor, here's how undoing with the History panel works:

1. **Click Expert in the Photo Editor and choose Window ⇨ History.**

   The History panel displays a record of each step you made in the current editing session, as shown in Figure 1-6.

2. **To undo one or more edits, click any item on the History panel.**

Elements reverts your image to that last edit. All edits that follow the selected item are grayed out.

3. **If you want to bring back the edits, click any grayed-out step on the panel.**

Elements reinstates your edits up to that level. If you make a new edit after going back a few steps, the grayed-out steps disappear.

FIGURE 1-6:
The History panel.

REMEMBER

All your steps are listed on the History panel if you remain in Elements and don't close the file. When the file is closed, all history information is lost.

TIP

Storing all this editing history can affect Elements' performance. If your computer slows to a snail's pace when you're using Elements, check out the following options:

» **Choose Edit ⇨ Clear ⇨ Clear History.** Elements flushes all the recorded history and frees some precious memory, which often enables you to work faster. Just be sure you're okay with losing all the history in the History panel thus far.

» **Eliminate Clipboard data from memory.** To do so, choose Edit ⇨ Clear ⇨ Clipboard Contents or Edit ⇨ Clear ⇨ All.

» **Restore the number of history states stored to the default of 50.** In Elements Performance Preferences, you can change the number of history states. You can ratchet this number up to 1,000 if you like, but realize that the more history states you record, the more memory Elements requires.

Reverting to the last save

While you edit photos in Elements, plan on saving your work regularly. Each time you save in an editing session, the History panel preserves the list of edits you make until you hit the maximum number or close the file.

If you save, perform more edits, and then want to return to the last saved version of your document, Elements provides you with a quick, efficient way to do so. If you choose Edit ⇨ Revert, Elements eliminates your new edits and takes you back to the last time you saved your file.

When you choose Revert, *Revert* appears in the History panel. You can eliminate the Revert command from the History panel by right-clicking (Windows) or Ctrl-clicking (on a Mac with a one-button mouse) the Revert item and choosing Delete from the contextual menu that appears.

Getting a Helping Hand

You probably bought this book because you're not a fan of sifting through Help files and want an expert guide to image editing. We share everything a beginner needs to get started in Elements, but Elements is too sophisticated a program to cover completely in the pages we have here. You may also need some quick help if you don't have this book nearby.

Whenever you need a hand, know that you can find valuable help information quickly and easily within Elements itself. If you're stuck on understanding a feature, ample help documents are only a mouse click away and can help you overcome some frustrating moments.

Your first stop is the Help menu, where you can find several commands that offer information:

>> **Photoshop Elements Help:** Choose Help ⇨ Photoshop Elements Help or press the F1 key (Windows) or the Help key (on a Mac with an extended keyboard) to open the Elements Help file. You can type a search topic and press Enter to display a list of search results.

>> **Getting Started:** From the Help menu, choose this item for tips and information on getting started in Elements.

>> **Key Concepts:** While you read this book, if we use a term that you don't completely understand, choose Help ⇨ Key Concepts. A web page opens in your default web browser and provides many web pages with definitions of terms and concepts.

>> **Support:** From the Help menu, this command launches your default web browser and takes you to the Adobe website (www.adobe.com), where you can find information about Elements, problems reported by users, and some work-around methods for getting a job done. You can find additional web-based help information by clicking Photoshop Elements Online and Online Learning Resources. The vast collection of web pages on Adobe's website offers assistance, tips and techniques, and solutions to many problems that come with editing images. Be sure to spend some time browsing these web pages.

>> **Video Tutorials:** Choose Help ⇨ Video Tutorials to open a web page where videos for common tasks are hosted on Adobe's website.

>> **Forum:** Choose Help ⇨ Forum to explore user comments and questions with answers to many common problems.

TIP

Tooltips can be another helpful resource. While you move your cursor around tools and panels, pause a moment before clicking the mouse. A slight delay in your actions produces a *tooltip,* which is a small box that describes the item your mouse is pointing to. Elements provides this sort of dynamic help when you pause the cursor before moving to another location.

You can also find help by searching in the Home screen, as mentioned in the "Getting Familiar with the Home Screen" section, earlier in this chapter.

Saving Files with Purpose

When you save a file after editing it, you might save the file in the same file format, or change the format to suit your photo service center's specifications or to ensure that your image downloads quickly on a website.

When you save, Elements also enables you to take advantage of special features, such as saving different versions of a file or including your edited file in the Organizer as well as saving it to your hard drive.

This section is your guided tour of the Save/Save As dialog box (or Save As dialog box, if you're saving a file for the first time) and the Save for Web dialog box.

Using the Save/Save As dialog box

NEW

Before you save a file, Elements offers you an option for where you want to save your file. Choose File ⇨ Save or File ⇨ Save As and the Save As dialog box opens, as shown in Figure 1-7.

Choices offered in this dialog box include saving your files to the cloud. You can choose to save files on Adobe's servers and access the file from any computer when you log on to Adobe Creative Cloud. Or you can choose to save files locally in your computer.

If you want to eliminate this dialog box from opening each time you save a file, select the check box at the bottom of the dialog box.

FIGURE 1-7:
The Save As
dialog box that
appears on
using your first
Save/Save As.

In almost any program, the Save (or Save As) dialog box is a familiar place where you make choices about the file to be saved. With Save As, you can save a duplicate copy of your image or save a modified copy and retain the original file. However, if you're planning to upload your final image to the web, skip the familiar Save (or Save As) dialog box and see the next section, "Saving files for the web."

To use the Save (or Save As) dialog box, choose File ➪ Save for files to be saved the first time, or choose File ➪ Save As when you want to make a copy of the open file, and a dialog box then opens.

TIP

As a matter of good practice, when you open an image, choose File ➪ Save As for your first step in editing a photo. Save with a new filename to make a copy and then proceed to edit the photo. If you don't like your editing results, you can return to the original, unedited photo and make another copy for editing.

The standard navigational tools that you find in any Save dialog box appear in the Elements Save/Save As dialog box. Here are two standard options in the Elements Save/Save As dialog box:

>> **Filename:** This item is common to all Save (Windows) or Save As (Mac) dialog boxes. Type a name for your file in the text box.

>> **Format:** From the drop-down list, you choose file formats. For more on file formats, see Chapter 2.

A few options make the Photoshop Elements Save/Save As dialog box different from other Save dialog boxes that you might be accustomed to using. The Save Options area in the Save As dialog box provides these choices:

- » **Include in the Elements Organizer:** If you want the file added to the Organizer, select this check box. (For more information about using the Organizer, see Part 2.)

- » **Save in Version Set with Original:** This choice is a bit odd. You won't see Version Set available for any photo you open in either Quick or Expert mode by choosing File ⇨ Open. You must load the file in the Organizer and open from the Organizer in the Photo Editor; then, when you save the file in either mode, you see Version Set available. This option provides you with opportunities to make multiple edits on a file and save as different versions all within the same file.

- » **Layers:** If your file has layers, selecting this check box preserves the layers. For more on Layers, see Chapter 9.

- » **As a Copy:** Use this option to save a copy without overwriting the original file.

- » **Color:** Color profiles help you maintain accurate color, and this box controls your image's color profile. Select the box for ICC (International Color Consortium) Profile. Depending on which profile you're using, the option appears for sRGB or Adobe RGB (1998). When the check box is selected, the profile is embedded in the image. Chapter 15 explains how to use color profiles with your prints.

- » **Thumbnail (Windows only):** If you save a file with a thumbnail, you can see a miniature representation of your image when viewing it in folders or on the desktop. If you select Ask When Saving in the Saving Files preferences, the check box can be enabled or disabled. If you select an option for Never Save or Always Save in the Preferences dialog box, this box is enabled or disabled (grayed out) for you. You need to return to the Preferences dialog box if you want to change the option.

Saving files for the web

The Save for Web command helps you prepare photos to show on the web or just onscreen. Choose File ⇨ Save for Web. In the Save for Web dialog box that opens (see Figure 1-8), you see your original image on the left, and you see the result of making changes for file format and quality settings on the right.

The standard rule with web graphics is to find the smallest file size for an acceptable image appearance. In the Save for Web dialog box, you have many choices for reducing file size. Notice in Figure 1-8 that you see the original image with the file size reported below the image on the left. After choosing JPEG for the file type, you can see that the image size is reduced from the original 11MB to 434.7K.

FIGURE 1-8:
The Save
for Web
dialog box.

You can also use the Quality item that appears to the right of the drop-down list to adjust the final quality of the saved file. Here, you need to find the right balance between quick download times and image appearance. Just keep an eye on the preview image as well as the download time information for your optimized file.

For the most accurate viewing, set the zoom size to 100 percent. In the lower-left corner of the dialog box, you can choose zoom levels from the drop-down list or just type a value in the field box. If your chosen settings noticeably degrade your image quality, you can easily discern the loss when viewing at a 100-percent view.

REMEMBER

Working in the Save for Web dialog box is a matter of making choices and viewing the results. Toggle the different file type choices and make adjustments for quality. If you see image degradation, change to a different quality setting or file format. Always look at the file-size item reported below the image on the right and try to find the lowest file size that produces a good-looking image.

Chapter **2**

Basic Image-Editing Concepts

When you open a picture in Photoshop Elements, you're looking at a huge grid of pixels. These *pixels* are tiny, colored squares, and the number of pixels in a picture determines the picture's *resolution.*

This relationship between pixels and resolution is important for you to understand in all your Elements work. You'll find the concepts covered in this chapter especially helpful when creating selections (as we explain in Chapter 8), printing files (Chapter 15), and sharing files (Chapter 16).

Additionally, you need to understand *color modes,* which define how many colors an image contains. Color modes are important when you're using tools in the Tools panel and Panel Bin and printing and sharing files. Basically, you want to choose a color mode for your image that is best suited for print or onscreen and the type of image you have (a photo with lots of colors versus a line drawing with only a few colors, for example).

Like resolution and color modes, the file format in which you save an image often depends on your desired output — print or screen — so this chapter concludes with an introduction to choosing a file format. Additionally, this chapter helps you understand the basics of working with resolution, color modes, and file formats that are essential to great results in your final images. We talk about changing resolution by resizing images, converting color modes, and saving the results in different file formats.

Grappling with the Ubiquitous Pixels

Most digital images are composed of millions of tiny, square pixels. Each pixel has one, and only one, color value. The arrangement of the pixels of different shades and colors creates an optical illusion when you view an image onscreen. For example, black-and-white pixels might create the impression that you're looking at something gray — not at tiny black-and-white squares.

Just about everything you do in Elements has to do with changing pixels:

» Surrounding pixels with selection tools to select what appear to be objects in your image

» Making pixels darker or lighter to change contrast and brightness

» Changing shades and tints of pixels for color correction

» Performing a variety of other editing tasks

An image made of pixels is a *raster image.* If you open a file in Elements that isn't made of pixels, you can let Elements rasterize the data. In other words, Elements converts other data to pixels if the document wasn't originally composed of pixels.

TECHNICAL STUFF

Images not made of pixels are typically *vector images.* You can also have vector content in an Elements file. Text added with the Type tool, for example, is a vector object. When you save an Elements file with the Text layer intact or save it as a Photoshop PDF file, the vector data is retained. We talk more about vector data in Chapters 13 and 14. For this chapter, you just need to focus on raster data.

REMEMBER

To use most of the tools and commands in Elements, you must be working on a raster image file. If your data isn't rasterized, many tools and commands are unavailable.

The pixels in an image determine an image's resolution and dimensions, as we explain in the following sections.

Understanding resolution

The number of pixels in an image file determines the image's resolution, which is measured in pixels per inch (ppi). For example:

» If you have 300 pixels across a 1-inch horizontal line, your image resolution is 300 ppi.

» If you have 72 pixels across 1 inch, your image resolution is 72 ppi.

Image resolution is critical to properly outputting files in the following instances:

>> **Printing images:** The optimal resolution for print is 300 ppi. If the image resolution is too low, the image prints poorly. If the resolution is too high, you waste time processing all the data that needs to be sent to your printer.

Note: Printing to inkjet printers in the best quality often does not require having a 300 ppi image. Much depends on the printer. Some printers can print perfectly at 35 ppi. Desktop printers can print optimally at a ppi of 180, 210, 280, and so on. When printing to a desktop printer, consult the printer's manual for the optimum printer resolution.

>> **Showing images onscreen:** The best resolution for onscreen images is a more complicated issue. There is no standard optimum resolution that fits all monitors. If you want to be precise, take the screen resolution described in your monitor's manual — say, 2,560 for the horizontal resolution — and divide that number by the actual width of your computer monitor. Say that your monitor width is 23.4 inches. The result of 2,560 ÷ 23.4 is 109. Optimum resolution for this kind of monitor is 109 ppi. The old standard of 72 ppi is outdated, but if you don't want to do the math, images will display just fine at 72 ppi on Mac computers and 96 ppi on Windows machines.

Zoom levels also impact viewing images. If you zoom in on an image, it appears more pixelated. When creating images for screen viewing, you might think about how much a user is likely to zoom in on a photo and set the resolution accordingly — such as 2x, 3x, and so on as the actual ppi.

To see how image resolution and screen resolution combine and impact what you see onscreen, look at Figure 2-1. You see an image reduced to 50 percent and then at different zoom sizes. When the size changes, the monitor displays your image at different resolutions. For example, if you view a photo with a resolution of 72 ppi and reduce the size to 50-percent view on your monitor, the resolution on the monitor appears as though the photo is at 144 ppi. When the size is 100 percent, the image resolution is the same as the monitor resolution. Table 2-1 provides a closer look at these differences in resolution.

This relationship between the image resolution and viewing the image at different zoom levels is an important concept to grasp. If you grab an image off the web and zoom in on it, you may see a view like the 800-percent view shown in Figure 2-1. If you acquire a digital camera image, you may need to zoom out to a 16-percent view to fit the entire image in the image window.

These displays vary so much because of image resolution. That image you grabbed off a web page might be a 216-pixel square image at 72 ppi, and that digital camera image might be a 2,400-x-3,120-pixel image at 240 ppi. To fill the entire window with the web image, you need to zoom in on the file. When you zoom in, the image appears as though it's reduced in resolution.

50%   100%

200%   400%   800%

FIGURE 2-1:
The same
image is
viewed at
different
zoom levels.

TABLE 2-1 **How Image and Display Resolutions Affect What You See Onscreen**

Image Resolution	Display Resolution	Zoom Level	How Image Appears Onscreen
72 ppi	72 ppi	100%	Image appears onscreen at its actual resolution, so the onscreen display is the same as what you'd see if you printed the image. The print won't be crisp, however, because the resolution is too low for print. A low resolution looks fine on a monitor but not on paper.
72 ppi	72 ppi	50%	Image appears smaller onscreen, as though it has a higher image resolution (144 ppi, or twice the resolution that it actually has).
72 ppi	72 ppi	200%	Image appears larger onscreen, as though it has a lower image resolution (36 ppi, or half of its actual resolution). The display needs to simulate "spreading out" the pixels to make the image appear bigger.
300 ppi	72 ppi	100%	Image appears larger onscreen than it will in print, because the monitor can display only 72 ppi. A print of this image will look clear and crisp, because 300 ppi is the ideal resolution for prints.
300 ppi	72 ppi	50%	Image appears smaller onscreen but will print larger than the monitor view.
300 ppi	72 ppi	200%	Image appears larger onscreen but will print smaller than the monitor view.

REMEMBER

When you zoom in to or out of an image, you change the resolution as it appears on your monitor. *No resolution changes are made to the file.* The image resolution remains the same until you use one of the Elements tools to reduce or increase the image resolution.

Understanding image dimensions

Image dimensions involve the physical size of your file. If the size is 4-x-5 inches, for example, the file can be any number of different resolution values. After the file is open in Elements, you can change the dimensions of the image, the resolution, or both.

When you change only the dimensions of an image (not the number of pixels it contains), an inverse relationship exists between the physical size of your image and the resolution. When image size is increased, resolution decreases. Conversely, when you raise resolution, you reduce image size.

The Art of Resampling

In some cases, images are too large, and you need to reduce their resolution and physical size. In other cases, you might need a higher resolution to output your images at larger sizes. This method of sizing — changing the size, as well as the number of pixels — is dubbed *resampling* an image. Specifically, reducing resolution is *downsampling,* and raising resolution is *upsampling.*

Here's a quick example to clarify the benefit of resampling. Say you have a photo taken with a digital single-lens reflex (DSLR) camera, which takes pretty high-resolution photos. The photo could easily have a resolution of 300 ppi and dimensions of 14 x 10 inches. If you just want to make a few color corrections in Elements and then make 7-x-5-inch prints for your family members, resampling the file keeps the file size manageable for both your computer's memory and for uploading to a printing service. Because you decreased the photo's dimensions, the photo still maintains the resolution you need for a high-quality photo print (that is, 300 pixels per inch or less, depending on the printer). If you just changed the photo's dimensions without resampling, the photo's resolution would almost double, making for an unnecessarily large file.

WARNING

Use caution when you resample images; when you resample, you either toss away pixels or manufacture new pixels. To protect your images during resampling, work on a copy of your image, instead of the original file.

You can change an image's size and resolution in a couple of different ways. One method is cropping images. You can use the Crop tool with or without resampling images. For more information on using the Crop tool, see Chapter 10. Another method is to use the Image Size dialog box, which you use in many of your editing sessions in Elements.

To resample an image with the Image Size dialog box, follow these steps:

1. **Choose Image ⇨ Resize ⇨ Image Size.**

   Alternatively, you can press Ctrl+Alt+I (⌘ +Option+I on the Mac). The Image Size dialog box opens, as shown in Figure 2-2.

   The Pixel Dimensions area in the Image Size dialog box shows the file size (in this example, 12.1M). This number is the amount of space the image takes up on your hard drive. The width and height values are fixed with the default Resample Image check box at the bottom of the dialog box enabled.

2. **In the Document Size area, redefine dimensions and resolution.**

   The options are

   - **Width:** Type a value in the text box to resize the image's width. Then press Tab to move out of the field and implement the change. From the drop-down list to the right of the text box, you can choose a unit of measure: percent, inches, centimeters, millimeters, points, picas, or columns.

   - **Height:** The Height options are the same as the Width.

     If you keep the sizing proportional, you typically edit either the Width or Height text box, but not both. When you alter either width or height, the resolution changes respectively.

TIP

   - **Resolution:** Type a value in the text box to change resolution and then press Tab to commit the change. After you edit the resolution, the Width and Height values are changed inversely (if the Constrain Proportions check box is selected).

3. **(Optional) If you're okay with resampling your image to get the desired size, select the Resample Image check box.**

   With this check box selected, you can change dimensions and pixels at the same time, which results in either reducing or increasing the number of pixels. When the check box is deselected, the values for dimensions are linked; changing one value automatically changes the other values.

4. **(Optional) If you select the Resample Image check box, choose a resampling method from the drop-down list below it or select the other resample options above it (or do both).**

From the drop-down list, you see three options for Bicubic plus Nearest Neighbor and Bilinear. Adjacent to the method name, Elements provides a description to help you know when to choose one over the other.

In the drop-down list, you find different choices for resampling. See Table 2-2 for details on each method.

When you select the Resample Image check box, the two check boxes above it become active. Here's what they do:

- **Scale Styles:** Elements has a Styles panel from which you can add a variety of different style effects to images. (See Chapter 12 for details.) When you apply a style, such as a frame border, the border appears at a defined width. When you select the Scale Styles check box and then resize the image, the Styles effect is also resized. Leaving the check box deselected keeps the style at the same size while the image is resized.

- **Constrain Proportions:** By default, this check box is selected, and you should leave it that way unless you want to intentionally distort an image.

5. **When you're done selecting your options, click OK to resize your image.**

FIGURE 2-2:
The Image Size
dialog box.

TABLE 2-2   **Resolutions and Printing**

Output Device	Optimum	Acceptable Resolution
Desktop laser printers	300 ppi	200 ppi
Desktop color inkjet printers	300 ppi	180 ppi
Large-format inkjet printers	150 ppi	120 ppi (some printers require much less)
Professional photo lab printers	300 ppi	200 ppi
Desktop laser printers (black and white)	170 ppi	100 ppi
Magazine quality — offset press	300 ppi	225 ppi
Screen images (web, slideshows, and video)	72 ppi	72 ppi
Tablet devices and smartphones	150+ ppi	150 ppi

Choosing a Resolution for Print or Onscreen

Resolution in your Elements work is paramount in printing files. Good ol' 72-ppi images can be forgiving, and you can get many of your large files scrunched down to 72 ppi for websites and slideshows. For a nice-looking print, however, you need a much higher resolution. Many different printing output devices exist, and their resolution requirements vary.

For your own desktop printer, plan to print a variety of test images at different resolutions and on different papers. You can quickly determine the best file attributes by running tests. When you send files to service centers, ask the technicians what file attributes work best with their equipment.

REMEMBER

White does not print as a color. When you use white, it appears transparent on your prints, and the color appears the same as the paper color you're using.

For a starting point, refer to Table 2-2 for the recommended resolutions for various output devices.

TIP

If you find choosing a resolution for printing to be confusing, just leave it all up to the printer driver to take care of the sampling.

Working with File Formats

Elements provides you with a long list of file formats, many of which are outdated. Although many different file formats are available, use only a few. Figure 2-3 shows the open Format drop-down list that you see in the Save or Save As dialog box.

In the following sections, we explain the formats you typically work with most often.

| TIFF (*.TIF;*.TIFF) |
| Photoshop (*.PSD;*.PDD) |
| BMP (*.BMP;*.RLE;*.DIB) |
| CompuServe GIF (*.GIF) |
| Photo Project Format (*.PSE) |
| GIF (*.GIF) |
| JPEG (*.JPG;*.JPEG;*.JPE) |
| Photoshop PDF (*.PDF;*.PDP) |
| Pixar (*.PXR) |
| PNG (*.PNG;*.PNS) |
| TIFF (*.TIF;*.TIFF) |

FIGURE 2-3:
The drop-down list of file formats that Elements supports.

JPEG (*.jpg, *.jpeg, *.jpe)

JPEG (Joint Photographic Experts Group) is perhaps the most common file format now in use. That's in large part because of smaller file sizes that make web viewing and exchanging files much easier. You can use JPEG files for prints or share them online via a web page or email attachment. Creative professionals wouldn't dream of using the JPEG format in design layouts, but everyone else uses the format for all kinds of documents.

You need to exercise some caution when you're using the JPEG format. JPEG files are compressed to reduce file size, so you can scrunch an image of several megabytes into a few hundred kilobytes. When you save a file with JPEG compression, however, you experience data loss. You might not see this on your monitor, or it might not appear noticeably on photo prints if you're using low compression while preserving higher quality. However, when you save with maximum compression, more pixels are tossed away, and you definitely notice image degradation.

REMEMBER

When you save, open, and resave an image in JPEG format, each new save degrades the image more. If you need to submit JPEG images to photo labs for printing your pictures, keep saving in the Photoshop PSD file format until you're ready to save the final image. Save in JPEG format when you want to save the final file for printing and use a low compression with high quality.

When you select JPEG for the format and click Save, the JPEG Options dialog box opens, as shown in Figure 2-4. You choose the amount of compression by typing a value in the Quality text box or by moving the slider below the Quality text box. The acceptable range is from 0 to 12 — 0 is the lowest quality and results in the highest compression, and 12 is the highest quality and results in the lowest amount of compression.

Notice that you also have choices in the Format Options area of the JPEG Options dialog box. The Progressive option creates a progressive JPEG file commonly used with web browsers. This file type shows progressive quality while the file downloads from a website. The image first appears in a low-quality view and shows higher-resolution views until the image appears at full resolution when it's completely downloaded in your browser window.

PNG (*.png)

PNG (Portable Network Graphics) is another format used with web pages. PNG supports all color modes, 24-bit images, and transparency. One disadvantage of using PNG is that color profiles can't be embedded in the images, as they can with JPEG. An advantage, however, is that PNG uses lossless compression, resulting in images without degradation.

FIGURE 2-4:
When saving in JPEG format, choose the amount of compression you want to apply to the saved image.

PNG is also an option in the Save for Web dialog box. Choose File ➪ Save for Web to export your photos as PNG.

TIP

When saving images for the web, if you have an image with just a few colors, such as a logo, try the GIF or PNG-8 format. If you need transparency in an image, you need to use either GIF or PNG-24. Quite often, you'll find that PNG-24 results in the best-looking image.

TIFF (*.tif, *.tiff)

TIFF (Tagged Image File Format) is the most common format used by graphic designers. TIFF is generally used for importing images in professional layout programs, such as Adobe InDesign and QuarkXPress, and when commercial photo labs and print shops use equipment that supports downloading TIFF files directly to their devices. (*Note:* Direct downloads are used in lieu of opening a Print dialog box.)

Inasmuch as creative professionals have used TIFF for so long, a better choice for designers using a program such as Adobe InDesign is to save in the native Photoshop PSD file format. This requires a creative professional to save only one file in native format without bothering to save both native and TIFF formats.

TIFF, along with Photoshop PSD and Photoshop PDF, supports saving layered files and works in all color modes. When you save in TIFF, you can also compress files in several different compression schemes, but compression with TIFF files doesn't lose data unless you choose a JPEG compression.

When you choose TIFF from the Format drop-down list and click Save in the Save/Save As dialog box, the TIFF Options dialog box opens. Your options for image compression include

» **NONE:** Selecting this option results in no compression. You use this option when sending files to creative professionals for creating layouts in programs such as Adobe InDesign. (None of the three compression schemes listed next is recommended for printing files to commercial printing devices.)

» **LZW:** This lossless compression scheme results in much lower file sizes without destroying data.

» **ZIP:** ZIP is also a lossless compression scheme. You can favor ZIP compression over LZW when you have large areas of the same color in an image.

» **JPEG:** JPEG is lossy and results in the smallest file sizes. Use JPEG here the same as when you apply JPEG compression with files saved in the JPEG format.

Leave the remaining items in the dialog box at defaults and click OK to save the image.

Getting Familiar with Color

In this section, you find some fundamental principles to make your work in Elements easier when you're editing color images.

REMEMBER

Your first level of understanding color is to understand what RGB is and how it works. *RGB* stands for *red, green,* and *blue.* These are the primary colors in the computer world. Forget about what you know about primary colors in an analog world; computers see primary colors as RGB. RGB color is divided into *color channels.* Although you can't see the individual channels in Elements, you still need to understand just a little about color channels.

When you see a color *pixel* (a tiny square), the color is represented as different levels of gray in each channel. This may sound confusing at first, but stay with us for just a minute. When you have a color channel, such as the red channel, and you let all light pass through the channel, you end up with a bright red. If you screen that light a little with a gray filter, you let less light pass through, thereby diluting the red color. This is how channels work. Individually, they all use different levels of gray that permit up to 256 levels of light to pass through them. When you change the intensity of light in the different channels, you ultimately change the color.

Each channel can have up to 256 levels of gray that mask out light. The total number of possibilities for creating color in an RGB model is achieved by multiplying the values for each channel ($256 \times 256 \times 256$). The result is more than 16.7 million; that's the total number of colors a computer monitor can display in RGB color.

This is all well and good as far as theory goes, but what does that mean in practical terms? Actually, you see some of this information in Elements' tools and dialog boxes. As an experiment, open a file in Elements and choose Enhance ⇨ Adjust Lighting ⇨ Levels; the Levels dialog box shown in Figure 2-5 opens.

FIGURE 2-5:
The Levels
dialog box.

Notice that the Channel drop-down list shows you Red, Green, and Blue as individual channels, as well as a composite RGB selection. Furthermore, the Output Levels area shows you values ranging from 0 on the left to 255 on the right. Considering that 0 is a number, you have a total of 256 different levels of gray.

REMEMBER

What's important is that you know that your work in color is related to RGB images that comprise three different channels. There are 256 levels of gray that can let through or hold back light and change brightness values and color. See Chapters 10 and 11 for more on using tools, such as levels, to adjust color in this way.

Getting Color Right

In Elements, when it comes to color, the challenge isn't understanding color theory or definitions, but rather matching the RGB color you see on your computer monitor as closely as possible to your output. *Output* can be a printout from a color printer or a screen view on a web page.

We say match "as closely as possible" because you can't expect to achieve an exact match. You have far too many printer and monitor variables to deal with. However, if you properly manage color, you can get a very close match.

To match color between your monitor and your output, you need to first calibrate your monitor and then choose a color workspace profile. In the following sections, you can find all the details.

Color the easy way

REMEMBER

The upcoming sections are complex and require some dedicated effort to follow the descriptions. If you're interested in sharing photos only onscreen (that is, on your own website or on Instagram, Facebook, Twitter, and so on) and you plan to leave the printing to others, you don't need to bother with color correction and going through a maze of steps to get the color perfected. In that case, you can skip the technical stuff in the following sections.

Your only consideration for onscreen viewing is your overall monitor brightness. If your monitor displays images darker or lighter than other computers viewing your images, you need to follow the upcoming sections and understand how to adjust your overall monitor brightness.

Calibrating your monitor

REMEMBER

Your monitor needs to be calibrated to adjust the gamma and brightness; correct any color tints or colorcasts; and generally get your monitor to display, as precisely as possible, accurate colors on your output. You can choose among a few tools to adjust monitor brightness. These tools range from a low-cost hardware device that sells for less than $100 to expensive calibration equipment for $3,000 or more.

Gamma is the brightness of midlevel tones in an image. In technical terms, gamma is a parameter that describes the shape of the transfer function for one or more stages in an imaging pipeline.

We skip the costly high-end devices and software utilities that don't do you any good and suggest that you make, at the very least, one valuable purchase for creating a monitor profile: a hardware profiling system. On the low end, some affordable devices go a long way toward helping you adjust your monitor brightness and color balance. The newest Datacolor Spyder (SpyderX) costs $170. Hardware tools of various kinds can help you create monitor profiles for working with color. The best way to find a device that works for you is to search the Internet for hardware descriptions, dealers, and costs.

On LCD/LED monitors, you need to adjust the hardware controls to bring your monitor into a match for overall brightness with your photo prints. Be certain to run many test prints and match your prints against your monitor view to make the two as similar as possible.

You have a lot to focus on when calibrating monitors and getting the color right on your monitor and your output. We talk more about color prints in Chapter 15.

Choosing a color workspace

After you adjust your monitor color by using a hardware profiling system, your next step is to choose your color workspace. In Elements, you have a choice between two workspace colors: either sRGB or Adobe RGB (1998). You access your color workspace settings by choosing Edit ➪ Color Settings. The Color Settings dialog box opens, as shown in Figure 2-6.

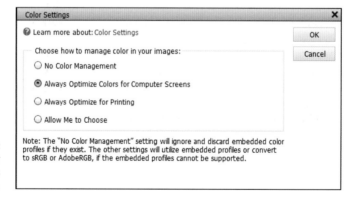

FIGURE 2-6:
The Color
Settings
dialog box.

The Color Settings dialog box gives you these options:

>> **No Color Management:** This choice turns off all color management. Don't choose this option for any work you do in Elements. When using No Color Management, you need to work with files that have color profiles embedded

in the photos. You most likely won't use these types of photos. For information on when you might use the No Color Management option, see Chapter 15.

» **Always Optimize Colors for Computer Screens:** Selecting this radio button sets your workspace to sRGB. sRGB color is used quite often for viewing images on your monitor, but this workspace often results in the best choice for color printing, too. Many color printers can output all the colors you can see in the sRGB workspace. In addition, many photo services we talk about in Chapter 15 prefer this workspace color.

» **Always Optimize for Printing:** Selecting this option sets your color workspace to Adobe RGB (1998). The color in this workspace represents the best color you can see on newer monitors, as well as many of the newer inkjet printers. As a default, this is your best choice.

» **Allow Me to Choose:** When you select this option, Elements prompts you for a profile assignment when you open images that contain no profile. This setting is handy if you work back and forth between screen and print images.

Understanding how profiles work

You probably created a monitor color profile when you calibrated your monitor. You probably also selected a color profile when you opened the Color Settings dialog box and selected your workspace color. When you start your computer, your monitor color profile kicks in and adjusts your overall monitor brightness and corrects for any colorcasts. When you open a photo in Elements, color is converted automatically from your monitor color space to your workspace color.

At print time, you use another color profile to output your photos to your desktop color printer. Color is then converted from your workspace color to your printer's color space. In Chapter 15, we show you how to use color profiles for printing. For now, just realize that each of these color profiles, and using each one properly, determine whether you can get good color output.

IN THIS CHAPTER

» **Examining the Editor workspace**

» **Using the Photo Bin**

» **Using Creative Effects**

» **Launching Preferences**

» **Customizing the presets**

Chapter **3**

Exploring the Photo Editor

Photoshop Elements has two workspaces: the Organizer, which we discuss in Chapter 4, and the Photo Editor, introduced in Chapter 1. You manage and arrange your photos in the Organizer, and you edit photos in the Photo Editor.

In this chapter, we continue our discussion of the Photo Editor so that you can refine your photo-editing skills. You discover the Photo Editor's workspace in depth and how to access the Photo Editor's three editing modes: Expert, Quick, and Guided.

Examining the Photo Editor

Before you begin editing photos, you'll find it helpful to look over the Photo Editor and figure out how to move around the workspace. When the Photo Editor is in Expert mode, you find the following (as labeled in Figure 3-1):

(A) **Menu bar:** As does just about every other program you launch, Elements supports drop-down lists. The menus are logically constructed and identified to provide commands for working with your pictures (including many commands that you don't find supported in tools and on panels). A quick glimpse at the menu names gives you a hint of what might be contained in a given menu list. Throughout this book, we point you to the menu bar whenever it's helpful. Most of the menu commands you find in Elements 2022 are the same as those found in earlier versions of Elements.

(B) Photo Editor modes: The Photo Editor has three modes. The Expert mode is shown in Figure 3-1. You find an introduction to Quick mode in Chapter 1 and a more detailed look at Quick mode in Chapter 10. An introduction to Guided mode appears later in this chapter, in the "Using Some Creative Features" section. Parts 3 and 4 cover all the different features of Expert mode, including making selections, creating composites from several images, drawing, adding text, and exploring creative flourishes with filters and effects.

(C) Create menu: When you open the Create menu and choose an option, you leave the current editing mode. For example, when in Expert mode, choose Create ⇨ Photo Collage, and all the options that were available in the Photo Editor temporarily disappear when the Creation Wizard opens. To return to the Photo Editor, complete the creation or cancel the wizard. Chapter 17 guides you through the options in the Create menu.

(D) Features buttons: On Windows, you find three buttons in the top-right corner. These buttons are used to (1) minimize the window; (2) maximize/minimize the window; and (3) close the application. On Apple Macintosh, the same three buttons appear, but they are placed in the top-left corner of the window.

(E) Share menu: The Share menu works similarly to the Create menu and offers options for sharing your images. Chapter 16 focuses on the Share menu.

(F) Panel Bin: Figure 3-1 shows the Layers panel. You change panels by clicking the icons at the bottom of the Panel Bin. (The icons are described in item S.) *Creations* (things you make) are also contained in the Panel Bin when you click the Create button (item E).

(G) Open menu: When you have several files open in the Photo Editor, the Open menu is one way to switch among these files. To use this menu, click the down-pointing arrow adjacent to the Open button and, from the drop-down list, choose the image you want to move to the foreground. ***Note:*** The Open menu also offers you an option to create a new, blank file.

In Figure 3-1, several files are open, indicated by the tabs at the top of the image window. You can also place an open file in the foreground in the image window in these other ways:

- Click a tab at the top of the image window to move the image to the foreground (item Q).

- Click a photo in the Photo Bin (see item J).

- Open the Window menu and choose a photo listed at the bottom of the menu.

FIGURE 3-1:
The Photo
Editor
workspace.

(H) File tabs: Multiple photos opened in the Photo Editor appear in different tabs at the top of the window by default.

In technical-speak, this is a *docked* position, meaning that the photos are docked in the image window. You can click a tab and drag it down to *undock* the photo To undock photos you must change a preference setting in the General Preferences by checking Allow Floating Windows in Expert Mode. (See "Controlling the Editing Environment," later in this chapter, for more on changing preferences.) Doing so makes the photo appear as a *floating window.* You might want to float windows when copying and pasting image data between two or more photos. You can also view all open files in a floating window without choosing All Floating from the Layout pop-up menu (item M). To use this menu command, you must first enable the Preferences to allow floating windows.

(I) Tools panel: Here you find the Photo Editor toolbox, where you click a tool and apply an edit to the photo. See "Selecting the tools" and "Selecting from the Tool Options," later in this chapter.

(J) Photo Bin/Tool Options: Figure 3-1 shows the Photo Bin open. Click the Tool Options button, and a set of Tool Options replaces the Photo Bin. You can also open the Tool Options by clicking a tool in the Tools panel.

Tool Options enable you to specify how the selected tool works. For example, the Tool Options for the Brush tool, as shown in Figure 3-2, enable you to select from a few different brush styles, set the size of your brush, and much more. (You discover how the specific tools work in the relevant chapters later in this book. For example, you find out how the Brush tool works in Chapter 13, which covers drawing and painting.)

Each tool in the Tools panel supports various tool options. To return to the Photo Bin, click the Photo Bin button at the bottom left of the window.

(K) **Undo/Redo:** These commands are so useful that they have an extra-prominent place in the Photo Editor interface. (See Chapter 1 to find out about other tools that help you undo or redo your work.) Click the respective tool for Undo or Redo. You can also press Ctrl+Z (⌘ +Z on the Mac) for Undo and Ctrl+Y (⌘ +Y) for Redo.

(L) **Rotate:** Click the Rotate left tool to rotate counterclockwise 90 degrees. Click the down-pointing arrow on the Rotate tool and choose the Rotate Right tool to rotate a photo 90 degrees clockwise.

(M) **Layout:** When you have multiple photos open in the Photo Editor, the Layout pop-up menu enables you to choose how the photos display in the image window (such as rows, columns, as a grid, and so on). To return to the tabbed view, choose Default from the Layout pop-up menu.

(N) **Organizer:** Click the Organizer button to open the Organizer, which we cover in detail in Chapter 4. Elements makes it very easy for you to toggle back and forth between the Organizer and the Photo Editor by clicking their respective buttons at the bottom of the windows.

(O) **Home Screen:** Opens the Elements Home Screen window.

(P) **Panel Bin icons:** Click an icon at the bottom of the Panel Bin to display a different panel. Your choices are the following panels: Layers, Effects, Filters, Styles, Graphics, and More. These panels are docked in the Panel Bin by default and can't be removed unless you choose Custom Workspace (item T). We talk more about these panels in the later section "Playing with panels."

(Q) **Image window:** In this window, you view a photo you want to edit. Likewise, you can view multiple photos you want to edit when viewing floating windows.

(R) **Photo Bin Options menu:** Click this icon to open a pop-up menu of tasks, such as saving the Panel Bin Photos in an Album, printing selected photos in the Panel Bin, and showing a Grid in the Panel Bin.

FIGURE 3-2:
Tool Options provide more editing features for tools selected in the Tools panel.

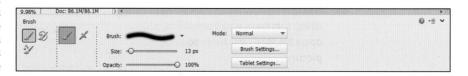

(S) **Panels:** Click the icons to open the panels that include Layers, Effects, Filters, Styles, Graphics, and a category named More that's a collection of other, different panels.

(T) **More menu:** To open additional panels, click the down-pointing arrow to open a pop-up menu of choices. The panels you open from the Panel Options menu appear as floating windows and can't be docked in the Panel Bin.

Notice at the bottom of the pop-up menu you find Custom Workspace. When you click Custom Workspace, you can move panels around and dock or undock them in the Panel Bin.

The description of the Photo Editor workspace is brief in this chapter. Most of the options you have for using tools, panels, and menu commands are discussed in later chapters. For now, try to get a feel for what the Photo Editor provides and how to move among many of the Photo Editor features.

Examining the image window

Not surprisingly, the image window's tools and features are most useful when an image is open in the window. To open an image in the image window, shown in Figure 3-3, follow these steps:

1. **Choose File ⇨ Open.**

The standard Open dialog box appears; it works like any ordinary Open dialog box that you find in other applications.

REMEMBER

You can always click one or more photos in the Organizer and click the Editor button to open the selected photos in the Photo Editor.

2. **Navigate your hard drive (by using methods you know to open folders) and then select a picture.**

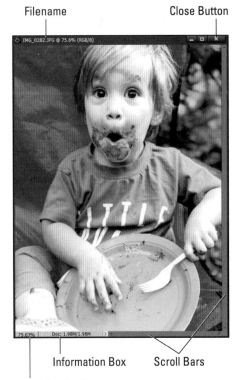

Filename   Close Button

IMG_0282.JPG @ 75.6% (RGB/8)

75.63%   Doc: 1.98M/1.98M

Information Box   Scroll Bars

Magnification Box

Photo: Courtany Jensen, Model: Hudson Jensen

FIGURE 3-3:
The image window displays an open file undocked within the Elements workspace.

If you haven't yet downloaded digital camera images or acquired scanned photos and want an image to experiment with, you can use a sample image. Both your operating system and Photoshop Elements typically provide sample images:

- On your operating system, sample images are typically found in your Pictures folder, which is one of the default folders in both Windows and macOS installations.

- In Elements, you can store photos anywhere on your hard drive and access them in your Organizer.

3. **Select a picture and click Open.**

The photo opens in a new image window in Elements.

You can open as many image windows in Elements as your computer memory can handle. When each new file is opened, a thumbnail image is added to the Photo Bin at the bottom of the workspace (refer to Figure 3-1).

Notice that in Figure 3-1, filenames appear as tabs above the image window when the indows are docked and not appearing as floating windows. Additionally, photo thumbnails appear in the Photo Bin. To bring a photo forward, click the filename in a tab or simply click a thumbnail in the Photo Bin. To close a photo, click the *X* adjacent to the filename or choose File ⇨ Close.

To close a photo in the image window but keep it open in the Panel Bin, click the minimize button in the top-right corner (Windows) or top-left corner (Mac). Refer to item D in Figure 3-1.

Here's a look at important items in the image window, as shown in Figure 3-3:

- ❯❯ **Filename:** Appears above the image window for each file open in the Photo Editor.

- ❯❯ **Close button:** Click the *X* to the right of the filename to close the file. (On the Mac, choose File ⇨ Close.)

- ❯❯ **Scroll bars:** These become active when you zoom in on an image. You can click the scroll arrows, move the scroll bar, or grab the Hand tool in the Tools panel and drag within the window to move the image.

    For Mac users: If you don't see scroll bars on your Finder windows, open the System Preferences by clicking the System Preferences icon on the Dock or choosing System Preferences from the Apple menu. In General Preferences, click Always in the Show Scroll Bars section.

- ❯❯ **Magnification box:** See at a glance how much you've zoomed in or out.

TIP

>> **Information box:** You can choose what information this readout displays by choosing one of the options from the pop-up menu, which we discuss in more detail later in this section.

When you're working on an image in Elements, you always want to know the physical image size, the image resolution, and the color mode. (Size is the physical size of the image. Image resolution is the number of pixels in your image. Color mode is a mode such as RGB for red, green, and blue, grayscale for black and white, and so on.) Regardless of which menu option you select from the status bar, you can quickly glimpse these essential stats by clicking the Information box (not the right-pointing arrow but the box itself), which displays a pop-up menu like the one shown in Figure 3-4.

```
Width: 6720 pixels (22.4 Inches)
Height: 4480 pixels (14.933 Inches)
Channels: 3 (RGB Color, 8bpc)
Resolution: 3 (RGB Color, 8bpc)
```

FIGURE 3-4:
Click the readout on the status bar to see file information.

>> **Sizing the Window:**

You can also resize the window by dragging any corner in or out when the image is undocked and not viewed as a tab.

TIP

To undock windows, press Ctrl/⌘ +K to open the Photo Editor Preferences. Click General in the Left pane and select the box where you see Allow Floating Documents in Expert Mode. You must be in Expert mode to view documents undocked.

Now that you're familiar with the overall image window, we want to introduce you to the Information box's pop-up menu, which enables you to choose what details appear in the Information box. Click the right-pointing arrow to open the menu, shown in Figure 3-5.

Here's the lowdown on the options you find on the pop-up menu:

```
✔ Document Sizes
  Document Profile
  Document Dimensions
  Current Selected Layer
  Scratch Sizes
  Efficiency
  Timing
  Current Tool
```

FIGURE 3-5:
From the pop-up menu on the status bar, choose commands to show more information about your file.

>> **Document Sizes:** Shows you the saved file size. For information on file sizes and resolutions, see Chapter 2.

>> **Document Profile:** Shows you the color profile used with the file. Understanding color profiles is important when printing files. Turn to Chapter 15 for more information on using color profiles.

>> **Document Dimensions:** When selected, this option shows you the physical size in your default unit of measure, such as inches.

>> **Current Selected Layer:** When you click a layer in the Layers panel and choose Current Selected Layer, the layer name appears as the readout.

>> **Scratch Sizes:** Displays the amount of memory on your hard drive that's consumed by all documents open in Elements. For example, 20M/200M indicates that the open documents consume 20 megabytes and that a total of 200 megabytes is available for Elements to edit your images. When you add more content to a file, such as new layers, the first figure grows while the second figure remains static. If you find that Elements runs slowly, check your scratch sizes to see whether the complexity of your file is part of the problem. If so, you might clear some of your history (see Chapter 1) or merge a few layers (see Chapter 9) to free space.

>> **Efficiency:** Indicates how many operations you're performing in RAM, as opposed to using your *scratch disk* (space on your hard drive). When the number is 100 percent, you're working in RAM. When the number drops below 100 percent, you're using the scratch disk.

TIP

If you continually work below 100 percent, it's a good indication that you need to buy more RAM to increase your efficiency. If you have multiple applications open, quit all other programs to conserve RAM.

>> **Timing:** Indicates the time it took to complete the last operation.

>> **Current Tool:** Shows the name of the tool selected from the Tools panel.

REMEMBER

Why is the information in this pop-up menu important? Suppose you have a great photo you want to add to your Facebook account and you examine the photo to find the physical size of 8 x 10 inches at 300 pixels per inch (ppi). You also find that the saved file size is more than 20MB. At a quick glance, you know you want to resize or crop the photo to perhaps 4 x 6 inches at 72 ppi. (Doing so drops the file size from more than 20MB to around 365K.) Changing the resolution dramatically reduces the file size. We cover file sizes and changing the physical dimensions of your photos in Chapter 2. For now, realize that the pop-up menu shows you information that can be helpful when preparing files for print and display.

Don't worry about trying to understand all these terms. The important thing to know is that you can visit the pop-up menu and change the items at will during your editing sessions.

Uncovering the contextual menus

Contextual menus are common to many programs, and Photoshop Elements is no exception. They're those little menus that appear when you right-click, offering commands and tools related to whatever area or tool you right-clicked. If you have a one-button mouse on the Mac, press Ctrl+click to open a context menu.

The contextual menus are your solution when you're in doubt about where to find a command on a menu. You just right-click an item and a pop-up menu opens.

Because contextual menus provide commands related to the tool you're using or the object or location you're clicking, the menu commands change according to the tool or feature you're using and where you click at the moment you open a contextual menu. For example, in Figure 3-6, you can see the contextual menu that appears after we create a selection marquee using the Rectangular Marquee Selection tool and right-click anywhere in the image window. Notice that the commands are all related to selections. Other selection tools, like the Quick Selection tool and Magic Wand, offer you different menu choices from a contextual menu.

| Deselect |
| Select Inverse |
| Feather... |
| Refine Edge... |
| Layer Via Copy |
| Layer Via Cut |
| New Layer... |
| Free Transform |
| Transform Selection |
| Fill Selection... |
| Stroke (Outline) Selection... |
| Last Filter |

FIGURE 3-6:
A contextual menu for a Rectangular Marquee selection.

Selecting the tools

More often than not, clicking a tool on the Tools panel is your first step in editing operations. (If you're not familiar with the Tools panel, refer to Figure 3-8.) In panel hierarchy terms, you typically first click a tool on the Tools panel and then use another panel to fine-tune how the tool works.

Sometimes when you select a tool in the Tools panel, you find additional tools in the Tool Options area. For example, you may click the Marquee Rectangle tool in order to access the Elliptical Marquee tool in the Tool Options, directly below the image window. The Quick Selection tool, the Selection Brush tool, the Refine Selection tool, and the Magic Wand tool, all shown in Figure 3-7, are all in the Tool Options. See the following section for more about the Tool Options area.

Keep in mind that if you don't find a tool in the Tools panel, look in the Tool Options for additional tools within a tool group.

FIGURE 3-7:
Additional tools within a tool group are available in the Tool Options.

You can easily access tools in Elements by pressing shortcut keys on your keyboard. For a quick glance at the key that selects each tool in the Tools panel, look over Figure 3-8.

TIP

The following tips can help you find your way around the Tools panel with keyboard shortcuts:

» **To select tools within a tool group by using keystrokes, press the respective key to access the tool.** For example, press the L key to select the Lasso tool. Press L again to select the Magnetic Lasso tool — the next tool in the group. Press L again and you select the Polygon Lasso tool.

» **Whether you have to press the Shift key to select tools is controlled by a preference setting.** To change the default setting so that you don't have to press Shift, choose Edit ➪ Preferences ➪ General or press Ctrl+K. (Choose Adobe Photoshop Elements Editor ➪ Preferences ➪ General or press ⌘ +K on the Mac.) Then, in General Preferences, deselect the Use Shift Key for Tool Switch check box.

» **The shortcuts work for you at all times, except when you're typing text with the cursor active inside a text block.** Be certain to click the Tools panel to select a tool when you finish editing text, or select the Commit green check mark to end using the Text tool.

The tools are varied, and you may find that you don't use all the tools in the Tools panel in your workflow. Rather than describe the tool functions here, we address the tools in the rest of this book as they pertain to their respective Elements tasks.

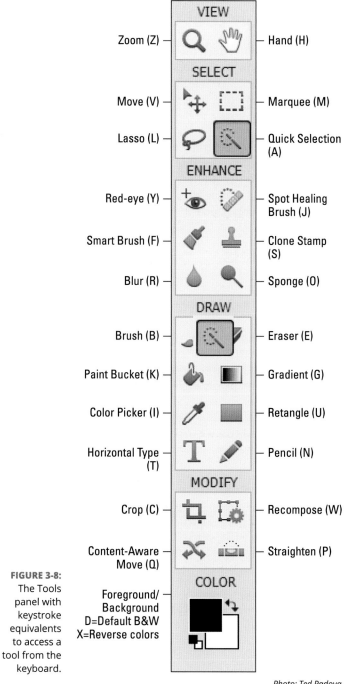

VIEW

Zoom (Z) — — Hand (H)

SELECT

Move (V) — — Marquee (M)

Lasso (L) — — Quick Selection (A)

ENHANCE

Red-eye (Y) — — Spot Healing Brush (J)

Smart Brush (F) — — Clone Stamp (S)

Blur (R) — — Sponge (O)

DRAW

Brush (B) — — Eraser (E)

Paint Bucket (K) — — Gradient (G)

Color Picker (I) — — Retangle (U)

Horizontal Type (T) — — Pencil (N)

MODIFY

Crop (C) — — Recompose (W)

Content-Aware Move (Q) — — Straighten (P)

COLOR

Foreground/ Background D=Default B&W X=Reverse colors

FIGURE 3-8: The Tools panel with keystroke equivalents to access a tool from the keyboard.

Photo: Ted Padova

Selecting from the Tool Options

When you click a tool on the Tools panel, the Tool Options box appears at the bottom of the workspace and offers you choices specific to the selected tool. (Refer to Figure 3-7, which shows the Quick Selection tool options.) In addition to providing you with choices for selecting tools within a tool group, you can adjust settings for a selected tool.

In Figure 3-7, you see choices for adjusting the Quick Selection tool, varying the size of the tooltip, and refining the selection.

You can find many of these fine-tuning adjustments in the Tool Options for most of the tools you select in the Tools panel.

Playing with panels

The panels are where you control features such as layers, effects, and more. In the Photo Editor, you open these panels in the Panel Bin:

» **Layers:** The Layers panel displays all the layers you've added to a photo. We talk much more about layers in Chapter 9. For now, look at how the different panels are designed. In the Layers panel, you find various tools at the top left and an icon with horizontal lines in the top-right corner, to the right of the Trash icon (as shown in Figure 3-9).

You can select multiple layers and click the folder icon at the top of the Layers panel to create a new layer group. All the grouped layers are nested in a folder.

When you click the icon at the top right, a pop-up menu appears (see Figure 3-10), which shows menu items supporting the tasks you perform in the Layers panel.

FIGURE 3-9:
The Layers panel with a Background and three layers.

» **Effects:** At the bottom of the Panel Bin, click the *fx* button to open the Effects panel. The Effects panel contains tabs offering a umber of choices for applying a number of different effects to your pictures. You simply click an effect thumbnail you want when you edit the photo. We cover applying effects in Chapter 12.

>> **Filters:** Click Filters to open the panel where you can apply a number of different filter effects to the open image. For more on using Filters, see Chapter 12.

>> **Styles:** Click Styles, and you find a drop-down menu listing numerous styles. Open a category and click a style to apply to an image. In some respects, this panel behaves similarly to Filters. For more on Styles, see Chapter 12.

>> **Graphics:** The Graphics panel contains several menus where you can choose among a huge assortment of graphic illustrations that can also be added to your photos. For more information on using the Graphics panel, see Chapter 17.

>> **More:** Click the down-pointing arrow at the bottom of the Panel Bin to the right of the More button, and a pop-up menu opens, allowing you to choose additional panels. The Layers, Effects, Filters, Styles, Graphics, and Favorites panels are docked in the Panel Bin and can't be removed.

FIGURE 3-10:
The Layers panel pop-up menu.

The panels you open from the pop-up menu shown in Figure 3-11 open as floating panels. These are your options:

● **Actions:** Actions enable you to automate a series of edits to your pictures. In Figure 3-11, you can see the Actions that are supported when you open the More menu and select the Actions tab. As with other panels, a pop-up menu is supported, and it offers Load, Replace, Reset, and Clear options so that you can modify Actions.

Elements still doesn't support recording your own series of editing steps and capturing the steps as an Action. However, most of the Actions that are created in Adobe Photoshop can be loaded in Elements.

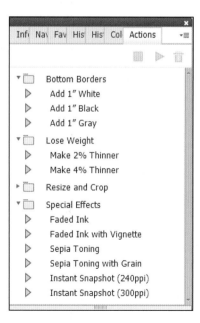

FIGURE 3-11:
Actions panel opened in a group of floating windows.

You can find a number of free downloadable Actions on the Internet. Just search for *Photoshop Actions* and explore the many downloads available to you.

- **Adjustments:** The Adjustments panel works only when you have an Adjustment layer. For details about using the Adjustments panel and Adjustment layers, see Chapter 9.

- **Color Swatches:** This panel displays color swatches you might use for coloring and painting that we cover in Chapter 13.

- **Favorites:** Opens the Favorites panel where you find a list of items you designated as a favorite edit.

- **Histogram:** Open this panel to display a histogram of the photo in the foreground. We talk more about histograms in Chapter 11.

- **History:** Choose this item to display the History panel. For more on using the History panel, see the section about retracing your steps in Chapter 1.

- **Info:** The Info panel provides readouts for different color values and physical dimensions of your photos.

- **Navigator:** The Navigator panel helps you zoom in and move around on a photo in the image window.

- **Custom Workspace:** When you choose Custom Workspace, you can dock and undock panels. This option enables you to configure a custom workspace to your liking.

» **Create/Share panel:** These panels also exist in the Organizer. Click Create at the top right of the Panel Bin to open the Create panel in the Photo Editor. In both the Photo Editor and the Organizer, the Create panel is used for making a number of creations such as calendars, photo books, greeting cards, photo collages, and more. The Share panel contains many options for sharing your photos. We talk more about making creations in Chapter 17, and we cover using the Share panel in Chapter 16.

When you open the additional panels as floating windows, the panels are docked in a common floating window. You can drag a panel out of the docked position and view it as a separate panel or move it to the docked panels.

When you open a panel in either the Organizer or the Photo Editor, you find other options available from tools, drop-down lists, and a menu you open by clicking the icon with horizontal lines in the top-right corner of the panel.

Using the Photo Bin

The Photo Bin displays thumbnail views of all your open images (see Figure 3-12). You can immediately see a small image of all the pictures you have open at one time, as shown earlier in Figure 3-1. You can also see thumbnail views of all the different views you create for a single picture. Find out all the details in the following sections.

TIP

If you want to rearrange the order of the thumbnails in the Photo Bin, you can click and drag any thumbnail to the left or right.

Creating different views of an image

What? Different views of the same picture, you say? Yes, indeed. You might create a new view when you want to zoom in on an area for some precise editing and then want to switch back to a wider view. Here's how you do it:

1. **Click a thumbnail image in the Photo Bin.**

   You must have a photo open in the Photo Editor Image window. The photo you click in the Photo Bin appears in the image window as the active document.

2. **Choose View ⇨ New Window for *<filename>*.**

   Note that *<filename>* is the name of the file in the image window.

3. **Zoom to the new view.**

   A new view appears for the active document, and you see another thumbnail image added to the Photo Bin.

TIP

   To zoom quickly, click the Zoom tool in the Tools panel and then click a few times on the picture in the image window to zoom in to the photo.

Viewing filenames

By default, photos open and are displayed in the Photo Bin without the associated filenames. However, if you mouse over a photo in the Photo Bin, a tooltip opens that displays the name of the file. If you want the name of each file shown in the Photo Bin without having to mouse over the files, open a contextual menu on a photo in the Photo Bin and choose Show Filenames.

Using Photo Bin Actions

On the Photo Bin Actions menu, you find handy tasks that you can perform on photos open in the Photo Editor. Click the Photo Bin Options menu to display the menu commands, as shown in Figure 3-12.

Here's what each Photo Bin Action does:

» **Print Bin Files:** Select the files in the Photo Bin that you want to print and then choose Print Bin Files. The selected files open in the Print dialog box, where you can make photo prints of the selected images.

» **Save Bin as an Album:** You can add photos to an existing album, or you can create a new album. You can do many wonderful things with Photo Albums.

» **Show Grid:** By default, no divider lines appear between photos in the Photo Bin. When you choose Show Grid, divider lines appear between the photos.

Using Some Creative Features

Adding some creative effects to your photos has long been a stellar aspect of Elements. Quite often, users explore many interesting edits in the Guided Edit panel. Guided Edits not only provide you with many interesting effects to apply to your photos but also offer you easy step-by-step instructions on how to use each effect.

New Guided Edit components have been introduced in each new upgrade to Elements over the past several years. However, this year we don't see a new Guided Edit in Elements, but we do see some interesting menu commands that provide you with sone fascinating results.

Using Guided Edits

Guided mode is a marvelous editing feature in Elements. To access Guided mode, click the Guided tab near the top of the Photo Editor workspace.

Guided mode is like having a personal assistant to walk you through several steps in an editing process. When you click the Guided tab in the Photo Editor, you find several tabs at the top of the window (see Figure 3-13). These tabs represent various categories. Click a tab, and below the tabs you find individual editing solutions represented as thumbnail images with names of the Guided mode and a description of what the edit provides you with.

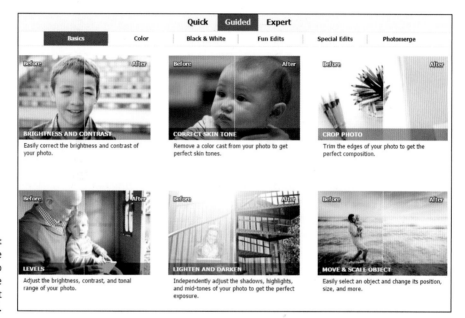

FIGURE 3-13: Click the Guided tab to open the Guided Edit panel.

When you click an editing option, a panel opens on the right side of the window. In the panel is a sequence of steps. Follow the steps, and you end up with a result similar to the example shown in the panel.

NEW

In Elements 2021, three new Guided Edits were introduced in the program: Perfect Landscape, for perfecting landscape photos; Creative Duotone Effect, for creating two-color images; and Move and Scale, for moving or scaling (or both) an object in a photo. The Move and Scale Guided Edit walks you through selecting an object and provides a choice for Moving or Duplicating the object.

TIP

The best way to discover what results you can achieve is to open photos and apply various edits using the Guided panel. Some of the more complicated options, such as creating Out of Bounds effects, offer you a link to online video tutorials to help you further simplify the process.

In Elements 2022, as we said, there are no new Guided Edits introduced in this current release. However, taking off from the Moving and Scaling Guided Edit introduced in Elements 2021, we find some menu commands that are similar to Moving Objects. The commands are found in the Enhance menu.

Moving Objects and Moving Photos

In the Enhance menu, you find two new menu commands: Moving Overlays and Moving Objects. Moving Overlays lets you choose from a variety of objects that you can apply to a photo, and through animation, you can choose to move the objects. The file is then exported as a movie file.

Moving Photos enables you to add some animation to a photo, You can, for example, zoon in, zoom out, move left, move right, and perform several more animated movements.

To use the menu commands, you begin by opening a photo in Expert editing mode. In Figure 3-14, you can see the Moving Overlays option that we chose from the Enhance menu. When using Moving Overlays, you choose an object from one of three menus at the top-right side of the window. You can choose to have the overlay appear in front of or behind a subject in your photo. To have the element appear behind the subject, select the check box for Protect Subject.

To add an overlay to the photo, double-click one of the elements in the Add Overlays panel, and an object appears in the photo. You can duplicate the object by simply clicking and dragging it away from the default placed objects.

To preview the results, click the Play button (the right-pointing arrow at the bottom of the window). When satisfied with the results, click Export. You can choose to export the file as an animated GIF or an MP4 movie file.

For more information on using these and other commands in the Enhance menu, see Chapter 11.

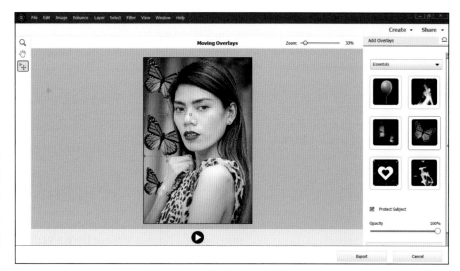

FIGURE 3-14:
Choose Moving
Overlays from
the Enhance
menu to
open the
Moving
Overlays
window.

Controlling the Editing Environment

Opening Elements for the first time is like moving into a new office. Before you begin work, you need to organize the office. At minimum, you need to set up the desk and computer before you can do anything. In Elements terms, the office organization consists of specifying preference settings. Preferences are settings that provide a means to customize your work in Elements and to fine-tune the program according to your personal work habits.

In the following sections, we explain the preference options that you most likely want to adjust. If you need more detail about a preference option than the following section provides, look at the help documents discussed in Chapter 1.

REMEMBER

Elements has two Preferences dialog boxes: one in the Photo Editor workspace and another in the Organizer workspace. The following sections cover the Preferences dialog box that you open when in the Photo Editor, whether you're using Windows or the Mac. See Chapter 4 for details about Organizer preferences.

Launching and navigating Preferences

The Photo Editor's Preferences dialog box organizes all the options into several panes. By default, when you open the Preferences dialog box, you see the General pane.

To open the Preferences dialog box, choose Edit ⇨ Preferences ⇨ General (or Photoshop Elements Editor ⇨ Preferences ⇨ General on the Mac). Alternatively, press Ctrl+K (⌘ +K on the Mac). Using either method opens the Preferences dialog box to the General pane, as shown in Figure 3-15.

FIGURE 3-15: The General pane in the Preferences dialog box.

In Figure 3-15, you see items on both the left and right sides of the dialog box that are common to all preferences panes. Here's a quick introduction to what these items are and how they work:

>> **Panes list:** Elements lists all the different panes along the left side of the Preferences dialog box. Click an item in the list to make the respective pane open on the right side of the dialog box.

>> **OK:** Click OK to accept any changes made in any pane and dismiss the Preferences dialog box.

>> **Cancel:** Click Cancel to return to the same settings as when you opened a pane and to dismiss the dialog box.

>> **Reset Preferences on Next Launch:** Clicking the Restore Default Settings button returns the dialog box to the same settings as when you opened the dialog box. The dialog box stays open for you to set new settings.

REMEMBER

Of particular importance in the General tab are the items you see for Allow Floating Documents in Expert Mode and Enable Floating Document Window Docking. As we discuss earlier in this chapter (see "Examining the image window"), select these check boxes if you want to undock the document windows from the tabs.

Checking out all the Preferences panes

The settings in the Preferences dialog box are organized into different panes that reflect key categories of preferences. The following list briefly describes the types of settings you can adjust in each preferences pane:

>> **General preferences,** as the name implies, apply to general settings you adjust for your editing environment.

>> **Saving Files preferences** relate to options available for saving files. You can change the case of existing filenames; save a file with layers or flatten layers (as we explain in Chapter 9); save files with image previews that appear when you're viewing files as icons on your desktop (Windows); and save with some compatibility options. On the Mac, the Finder generates thumbnails automatically, so you don't need to specify thumbnails in a Save dialog box.

>> **Performance preferences:** This pane is where you find history states (explained in Chapter 1) and memory settings, such as allocating memory to Elements.

>> **Scratch Disks preferences:** Below Performance, you find scratch disk options. (See the nearby sidebar "What's a scratch disk?" for more on scratch disks.) You can monitor how your scratch preferences are working in the image window. See the earlier section, "Examining the image window," for details.

>> **Display & Cursors preferences:** This pane offers options for how certain tool cursors are displayed and how you view the Crop tool when you're cropping images. Chapter 10 explains how cropping works.

>> **Transparency preferences:** These require an understanding of how Elements represents transparency. Imagine painting a portrait on a piece of clear acetate. The area you paint is opaque, and the area surrounding the portrait is transparent. To display transparency in Elements, you need some method to represent transparent areas. (Chapter 8 has more details.) Open the Transparency preferences and make choices for how transparency appears in Elements.

>> **Units & Rulers preferences:** Here you can specify settings for ruler units, column guides, and document preset resolutions.

>> **Guides & Grid preferences:** This pane offers options for gridline color, divisions, and subdivisions. A grid shows you nonprinting horizontal and vertical lines. You use a grid to align objects, type, and other elements. You can snap items to the gridlines to make aligning objects much easier. You can drag guides (sometimes called guidelines) from the ruler and position them between gridlines.

- » **Plug-Ins preferences:** These preferences include options for selecting an additional Plug-Ins folder. Plug-ins are third-party utilities that work with Elements. For example, you can find plug-ins that offer editing features not found in Elements, enable many different adjustments for brightness/contrast and color correction, and provide some nifty special effects. You can find many free plug-ins on the Internet by searching for *Photoshop Elements Plug-Ins.*

- » **Adobe Partner Services:** Here you can control whether Elements automatically checks for new services, clears the online stored data, and resets your account information for all services.

- » **Application Updates:** You can choose to automatically update Elements or receive a notification that an update is available.

- » **Type preferences:** This pane provides options for setting text attributes. You have options for using different quotation marks, showing Asian characters, showing font names in English, and previewing font sizes.

- » **Country/Region Selection:** You can select your country or region from the drop-down menu.

WHAT'S A SCRATCH DISK?

Assume that you have 1GB of free RAM (your internal computer memory) and you want to work on a picture that consumes 1.25GB of hard drive space. Elements needs to load all 1.25GB of the file into RAM. Therefore, an auxiliary source of RAM is needed for you to work on the image. Elements uses your hard drive. When a hard drive is used as an extension of RAM, this source is a *scratch disk.*

If you have more than one hard drive connected to your computer, you can instruct Elements to use all hard drives, and you can select the order of the hard drives that Elements uses for your extension of RAM. All disks and media sources appear in a list as 1, 2, 3, 4, and so on.

Warning: Don't use USB 1.1 external hard drives or other drives that have connections slower than USB 2.0, Thunderbolt, or FireWire. Using slower drives slows Elements' performance. USB 2.0 drives are being phased out and giving way to the newer, faster USB 3.0 drives.

Perusing preset libraries

Part of the fun of image editing is choosing brush tips, swatch colors, gradient colors, and patterns to create the look you want. To get you started, Elements provides you with a number of preset libraries that you can load and use when you want. For example, you can load a Brushes library to acquire different brush tips that you can use with the Brush tool and the Eraser tool. But you're likely to want to customize the preset libraries at least a little bit, too.

You can change libraries individually in respective panels where the items are used. For example, you can change color swatch libraries on the Color Swatches panel or choose brush-tip libraries in the Tool Options. Another way you can change libraries is to use the Preset Manager dialog box, as shown in Figure 3-16.

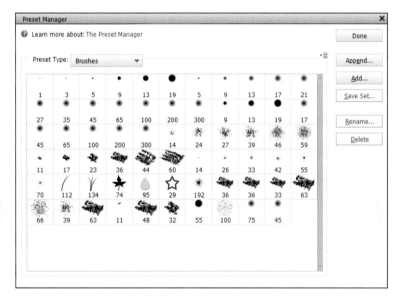

FIGURE 3-16: The Preset Manager dialog box provides a central area where you can change libraries.

We cover using the presets in Chapter 13, which is where you can find out how to use the many presets that Elements provides. The important thing to note here is that you can change the presets according to your editing needs.

To open the Preset Manager dialog box, choose Edit ➪ Preset Manager. The available options in the dialog box are

> **»** **Learn More About: The Preset Manager:** Click the blue Preset Manager hyperlinked text to open the Help document and find out more about managing presets.

» **Done:** Any changes you make in the Preset Manager are recorded and saved when you click Done.

» **Preset Type:** Open the drop-down list to choose from Brushes, Swatches, Gradients, Styles, Patterns, and Effects.

» **Append:** Click the Append button to append a library to the existing library open in the Preset Manager.

» **Add:** Click this button to open another library. Elements allows you to choose from several libraries for each preset type. When you choose Add, the open library closes as a new library opens. If you added a new item, such as a brush, it's lost when you click Add unless you saved the new brush. For more on brushes, see Chapter 8.

» **Save Set:** You can save any changes you make in the Preset Manager as a new library. If you make a change, use this option so that you don't disturb the original presets.

» **Rename:** Each item in a library has a unique name. If you want to rename an item, click the thumbnail in the Preview pane, click Rename, and then type a new name in the dialog box that appears.

» **Delete:** Click an item in the Preview window and click Delete to remove the item from the library.

2

Managing Media

IN THIS PART . . .

Discover the basic features of the Organizer interface.

Import images from your computer, camera, or scanner into the Organizer.

Tag images with keywords, faces, places, or events so that you can easily find images.

View your pictures in the Media Browser and change views.

Use the Organizer's search features to pinpoint the images you need.

IN THIS CHAPTER

» Organizing your photos on your computer

» Importing photos into the Organizer

» Exploring the Media Browser

» Scanning photos and artwork

» Acquiring photos from cellphones and tablets

» Using Preferences

Chapter **4**

Navigating the Organizer

D o you treasure your color-coded filing system and own a special sock drawer organizer? Or are you more inclined to hand your accountant a plastic grocery sack of statements and receipts to sort out for you when tax-filing season comes around?

We're not here to judge. Whatever your organizational style, you'll like the Elements Organizer. The Organizer gives you myriad ways to tag and rate your images, but it also provides tools that automate some of the work.

Before you get started with all the organizational tools, you need to import images into the Elements Organizer. That's what this chapter is all about.

You have many ways to import a picture into Elements. We walk you through an easy method for importing images from cameras and card readers into the Organizer. We also help you import images from CDs, DVDs, a scanner, or your phone and tablet.

Organizing Photos and Media on a Hard Drive

Photos and media hog most of the available storage space on the average consumer's computer. If you're anything like us, you grab a ton of photos and videos with your digital camera, smartphone, and maybe a tablet, too. Even if you faithfully transfer images from all these different sources to your computer, you can end up with a real mess of photos — all with inscrutable filenames such as DS603_Azb42.jpg.

REMEMBER

If all the photos on your hard drive are organized into folders, you'll have an easier time managing those photos in the Elements Organizer. We recommend that you organize your image files in folders before you start working with Elements.

How you label your folders is a personal choice. You may want to name the folders by year and use subfolders for organizing photos by events, locations, photo content, and so on. In Figure 4-1, you can see just one example of how you might organize your photos on a hard drive.

After you organize your photos into folders, you can use the Organizer to import files from folders, as we explain later, in the section "Adding files from folders and removable media."

TIP

If your image files gobble up too much space on your computer's hard drive, we recommend storing all your photos on an external drive instead. Fortunately, the price of large-capacity drives is well within the reach of most people who own a computer, digital camera, or smartphone. Depending on how many photos you take (or image files you create), look for a 1TB to 4TB USB drive that attaches to your computer. Use the drive only for your photos, videos, and other media, and don't copy other data files to it. When all your image and media files are in one place, keeping them organized on that drive becomes much easier.

FIGURE 4-1:
Organize
photos and
media in
folders and
subfolders
on your hard
drive.

Adding Images to the Organizer

To use the Elements Organizer, you need to import the images into the Organizer.

You have several options for downloading photos from your camera and other devices to your computer:

» Using AutoPlay Wizards for Windows and Assistants on the Mac

» Importing photos directly from Photos (formerly iPhoto) if you use a Mac

» Using the Photoshop Elements Downloader

The built-in downloaders from your operating system attempt to make your life easier, but in reality, it may be more difficult to struggle with a downloader application and later organize files in folders (as we recommend earlier in this chapter).

TIP

Perhaps the easiest method for transferring photos from a camera or card reader is to quit the operating system's downloader application or any camera-specific applications and just stay with the tools that Photoshop Elements provides.

The following sections introduce you to the tools available for adding images to the Organizer. If you've already organized images on your hard drive or other media into folders, the Get Files from Folders command can help. If images are still on your camera, the Elements Downloader enables you to download images from your camera into the folder where you want to keep the images, using whatever folder organization system you've created; the Elements Downloader also imports the images into the Organizer at the same time.

Adding files from folders and removable media

Most people have photos on their computer's hard drive, as well as on removable media, such as external hard drives, media cards, or maybe even a USB flash drive. Adding images from your hard drive to the Organizer is easy. If you have a source, such as a USB flash drive, media card, or external hard drive, you copy files from the source to the drive where you store photos. Or you can copy files into the Organizer directly from the removable media.

The following steps explain how to import images from your hard drive into the Organizer Media Browser:

1. **Click the Import button in the top-left corner of the Organizer to open the drop-down list and choose From Files and Folders.**

   Alternatively, you can choose File ⇨ Get Photos and Videos ⇨ From Files and Folders.

   The Get Photos and Videos from Files and Folders dialog box opens, as shown in Figure 4-2.

   When you first click the Import button or choose File ⇨ Get Photos and Videos ⇨ From Files and Folders, the dialog box appears, showing you some information regarding importing photos. Click the Start Importing button or the Skip button to continue importing photos. After you click the Start Importing button, another dialog box appears, prompting you to use the Auto Tagging feature. For more on creating tags, see Chapter 5.

2. **Browse your hard drive for the photos you want to add.**

   You can navigate your computer and any connected external drives or media devices in the left-hand pane. (For example, if you've connected a USB drive of photos or loaded a CD of images into your CD drive, you can navigate to those photos here.) The contents of the selected drive or folder appear in the middle pane of the dialog box.

FIGURE 4-2:
The Get Photos and Videos from Files and Folders dialog box.

If you're importing photos directly from the external device, by default, the Get Photos and Videos from Files and Folders dialog box copies your media to your hard drive when you click the Get Media button. You can deselect the Copy Files on Import check box so that only thumbnail images will appear in the Media Browser. To edit a photo, you have to reconnect the drive, CD, or DVD to your computer. If you elect to copy the images, the photos are available for editing each time you start a new Elements session.

You can keep photos and videos on external drives and don't need to copy the images to your internal hard drive. Create a catalog specifically for a particular drive and open that catalog when you connect the drive. In this regard, you can have several external drives, each with its own catalog. For information on creating a new catalog, see Chapter 6.

3. **Select the files or a folder that you want to import.**

   You can import individual images, a single folder of photos, or a folder and all its subfolders.

4. **Click the Get Media button.**

When you add files to the Organizer, the image thumbnails are links to the files stored on your drive. They aren't the complete image data.

If you want to import a single photo and you want to know the file attributes of the targeted photo, place the cursor over a photo; a tooltip displays file attribute information.

Downloading camera images with the Elements Downloader

Import photos from your camera to the Organizer as follows:

1. **Insert a media card from a camera or attach a camera to your computer via a USB port.**

   We recommend using a media card instead of attaching your camera, in case the battery is low on your camera. (If the battery runs out, the import stops.) If you have a media card for your camera, take it out and insert it into a card reader that you attach to your computer via a USB port or a built-in card reader in your computer.

2. **If you see an Autoplay Wizard on Windows or a dialog box for importing photos into Photos on the Mac, cancel out of the dialog box and let Elements control your import. Otherwise, skip to Step 3.**

3. **In Elements, open the Organizer workspace and choose Import ⇨ From Files and Folders. Or choose File ⇨ Get Photos From Camera or Card Reader.**

The Elements Organizer – Photo Downloader opens, as shown in Figure 4-3.

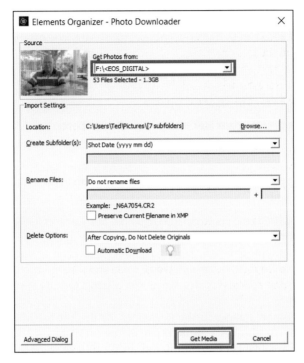

FIGURE 4-3:
The Elements
Organizer –
Photo
Downloader
opens.

4. **From the Get Photos From drop-down list at the top of the dialog box, choose your media card.**

5. **Click the Browse button (Choose on Mac) and locate the folder on your drive to which you want to copy the photos.**

REMEMBER

If you don't click the Browse button and select a folder, all files copied to your hard drive are copied to the User Pictures folder. This is the default for Photoshop Elements. If you use an external hard drive to store your photos, you'll want to copy photos to the external drive. When you select a folder, select the one that fits the overall folder organizational structure for your images so that your image files stay organized.

TIP

You can also create a new folder and add files from your media to the new folder. Click Advanced Dialog in the lower-left corner. Another dialog box opens. Click Browse and create a new folder in the Browse dialog box.

You can leave the rest of the settings at the defaults or rename the photos here. You can also take care of file renaming in the Organizer later. Don't delete the photos from your card just in case you delete some photos in the Organizer and want to retrieve them. After you're certain everything in Elements is to your liking, you can later delete photos by using your camera.

TIP

When renaming images, try to use a system that you easily comprehend. Use descriptive names such as family_2.20, Spain_3.19, photoshoot_Kelley, and so on, including dates or other descriptors such as the kind of event or the people photographed.

The Downloader has an Advanced dialog box that you access by clicking the Advanced Dialog button. In the Advanced settings, you can make choices for things like correcting for red eye, creating photo stacks, and editing photo data that we call metadata. (We explain metadata in Chapter 6.) Because you can handle all these tasks in Elements, just leave the Advanced settings at their defaults.

6. **Import photos by clicking the Get Media button in the Photo Downloader dialog box.**

Elements adds the photos to the Organizer, and you eventually see thumbnail images in the Organizer's Media Browser after the upload completes. Give Elements some time to finish. If the Auto-Analyzer is on in your Preferences, Elements will run through facial recognition and add similar faces to different clusters. We address facial recognition in depth in Chapter 5.

REMEMBER

When you import images in the Organizer, by default the images are auto analyzed for visual similarity in addition to the facial recognition analysis. When these items are enabled in the Preferences, it can take some time to complete the import if you have a lot of files.

Importing additional photos from folders

Suppose you have your folders organized and photos copied to various folders. You take some more pictures of the same location and want to add these photos to a folder you already have labeled as a location name. To add pictures to a folder on your hard drive or external drive, follow these steps:

1. **Copy photos from a media card to your hard drive or external drive.**

In this example, we want to copy photos to a folder we have labeled Portraits.

TIP

2. **In the Organizer, choose File ⇨ Get Photos and Videos ⇨ From Files and Folders.**

The Get Photos and Videos from Files and Folders dialog box opens.

3. **Select the folder on your hard drive where you copied the new photos.**

   In this case, we select the folder containing the files we want to import.

4. **Click the Get Media button.**

   The Getting Media dialog box appears, and the photos are added to the Organizer (see Figure 4-4).

5. **Click OK in the Getting Media dialog box.**

   Photoshop Elements is smart enough to import only new images into the Organizer. Any images you previously imported from a given folder are listed in the Getting Media dialog box, and you're informed that the old images will not be imported.

FIGURE 4-4: Folder names appear in the Import panel.

Navigating the Media Browser

When you add photos to the Organizer, the photos and any additional media appear as thumbnails in the central portion of the Organizer — known as the *Media Browser.*

After files are imported into the Organizer, you see just those photos you imported in the Media Browser. Similarly, when you click a folder in the Import panel, only the photos within the selected folder display in the Media Browser. To see all the photos in your catalog, click the All Media button at the top of the Media Browser.

The Import panel is the list of folders on the left. You can collapse the panel to provide more viewing area in the Media Browser. Just click the Hide Panel button in the lower-left corner of the Organizer workspace (see Figure 4-5).

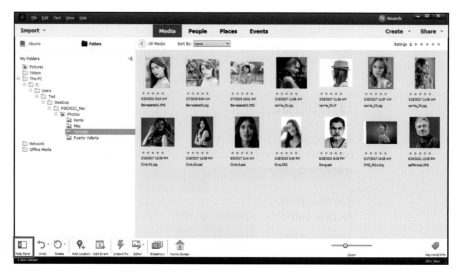

FIGURE 4-5:
Photos are displayed in a Tree view in the Import panel. The Hide Panel appears in the lower-left corner of the window.

The Import panel offers two different views:

» **List view:** By default, you see the folder List view that shows all folders imported in alphabetical order. If you have photos in subfolders, the Folder List view doesn't reflect the hierarchy for how your photos are organized on your hard drive.

TIP

» **Tree view:** To see a different view in the Organizer, click the drop-down list and choose View as Tree, and you change the Import panel view to the hierarchy view, as shown in Figure 4-5.

REMEMBER

If you have a touchscreen monitor or device, you can swipe photos to view them one at a time.

If you don't see the details below the photos, or the photos don't appear in grid view, press Ctrl+D (⌘ +D) to change the Media Browser view.

Using a Scanner

Scanners connect through the same ports as cameras and card readers — typically a USB port.

Even the lowest-end scanners provide 16-bit scans that help you get a little more data in the shadows and highlights. As with a digital camera, a scanner's price is normally in proportion with its quality.

Understanding image requirements

All scanning software provides you with options for determining resolution and color mode before you start a new scan. Chapter 2 introduces you to choosing a resolution and color mode.

REMEMBER

You should decide what output you intend to use and choose your resolution based on that output. Some considerations include the following:

>> **Scan the artwork or photo at the size and resolution for the final output.** If you have a 3-x-5 photo (216 x 360 pixels) that needs to be half the size (108 x 180 pixels) on a web page, scan the original with a 50-percent reduction in size at 72 ppi (the desired resolution for images on the web).

>> **Size images with the scanner software.** If you have a 4-x-6 photo that needs to be output for prepress and commercial printing at 8 x 12 inches, scan the photo at 4 x 6 inches at 600 ppi (a resolution that's large enough to increase the image size to 200 percent and still have a 300 dpi [dots per inch] image, which is the desired resolution for a print).

>> **Scan properly for line art.** *Line art* is 8-bit black and white only and should be used for scanning not only black-and-white artwork but also text. When you print line art on a laser printer or prepare files for commercial printing, the line-art resolution should match the device resolution. For example, printing to a 600 dpi laser printer requires 600 ppi for an 8-bit line-art image.

>> **Scan grayscale images in color.** In some cases, it doesn't matter, but with some images and scanners, you can get better results by scanning grayscale images in RGB (red, green, and blue) color and converting to grayscale, as we explain in Chapter 11.

>> **Scan in high-bit depths.** If your scanner is capable of scanning in 16- or 32-bit, by all means scan at the higher bit depths to capture the most data. A higher bit depth gives you more latitude when editing photos.

Using scanner plug-ins (Windows)

Generally, when you install your scanner software, a stand-alone application and a plug-in are installed to control the scanning process. *Plug-ins* work inside other software programs, such as Photoshop Elements. When you're using the plug-in, you can stay right in Elements to do all your scanning. Here's how it works:

1. **After installing a new scanner and the accompanying software, open the Organizer.**

2. **Press Ctrl+K to open the Preferences dialog box.**

   The Preferences dialog box opens.

3. **Click Scanner in the left column and adjust the Scanner preferences, such as by choosing your scanner, setting the quality, and choosing a target destination for your scans.**

When the Preferences dialog box displays your scanner, you know that the connection is properly set up and you're ready to scan. Here's how to complete your scan:

1. **In the Organizer, choose File ⇨ Get Photos ⇨ From Scanner (Windows).**

2. **In the Get Photos from Scanner dialog box that appears (as shown in Figure 4-6), make your choices and then click OK.**

   Here you can choose your scanner in the Scanner drop-down list, a location on your hard drive for saving the scanned images, a quality setting, and an option to automatically correct red eye.

   Elements may churn a bit, but eventually your scanner software window appears atop the Organizer, as you can see in Figure 4-7. The window is the scanner software provided by your scanner manufacturer. (Your window will look different from Figure 4-7 unless you use the same scanner we use.)

FIGURE 4-6: Make choices in the Get Photos from Scanner dialog box and click OK.

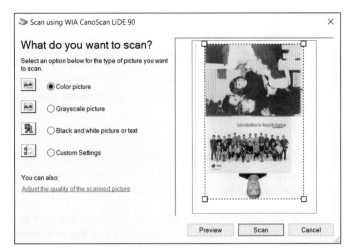

FIGURE 4-7:
When you scan
from within
Elements, your
scanner
software
window loads
on top of the
Elements
workspace.

3. **Preview the scan.**

   Regardless of which software you use, you have similar options for creating a preview; selecting resolution, color mode, and image size; scaling; and other options. If you click the Preview button, you see a preview before scanning the photo(s).

4. **Adjust the options according to your output requirements and the recommendations made by your scanner manufacturer.**

5. **When everything is ready to go, click the Scan button.**

   The final image drops into an Elements image window.

Scanning on the Mac

Photoshop Elements doesn't support scanning on the Mac as it does for Windows. On the Mac, you have a few options:

>> **Scanner software:** You can use your scanner software and open the resulting scan in the Elements Photo Editor.

>> **Image Capture:** With Image Capture (found in your Applications folder), you can complete a scan and open the file directly in Elements. Image Capture provides options for saving scans as JPEG, TIFF, PNG, or PDF. Quite often, you'll find best results when saving as PNG.

Scanning many photos at a time

If you have several photos to scan, you can lay them out on the scanner bed and perform a single scan to acquire all images in one pass. Arrange the photos to scan on the glass and set up all the options in the scanner window for your intended output. When you scan multiple images, they form a single scan, similar to what you see in Figure 4-7.

TIP

After you scan multiple images, Elements makes it easy for you to separate each image into its own image window, where you can save the images as separate files. In the Photo Editor, choose Image ⇨ Divide Scanned Photos to make Elements magically open each image in a separate window while your original scan remains intact. The images are neatly tucked away in the Photo Bin, where you can select them for editing, as shown in Figure 4-8. (For more information on using the Photo Editor and working with the Photo Bin, see Chapter 3.)

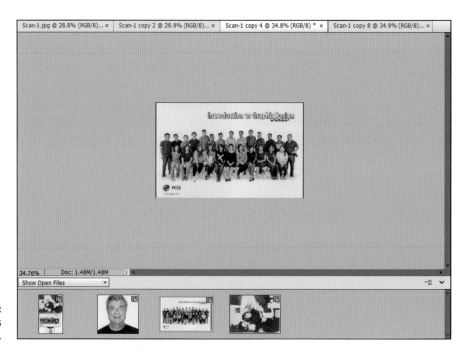

FIGURE 4-8:
The scan is split.

TIP

When scanning multiple images and using the Divide Scanned Photos command, be sure to keep your photos on the scanner bed aligned vertically, horizontally, and parallel to each other the best you can. Doing so enables Elements to do a better job of dividing and straightening your photos.

If you close one of the images that were divided, Elements prompts you to save the image. Only the scan was saved when you started the process. You still need to save the divided scans.

After dividing the images, choose File ⇨ Close All. Elements closes all files that have been saved and individually prompts you to save all unsaved images.

Phoning in Your Images

You can acquire images from iPhones, iPods, iPads, Androids, and a variety of different handheld devices. As a matter of fact, you can do quite a bit with uploading, downloading, and preparing photos for handheld devices.

If you want to add images from a mobile device to the Organizer or open images in one of the editing modes, you need to copy files to your hard drive via a USB or Bluetooth connection, or download an email attachment of the photos if your phone can use email.

Follow these steps after copying files to your hard drive:

1. **Choose File ⇨ Get Photos and Video ⇨ From Files and Folders.**

   The Elements Organizer – Photo Downloader dialog box opens.

2. **Locate the folder into which you copied the files and add them to your Organizer.**

   Or you can open them in one of the editing modes.

   With an iPhone, iPod touch, or iPad, you can use the Photo Downloader to transfer media.

3. **Hook up the device with a USB cable.**

   The Photo Downloader opens automatically. If the downloader doesn't open automatically, you may have to open it manually.

4. **Click the Browse button, as shown in Figure 4-9, to open the Select Directory to Store Files window and select a destination folder.**

5. **Click the Select Folder button to identify where the photos are saved.**

6. **Click the Get Media button to download the photos to your computer.**

FIGURE 4-9:
Get media
from your
phone to your
computer.

To upload Elements creations and edited photos to your iPhone, iPad, or iPod touch, use Apple's iTunes:

1. **In iTunes, choose File ⇨ Add Files to Library.**

2. **Select the images and videos from a folder on your hard drive that you want to upload to the device.**

   REMEMBER

   When uploading photos to an iPhone or iPad, use only the formats these devices support, such as JPEG, TIFF, GIF, and PNG.

3. **Hook up the iPhone or iPad and then click the Photos and/or Videos tab at the top of the iTunes window.**

4. **Select the check box for each item you want to upload and then click the Sync button.**

   Your files are uploaded to your device while the sync is in progress.

TIP

You can bypass iTunes with the iPad by using the Camera Connection Kit (older iPads) or the Lightning Adapter (newer iPads), provided by Apple for $29.95 (39.95 for USB 3). The kit supports only SD cards, but you can attach many different types of card readers to the USB port on the Camera Connection Kit and use other media cards. Copy files from the Organizer to the media card and use it as you would use an external media source to share photos back and forth between your computer and the iPad.

Setting Organizer Preferences

Throughout this book, we often refer to making some choices in the application Preferences. The Organizer and the Photo Editor have a set of preferences that you open by choosing Edit ⇨ Preferences (Windows) or Photoshop Elements Organizer ⇨ Preferences (Mac), or by pressing Ctrl/⌘+K. Each set of preferences has several panels. When you click an item in a panel's left pane, options for the respective item appear in the right pane. After making your choices, click OK, and the preferences remain for all subsequent sessions in the Organizer.

If your computer has only 8G or less of RAM, you may find Elements performing very slowly. One of the items that slows down a computer running Elements with less than 16G of RAM is Media-Analysis. By default, Face Recognition and Media-Analysis are turned on. To turn off the auto analysis operations, be in the Organizer and press Ctrl/⌘ +K to open the Organizer Preferences panel. Click Media-Analysis and deselect all the check boxes, as shown in Figure 4-10. Click OK, and the auto run operations of Media-Analysis will stop.

Many preference items are self-explanatory. When you need some detail on making a preference choice, refer to the Adobe Help file, which you can find by choosing Help ⇨ Elements Organizer Help.

FIGURE 4-10: Open the Organizer's Preferences and deselect all the Media-Analysis items.

IN THIS CHAPTER

» **Creating keyword and People tags**

» **Using the Auto Curator and Auto Creations**

» **Rating your images and placing them on maps**

» **Working with albums**

» **Working with Events**

Chapter **5**

Organizing Your Pictures

ownloading a bunch of media cards filled with photos and leaving them in folders distributed all over your hard drive is like having a messy office with papers stacked haphazardly all over your desk. Trying to find a file, even with all the great search capabilities we cover in Chapter 6, can take you as much time as sorting through piles of papers. What you need is a good file-management system.

In this chapter, we talk about tagging photos, organizing and annotating files, creating versions and stacks, creating photo albums, and performing other tasks so that you can quickly sort through large collections of photos. Be certain to take some time to understand the organizational methods that Elements offers, and keep your files organized when you copy them to your hard drive. Sharpening your photo-management skills enables you to easily find photos you want to edit, add photos to a new creation, or share photos with friends and family.

Touring the Organizer

To help you start using the Organizer's photo-management tools, we begin this chapter about more Organizer tasks by first offering a glimpse at the Organizer workspace.

Figure 5-1 shows you an Organizer view. The various items in the Organizer include the following:

(A) Menu bar: The Organizer menus appear in the top-left section of the menu bar. In Windows, the menus belong to the application. On the Mac, the menu bar is part of the operating system's menus.

(B) Sort By: When you click a folder, as you see in item J, the thumbnail images shown in the Media Browser (item K) display only those photos within the selected folder. Figure 5-1 shows the Outdoors folder selected. Note that when the cursor appears over the folder, a tooltip displays the directory path for the folder.

The Sort By drop-down list is where you can sort the thumbnails in the Media Browser according to Newest, Oldest, and Batches of photos that you imported.

(C) Media/People/Places/Events: At the top of the Organizer window, you find four tabs:

- **Media:** The first tab is Media. Click the Media tab to display thumbnails of photos either in a folder or in the entire catalog. (See Chapter 6 for more on catalogs.)

- **People:** Click this tab to display photos where you have tagged faces, as we discuss later in this chapter.

- **Places:** Click this tab, and a Google map appears in the Panel Bin. You can tag photos according to map coordinates by using Google Maps. Click the Add Location button (item O) to tag an image with a place on the map. See Chapter 6 for more on adding places.

- **Events:** Click this tab to display photos that have been tagged as Events. To tag a photo with an Event, click the Add Event button (item P). See the section "Working with Events," later in this chapter.

We talk more about tagging photos later in this chapter, in the section "Organizing Groups of Images with Tags."

(D) Search: Click this button to open the Search pane.

When you click the Search button, a window opens, from which you can choose from a number of different search options. We cover the new Search features in Chapter 6.

(E) Features buttons: In Windows, you find Maximize, Minimize, and Close buttons in the top-right corner of the Organizer. On the Mac, in the top-left corner you find Close, Minimize to Dock, and Maximize.

(F) Import: From the drop-down list, you can choose to import photos from Files and Folders, Camera or Card Reader, or Scanner. Another option enables you to search your hard drive. On the Mac, you have an additional option. Choose File ⇨ Get Photos and Videos ⇨ in Bulk. A dialog box opens and lets you import files from folders.

(G) Create/Share: These two items are drop-down lists. You choose a menu item that takes you either to the Photo Editor or to a wizard where you work step-by-step to complete a task. For more information on making creations, see Chapter 17. For more information on sharing photos, see Chapter 16.

(H) Albums/Folders tabs: Click Albums to view any Photo Albums you have created. Click Folders to display a folder view as shown in Figure 5-1.

(I) Ratings/Auto Curator: Ratings are denoted as stars from 1 to 5. Click a star, and those images identified with a given rating are displayed in the Media Browser. Select the Auto Curate check box to automatically choose to auto analyze photos for visual similarities.

(J) Folders view: Click a Folder name to display just the photos within the respective folder. In Figure 5-1, you see the Outdoors folder selected in the My Folders panel.

(K) Media Browser: The Media Browser shows thumbnails of your images.

(L) Keyword/Info: Click the Keyword/Info button to open the Panel Bin and choose options from the Tags or Information panels. The current view in Figure 5-1 shows the panels hidden.

FIGURE 5-1:
The Organizer workspace.

Photos: Ted Padova

(M) **Catalog Name:** The name of the current catalog is reported here.

(N) **Hide Panel:** Click this button to hide the left panel. Doing so provides you with a maximum viewing area for the photo thumbnails.

(O) **Undo:** This item and (P) Rotate go hand in hand. When you Rotate an image using the Rotate tool (item P), you can Undo by clicking this tool.

(P) **Rotate:** When you click the arrow, you can choose to rotate a photo clockwise or counterclockwise. To use either tool, you must first select a thumbnail in the Media Browser.

(Q) **Add Location:** When you click Add Locations, a window opens atop the Organizer. Type a location name (as it appears on a map), and the new location is added to the Places panel. For more on adding photos to maps, see the section "Placing Pictures on Maps," later in this chapter.

(R) **Add Event:** Add Event is yet another item that helps you organize your photos. You can add tags for people, places, and then events to help narrow down a large collection of photos. Each of these items can be sorted by clicking the respective tab at the top of the Organizer. For more on adding Event tags, see the section "Adding new Events," later in this chapter.

(S) **Instant Fix:** Click this button to apply Quick Edit fixes to your photographs. You can crop, adjust lighting, fix red-eye problems, and apply some smart fixes to your photographs without opening them in the Photo Editor.

(T) **Editor:** Click to return to the Photo Editor.

(U) **Slideshow:** Click this button to begin a new project called Memories. Memories displays selected images as a video. For more on Memories, see Chapter 17.

(V) **Home Screen:** Click this button and the Home Screen appears.

(W) **Zoom:** Adjust the slider to make thumbnails larger or smaller.

REMEMBER

This overall description of the Organizer can be helpful when you perform tasks related to the Organizer. Earmark this page and use it as a reference to quickly identify items contained in the Organizer.

Organizing Groups of Images with Tags

Tags are a great way to organize your files. After you acquire your images in the Organizer, as we discuss in Chapter 4, you can tag images according to the dates when you took the pictures, the subject matter, or some other categorical arrangement so that the images are easy to sort.

The Organizer's Tags panel helps you tag your photos and gives you the flexibility to customize your tags.

The Tags panel is divided into four categories: Keywords, People Tags, Places Tags, and Events Tags (see Figure 5-2).

The Organizer helps you organize your photos into these four main categories, and each category has a drop-down list that you can use to create new tags and add new sub-categories. In the following sections, you can find out how to create and manage tags.

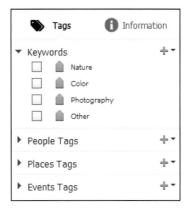

FIGURE 5-2:
The Tags panel in the Organizer.

Creating and viewing a tag

To create a new tag and add tags to photos, follow these steps:

1. **Open the Media Browser and select photos you want to tag.**

   See Chapter 4 for details about opening images in the Organizer.

2. **To create a new tag, choose which category you want to use (Keywords, People Tags, Places Tags, or Events Tags) and then click the down-arrow adjacent to the plus (+) icon next to that category to open a drop-down list.**

3. **From the Tags panel, choose the type of tag you want:**

   - **Keywords:** Choose New Keyword Tag.

   - **People Tags:** Choose New Person.

   - **Places Tags:** Choose Add a New Place.

   - **Events Tags:** Choose Add an Event.

   When you add a new Keyword tag, the Create Keyword Tag dialog box opens, as shown in Figure 5-3, where you can add information about the tag attributes.

FIGURE 5-3:
The Create Keyword Tag dialog box.

Depending on what category you choose, the information you fill into the dialog box varies. For example, when you add a new tag in the Keywords category, the Create Keyword Tag dialog box provides options for editing the tag icon, specifying a category, typing a name, and adding comments. If you add a People tag, you type a person's name and choose a group such as family, friends, and so on. If you add a Places tag, you can choose to map the location. If you add an Events tag, you type the tags for the event, choose dates, and add a description. Hence, the attributes change according to the type of tag you create.

In our example, we add a new tag to the Keywords category.

4. **Specify a category.**

   Click the Category drop-down list and choose one of the preset categories listed in the menu. (See the later section "Working with sub-categories" for instructions on customizing categories.) In our example, we chose Nature for the Category.

5. **Type a name for the tag in the Name text box and add a note to describe the tag.**

   You might use the location where you took the photos, the subject matter, or other descriptive information for the note.
   In our example, we chose Sunset.

6. **Click OK.**

   You return to the Organizer.

7. **In the Organizer, select the photos to which you want to add tags.**

   Click a photo and Shift-click another photo to select photos in a group. Click a photo and Ctrl-click (⌘-click) different photos scattered around the Organizer to select nonsequential photos.

8. **To add a new tag to a photo, first click the plus (+) symbol in the Tags panel to name a new tag, as shown in Figure 5-4. After a tag has been created, drag photos to the tag to tag them.**

   Alternatively, you can drag a tag to the selected photos.

   When you release the mouse button, the photos are tagged.

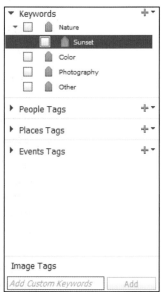

FIGURE 5-4:
The Tags panel after adding a tag in the Keywords category.

The check box adjacent to the tag name is used to display all photos with the respective tag in the Media Browser.

9. **Repeat Steps 2–8 to create tags for all the images you want to organize.**

REMEMBER

Multiple keyword tags can be added to the same image.

Tags help you in many ways, as we explain later in this chapter, in the sections "Sorting photos according to tags" and "Creating an album." The more you become familiar with tagging photos, the more opportunities you have for sorting and finding photos and adding found photos to albums. We encourage you to play with the Tags panel and explore creating tags and tagging photos in each of the different categories.

Adding icons to tags

By default, Elements provides a set of icons displayed adjacent to all tag names. You can change the icon appearance to match a view similar to one of the photos you tag for a given keyword.

If you want to add an image to the tag icon, you can handle it in a few ways. Perhaps the most reliable is to edit the tag as follows:

1. **Right-click a tag in the Tags panel and choose Edit.**

   The Edit Keyword Tag dialog box opens.

2. **Click the Edit Icon button.**

   The Edit Keyword Tag Icon dialog box opens, as shown in Figure 5-5.

3. **Select an image for the tag icon.**

   Click the Import button to import an image for the icon. Or click the left and right arrows to scroll through all the images with this tag and choose one for an icon.

   Additionally, you can click the Find button to open a window displaying thumbnail images of all the photos with this tag.

4. **(Optional) Crop the image by moving handles on the rectangle displayed in the Edit Keyword Tag Icon dialog box.**

FIGURE 5-5:
The Edit Keyword Tag Icon dialog box enables you to add or change a tag icon.

5. **Click OK when you finish editing the icon.**

The icon displays in the Tags panel.

REMEMBER

To view the icons appearing in the Tags panel with the custom appearance you add in the Edit Keyword Tag Icon dialog box, you need to view the Tags panel with Large Icons. See the next section, "Working with custom tags," to change the view.

Working with custom tags

We refer to *custom tags* as those tags you create in the Tags panel. Elements offers you a number of preset tags that you can use to tag your photos, and we refer to those as the *default tags.* In this section, we look at creating and editing custom tags.

You can manage tags by using menu commands from the Tags panel drop-down list (click the down arrow adjacent to one of the + icons) and other commands from a contextual menu that you open by right-clicking a tag on the Tags panel.

In the Tags panel in the Keywords tags drop-down list, you can access these commands:

- >> **New Keyword Tag:** Create a new tag, as we describe in the steps in the "Creating and viewing a tag" section, earlier in this chapter.

- >> **New Sub-Category:** A *sub-category* is a tag nested inside another tag. Create a sub-category by choosing New Sub-Category from the New menu; a dialog box opens, prompting you to type a name for the new sub-category. As an example of how you'd use tags and sub-categories, you might have a tag named Uncle Joe's Wedding. Then you might create sub-categories for Bride Dressing Room, Ceremony, Family Photos, Reception, and so on.

- >> **New Category:** Choose New Category to open a dialog box that prompts you to type a name for the new category. By default, you can find predefined category names for People, Places, Events, and Other. If you want to add your own custom categories, use this menu command.

- >> **Edit:** Choose Edit to open the Edit Keyword Tag dialog box. This dialog box appears exactly the same as the Create Keyword Tag dialog box (refer to Figure 5-3).

- >> **Import Keyword Tags from File:** If you export a tag, the file is written as XML (eXtensible Markup Language). When you choose From File, you can import an XML version of a tags file. This can be helpful if you've spent a lot of time tagging files, creating a new catalog, importing photos, and then importing the tags associated with the photos.

>> **Save Keyword Tags to a File:** You can save tags to a file that you can retrieve with the Import Keyword Tags from File command. This option is handy when you open a different catalog file and want to import the same collection names created in one catalog file to another catalog file.

>> **Collapse All Keyword Tags:** Tags appear in lists that can be collapsed and expanded. An expanded list shows you all the sub-category tags. Choose Collapse All Keyword Tags to collapse the list.

>> **Expand All Keyword Tags:** This command expands a collapsed list.

>> **Show Large Icons:** Click this option to display the tag icons larger in the Tags panel. When you change the view to large icons, you see the custom edits you make when editing an icon.

TECHNICAL
STUFF

Tags are saved automatically with the catalog you work with. By default, Elements creates a catalog and automatically saves your work to it. If you happen to create another catalog, as we explain in Chapter 6, your tags disappear. Be aware of which catalog is open when you create tags in order to return to them.

Working with default tags

When you create a custom tag, you can modify its appearance. With the default tags that Elements provides, you can make some changes to the tags' appearances, but in limited ways. For example, you cannot add a custom image for the tag icon. However, you can modify the names for the preset tags, and you can add custom sub-categories.

To edit a preset category tag, follow these steps:

1. **On one of the predefined categories, right-click and choose Edit.**

   The Edit Category dialog box opens, as shown in Figure 5-6.

2. **Click the Choose Color button to change the color of the tag icon.**

FIGURE 5-6:
In the Edit Category dialog box, you can make some changes to the tag icon.

3. **To choose an icon for the preset category, move the scroll bar horizontally and click the icon you want to use.**

   You're limited to the images Elements provides you with for displaying icons on the predefined categories.

4. **Click OK when you're done.**

Working with sub-categories

A category tag is at the top of the tag hierarchy. As we mention earlier, there are four main categories. Below a category, you can add sub-categories, and each sub-category can have sub-categories below it. For example, you may want to create separate tags for different people in the People Tags category. You can't use custom icons, and you're restricted to using the icons provided by Elements, as shown in Figure 5-6. Here's how to add a new category and sub-category:

1. **In the Tags panel click an existing category for which you want to add a sub-category, or choose New Keyword Tag to create a New Keyword Tag from the drop-down lists (+ icon).**

   In this case, we're working with existing Keywords Tags, so we click Photography to add a sub-category to the Photography Group Colleagues and then click New Person. The Create Sub-Category Name dialog box then opens.

2. **Provide a name in the Sub-Category Name dialog box and choose a group from the Parent Group or Sub-Category drop-down list.**

   In our example, we add one sub-category to the Photography tag. The sub-category is named Portraits, as shown in Figure 5-7.

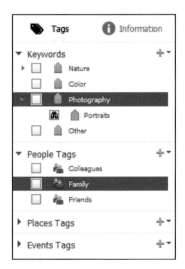

FIGURE 5-7:
Add a sub-category in the Keywords Tags panel.

3. **Click OK and then drag all the photos you want tagged with the new sub-category.**

   Notice that you don't have options for creating custom icons or for adding icons provided by Elements. All the sub-category icons are predefined for you.

Sorting photos according to tags

Tagging photos is useless unless you have a way to view the photos according to their tags. The Organizer makes it easy to view your tagged photos. Simply select the check box next to a tag name (the check box occupies a tiny pair of binoculars when selected). The Media Browser view changes to show you all the photos that have been tagged with the respective tag name, as shown in Figure 5-8.

FIGURE 5-8: The Media Browser displays photos that have been tagged with the item you selected in the Tags panel.

Auto Generating Tags

Elements provides many different kinds of automated features. Among some automated features using Adobe Sensei technology, you find some impressive options for auto creating various kinds of tags.

Working with Auto Creations

NEW

Building upon the auto curating feature introduced in Elements 2018 and further developed in Elements 2019 is the Auto Creation feature, which is based on various events among your photos. You turn on Auto Creations by opening the Organizer Preferences (⌘ + K [Mac] or Ctrl+K [PC]) and click Media-Analysis in the left pane. Select Generate Auto Creations in the right pane, as shown in Figure 5-9. When enabled, Elements analyzes all Photos, Videos, or both in the Media Browser and automatically tags like files.

FIGURE 5-9:
Select
Generate
Auto
Creations
in the
Preferences
dialog box.

REMEMBER

If you run into memory problems, turn off all the options in the Media-Analysis Organizer Preferences after running Auto Creations.

Adding new Events

Select a photo in the Media Browser and click the + (plus) icon in the Events panel. From the drop-down menu, choose New Event. A side panel opens, as shown in Figure 5-10. Provide a name and description and click Done. The new event is added as an Event tag, and items related to the Event are grouped together.

For more on Event tags, see the section "Working with Events," later in this chapter.

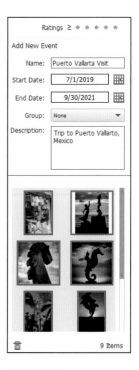

FIGURE 5-10:
Add a new Event in the side panel.

Rating Images with Stars

You can rate photos in the Organizer by assigning images a number of stars, from one to five. You might have some photos that are exceptional, which you want to give five-star ratings, whereas poor photos with lighting and focus problems might be rated with one star.

To assign a star rating to a photo, select a photo in the Media Browser and click a star in the Tags panel, as shown in Figure 5-11. One star is the lowest rating, and five stars is the highest.

FIGURE 5-11:
Rating photos with stars in the Information panel.

Photos can be rated with stars by clicking a star below a photo in the Media Browser. To see the stars below photos, you must be viewing your photos with Details. If the stars are not currently visible in the Media Browser, choose View Details or press Ctrl/⌘ +D.

You can rate multiple photos by showing Details, select photos you want rated with the same start rating, and click the star you want to use for the rating. All photos take on the same rating.

TIP

Some DSLR and mirrorless cameras enable you to rate images with stars in-camera. You can quickly select images you think are some of the better photos of a given shoot. When you import the photos in Elements, the metadata for the files are also imported, including your star ratings.

After assigning star ratings to photos, you can sort photos according to their ratings. For example, click a star that appears in the Ratings at the top of the Media Browser (refer to Figure 5-11). If you click the third star, all photos rated with three, four, and five stars appear in the Media Browser. If you click the fifth star, only those photos rated with five stars appear in the Media Browser.

REMEMBER

Be certain to click the star value in the Information panel when rating a photo with a star rating. If you click a star next to the Ratings label at the top of the Media Browser, Elements thinks you want to sort photos in the Media Browser according to the star rating.

Adding Images to an Album

Albums offer another way to organize your images. You can use albums to store photos that meet a specific set of criteria. For example, you might use your tags and star ratings to easily find all the five-star photos of your family. Or use your Events and Places tags to find all the photos you took at a conference in Paris. However, the photos you put in an album don't need to be tagged or starred. When you need a folder for a special stash of digital photos, the Organizer's albums feature is there for you.

Creating an album

With albums and star ratings, you can further break down a collection into groups that you might want to mark for printing, sharing, or onscreen slideshows.

To create an album, follow these steps:

1. **Sort photos in the Media Browser to determine what photos you want to include in a new album.**

   In our example, we clicked the third star to sort photos ranked with three or more stars.

2. **Click Albums at the top left of the Organizer and then click the plus (+) icon next to My Albums, as shown in Figure 5-12. From the drop-down list, choose New Album.**

3. **Name the new album.**

In the Panel Bin, you see the Add New Album panel. Type a name for the album in the Album Name text box in the New Album panel on the right side of the Organizer window, as shown in Figure 5-13.

If you didn't sort files in Step 1, you can do so now, or simply pick and choose which photos to add to the new album from photos appearing in your catalog.

4. **By default, any photos selected in the Media Browser are added to the new Album. To add more photos, drag photos from the Media Browser to the Content tab in the Edit Album panel, as shown in Figure 5-13.**

If photos are sorted and you want to include all photos in the Media Browser, press Ctrl+A/⌘ +A to select all the photos, or choose Edit ⇨ Select All. After the files are selected, drag them to the Content pane in the Edit Album panel. (See Figure 5-13.)

If you don't have files sorted, click one or more photos and drag them to the Content pane. Repeat dragging photos until you have all photos you want to include in your new album.

5. **Click OK at the bottom of the panel.**

Your new album now appears listed in the Albums category on the Import panel.

FIGURE 5-12: Click the plus (+) icon to open the drop-down list and then choose New Album.

That's it! Your new album is created, and the photos you dragged to the album are added to it. You can display all the photos within a given album in the Media Browser by clicking the album name in the Albums panel.

REMEMBER

Creating multiple albums uses only a fraction of the computer memory that would be required if you wanted to duplicate photos for multiple purposes, such as printing, web hosting, sharing, and so on.

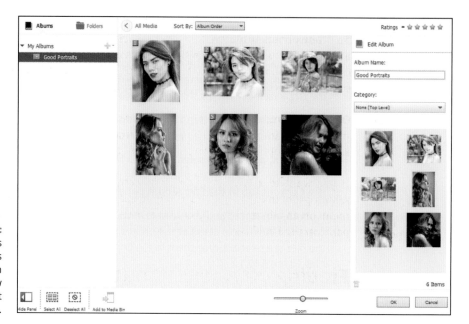

FIGURE 5-13:
Drag photos
to the items
window in
the Add New
Album Content
panel.

Using albums for temporary work

You can add an album for temporary work and then delete the album when you no longer need it.

For instance, you may want to explore some of the creation and sharing items in the Create and Share panels. Before you peruse the options, create an album and add photos to it. Then proceed to use the sharing feature that interests you. When you finish, right-click to open a contextual menu and choose Delete *<album name>*.

Editing an album

After creating an album, you may want to change the album name, add more photos to an album, delete some photos from an album, change the album category, or make some other kind of edit.

Your first step in performing any kind of edit to an album is to look at the left side of the Organizer. In the Import panel, you see a list of albums under the Albums category like those shown in Figure 5-13, in the previous section. To edit an album, right-click the album name and choose Edit. After clicking Edit, the album appears in the Panel Bin on the right side of the Organizer. Drag images from the Media Browser to the album. You can also drag images from the Media Browser to an album name to add photos to an album.

To delete photos from an album, right-click an album name and choose Edit from a context menu. When the album opens as a panel on the right, select a photo and click the Trash icon at the bottom of the panel. Note that you cannot drag a photo to the Trash icon. You must select a photo and click the Trash icon.

Other commands are available in the context menu that you open from an album name in the Import panel. You can rename an album, delete an album, explore some export options, share an album, and add more media to your album.

REMEMBER

If you want to use the context menu commands, you must close the Add New Album panel in the Panel Bin. While this panel is open, you cannot open a context menu on an album name. Click either Done or Cancel to close the Add New Album panel in the Panel Bin.

Finding out more about sharing your albums

An album is a starting point for many exciting things you can do with a collection of photos. Albums help you assemble a collection of photos that can be viewed on many devices and shared with others. Later in this book, we explore many ways you can share your albums with friends, family, and even the world, if you like:

>> Host albums online for others to view your photos.

>> Save the albums to a file on your hard drive.

>> Organize an album for sharing photos with others.

>> View albums as slideshows.

Chapter 16 gives you the details on all these sharing tricks, except the one in the last bullet. To find out how to view albums as slideshows, see Chapter 17.

Adding People in the Media Browser

For most people, the most enjoyable pictures are those of family and friends. You may take photos of landscapes and wonderful places, but quite often you'll ask someone to stand in front of the Colosseum, Louvre, Grand Canyon, or other notable landmark.

For just that reason, Photoshop Elements makes it easy for you to identify, sort, and view pictures with people.

Elements groups photos of the same person into clusters, even before you start adding names to faces in the Media Browser. What this means for you is a much easier time tagging people when you import pictures of your family and friends.

You know that you can add folders of pictures to the Organizer to help manage photos. After you add new pictures to the Organizer, you can select a folder in the Import panel and label all the people in the photos. Elements makes it easy to label people's faces:

1. **Open Preferences (Ctrl/⌘ +K) and click Media-Analysis.**

2. **Be sure the Run Face Recognition Automatically check box is selected.**

3. **Import photos into the Organizer.**

4. **After you import photos, click the People tab.**

   Elements shows you several clusters of photos.

5. **Click Add Name.**

   Type a name and click the check mark to accept the name, as shown in Figure 5-14.

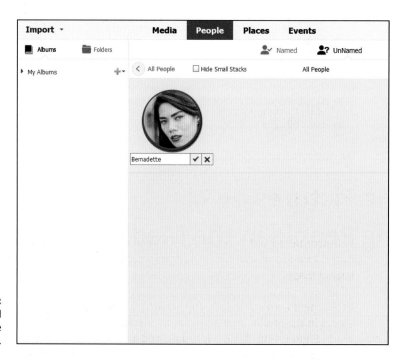

FIGURE 5-14:
Click Add Name and type a name.

6. **Continue adding names.**

   This process is manual, and you may have to continue adding names even when photos appear the same as others you've named.

7. **When you're finished, click Named at the top of the panel to see all the clusters you've named, as shown in Figure 5-15.**

   The number adjacent to the name indicates the number of photos tagged with the same name.

8. **Click a cluster to show all the photos within the group.**

   That's it! After you label the photos, you can easily search, sort, and locate photos of specific people. You can even download your Facebook friends list to the Organizer to help simplify labeling people.

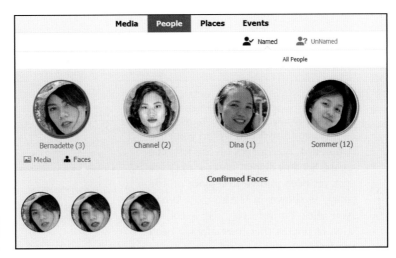

FIGURE 5-15: Photos tagged with names.

Placing Pictures on Maps

You may take vacations to interesting places and want to sort photos according to the location where the photos were shot. You can easily place photos on geo-spatial maps.

In Elements, the methods for pinning photos to a map is an easy task. Click Places in the Media Browser, and the Media Browser window changes to what you see in Figure 5-16. Type a location, and a submenu displays a map location. Click the map location, and the map changes the view with the photos shown at the left side of the Media Browser.

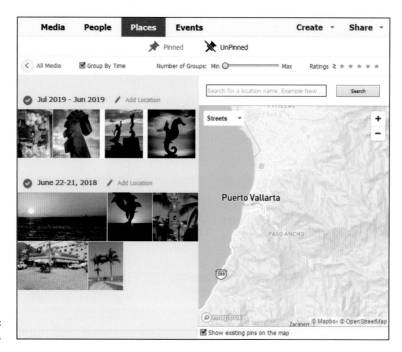

FIGURE 5-16:
The Places tab.

At the top of the window, you see Pinned and Unpinned. When you click Unpinned, the images on the left side of the window display photos that have not yet been pinned to a place on the map, as shown in Figure 5-17. When you click Pinned, you see a collection of photos that have already been pinned to map locations.

To see how easy placing photos on maps is, do the following:

1. **Click Places at the top of the Media Browser.**

2. **Click the photos in the Media Browser that you want to add to a new place.**

3. **Click the Add Location icon at the bottom of the Media Browser.**

FIGURE 5-17:
Search for a location and click Unpinned at the top of the Media Browser to display a collection of unpinned photos.

A window appears, prompting you to type a name for the location.

4. **Type the location name (the city or other location type).**

5. **Click Apply.**

   The selected images are pinned to the map location.

6. **To locate the pinned photos, type the location name in the Search text field and press Enter.**

   The map changes to the location you add to the Search text field. Click Pinned and you see the pinned photos.

TIP

When you press Enter after completing a search and click Pinned, the Places window defaults back to All Places.

If you want to sort photos according to location, choose Find ⇨ Using Advanced Search. The Organizer view changes and a column labeled Places appears. All photos assigned to specific locations are listed in this column. You can easily select the check boxes to find photos assigned to a given place or select multiple check boxes to find photos from several places.

Working with Events

You may have photos taken at special occasions or during holidays. You can add more organization opportunities to your Organizer management by assigning photos to different Events.

An *Event* can be any function of your choosing, such as a Christmas party, a ski trip, or an anniversary celebration. To create an Event and assign photos to it, do the following:

1. **Click the Events tab at the top of the Organizer window.**

2. **Select photos and click the Add Event icon at the bottom of the Media Browser.**

   When you add a new Event, a Name Event pop-up appears, where you can enter the event name, dates, and a description.

3. **Type a name for the Event in the Event text field in the Add New Event panel.**

4. **Type a description in the Description text box.**

5. Add photos to the Event.

Drag photos from the Media Browser (the right side of the Organizer window) to the Events panel. When you create Events, dates are automatically added in the Events panel.

6. Click Done.

The photos are now assigned to an Event. To view Events, click the Events tab at the top of the Organizer. You see collections of photos if you added several Events, with the first photo in the Event appearing on top. To view all photos, double-click the Event thumbnail that you want to view.

When you click the Events tab and then click Named at the top of the Organizer window, you see the Events you added, as shown in Figure 5-18. Double-click a cluster to display the images assigned to the Event.

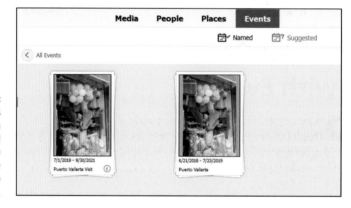

FIGURE 5-18:
Click the Events tab and then click Named to display the Events you've added in the Organizer.

IN THIS CHAPTER

» **Working with catalogs**

» **Switching to different views**

» **Viewing Memories**

» **Searching for your photos**

» **Grouping your files in stacks**

Chapter **6**

Viewing and Finding Your Images

Photo organization begins with adding images to a catalog. By default, the Organizer creates a new catalog for you (so you might not even notice the presence of your catalog without reading this book). As your catalog grows with the addition of more files, you'll want to discover ways to search and use a given set of images for a project.

In this chapter, we begin by talking about catalogs and then look at how to view and organize your pictures in the Organizer and the Media Browser. We show how the many options help speed up your work in Photoshop Elements. Before tackling this chapter, get familiar with the Organizer. Chapter 4 offers a brief glimpse of the Organizer and looks at a few different views; Chapter 5 explains how to tag photos and create photo albums in the Organizer.

Cataloging Files

When you import files in the Organizer, all your files are saved automatically to a catalog. The files themselves aren't really saved to the catalog; rather, links from the catalog to the individual files are saved. In Elements, *links* are like pointers that tell the catalog where to look for a file. When you add and delete files within the Organizer, the catalog is updated continually.

REMEMBER

After you import files in the Organizer, the Organizer maintains a link to the media. If you move the media on your hard drive, the link is broken. You need to reestablish the link by opening the file in the Photo Editor. The Find Offline Drives – Edit dialog box opens so that you can reconnect the file by browsing for its new location.

Your default catalog is titled *My Catalog* by the Organizer. As you add photos in the Organizer, your default catalog grows and may eventually store thousands of photos. At some point, you may want to create one or more additional catalogs to store photos. You may want to use one catalog for your family's and friends' photos and another for business or recreational activities. You may want to create separate catalogs for special purposes such as business, family, social networking, or other kinds of logical divisions. To further segregate images, you might create a number of different albums from a given catalog.

Using the Catalog Manager

Catalogs are created, deleted, and managed in the Catalog Manager. To access the Catalog Manager, choose File ➪ Manage Catalogs. The Catalog Manager opens, as shown in Figure 6-1.

FIGURE 6-1:
The Catalog Manager dialog box.

To keep your photos organized and your catalog files small, you can start a completely new catalog before you import photos. Follow these steps:

1. **Choose File ➪ Manage Catalogs and click the New button in the Catalog Manager dialog box, as shown in Figure 6-1.**

2. **When the New Catalog dialog box opens, type a name for the new catalog in the File Name text box.**

3. **(Optional) If you want to add the free music files that installed with Elements, select the Import Free Music into All New Catalogs check box.**

   We recommend selecting the Import Free Music into All New Catalogs and Import Music Files check box. The Organizer ships with free music files that you can use in a variety of creations. See Chapter 17 for more on making creations.

TIP

4. **Click OK to create the new catalog.**

5. **Choose File ➪ Get Photos and Videos ➪ From Files and Folders to add files to the new catalog. Alternatively, you can click the Import button above Albums and Folders in the left panel.**

   The Get Photos and Videos from Files and Folders dialog box opens.

6. **Navigate your hard drive and select the photos you want to add. After you identify all the files, click Get Media.**

   The selected photos are added to your new collection of media contained in the catalog.

Working with catalogs

After you create different catalogs for your images, the following tips for working with catalogs will come in handy:

» **Understanding how you want to organize your photos before creating your first catalog:** Unfortunately, Elements doesn't provide you with a command to split large catalogs into smaller ones. However, if you've created a large catalog and want to split it into two or more separate catalogs, you can manually add new photos to a new catalog and delete photos from the older catalog.

» **Switching to a different catalog:** When you need to open a different catalog file, choose File ➪ Manage Catalogs and select the name of the catalog you want to open. Click Open at the bottom of the dialog box to open the selected catalog. The Organizer window changes to reflect files contained in that catalog.

» **Fixing a corrupted catalog:** Notice the Repair button in Figure 6-1. If you can't see thumbnail previews of images or open them in one of the editing modes, your catalog file might be corrupted. Click the Repair button to try to fix the problem.

>> **Improving catalog performance:** When catalogs get sluggish, you might need to optimize a catalog to gain better performance. You should regularly optimize your catalog (by clicking the Optimize button in the Catalog Manager) to keep your catalog operating at optimum performance.

Backing up your catalog

Computer users often learn the hard way about the importance of backing up a hard drive and the precious data they spent time creating and editing. We can save you that aggravation right now, before you spend any more time editing your photos in Elements.

We authors are so paranoid when we're writing a book that we back up our chapters on multiple drives when we finish them. The standard rule is that if you spend sufficient time working on a project and it gets to the point where redoing your work would be a major aggravation, it's time to back up files.

When organizing your files, adding keyword tags, creating albums, and creating stacks and version sets, you want to back up the catalog file in case it becomes corrupted. Fortunately, backing up catalogs is available to both Windows and Mac users. For optimum performance, backing up to a 1TB USB drive will serve you best.

Here's how you can use Elements to create a backup of your catalog:

1. **Choose File ⇨ Backup Catalog to open the Backup Catalog Wizard.**

   This wizard, shown in Figure 6-2, has several choices for backing up catalogs.

2. **Select the source to back up.**

   The first pane in the Backup Catalog to Hard Drive Wizard offers three options:

NEW

- **Backup Catalog Structure:** When you choose this option, you back up the structure of the catalog that contains tags, people, places, events, and so on. No photos or videos are backed up when you make this choice.

- **Full Backup:** Use this choice when you want to back up everything, including your photos and videos.

- **Incremental Backup:** Select this radio button if you've already performed at least one backup and you want to update the backed-up files.

FIGURE 6-2:
The wizard
provides
options for
selecting the
destination
media for the
backup.

3. **Click Next and select a target location for your backed-up files.**

   Active drives, external hard drives attached to your computer, or mounted network drives available to your computer appear in the Select Destination Drive list. Select a drive, and Elements automatically assesses the write speed and identifies a previous backup file if one was created.

   The total size of the files to copy is reported in the wizard. This information is helpful so that you know whether more than one drive is needed to complete the backup (on Windows) or a backup drive has enough space to complete the backup.

4. **If you intend to copy files to your hard drive or to another hard drive attached to your computer, click the Browse button and identify the path.**

5. **Click Save Backup.**

   The backup commences. Be certain to not interrupt the backup. It might take some time, so just let Elements work away until you're notified that the backup is complete.

Backing up photos and files

With files stored all over your hard drive, manually copying files to a second hard drive, CD, or DVD would take quite a bit of time. Fortunately, Elements makes finding files to back up a breeze.

Choose File ➪ Copy/Move to Removable Drive and then, in the dialog box that opens, select the Copy Files check box and click Next. Select a hard drive, type a name for the backup folder, and click OK. Elements goes about copying all files shown in the Organizer to your backup source.

TIP

Mac users don't have an option for backing up photos from the Organizer to CDs or DVDs. On the Mac, you can create a burn folder in the Finder, select all photos in the Organizer, and drag the selected files to the burn folder. Click the Burn button, and the files are copied to a CD or DVD.

Switching to a Different View

The Organizer provides you with several different viewing options. In Chapter 4, you find out about viewing files in the Media Browser and look at viewing recent imports and all files. You can also view files according to a timeline, certain media types such as those media types listed in the View ➪ Media Types menu, and places and events. Here you find a quick tour of the View menu.

On the View menu, you have choices for sorting files that are displayed in the Media Browser. Some of the menu choices you have are

- **» Media Types:** Choose View ➪ Media Types and look over the submenu. You can eliminate video, audio, and projects by selecting the respective items if you want to view just photos in the Media Browser. Likewise, you can eliminate photos and explore the other choices by selecting or deselecting the submenu items.

- **» Hidden Files:** If files are hidden, you can view all files by choosing View ➪ Hidden Files, and then you can choose (in the submenu) to view All Files, view Hidden Files, or (if files are in view) to hide Files.

- **» Details:** By default, file details, such as file creation dates and star ratings, are hidden. You can show file details by choosing View ➪ Details or pressing Ctrl+D/⌘ +D.

- **» File Names:** By default, the filenames of the photos appearing in the Media Browser are hidden. You can show filenames by choosing View ➪ File Names.

- **» Timeline:** Choose View ➪ Timeline, and a horizontal bar opens at the top of the Organizer. A slider appears on the bar that you can drag left and right to select a time when your photos were taken, as shown in Figure 6-3.

FIGURE 6-3:
The Media
Browser
displaying a
timeline.

Viewing Photos in Memories (Slideshow)

Elements offers essentially three different slideshow-type viewing options:

» In the Media Browser, you'll notice a button called Slideshow (after the slideshow is created, it's known as Memories) where Elements creates a video of selected photos in the Media Browser. You also find a Slideshow option in the Create panel. Both options are used to create animated videos of your cherished photos that you can export as a movie file and share with friends and family. We cover creating Memories videos in Chapter 17, where we discuss many different creation options.

» The other slideshow option you have is to view selected photos as a slideshow on your computer. Naturally, you find this option as a menu command in the View menu. However, the command you want is not called Slideshow. Elements provides you with a Full Screen command, which you use to view your pictures in Full Screen view as a slideshow.

Here's how you create a slideshow using Full Screen view from the View menu:

1. **Select photos in the Organizer and choose View ⇨ Full Screen (or press F11 on Windows or ⌘+F11 on Mac).**

   The first photo appears with a tools panel and two panels with various editing options. You can organize, edit, transform, tag, and add metadata to your photos while in Full Screen view. Click Organize and then click Edit to open panels with editing options, as shown in Figure 6-4.

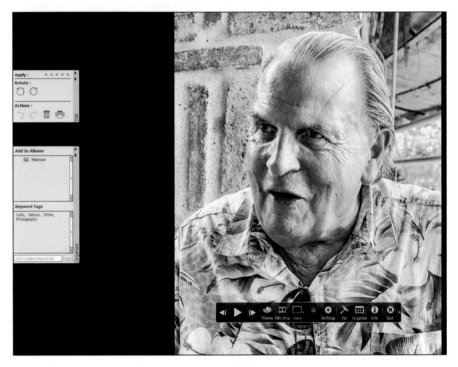

FIGURE 6-4:
The first photo in Full Screen view opens with a number of tool and panel options.

2. **Click the Film Strip button on the lower-left side in the horizontal tools strip and click Organize to expand the panel (see Figure 6-5).**

   The Full Screen viewer appears, as shown in Figure 6-5. Your photos are displayed as thumbnails at the bottom of the window. Click a photo to jump to the respective image.

Keep in mind that Elements provides you with view options when you use various menu commands in the View menu. When you view photos in Full Screen view, you don't have any export or saving opportunities. Once again, to save a slideshow, turn to Chapter 17.

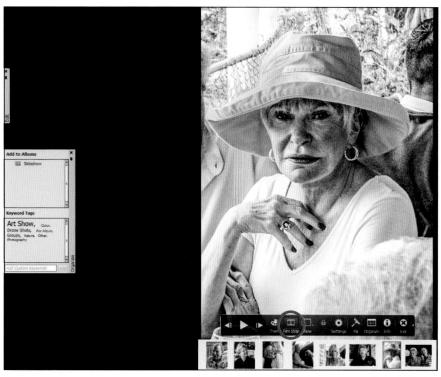

Photos: Ted Padova

FIGURE 6-5:
Click Film Strip to see mini thumbnails of the photos in the slideshow.

Searching for Photos

When you're looking for a photo but aren't quite sure how you filed it away, the Elements search options are a great tool. You probably remember some detail that can help you find the photo or photos you're looking for. In Elements, you'll likely find a search tool that can look for that specific detail or details so that you locate your photo in no time.

Using Search

Before we explore the many options you have from menu commands on the Find menu, look at the Media Browser. At the top, you find the word *Search* and a magnifying glass.

When you click Search at the top of the Media Browser window, the interface changes to an overlay with a series of buttons along the left side of the window, and the thumbnails in the Media Browser are dimmed, as shown in Figure 6-6.

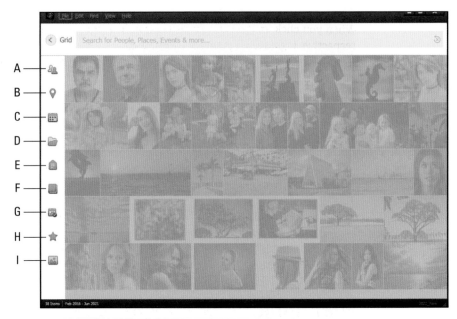

FIGURE 6-6:
Click Search
to display the
Search overlay
window.

TIP

Before we go too far, you should know that you can exit the overlay window at any time by clicking Grid in the upper-left corner or pressing the Esc key. You're then returned to the normal Media Browser window.

You can explore the various options by mousing over the icons at the left side of the window, such as the Smart Tags (top), shown in Figure 6-6. The search options available to you include the following:

(A) **People:** All the people you've tagged are shown in people clusters.

(B) **Places:** Photos you have tagged with locations are shown according to geographic location.

(C) **Date:** Search by the date when the photo was taken.

(D) **Folders:** You can restrict searching to photos from given folders in your catalog by clicking the Folders icon.

(E) **Keywords:** Any photos you've tagged with Keyword tags are shown.

(F) **Albums:** Click this icon and all the albums you've created are shown.

(G) **Events:** All events tagged with Event tags are shown.

(H) **Ratings:** You can search for photos you've tagged with star ratings.

(I) **Media Types:** Mouse over Media Types, and you find options for searching photos, audio files, videos, and projects.

When you click an item in any of the search categories, only those items with the respective tags are displayed in the Media Browser. To return to a full catalog view, click Grid at the upper-left side of the Media Browser window.

Searching for untagged items

You can tag files with a number of different criteria, as we explain in Chapter 5. When tags are added to images, you can sort files according to tag labels. We also cover sorting by tag labels in Chapter 5. For now, look at the Find menu and notice the Untagged Items command.

TIP

If you haven't added tags to some items and want to show only the untagged files so that you can begin to add tags, choose Find ⇨ Untagged Items or press Ctrl+Shift+Q on Windows or ⌘ +Shift+Q. Elements displays all files without tags in the Media Browser so that you can easily see which photos need to be tagged.

Searching captions and notes

Captions and notes are added in the Information panel. When captions or notes are added to files, you can search for the caption name, contents of a note, or both. To search caption names and notes, follow these steps:

1. **Make sure you have media added to the Organizer.**

    See Chapter 4 for details.

2. **Add captions, notes, or both.**

    If you don't have any files tagged with captions or notes, you need to add them in the Information panel. Open the Information panel and type captions and notes in the respective text boxes. (Chapter 5 tells you how to add your captions and notes.)

3. **Choose Find ⇨ By Caption or Note.**

    The Find by Caption or Note dialog box opens, as shown in Figure 6-7.

FIGURE 6-7: In the Find by Caption or Note dialog box, specify search criteria.

4. **In the Find Items with Caption or Note text box, type the words you want to locate and choose to match all or part of the word or words you typed.**

   Options in the dialog box are

   - **Match Only the Beginning of Words in Captions and Notes:** Select this radio button when you know that your caption or note begins with words you type in the text box.

   - **Match Any Part of Any Word in Captions and Notes:** Select this radio button if you're not sure whether the text typed in the box is used at the beginning of a caption or note, or whether it's contained within the caption name or note text.

5. **Click OK.**

   The results appear in the Organizer.

Searching by history

Searching *history* is searching for chronologically ordered information about operations performed on your media, such as printing, emailing, sharing, and so on. Elements keeps track of what you do with your photos when you perform a number of different tasks. You can search for files based on their file history by choosing Find ⇨ By History. Select the options you want on the By History submenu, and Elements reports files found on date searches that meet your history criteria.

Searching metadata

Metadata includes information about your images that's supplied by digital cameras, as well as custom data you add to a file. Metadata contains descriptions of the image, such as your camera name, the camera settings you used to take a picture, copyright information, and much more.

Metadata also includes some of the information you add in Elements, such as keyword tags, albums, People tags, and so on. You can combine various metadata items in your search, such as keyword tags, camera make and model, f-stop, ISO setting, and so on. Searching for metadata might be particularly helpful when you have photos taken during an event by several family members and friends. In this example, you might want to isolate only those photos taken with a particular camera model.

To search metadata, follow these steps:

1. **Choose Find ⇨ By Details (Metadata) in the Organizer.**

   The Find by Details (Metadata) dialog box, shown in Figure 6-8, opens.

2. **Choose to search for one criterion or all your criteria by selecting a radio button.**

   The first two radio buttons in the dialog box offer choices for Boolean OR and Boolean AND. In other words, do you want to search for one item *or* another, or to search for one item *and* another. The results can be quite different depending on the criteria you identify in the menus below the radio buttons.

3. **Choose an item from the first menu (we used Filename in Figure 6-8) and then choose to include or exclude the item. Next fill in the third column.**

   How you fill in the third column depends on your selections in the first two columns.

   Items are listed as menus in horizontal rows. The third column can be a menu or a text box, as shown in Figure 6-8.

4. **(Optional) To add criteria (in our example, we use two items for our search), click the plus (+) symbol.**

   Another row is added to the dialog box, and you select your choices, as explained in Step 3.

5. **If you want to save the Search attributes, check Save this Search Criteria as Saved Search.**

6. **After identifying your search criteria, click Search.**

   The media matching the criteria is shown in the Media Browser.

FIGURE 6-8: Choose Find ⇨ By Details (Metadata) in the Organizer to open the dialog box in which metadata are specified.

Searching similarities

We discuss tagging people in Chapter 5. When you have people tagged, you can easily click the People tab at the top of the Organizer and locate all the people you have tagged. Not all the search options are perfect. You may find that some photos are missed; however, the search features offer you a more than reasonable effort at finding the photos you want to use.

Searching visually similar photos

Elements also lets you search photos for visual similarities. You may have group shots, architecture, animal life, and so on and want to search for photos containing objects that are visually similar.

To search for photos with visual similarities, choose Find ⇨ By Visual Searches, Visually Similar Photos and Videos, Objects appearing in Photos, and Duplicate Photos.

Searching duplicates

You may have a number of photos that are duplicates or are very close to being duplicate images. You might want to locate duplicates or near-duplicate images and delete some from your catalog or stack the photos. (See "Stackin' 'em up," later in this chapter.) To find duplicate photos, choose Find ⇨ By Visual Searches menu and choose Duplicate Photos.

Photos that are visually similar appear in horizontal rows. Click Stack, and the photos are stacked.

If you want to delete photos, click a photo and then click the Remove from Catalog button at the bottom of the window.

Searching objects

You may want to stack or delete photos that contain similar objects, such as buildings, automobiles, trees, groups of people, and so on. To search for objects, follow these steps:

1. **Choose Find ⇨ By Visual Searches ⇨ Objects appearing in photo.**

2. **Double-click a photo containing the desired object.**

   A rectangle appears for selecting a photo that contains the object you want to search.

3. **Move the rectangle and resize it so that it surrounds the object you're looking for, as shown in Figure 6-9.**

4. **Click the Search Object button.**

   Elements displays its search results.

Grouping Files That Get in the Way

Elements offers a few ways to organize images that are getting in the way. You can hide files, stack files, or create versions, as we explain in the following sections.

Marking files as hidden

With a simple menu command, you can mark selected files in the Organizer as *hidden.* Select files you want to hide, and, from either the Edit menu or a contextual menu, choose Visibility ➪ Mark as Hidden. To see the files you mark for hiding, return to the same Visibility menu and choose Show Hidden. Essentially, you remove the check mark for Show Hidden, which results in hiding the files hidden. To easily toggle between showing and hiding files marked for hiding, choose View ➪ Hidden Files.

Stackin' 'em up

Think of a *stack* of images as being like a stack of cards that are face up: You see only the front card, with all the other cards hidden under that top card. Stacks in the Organizer work the same way. You hide different images behind a foreground image. At any time, you can sort the images or display all images in the stack in the Organizer.

To create a stack, follow these steps:

1. **In the Organizer, select several photos.**

   You can select any number of photos in the Media Browser, as shown in Figure 6-10. However, you can't stack audio or movie files.

FIGURE 6-10:
In the Media Browser, select a group of images you want to stack.

2. **Choose Edit ⇨ Stack ⇨ Stack Selected Photos.**

   Elements stacks your photos. The first image you select remains in view in the Media Browser. In the upper-right area, an icon that looks like a stack of cards appears on the image thumbnail when you've stacked some images, as you can see in Figure 6-11.

To unstack photos, do the following:

1. **Set the view to Detail view.** Detail view displays detail information below the thumbnail images in the Media Browser. If you are not in Detail view, press Ctrl/⌘ +D or choose View ⇨ Details. You must be in Detail view to proceed.

2. **Select Unstack Photos.**

   Right-click a group of stacked photos and choose Stack ⇨ Unstack Photos. Alternatively, you can choose Edit ⇨ Stack ⇨ Unstack Photos. If you want to unstack multiple stacks, again you must be in Detail view and then choose View ⇨ Expand All Stacks.

FIGURE 6-11:
Set the View to
Details, right-
click a stack,
and choose
Stack ➪
Unstack
Photos.

After you stack a group of images, you can use the Stack submenu commands to manage the photos. Click a stack to select it and then choose Edit ➪ Stack. The available submenu commands are as follows:

>> Automatically Suggest Photo Stacks

>> Stack Selected Photos

>> Unstack Photos

>> Expand Photos in Stack

>> Collapse Photos in Stack

>> Flatten Stack

>> Remove Selected Photos from Stack

>> Set as Top Photo

WARNING

When you flatten a stack, all photos except for the top photo are deleted from the catalog but not from your hard drive.

TIP

To view all stacks in the Media Browser in expanded form, choose View ➪ Expand All Stacks. Using this command doesn't require you to individually select stacks in the Media Browser before expanding them.

Creating versions

Versions are similar to stacks, but you create versions from only one file. You can edit an image and save both the edited version and the original as a version set.

Also, you can make additional edits in either editing mode and save to a version set. To create a version set, follow these steps:

1. **Select an image by clicking it in the Media Browser.**

2. **Apply an edit.**

   For example, right in the Organizer, you can correct some brightness problems in your image. Click Instant Fix to open the Instant Fix panel and click one of the tools in the panel. See Chapter 10 for more details on using the Instant Fix tools or any other editing tool.

3. **Save the edited file in a version set.**

   Choose File ➪ Save. In the Save dialog box under Save Options, select Save in Version Set with Original.

   If you don't use Instant Fix and make an edit, you need to choose Save As and save your file in a Version Set. Don't make an edit and click Save. It will overwrite your original file.

4. **View the items in the version set by clicking the image in the Media Browser and choosing Edit ➪ Version Set ➪ Expand Items in Version Set.**

   Elements automatically creates a version set for you when you apply the Instant Fix to the file. The Media Browser shows two thumbnail images — one representing the original image and the other representing the edited version.

5. **To open the original image in the Photo Editor, select the image in the Media Browser and then click the Editor button.**

6. **Edit the image in Expert mode.**

   You can choose from many different menu commands to edit the image. For example, suppose you want an image for printing and a lower-resolution image for posting on your Facebook page. Choose Image ➪ Resize ➪ Image Size, as we explain in Chapter 2, to resample an image.

7. **Save a version by choosing File ➪ Save As.**

8. **In the Save Options area of the Save As dialog box, select the Include in the Organizer and Save in Version Set with Original check boxes.**

   Chapter 1 also explains the options for saving files.

9. **Click Save.**

   The edits made in the Photo Editor are saved as another version in your version set.

   After you create a version set, you find additional submenu commands that you can use to manage the version set. Choose Edit ➪ Version Set or right-click a version set and then choose Version Set.

3

Selecting and Correcting Photos

IN THIS PART . . .

Work with the Camera Raw Editor.

Change, optimize, perfect, and combine images into composite designs.

Select image content and then alter that content for a variety of purposes, such as correcting the color, changing the appearance, and extracting the content so that you can add it to other photos.

Correct an image's contrast, brightness, and color irregularity.

Convert one color mode to another.

IN THIS CHAPTER

» Getting familiar with Camera Raw

» Understanding panels and profiles

» Editing non-Raw Images

» Examining default settings

» Using sidecar files and preferences

Chapter **7**

Editing Camera Raw Images

A s we state in the Introduction, our apologies for not including Camera Raw adjustments in some earlier releases of this book. As you find out in this chapter, using the Camera Raw Editor should be one of your frequent tasks for beginning most image editing tasks.

The forthcoming chapters (8 through 11) deal with making tonal adjustments, correcting brightness and contrast, and working with color. You should look at these chapters as using techniques to tweak your photos or add special effects. Your first stop, however, when it comes to improving your photos' overall brightness and contrast is the Camera Raw Editor.

You may often hear people refer to this separate application, included with your purchase of Photoshop Elements, as the Camera Raw Converter, the Camera Raw Dialog, the Raw Editor, the Raw Converter, and other such names. For our purposes here, we refer to the application as the Camera Raw Editor or simply the Raw Editor.

Launching the Camera Raw Editor

NEW

In Elements 2021, Adobe made a major change to the Camera Raw Editor user interface. If you used the Camera Raw Editor in previous versions of Elements, you'll immediately notice the difference in the user interface (UI) when you open a file in the Raw Editor in Elements 2021 and later.

The first time you launch the Camera Raw Editor, a Setup Camera Raw screen opens and prompts you to make a choice for the UI you want to use. In Figure 7-1, you can see the initial screen after launching the Camera Raw Editor.

As shown in Figure 7-1 you have a choice to use the new Adobe Camera Raw (ACR) or use the legacy UI. The new UI displays the film strip at the bottom of the ACR window by default, and you can view multiple panel settings simultaneously in the Panel Bin. You can change the filmstrip orientation from horizontal to vertical.

FIGURE 7-1:
The Camera
Raw Editor
Setup screen.

The legacy UI displays the filmstrip, by default, on the left side of the ACR window, and you can work in only a single panel at a time.

In this chapter, we look at using the new ACR UI. The new ACR UI is the default. Double-click a raw file or choose File ➪ Open in Camera Raw Click in the Photo Editor. The first screen you see is the Camera Raw Set Up screen, shown in Figure 7-1. Click OK to accept defaults and open the raw file in the Raw Editor. As you can see in Figure 7-2, much has changed in the user interface. All the features and tools you may have used in previous versions of the Camera Raw Editor are available in this upgrade. The settings have just been moved around a bit.

FIGURE 7-2:
The Camera
Raw Editor
user interface.

Understanding Camera Raw

First and foremost, a Camera Raw file is a file format. Most DSLRs, many mid- to high-end mirrorless cameras, and more than 20 different cellphone cameras can save data in the Camera Raw format. Unfortunately almost all developers use their own unique file extension when saving files. For example, Canon raw files are saved as .crw or .cr2, Sony's files are saved as .arw, Nikon's files are saved as .nef, and Fuji files are saved with an .raf extension. Likewise, other developers use unique naming conventions.

Dealing with myriad different Raw file formats has been a challenge for Adobe. With each release of the Camera Raw Editor, Adobe needs to ensure compatibility with all the developers supporting Camera Raw.

One solution provided by Adobe is Adobe's own Raw file format, which uses a .dng extension (Digital Negative). In the event that you acquire an update to Lightroom, Photoshop, or Photoshop Elements and your camera's Raw format is not supported, you can download the free DNG converter from Adobe at https:// helpx.adobe.com/photoshop/using/adobe-dng-converter.html. You may be able to convert to DNG until Adobe supports your camera's Raw files. In the section "Changing program defaults," later in this chapter, we talk a little bit more about Adobe DNG.

Learning Raw file format attributes

There are several reasons you should make all your first attempts at improving your images in the Raw Editor. These include:

>> **Working with non-destructive editing.** When you open a Camera Raw image in the Raw Editor, all the edits you make for everything, including brightness/contrast, color corrections, tonal corrections, cropping, straightening, sharpening, and so on, are nondestructive. This means that you can always return to the original raw image, dismiss all previous edits, and start over. You don't need to save a copy. Moreover, you can share the Raw file with another user, who can work with your edited image or also dismiss all the edits and start with a fresh unedited version.

>> **Working with higher bit depths.** Inasmuch as you can also use some editing features in the Elements Photo Editor on 16-bit images, in the Raw Editor, all the edits you make can be made on either 8-bit or 16-bit images. To understand more about bit depth, you first need to understand dynamic range.

Dynamic range is the range of *f*-stops between the brightest areas of a photo (the highlights) and the darkest areas (the shadows) where you can detect detail. The human eye can detect roughly 18 different *f*-stops. Translated into practical terms, this means that we can see some detail in the lightest areas of things like cloud formations, and we can see some detail in some dark shadows, as in a tunnel.

Higher-end DSLR and mirrorless cameras capture an average of 10–12 *f*-stops. One camera that captures 15 stops is the Sony A7RIV. The Canon 5D Mark IV captures 12 stops; the Nikon D810 captures 14.8 stops. Smartphone cameras are becoming increasingly better, capturing images at higher dynamic ranges as well. For example, some iPhone, Google, and Samsung devices capture respectable dynamic ranges. Improvements in technology are bringing cameras closer to capturing detail in highlights and shadows that approach the ability of the human eye — but they're not there yet.

When you take a picture in Raw format, your camera captures all the data the sensor can handle. You open the higher bit image in the Raw Editor and decide on the compromises you're willing to make, such as more detail in shadows or more detail in highlights. Your final images need to be reduced to 8-bit for printing or sharing on social media websites, so you must make some decisions about where to clip the image. In other words, you decide what parts of the data you will cut off.

Because Raw editing is a post-processing task, you start with all the original data and decide what data remains and what data are tossed. Sixteen-bit images offer you much more data to work with than 8-bit images do. JPEG images, on the other hand, are processed by the camera, and many of those decisions are made for you. You have more limited control over the data with JPEG files than with Raw files. Furthermore JPEG files are only 8-bit and hold much less data than the Raw files do.

>> All editing is accessible in a single dialog box. If, for the moment, you consider the Raw Editor as a dialog box, all image editing is handled within the editor. In the Elements Editor in Expert mode, you need to address several different menu commands to perform edits in different dialog boxes. The Raw Editor offers you a panel with sliders, where you can make changes to white balance, contrast, exposure, highlights, shadows, saturation, vibrance, and more, all from within a single panel and without the need to open multiple dialog boxes.

Opening images in the Camera Raw Editor

From the desktop, you can open Camera Raw images by double-clicking the mouse button on a Raw image. The image opens in the Raw Editor. If you see a dialog box indicating that the image can't be opened, it means that Adobe has not yet included support for your camera. This is sometimes the case with new.

Camera Raw Editor releases. If your camera isn't supported, you can convert the image to a DNG file and open the DNG in the Raw Editor. For more information on Adobe Digital Negative (DNG), see the section "Changing program defaults," at the end of this chapter.

You can also open the Elements Photo Editor and choose File ⇨ Open or press Ctrl/⌘ + O, select a Raw image, and click OK, and the image opens in the Raw Editor.

You also have a File ⇨ Open in Camera Raw menu command. You can open JPEGs, TIFFs, and PSD files in the Camera Raw Editor. Files saved as TIFF and PSD as 16-bit images can be edited in 16-bit. JPEG files are always 8-bit.

REMEMBER

You may see some YouTube videos or read articles in which authors claim that the difference between JPEG and Raw is that Raw files are not compressed and JPEG files are compressed. This is not true. Today, Raw files can be compressed with lossless or lossy compression. The distinguishing factor between JPEG and Raw is that Raw holds all data captured from the image sensor, and the camera does not process the file. JPEG files are processed by the camera, and data are clipped. When the files are saved, they are always saved with lossy compression, meaning that additional data loss occurs.

Getting Familiar with the Raw Editor

When you open a file (or multiple files) in the Raw Editor, you find a number of tools and buttons as well as several panels. You also notice that the Raw Editor has no menu. All tasks are performed within the Editor workspace.

This section familiarizes you with the tools and buttons available to you in the Raw Editor. In Figure 7-3, you can see the tools appearing at the top-right side of the Editor window and various buttons around the interface. For the moment, we skip the Panel Bin on the right and address it later, in the section "Getting Familiar with the Panels."

FIGURE 7-3:
The Camera Raw Editor tools.

Beginning with the tools at the top right of the window, you find:

(A) **Camera Data Readout**

(B) **Histogram:** The Histogram displays data in your image. In the three RGB channels, you can see how the data falls across a measure of grays from 0 to 255. You can also see whether clipping (cutting off data) occurs if there is a spike (high column) on either side of the Histogram.

(C) **Convert and save image:** Clicking this icon opens the Save Options dialog box. For more on Save Options, see the section "Using Save Options," later in this chapter.

(D) **Open Preferences (Ctrl/⌘ + K):** Rather than describe the Raw Editor Preferences here, we take a look at the preference choices later in the chapter, in the section "Using sidecar files."

(E) **Toggle full screen mode (F):** Press the F key or click this button to expand the Raw Editor workspace to full-screen view. Press F again and you return to the default view.

(F) **Shadow clipping warning (U):** When you click this button, you see clipping in an image for shadows, represented by blue areas. *Clipping* means that no detail is shown in that area of the image.

(G) **Highlight clipping warning (O):** Click this button, and you see clipping of highlights, represented as red areas.

(H) **Edit:** If you click the Crop tool (item H) or the Red Eye Removal tool (item I) and you want to return to the default edit mode, click this tool.

(I) **Crop & Rotate tool (C):** You can crop images in the Camera Raw Editor much the same as you crop in the Elements Photo Editor. If you click the Crop tool, another panel opens in the Panel Bin (item K), as shown in Figure 7-4. Settings you have available in the Crop panel include:

- **Aspect Ratio:** Click the default size and a drop-down list opens, where you can choose from a number of different crop ratios.

- **Angle:** Move the slider to change the angle for the crop.

- **Straighten tool (A):** The Straighten tool functions the same in the Raw Editor as in the Elements Photo Editor. For more on straightening images, see Chapter 10.

- **Rotate Left (L):** Click the tool button or press the L key to rotate the image 90° left. Keep pressing L to rotate the image at 90° movements.

- **Rotate Right (R):** Click the tool button or press the R key to rotate the image 90° right.

- **Flip Horizontal:** Click the button adjacent to the Rotate Right button, and the image flips horizontal.

- **Flip Vertical:** Click the last button in the Rotate & Flip category to flip the image vertically.

- **Crop Adjustments:** In Figure 7-4, you can see some marks at the corners and along the horizontal and vertical centers at the edges of the photo. Click and drag a corner or center item to shape the crop. If you move the cursor outside the marks, you see a semicircle with two arrowheads. Click and drag to rotate the image. If you place the cursor at the corners, you see a diagonal line with two arrowheads. Click and drag to crop down or up.

To return to the default editing mode, click the Edit button (item F). For more on using the Crop tool, see Chapter 10.

(J) **Red Eye Removal tool (Shift+E):** Removes red eye from a subject's eyes. For more on Red Eye Removal, see Chapter 10.

(K) **More image settings:** The flyout menu offers options for changing default settings for the open image.

(L) **Panel Bin:** By default, the Basic panel is open. For more on using the panels, see the section "Getting Familiar with the Panels," later in this chapter.

(M) **Zoom tool:** Click the tool, move it to the document, and click to zoom in. Press Ctrl/⌘ and click and drag to zoom into an area.

(N) **Hand tool (H):** Press the H key on your keyboard or click the Hand icon in the toolbar to access the Hand tool. Alternatively, you can press the spacebar to access the tool. Click and drag around an image to move it within the editor workspace.

(O) **Zoom options:** If you move the cursor into the document window, the cursor changes to a Zoom tool. Press the Alt/Option key and click and you can zoom out. You also have fixed zoom option choices in the pop-up menu. Click to open the menu and make choices for the zoom level you want. You can also zoom in and out of an image by pressing Ctrl/⌘ + – (minus sign) to zoom out, and Ctrl/⌘ ++ (plus sign) to zoom in.

TIP

Choose 100% views or greater when you make adjustments to sharpness and noise reduction.

(P) **Help:** Click this button to open Adobe's web pages, where help information related to the Raw Editor is provided.

(Q) **Change Views:** These three items appear only when you have more than one image open in the raw editor. You click the first icon to toggle the filmstrip on and off. Click the middle icon to open a menu where you choose to sort according to Date, File Name, Star Rating, and Color Label. Click the third icon to open a menu to filter views according to Star rating, Color Label, and files marked for deletion and rejection.

(R) **Stars:** Click a star to rate the photo. When you open the file in the Organizer, you can sort photos by star ratings. For more on rating photos with stars, see Chapter 5.

(S) **Depth:** For 16-bit images, choose 16Bits/Channel. The alternative choice is editing in 8-bit mode.

(T) **Image Thumbnails:** When you open multiple images, a thumbnail is displayed horizontally across the bottom of the Editor window.

(U) **Image Window:** The current active document appears here.

(V) Before/After (Q): Click this button to cycle through before and after views displayed adjacent to each other vertically, horizontally, and on split screen.

(W) Toggle between current settings and defaults: Click this button to see your image at the defaults. Click again and you see the image with the edits you made.

Defaults are not necessarily the original image captured by your camera. You can, for example, choose to open images with some auto corrections applied. When you toggle this button, you see the defaults after auto corrections were applied.

To learn more about changing defaults, see the section "Changing Image Defaults," later in this chapter.

(X) Open: Click Open, and the image opens in the Elements Photo Editor with the edits you applied.

Alt/Option+Open: When you press Alt/Option, the button changes to Open Copy. When you press Alt/Option and click Open Copy, a copy of the edited Raw image opens in the Elements Photo Editor. The original Raw image remains unaffected and is closed as the copy is opened.

(Y) Cancel: Click Cancel, and the image closes with no edits applied.

Alt/Option+Cancel: The Cancel button changes to Reset. When you press Alt/ Option and click Reset, all edits from the time you opened the image are returned to defaults.

(Z) Done: Click Done, and all your edits are applied and the image is closed. When you open the image, it is shown in the Raw Editor with the last edits you made.

FIGURE 7-4:
The Crop
panel.

Getting Familiar with the Panels

On the right side of the Raw Editor below the Histogram, you see, by default, the Basic panel. If you don't see the Basic panel open, you may see a list of the available panels, as shown in Figure 7-5.

Below the Profile drop-down list you see three items with right-pointing chevrons. At the top of the list is the Basic panel, followed by the Detail panel and finally the Calibration panel. Click one of the chevrons and the respective panel opens in the Panel Bin.

The next section takes a look at each of these panels individually.

FIGURE 7-5:
The Panel Bin showing a list of panels.

Using the Basic panel

The Basic panel is the center of your Camera Raw Editor world. The lion's share of the edits you make are handled in the Basic panel. Adobe logically positions tools and panels across an application interface. In normal workflows, you begin on the left and work toward the right or at the top and work down through tools and settings.

In the Basic panel, you make edits starting at the top of the panel and working down. Furthermore, many settings need to be finessed by toggling between different adjustments. For example, you can adjust Contrast and then later, when you get to Clarity, you can make an adjustment and see that Clarity also adds some contrast. Therefore, you may need to return to the Contrast slider and tweak the contrast a bit. This back-and-forth editing is common for many adjustments. Start at the top of the panel and realize that you may need to return to previous adjustments to fine-tune your editing.

Figure 7-6 shows the Basic panel with all the sliders set to default values.

Here's a description of each of the different settings for the Basic panel, as identified in the figure:

(A) **Histogram:** When you open an image in the Raw Editor, first take a look at the Histogram. You want to see whether the image is skewed to the left (where more shadows appear) or to the right (where more highlights exist). The ideal image will have no clipping on either side of the Histogram and more data appearing in the center (something like a bell curve). As a start, click the clipping warning buttons to show clipping in highlights and shadows. In Figure 7-7, the clipping indicators are selected. When the indicators are selected, you see a visual for areas of a photo that's clipped. In Figure 7-7, the red overlay on the photo shows highlights clipped.

(B) **Auto/B&W:** If you want the Raw Editor to make its best guess for all the adjustments, click the Auto button. Click B&W to convert from RGB Color to Grayscale.

Generally speaking, it's a good idea to begin your edits by clicking Auto and then working your way down the panel to fine-tune the settings.

(C) **Profile:** The drop-down menu displays choices for a number of profiles from which you can choose to begin your editing tasks. To the right of the menu is a grid icon that displays thumbnail views of each profile. The default profile is Adobe Color. We stay with the default in this section and look at working with profiles in the section "Working with Profiles," later in this chapter.

(D) **White Balance:** The default white balance is As Shot, meaning that the white balance you chose in your camera settings is used as the default here in the editor. You can change the white balance in several ways. Click the Eyedropper tool in the toolbar and locate a white, medium gray, or black area in the photo and click with the Eyedropper tool. Clicking with the Eyedropper tool sets a custom white balance. If you click several times, you can scroll back through your edits using the Undo command by pressing Ctrl/⌘ +Z to undo each edit. Each successive Undo takes you back one step. Hence you can, for example, click with the Eyedropper tool 10 times and undo 10 times to return to the original setting.

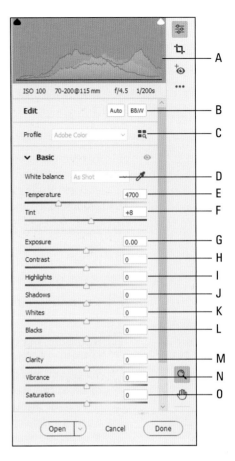

FIGURE 7-6:
The Basic panel with the sliders at defaults.

The other means for changing white balance is to adjust the Temperature and Tint sliders.

(E) Temperature: As you move the Temperature slider to the left, your image appears with more blue, resulting in a cooler image. Conversely, moving the slider to the right adds more yellow, resulting in a warmer image.

(F) Tint: You move this slider to the left to add more green. Move to the right to add more magenta.

To return to the defaults, you can choose As Shot from the White Balance menu, or you can double-click a slider to return its setting to the default. For example, if you move the Temperature slider from its default value of 5500 to 7000, double-clicking the slider returns you to the default 5500 value.

(G) Exposure: Move the slider left to darken the image. Move the slider right to lighten the image. Press Alt/Option and drag a slider to see any clipping as you make the adjustments. Clipping will appear as white when you depress the Alt/Option key and move the slider.

(H) Contrast: Move the slider left to decrease contrast. Move the slider right to increase contrast.

(I) Highlights: This slider enables you to adjust highlights. In some cases where highlights are blown out (that is, no data appears in the white areas of the image), you may be able to bring in some detail. Press the Alt/Option key and move left to see any clipping warnings as you add more highlight data or right to decrease highlights. When you see clipping, move the slider to the point where the clipping first begins to appear. Be sure to press the Alt/Option key down as you drag a slider to see clipping.

(J) Shadows: This features works in the opposite way to the Highlight slider. To increase detail in shadows, move the slider right. To decrease detail, move the slider left. Holding the Alt/Option key down displays clipping if it occurs in the image.

(K) Whites: This slider brightens whites in the image. Press Alt/Option and move the slider to detect clipping. When you see clipping occur, make the final adjustment just before you see the clipping.

(L) Blacks: This slider helps add richer blacks in an image. Press Alt/Option to detect clipping. When you see clipping occur, make the final adjustment just before you see the clipping.

(M) Clarity: Move this slider to the right to adjust midtones and add more contrast to the midtones.

(N) Vibrance: Adjusting Vibrance can add some snap to your photos by brightening colors.

(O) Saturation: Moving the Saturation slider left desaturates the image. Moving the slider right increases saturation. You can convert the image to grayscale by moving the Saturation slider all the way to the left, thus eliminating all color.

Note: Double-clicking a slider reverts to the default.

Sharpening and reducing noise

The second panel in the Panel Bin is the Detail panel. Click Detail to open the Detail panel. This panel has three sections, as you can see in Figure 7-8. At the top you find adjustments for Sharpening. Below Sharpening is Noise Reduction and the final group is Color Noise Reduction.

Sharpening images

By default, some sharpening is applied to images when you open them. Figure 7-8 shows you default slider adjustments when an image is opened in the Raw Editor. If you want to eliminate the default amount of sharpening, move the sliders to zero.

Before making any adjustments in this panel, you should view your image at a 1:1 ratio. Open the zoom menu from the lower-left corner of the editor window and choose 100%. This adjustment zooms the image to an actual size. In an actual-size view, you can see more clearly any artifacts that might appear if you sharpen too much. Use the Hand tool to move the image around and locate an area such as a subject's eye or contrasting colors in images. Sharpening actually increases contrast along edges of subjects and the background, or along edges of contrasting colors.

The sliders provide you adjustments for:

» **Sharpening:** The Sharpening slider increases contrast between colors and at the edges of color transitions. As a general rule, keep the Sharpening slider between 70 and 90. If you're sharpening portraits or shots with people, keep the Amount to 50 or less.

FIGURE 7-8:
Click the Detail text in the Panel Bin to open the Detail panel.

» **Radius:** Radius is the number of pixels the editor looks at on either side of the line of contrast between two contrasting colors or along the edges of subjects. Increasing radius will show strong contrast along lines of contrasting pixels. It's best to keep this adjustment low, such as at values between .8 and 1.2.

» **Detail:** This adjustment increases sharpness in detail. Although it increases sharpness, it may also result in adding more noise to images shot at higher ISOs. In many cases, you want to keep this setting off or at least keep it to 20 or below.

» **Masking:** Masking looks at the solid colors in the image where no contrasting values exist. To use this slider, press the Alt/Option key. The image area turns white. As you move the Masking slider to the right while keeping the Alt/Option key depressed, you begin to see solid colors appear as black (see Figure 7-9). Black areas are where no sharpening is applied. The white areas are where sharpening occurs. Move this slider to the right as far as needed to eliminate sharpening in solid colors.

FIGURE 7-9:
Press Alt/
Option when
adjusting
Masking.

Adjusting noise

By default, adjustments are made to reduce color noise. You see noise in color areas represented by varying colors of different pixels. As you reduce the noise, the colors disappear in solid color areas.

>> **Noise Reduction:** Move this slider to reduce overall noise.

>> **Detail:** This item represents how much detail remains in the color noise area. As you increase the adjustment, you regain some detail. Keep this adjustment low to avoid emphasizing the color noise.

>> **Contrast:** Zoom in to an 800–1600 percent view to see the results of moving this slider. You can make some adjustments for the contrast in the noise areas. Move the slider to around 50 to bring back some detail in the highlights.

Noise often shows up in images shot at high ISOs as well as when you expand the dynamic range to capture more detail in highlights and shadows. For example, when you move the Highlight and Shadow sliders in the basic panel to the far edges, you usually see some noise.

When you make adjustments on images with a lot of noise, first set all the sharpening sliders to zero and start your editing in this section. You don't want to sharpen the noise. Doing so introduces more noise in your image. First make all noise adjustments and then go to the sharpening sliders and make those adjustments.

Slider adjustments you can make to reduce color noise include:

>> **Color Noise Reduction:** Move this slider to adjust overall color noise.

>> **Detail:** Move this slider up to regain some detail that was lost after reducing color noise. Whereas the Color Noise Reduction adjustment blurs the image, this adjustment results in sharpening the softness introduced with the Color Noise Reduction adjustment.

>> **Smoothness:** This adjustment blurs the color noise so that it appears as if the color noise disappears. Add a little bit of color smoothness to further reduce the color noise.

Using the Calibration panel

There's not much to do in the Calibration panel. Your only adjustment is to choose a version of the Raw Editor. Most of the time you leave this menu command at the default, which is the current version of the Raw Editor. If you have legacy files edited in earlier versions of the Raw Editor, you might choose a menu option equivalent to the version from which the file was edited.

Working with Filmstrips

When you select multiple Raw files in the Organizer, or you select multiple Raw files in the Open dialog box and click Open, the files are all opened in the Raw Editor and are seen in the Raw Editor filmstrip. You can select photos in a contiguous or noncontiguous order in the filmstrip. To select photos in a noncontiguous order, click a photo in the filmstrip and press Ctrl/⌘ +. Click and select additional photos. In Figure 7-10, you can see photos selected in a noncontiguous order.

The files appear in a filmstrip. By default, the filmstrip is across the bottom of the ACR window. If you want to view the files vertically on the left side of the ACR window, you can open a context menu on an image thumbnail and choose Film Strip Orientation ⇨ Vertical, as shown in Figure 7-11. You can also press Shift + Ctrl/⌘+F and toggle back and forth between vertical and horizontal filmstrips.

FIGURE 7-10:
To make a
noncontiguous
selection,
press Ctrl/⌘
and click
each image
to add to the
selection.

As you can see in Figure 7-11, the context menu offers a number of options, as follows:

>> **Select All:** Click the menu command or press Ctrl/⌘ +A to select all photos in the filmstrip.

>> **Set Rating:** From the submenu, you can choose a star rating the same way you can at the bottom of the ACR window. Star ratings are the same as the star ratings you can use in the Organizer. For more on star ratings, see Chapter 5.

FIGURE 7-11:
Right-click a thumbnail to open a context menu.

>> **Set Label:** Mark images with a color label.

>> **Set Reject:** This choice places a check mark *in the context* menu. If you open the menu again, a check mark is shown, indicating that you rejected the image.

- >> **Mark for Deletion:** If you have a photo in the group that you don't want to use, click this command, and the photo is moved to the Recycle Bin/Trash Can. Be careful. If you click Mark for Deletion, the photo is moved out of its folder and to the trash. If you empty the Recycle Bin (Windows) or Trash Can (Mac) the file is deleted.

- >> **Filmstrip Orientation:** Choose the orientation in the submenu.

- >> **Show Filename:** Click this command to display the filenames of the photos below each thumbnail.

- >> **Show Ratings & Color Labels:** Displays star ratings and color labels.

- >> **Filter By:** You can select only those images containing items you marked, such as Star Rating values, Color Labels, Marked or Not Marked for Deletion, Rejected, or Not Rejected. For example, if you mark three out of seven images as Rejected, and you filter the files, you see only the four nonrejected files in the film strip.

- >> **Sort by:** Images in the filmstrip are sorted by Star Rating, Color Label, and all the other options you have available similar to filtering.

Working with Profiles

Earlier in this chapter, in the "Using the Basic panel" section, we look at choosing settings using the default Adobe Color profile. When you open a Raw image, the Adobe Color profile is selected by default. There are, however, many other profiles you can use. You can install custom profiles created by third parties; you can set up a number of favorites to access the profiles you use more frequently; and you can create your own custom profiles.

There's quite a bit to understand with regard to Camera Raw profiles. You can start by looking at the panels that Adobe provides you with when you first install Elements.

Looking at the Adobe Camera Raw profiles

When you install Photoshop Elements, Adobe installs many different profiles. As stated elsewhere in this chapter, Adobe Color is the default profile. If you click the down-pointing arrow adjacent to the Adobe Color text, the drop-down menu opens and reveals five additional profiles. The menu shows a list of additional profiles that you can use. You can also click the Browse Profiles icon adjacent to the drop-down list, or you can choose Browse from the drop-down list to see thumbnail images displayed for the profiles. Mousing over a thumbnail reveals a dynamic preview for how your photo would look if you use the respective profile. Figure 7-12 shows some of the thumbnails for the Adobe Color group along with other groups that are shown as collapsed.

The default Adobe Color group profiles include:

>> **Adobe Color:** This profile is Adobe's default profile intended for general use.

>> **Adobe Monochrome:** This profile renders an image as black and white with optimized sensitivity for how RGB values render as different tones. It also increases contrast.

>> **Adobe Landscape:** This profile adds enhancements to sky hues (blues) and foliage hues (greens).

>> **Adobe Portrait:** This profile provides optimum protection and enhancements for skin tones.

>> **Adobe Standard:** Adobe Standard adds subtle tonal and color adjustments to the image. Like Adobe Color, this is generally a good starting point for many images.

>> **Adobe Vivid:** Adobe Vivid adds an increased level of contrast and saturation.

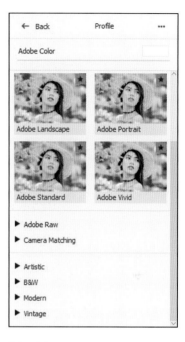

FIGURE 7-12:
Profile thumbnails displayed after clicking the Browse icon.

Additionally, you'll notice items such as Camera Matching, Artistic, B&W, Modern, and Vintage. To get familiar with these other choices, open some images and poke around by applying different profile settings to different images.

Managing profiles

If you right-click a profile (or Control+click on a Mac with a one-button mouse), a context menu opens. The menu shown in Figure 7-13 offers some options for managing profiles. These include:

>> **Profile Info:** Clicking this item in the menu opens a dialog box that provides a very brief description of the profile.

>> **Remove from Favorites:** If you added a profile to your Favorites list, this menu command enables you to delete the item from the Favorites. To learn more about Favorites, see "Creating a Favorites list," later in this chapter.

» **Manage Profiles:** Choose Manage Profiles to open the Manage Profiles dialog box which lists all profile groups. To hide or display a group, select the check box. If a check mark is already in a check box, you click it to hide the profile. Any profiles you select are visible in the Basic panel.

» **Reset Favorite Profiles:** If you add a number of profiles and want to return to defaults, click this item.

» **Rest Hidden Profiles:** If you hide any profiles, clicking this menu item brings them back and unhides them.

» **Import Profiles and Presets:** Choose this menu command to open the Import Profile and Presets dialog box. You can load custom profiles by selecting a profile and clicking the Open button. If you click the Browse icon and show thumbnails but then want to return to the List option, click the Back button at the top of the Basic panel. The Back button appears after you click Browse in the Profile area of the Basic panel.

Profile Info...
Remove from Favorites
Manage Profiles...
Reset Favorite Profiles
Reset Hidden Profiles
Import Profiles & Presets...

FIGURE 7-13:
Open a context menu on a profile thumbnail.

Creating a Favorites list

By default, the installed profiles appear in a Favorites list. You can open the list by clicking the down-pointing arrow adjacent to Favorites at the top of the Profile Browser panel. As you view different profiles notice the star icon in the top-right corner of each profile thumbnail. Clicking the star adds that profile to your Favorites list. To eliminate a profile from your Favorites list, click the star icon in the Favorites panel.

Adding profiles to a Favorites list enables you to quickly access those profiles that you use most often. As shown in Figure 7-14, we added a number of different profiles to our Favorites list, including a custom profile we created.

FIGURE 7-14:
A number of profiles added to the Favorites list.

Opening Non-Raw Images in the Camera Raw Editor

The Camera Raw adjustments are not limited to Raw files. Any JPEG, TIF, or PSD file can also be opened in the Raw Editor, and all the adjustments are available to all these image formats.

Camera Raw offers you images with all the data captured by the image sensor in the camera. Uncompressed Raw files have all the original camera sensor data. There are cameras that can save Raw files compressed with lossy compression or lossless compression. If a Raw file is compressed with lossy compression, some data is tossed during compression.

With other formats, some processing is performed, and no image format matches optimum data as Camera Raw uncompressed files do. However, you may not have images that were available in Raw format, or you may not have a camera or cell-phone that can save in a Raw format. If JPEG or one of the other formats is your only option, you can easily open the images in the Camera Raw Editor.

In the Photoshop Elements Photo Editor, choose File ⇨ Open in Camera Raw. In the Open dialog box, choose a JPEG file and open it using this command. The file opens in the Raw Editor, and you can go about making adjustments as described in this chapter.

Changing Image Defaults

Suppose you make some adjustments to a Raw image and then want to return to the original, unedited file. You have several ways to accomplish this task. From the Panel Bin, which is available when viewing all three panels, you can click the three bullet icons to open the menu (refer to Figure 7-14).

The choices you have for this menu include:

>> **Reset to Open:** Resets to the last time the file was opened.

>> **Reset to Default:** Returns the settings to the original file captured by the camera.

>> **Previous Conversion:** Uses the same settings as the previously used when file was edited.

>> **Clear Imported Settings:** Clears settings that you may have imported.

Working with XML Files and Preferences

There are a few things you should understand when it comes to sharing edited Raw images and changing default settings. You can start by examining the Preferences dialog box in the next section.

Changing program defaults

You can apply some default settings in the Camera Raw Editor Preferences dialog box. To open the Preferences dialog box, you must open an image in the Raw Editor. You can't launch the Editor without opening an image first. Any settings you make in the Preferences dialog box won't affect the open image. Preference settings take effect only when you quit and reopen the Raw Editor.

With the Raw Editor open, click the Open Preferences tool in the toolbar or press Ctrl/⌘ +K. The Preferences dialog box opens, as shown in Figure 7-15.

FIGURE 7-15:
Press Ctrl/⌘ +K to open the Preferences dialog box.

There are three individual areas in the Preferences dialog box with different settings. These include:

» **General:** In the General area, you make choices for Raw default settings. Choose from Adobe Default or Camera Settings. If you prefer your Camera Raw settings, open the drop-down list and choose Camera Settings.

» **DNG File Handling:** This section covers working with Adobe Digital Negative (DNG) files.

- **Embed XMP in DNG:** When you make edits in the Raw Editor, by default a text file called an XMP file known as a sidecar file is created that holds all your edit information. The Raw file itself is not edited. The XMP file holds the edit information apart from the photo itself. Choose this item if you want to embed the XMP file inside the DNG file.

- **Always Use Sidecar XMP File:** As the name implies, sidecar XMP files are always used.

- **Ignore Sidecar XMP Files:** The sidecar XMP file data are ignored.

- **Update Embedded JPEG Previews:** Updates thumbnails to updated images.

» **Panels:** If your screen resolution is such that items in the Basic panel are cut off and you have to scroll to see all settings in the Basic panel, select the Use Compact Layout box. The window items are resized slightly so that all settings are visible without the need for scrolling.

» **Orientation:** The default is Horizontal. The filmstrip appears horizontally at the bottom of the ACR window. Choose Vertical from the menu to view the thumbnails vertically along the left side of the image window.

- **Show Filenames:** Filenames appear below the thumbnails in the filmstrip.

- **Show Ratings & Color Labels:** Star ratings appear below the thumbnails in the filmstrip, and the stars appear with any assigned color specified when adding Color Labels.

» **Zoom and Pan:** You have an option to set the zoom level by editing the text box.

When enabled, you can click and drag to pan around an image that's zoomed in. If this preference is not enabled, you can press the spacebar or use the Hand tool to pan around a zoomed in image.

>> **Keyboard shortcuts:** This section has a single setting. Using legacy shortcuts literally has no effect. You can use Ctrl/⌘ +Z or Ctrl/⌘ +Alt/Option+Z to step back through edits in the panels. Legacy files are treated identically when the shortcuts work the same.

Using Save Options

At the top of the ACR window, the first icon at the top-right corner of the ACR window is the Convert and Save Image icon. When you click this item, the Save Options dialog box opens, as shown in Figure 7-16. In this dialog box, you have choices for the location where you want to save photos, file naming conventions, file extension choices, and some specifics related to the Adobe Digital Negative format. Most of these options are self-explanatory.

FIGURE 7-16: Click the first icon in the top-right corner to open the Save Options dialog box.

Using sidecar files

In the Preferences dialog box, you have some choices for handling sidecar files. Sidecar files are text files written in XML, and they contain all the data related to editing a Raw file. You can actually examine an XMP file by opening it in a text editor.

XMP files are like tape recordings. All the edits are reordered and documented for each edit you make. When you click Done or Open Image in the Raw Editor, the sidecar file is written. In a desktop view, you can see the sidecar file adjacent to the Raw image.

If you delete the sidecar file, all edits are deleted and the original Raw image remains in an unedited version. It's the same file you copied from your memory card to your computer.

It's important to understand that the sidecar file needs to accompany your original Raw image when you copy the image to another computer or share the image with another user. It's important, that is, if you want to retain all the edits you made in the Raw file.

Chapter **8**

Making and Modifying Selections

I f all you want to do is use your photos in all their unedited glory, feel free to skip this chapter and move on to other topics. But if you want to occasionally pluck an element out of its environment and stick it in another or apply an adjustment to just a portion of your image, this chapter's for you.

Finding out how to make accurate selections is one of those skills that's well worth the time you invest. In this chapter, we cover all the various selection tools and techniques. We also give you tips on which tools are better for which kinds of selections. But remember that you usually have several ways to achieve the same result. Which road you choose is ultimately up to you.

Defining Selections

Before you dig in and get serious about selecting, let us clarify for the record what we mean by "defining a selection." When you *define* a selection, you specify which part of an image you want to work with. Everything within a selection is considered selected. Everything outside the selection is unselected. After you have a selection, you can then adjust only that portion, and the unselected portion remains unchanged. Or you can copy the selected area into another image altogether. Want to transport yourself out of your background and onto a white, sandy beach? Select yourself out of that backyard BBQ photo, get a stock photo of the tropical paradise of your choice, and drag and drop yourself onto your tropics photo with the Move tool. It's that easy.

When you make a selection, a dotted outline — dubbed a *selection border,* an *outline,* or a *marquee* — appears around the selected area. Elements, sophisticated imaging program that it is, also allows you to partially select pixels, which allows for soft-edged selections. You create soft-edged selections by feathering the selection or by using a mask. Don't worry: We cover these techniques in the section "Applying Marquee options," later in this chapter.

REMEMBER

For all the selection techniques described in this chapter, be sure that your image is in Expert mode in the Photo Editor and not in Quick or Guided mode or in the Organizer.

Creating Rectangular and Elliptical Selections

If you can drag a mouse, you can master the Rectangular and Elliptical Marquee tools. These are the easiest selection tools to use, so if your desired element is rectangular or elliptical, by all means, grab one of these tools.

The Rectangular Marquee tool, as its moniker implies, is designed to define rectangular (including square) selections. This tool is great to use if you want to home in on the pertinent portion of your photo and eliminate unnecessary background.

Here's how to make a selection with this tool:

1. **Select the Rectangular Marquee tool from the Tools panel.**

   The tool looks like a dotted square. You can also press M to access the tool. If the tool isn't visible, press M again.

2. **Drag from one corner of the area you want to select to the opposite corner.**

   While you drag, the selection border appears. The marquee follows the movement of your mouse cursor.

3. **Release your mouse button.**

   You have a completed rectangular selection, as shown in Figure 8-1.

The Elliptical Marquee tool is designed for elliptical (including circular) selections. This tool is perfect for selecting balloons, clocks, and other rotund elements.

Here's how to use the Elliptical Marquee:

1. **Select the Elliptical Marquee tool from the Tools panel.**

   The tool looks like a dotted ellipse. You can also press M to access this tool if it's visible; if it isn't, press M again.

   If pressing the keyboard shortcut doesn't cycle through the tools, choose Preferences ⇨ General and make sure Use Shift Key for Tool Switch is deselected.

2. **Position the crosshair near the area you want to select and then drag around your desired element.**

   With this tool, you drag from a given point on the ellipse. While you drag, the selection border appears.

3. **When you're satisfied with your selection, release the mouse button.**

   Your elliptical selection is created, as shown in Figure 8-2. If your selection isn't quite centered around your element, simply move the selection border by dragging inside the border.

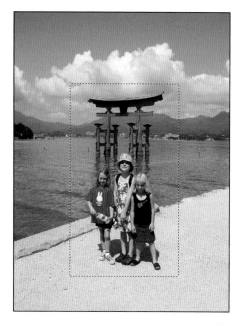

FIGURE 8-1:
Use the Rectangular Marquee tool to create rectangular selections.

You can move a selection while you're making it with either of the Marquee tools by holding down the spacebar while you're dragging.

Perfecting squares and circles with Shift and Alt (Option on the Mac)

Sometimes you need to create a perfectly square or circular selection. To do so, simply press the Shift key after you begin dragging. After you make your selection, release the mouse button and then release the Shift key. You can also set the aspect ratio to 1:1 in the Tool Options.

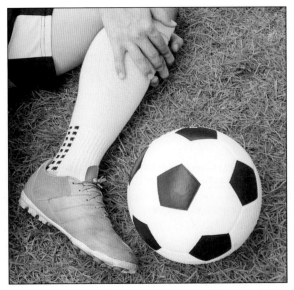

FIGURE 8-2:
The Elliptical Marquee tool is perfect for selecting round objects.

TIP

When you're making an elliptical selection, making the selection from the center outward is often easier. To draw from the center, first click the mouse button where you want to position the center, press Alt (Option on the Mac), and then drag. After making your selection, release the mouse button and then release the Alt (Option on the Mac) key.

If you want to draw from the center outward *and* create a perfect circle or square, press the Shift key as well. After you make your selection, release the mouse button and then release the Shift+Alt (Shift+Option on the Mac) keys.

Applying Marquee options

The Marquee tools offer additional options when you need to make precise selections at specific measurements. You also find options for making your selections soft around the edges.

REMEMBER

The only thing to remember is that you must select the options in the Tool Options, as shown in Figure 8-3, before you make your selection with the Marquee tools. Options can't be applied after the selection has already been made. The exception is that you can feather a selection after the fact by choosing Select ⇨ Feather.

FIGURE 8-3:
Apply Marquee
settings in the
Tool Options.

Here are the various Marquee options available to you:

» **Feather:** Feathering creates soft edges around your selection. The amount of softness depends on the value, from 0 to 250 pixels, that you enter by adjusting the slider. The higher the value, the softer the edges, as shown in Figure 8-4. Very small amounts of feathering can be used to create subtle transitions between selected elements in a collage or for blending an element into an existing background. Larger amounts are often used when you're combining multiple layers so that one image gradually fades into another. If you want a selected element to have just a soft edge without the background, simply choose Select ⇨ Inverse and delete the background. See more on inversing selections in the "Modifying Your Selections" section, later in this chapter. For more on layers, see Chapter 9.

REMEMBER

Don't forget that those soft edges represent partially selected pixels.

» **Anti-aliasing:** Anti-aliasing barely softens the edge of an elliptical or irregularly shaped selection so that the jagged edges aren't quite so obvious. An anti-aliased edge is always only 1 pixel wide. We recommend leaving this option chosen for your selections. Doing so can help to create natural transitions between multiple selections when you're creating collages.

» **Aspect:** The Aspect drop-down list contains three settings:

- **Normal:** The default setting, which allows you to freely drag a selection of any size.

- **Fixed Ratio:** Lets you specify a fixed ratio of width to height. For example, if you enter **3** for width and **1** for height, you get a selection that's three times as wide as it is high, no matter what the size.

- **Fixed Size:** Lets you specify desired values for the width and height. This setting can be useful when you need to make several selections that must be the same size.

» **Width (W) and Height (H):** When you choose Fixed Ratio or Fixed Size from the Aspect drop-down list, you must also enter your desired values in the Width and Height text boxes. To swap the Width and Height values, click the double-headed arrow button between the two measurements.

TIP

>> **Refine Edge:** For details on this great option, see "Refining the edges of a selection," later in this chapter.

The default unit of measurement in the Width and Height text boxes is pixels (px), but that doesn't mean that you're stuck with it. You can enter any unit of measurement that Elements recognizes: pixels, inches (in), centimeters (cm), millimeters (mm), points (pt), picas (pica), or percentages (%). Type your value and then type the word or abbreviation of your unit of measurement.

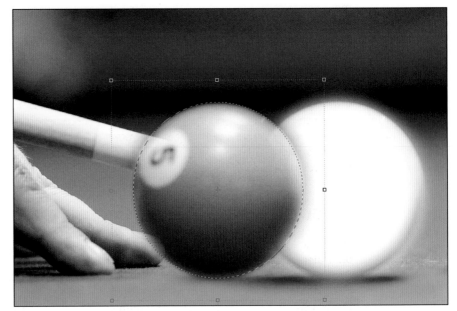

FIGURE 8-4:
Feathering
creates
soft-edged
selections.

© Mikadun/Shutterstock Image #65367541

Making Freeform Selections with the Lasso Tools

You can't select everything with a rectangle or an ellipse. Life is just way too free-form for that. Most animate, and many inanimate, objects have undulations of varying sorts. Luckily, Elements anticipated the need to capture these shapes and provided the Lasso tools.

The Lasso tools enable you to make any freehand selection you can think of. Elements generously provides three types of Lasso tools:

- » Lasso
- » Polygonal
- » Magnetic

Although all three tools are designed to make freeform selections, they differ slightly in their methodology, as we explain in the sections that follow.

To use these tools, all that's really required is a steady hand. You'll find that the more you use the Lasso tools, the better you become at your tracing technique. Don't worry if your initial lasso selection isn't super accurate. You can always go back and make corrections by adding and deleting from your selection. To find out how, see the section "Modifying Your Selections," later in this chapter.

TIP

If you find that you really love the Lasso tools, you may want to invest in a digital drawing tablet and stylus. This device makes tracing (and also drawing and painting) on the computer more comfortable. It better mimics pen and paper, and after trying it, many users swear that they'll never go back to a mouse. This is especially handy for laptop users. Attempting to draw accurately on a trackpad can make you downright cranky.

Selecting with the Lasso tool

Using the Lasso tool is the digital version of tracing an outline around an object on a piece of paper. It's that easy. And you have only three choices in the Tool Options — Feather, Anti-aliasing, and Refine Edge. To find out more about the Feather and Anti-aliasing tools, see the section "Applying Marquee options," earlier in this chapter. For the scoop on Refine Edge, see the section "Refining the edges of a selection," later in this chapter.

Here's how to make a selection with the Lasso tool:

1. **Select the Lasso tool from the Tools panel.**

   It's the tool that looks like a rope. You can also just press the L key. If the Lasso tool isn't visible, press L to cycle through the various Lasso flavors. Note that you can also access any of the Lasso tools in the Tool options located under the image.

2. **Position the cursor anywhere along the edge of the object you want to select.**

   The leading point of the cursor is the protruding end of the rope, as shown in Figure 8-5. Don't be afraid to zoom in to your object, using the Zoom tool — or, more conveniently, pressing Control++ (⌘ ++ on the Mac) — if you need to see the edge more distinctly. In this figure, we started at the top of the sunflower.

3. **Hold down the mouse button and trace around your desired object.**

Try to include only what you want to select. While you trace around your object, an outline follows the mouse cursor.

WARNING

Try not to release the mouse button until you return to your starting point. When you release the mouse button, Elements assumes that you're done and closes the selection from wherever you released the mouse button to your starting point; if you release the button too early, Elements creates a straight line across your image.

4. **Continue tracing around the object and return to your starting point; release the mouse button to close the selection.**

You see a selection border that matches your lasso line. Look for a small circle that appears next to your lasso cursor when you return to your starting point. This icon indicates that you're closing the selection at the proper spot.

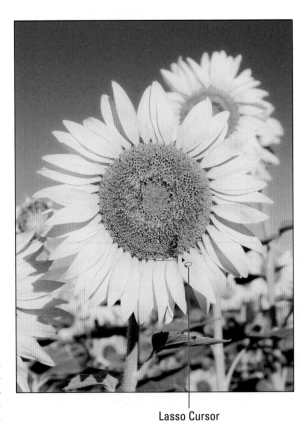

FIGURE 8-5:
The Lasso tool makes freeform selections.

Lasso Cursor

© Aleksey Stemmer/Shutterstock Image #80233594

Getting straight with the Polygonal Lasso tool

The Polygonal Lasso tool has a specific mission in life: to select any element whose sides are straight. Think pyramids, stairways, skyscrapers, barns — you get the idea. It also works a tad differently from the Lasso tool. You don't drag around the element with the Polygonal Lasso. Instead, you click and release the mouse button at the corners of the element you're selecting. The Polygonal Lasso tool acts like a stretchy rubber band.

Follow these steps to select with the Polygonal Lasso tool:

1. **Select the Polygonal Lasso tool from the Tools panel.**

   You can also press the L key to cycle through the various Lasso tools. The tool looks like a straight-sided lasso rope.

2. **Click and release at any point to start the Polygonal Lasso selection line.**

   We usually start at a corner.

3. **Move (don't drag) the mouse and click at the next corner of the object. Continue clicking and moving to each corner of your element.**

   Notice how the line stretches out from each point you click.

4. **Return to your starting point and click to close the selection.**

   Be on the lookout for a small circle that appears next to your lasso cursor when you return to your starting point. This circle is an indication that you're indeed closing the selection at the right spot.

   Note: You can also double-click at any point, and Elements closes the selection from that point to the starting point.

   After you close the polygonal lasso line, a selection border appears, as shown in Figure 8-6.

REMEMBER

Snapping with the Magnetic Lasso tool

The third member of the Lasso team is the Magnetic Lasso. We aren't huge fans of this Lasso tool, which can sometimes be hard to work with. However, we show you how it works so that you can decide whether to use it. The Magnetic Lasso tool works by defining the areas of the most contrast in an image and then snapping to the edge between those areas, as though the edge has a magnetic pull.

Polygonal Lasso selection border

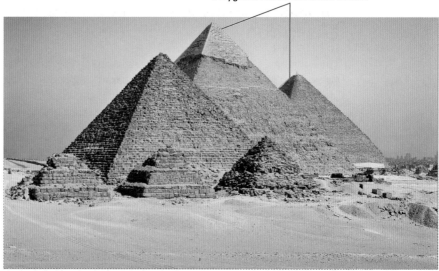

© WitR/Shutterstock Image #91826000

FIGURE 8-6:
After you close the polygonal lasso line, Elements creates a selection border.

TIP

You have the most success using the Magnetic Lasso tool on an image that has a well-defined foreground object and high contrast between that element and the background — for example, a dark mountain range against a light sky.

The Magnetic Lasso tool also has some unique settings, which you can adjust in the Tool Options before you start selecting:

» **Width:** Determines how close to the edge (between 1 and 256 pixels) you have to move your mouse before the Magnetic Lasso tool snaps to that edge. Use a lower value if the edge has a lot of detail or if the contrast in the image is low. Use a higher value for high-contrast images or smoother edges.

» **Contrast:** Specifies the percentage of contrast (from 1 percent to 100 percent) that's required before the Magnetic Lasso snaps to an edge. Use a higher percentage if your image has good contrast between your desired element and the background.

» **Frequency:** Specifies how many fastening points (from 1 to 100) to place on the selection line. The higher the value, the greater the number of points. As a general rule, if the element you want to select has a smooth edge, keep the value low. If the edge has a lot of detail, try a higher value.

>> **Tablet Pressure (pen icon):** If you're the proud owner of a pressure-sensitive drawing tablet, select this option to make an increase in stylus pressure cause the edge width to decrease.

Follow these steps to use the Magnetic Lasso tool:

1. **Select the Magnetic Lasso tool from the Tools panel.**

You can also press the L key to cycle through the various Lasso tools. The Magnetic Lasso tool looks like a straight-sided lasso with a little magnet on it.

2. **Click the edge of the object that you want to select to place the first fastening point.**

Fastening points anchor the selection line, as shown in Figure 8-7. You can start anywhere; just be sure to click the edge between the element you want and the background you don't want.

3. **Continue to move your cursor around the object without clicking.**

While the selection line gets pinned down with fastening points, only the newest portion of the selection line remains active.

If the Magnetic Lasso tool starts veering off the desired edge of your object, back up your mouse and click to force down a fastening point. Conversely, if the Magnetic Lasso tool adds a fastening point where you don't want one, press Backspace (Delete on the Mac) to delete it. Successive presses of the Backspace or Delete key continue to remove the fastening points.

TIP

If the Magnetic Lasso isn't cooperating, you can temporarily switch to the other Lasso tools. To select the Lasso tool, hold down Alt (Option on the Mac), click the mouse button, and drag. To select the Polygonal Lasso tool, hold down Alt (Option on the Mac) and click.

4. **Return to your starting point and click the mouse button to close the selection.**

You see a small circle next to your cursor, indicating that you're at the right spot to close the selection. You can also double-click, whereby Elements closes the selection from where you double-clicked to your starting point. The selection border appears when the selection is closed.

Magnetic Lasso fastening points

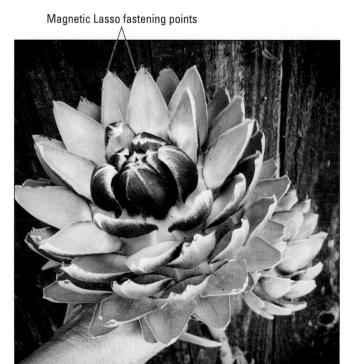

FIGURE 8-7:
The Magnetic Lasso tool snaps to the edge of your element and places fastening points to anchor the selection.

Working Wizardry with the Magic Wand

The Magic Wand tool is one of the oldest tools in the world of digital imaging. This beloved tool has been around since Photoshop was in its infancy and Elements was not yet a twinkle in Adobe's eye. It's extremely easy to use, but you'll have a somewhat harder time predicting what selection results it will present.

Here's how the Magic Wand tool works: You click inside the image, and the Magic Wand tool makes a selection. This selection is based on the color of the pixel you clicked. If other pixels are similar in color to your target pixel, Elements includes them in the selection. What's sometimes hard to predict, however, is how to determine *how* similar the color has to be to get the Magic Wand tool to select it. Fortunately, that's where the Tolerance setting comes in. In the sections that follow, we first introduce you to this setting and then explain how to put the Magic Wand to work.

Talking about Tolerance

The Tolerance setting determines the range of color that the Magic Wand tool selects. The range of color is based on brightness levels, ranging from 0 to 255:

» Setting the Tolerance to 0 selects one color only.

» Setting the Tolerance to 255 selects all colors, or the whole image.

The default setting is 32, so whenever you click a pixel, Elements analyzes the value of that base color and then selects all pixels whose brightness levels are between 16 levels lighter and 16 levels darker.

What if an image contains a few shades of the same color? It's not a huge problem. You can click the Magic Wand multiple times to pick up additional pixels that you want to include in the selection. You can find out how in the section "Modifying Your Selections," later in this chapter. Or you can try a higher Tolerance setting. Conversely, if your wand selects too much, you can lower your Tolerance setting.

TIP

So you can see by our talk on tolerance that the Magic Wand tool works best when you have high-contrast images or images with a limited number of colors. For example, the optimum image for the Wand would be a solid black object on a white background. Skip the wand if the image has a ton of colors and no real definitive contrast between your desired element and the background.

Wielding the Wand to select

To use the Magic Wand tool and adjust its Tolerance settings, follow these steps:

1. **Select the Magic Wand tool from the Tools panel.**

It looks like a wand with a starburst on the end. You can also just press A to cycle through the Magic Wand, Quick Selection, and Selection Brush tools. Or you can choose any of the tools and then select your desired tool in the Tool Options.

2. **Click anywhere on your desired element, using the default Tolerance setting of 32.**

REMEMBER

The pixel you click determines the base color.

If the Pixel Gods are with you and you selected everything you want on the first click, you're done. If your selection needs further tweaking, like the top image shown in Figure 8-8, continue to Step 3.

3. **Specify a new Tolerance setting in the Tool Options.**

If the Magic Wand selects more than you want, lower the Tolerance setting. If the wand didn't select enough, increase the value. While you're poking around in the Tool Options, here are a couple more options to get familiar with:

- **Sample All Layers:** If you have multiple layers and enable this option, the Magic Wand selects pixels from all visible layers. Without this option, the tool selects pixels from the active layer only. For more on layers, see Chapter 9.

- **Contiguous:** Forces the Magic Wand to select only pixels that are adjacent to each other. Without this option, the tool selects all pixels within the range of tolerance, whether or not they're adjacent to each other.

- **Anti-aliasing:** Softens the edge of the selection by one row of pixels. See the section "Applying Marquee options," earlier in this chapter, for details.

- **Refine Edge:** Click the Refine Edge button. In the Refine Edge dialog box, clean up your selection by moving the Smooth slider to reduce the amount of jagginess in your edges. Feather works like the Feather option discussed in the "Applying Marquee options" section, earlier in the chapter. Move the Shift Edge slider to the left or right to decrease or increase the selected area, respectively. For even more details, see the section "Refining the edges of a selection," later in this chapter. We explain yet another way to refine edges (which you don't find in the Tool Options) in "Applying the Grow and Similar commands," also later in this chapter. Finally, see how to use the Select Subject option, later in this chapter, in "Selecting Your Subject."

4. **Click your desired element again.**

Unfortunately, the Magic Wand tool isn't magical enough to modify your first selection automatically. Instead, it deselects the current selection and makes a new selection based on your new Tolerance setting. If it still isn't right, you can adjust the Tolerance setting again. Try, try again.

Tolerance 32

Tolerance 90

© *Brocreative/Shutterstock Image #264071576*

FIGURE 8-8:
The Magic
Wand selects
pixels based
on a specified
Tolerance
setting.

Modifying Your Selections

It's time for a seventh-inning stretch in this chapter on selection tools. In this section, you find out how to refine that Marquee, Lasso, or Magic Wand selection to perfection.

TIP

You're not limited to the manual methods described in the following sections, or even to keyboard shortcuts. You can also use the four selection option buttons on the left side of the Tool Options to create a new selection (the default), add to a selection, subtract from a selection, or intersect one selection with another. Just choose your desired selection tool, click the selection option button you want, and drag (or click if you're using the Magic Wand or Polygonal Lasso tool).

Adding to, subtracting from, and intersecting a selection

Although the Marquee, Lasso, and Magic Wand tools do an okay job of capturing the bulk of your selection, if you take the time to add or subtract a bit from your selection border, you can ensure that you get only what you really want:

>> **Add:** If your selection doesn't quite contain all the elements you want to capture, you need to add those portions to your current selection border. To add to a current Marquee selection, simply press the Shift key and drag around the area you want to include. If you're using the Polygonal Lasso, click around the area. And if you're wielding the Magic Wand, just press the Shift key and click the area you want.

REMEMBER

You don't have to use the same tool to add to your selection that you used to create the original selection. Feel free to use whatever selection tool you think can get the job done. For example, it's very common to start off with the Magic Wand and fine-tune with the Lasso tool.

>> **Subtract:** Got too much? To subtract from a current selection, press the Alt (Option on the Mac) key and drag the marquee around the pixels you want to subtract. With the Alt (Option on the Mac) key, use the same method for the Magic Wand and Polygonal Lasso as you do for adding to a selection.

>> **Intersect two selections:** Get your fingers in shape. To intersect your existing selection with a second selection, press Shift+Alt (Shift+Option on the Mac) and drag with the Lasso or Marquee tools. Or, if you're using the Magic Wand or Polygonal Lasso, press those keys and click rather than drag. Your selection now includes only the area common to both selections.

Avoiding key collisions

If you read the beginning of this chapter, you found out that by pressing the Shift key, you get a perfectly square or circular selection. We tell you in the preceding section, "Adding to, subtracting from, and intersecting a selection," that if you want to add to a selection, you press the Shift key. What if you want to create a perfect square while adding to the selection? Or what if you want to delete part of a selection while also drawing from the center outward? Both require the use of the Alt (Option on the Mac) key. How in the heck does Elements know what you want? Here are two tips to avoid keyboard collisions — grab your desired Marquee tool:

>> **To add a square or circular selection, press Shift and drag.** While you drag, keep the mouse button pressed, release the Shift key for just a second, and then press it again. Your added selection area suddenly snaps into a square or circle. You must then release the mouse button and then release the Shift key. Make sure your Aspect option is set to Normal.

>> **To delete from an existing selection while drawing from the center outward, press Alt (Option on the Mac) and drag.** While you drag, keep the mouse button pressed, release the Alt (Option on the Mac) key for just a second, and then press it down again. You're now drawing from the center outward. Again, release the mouse button first and then release the Alt (Option on the Mac) key.

REMEMBER

You can also use the selection option buttons in the Tool Options.

Painting with the Selection Brush

If you like the organic feel of painting on a canvas, you'll appreciate the Selection Brush. Using two different modes, you can either paint over areas of an image that you want to select or paint over areas you don't want to select. This great tool also lets you first make a basic selection with another tool, such as the Lasso, and then fine-tune the selection by brushing additional pixels into or out of the selection.

Here's the step-by-step process of selecting with the Selection Brush:

1. **Select the Selection Brush from the Tools panel.**

It looks like a paintbrush with a dotted oval around the tip. Or simply press the A key to cycle through the Selection Brush, Quick Selection, and Magic Wand tools. You can also select any of these tools and then choose your desired tool in the Tool Options.

TIP

This tool works in either Expert or Quick mode.

2. **Specify your Selection Brush options in the Tool Options.**

Here's the rundown on each option:

- **Mode:** Choose Selection if you want to paint over what you *want* to select or Mask if you want to paint over what you don't want.

  If you choose Mask mode, you must choose some additional overlay options. An overlay is a layer of color (that shows onscreen only) that hovers over your image, indicating protected or unselected areas. You must also choose an overlay opacity between 1 and 100 percent (which we describe in the Tip at the end of these steps). You can change the overlay color from the default red to another color. This option can be helpful if your image contains a lot of red.

- **Brush Presets Picker:** Choose a brush from the presets drop-down list. To load additional brushes, click the downward-pointing arrow to the right of Default Brushes and choose the preset library of your choice. You can select the Load Brushes command from the panel menu (top-right down-pointing arrow).

- **Size:** Specify a brush size, from 1 to 2,500 pixels. Enter the value or drag the slider.

- **Hardness:** Set the hardness of the brush tip, from 1 to 100 percent. A harder tip creates a crisper, more defined stroke.

3. **Paint the appropriate areas:**

- **If your mode is set to Selection:** Paint over the areas you *want* to select.

  You see a selection border. Each stroke adds to the selection. (The Add to Selection button in the Tool Options is selected automatically.) If you inadvertently add something you don't want, simply press the Alt (Option on the Mac) key and paint over the undesired area. You can also click the Subtract from Selection button in the Tool Options. After you finish painting what you want, your selection is ready to go.

- **If your mode is set to Mask:** Paint over the areas that you *don't* want to select.

  When you're done painting your mask, choose Selection from the Selection/Mask drop-down list or simply choose another tool from the Tool Options, in order to convert your mask into a selection border. Remember that your selection is what you *don't* want.

  While you paint, you see the color of your overlay. Each stroke adds more to the overlay area, as shown in Figure 8-9. In the example, the sky is masked (with a red overlay) to replace it with a different sky. When working in Mask mode, you're essentially covering up, or *masking,* the areas you want to protect from manipulation. That manipulation can be selecting, adjusting color, or performing any other Elements command. Again, if you want to remove parts of the masked area, press Alt (Option on the Mac) and paint.

REMEMBER

If you painted your selection in Mask mode, your selection border is around what you *don't* want. To switch to what you do want, choose Select ⇨ Inverse.

FIGURE 8-9:
The Selection Brush allows you to make a selection (right) by creating a mask (left).

© Hanis/iStockphoto #2054524

TIP

Which mode should you choose? Well, it's up to you. But one advantage to working in Mask mode is that you can partially select areas. By painting with soft brushes, you create soft-edged selections. These soft edges result in partially selected pixels. If you set the overlay opacity to a lower percentage, your pixels are even less opaque, or "less selected." If this partially selected business sounds vaguely familiar, it's because this is also what happens when you feather selections, as we discuss in the section "Applying Marquee options," earlier in this chapter.

Painting with the Quick Selection Tool

Think of the Quick Selection tool as a combination Brush, Magic Wand, and Lasso tool. Good news — it lives up to its "quick" moniker. Better news — it's also easy to use. The best news? It gives pretty decent results, so give it a whirl.

Here's how to make short work of selecting with this tool:

1. **Select the Quick Selection tool from the Tools panel.**

   The tool looks like a wand with a marquee around the end. It shares the same Tools panel space with the Selection Brush tool and the Magic Wand tool. You

TIP

can also press the A key to cycle through the Quick Selection, Selection Brush, and Magic Wand tools.

This tool works in either Expert or Quick mode.

2. **Specify the options in the Tool Options.**

Here's a description of the options:

- **New Selection:** The default option enables you to create a new selection. There are also options to add to and subtract from your selection.

- **Size:** Choose your desired brush size. Specify the diameter, from 1 to 2,500 pixels.

- **Brush Settings:** With these settings, you can specify hardness, spacing, angle, and roundness. For details on these settings, see Chapter 13.

- **Sample All Layers:** If your image has layers and you want to make a selection from all the layers, select this option. If you leave it deselected, you will select only from the active layer.

- **Auto-Enhance:** Select this option to have Elements automatically refine your selection by implementing an algorithm.

3. **Drag or paint the desired areas of your image.**

Your selection grows as you drag, as shown in Figure 8-10. If you stop dragging and click in another portion of your image, your selection includes that clicked area.

4. **Add to or delete from your selection, as desired:**

- **To add to your selection,** press the Shift key while dragging across your desired image areas.

- **To delete from your selection,** press the Alt (Option on the Mac) key while dragging across your unwanted image areas.

You can also select the Add to Selection and Subtract from Selection options in the Tool Options.

5. **If you need to fine-tune your selection, click the Refine Edge option in the Tool Options and then change the settings, as desired.**

The settings are explained in detail in the "Refining the edges of a selection" section, later in this chapter.

Note: If your object is fairly detailed, you may even need to break out the Lasso or another selection tool to make some final cleanups. Eventually, you should arrive at a selection you're happy with.

The selected portion is surrounded by a border

FIGURE 8-10:
Paint a selection with the Quick Selection tool.

Selecting with the Auto Selection Tool

If the selection tools described so far in this chapter seem a little too taxing, this tool is made for you. The Auto Selection tool lives up to its name by quickly and easily selecting your desired object. This intelligent tool takes your rough selection, analyzes the pixels, and determines the object it thinks you want within that rough selection. It then snaps to that object.

Here's how to use this genius tool:

1. **Select the Auto Selection tool from the Tools panel.**

The tool looks like a wand with three small yellow stars around the end, as shown in Figure 8-11. It shares the same Tools panel space with the Quick Selection, Selection Brush, and Magic Wand tools. You can also press the A key to cycle through those tools. Note that, by default, the New Selection option is highlighted.

This tool works in either Expert or Quick mode.

TIP

2. **Choose which tool you want to use to make your rough selection in the Tool Options.**

   You can choose from the Rectangular and Elliptical Marquee tools or the Lasso and Polygonal Lasso tools.

3. **Specify other options in the Tool Options:**

   - **Sample All Layers:** If your image has layers and you want to make a selection from all the layers, select this option. If you leave it deselected, you will select only from the active layer.

   - **Constrain Selection:** This option will keep your marquee selections perfectly square or circular.

4. **Make a rough selection around the desired object in your image.**

   We used the Lasso tool and selected the girl, as shown in Figure 8-11.

   When you release your mouse after making the selection, Elements smartly analyzes the pixels and snaps to your selected object, as shown in Figure 8-11.

5. **Add or subtract from your selection as needed.**

   - **To add to your selection,** press the Shift key while dragging across your desired image areas.

   - **To delete from your selection,** press the Alt key (Option key on the Mac) while dragging across your unwanted image areas.

   You can also select the Add to Selection and Subtract from Selection options in the Tool Options.

6. **If you need to fine-tune your selection, click the Refine Edge option in the Tool Options and adjust the settings, as desired.**

   The settings are explained in detail in the "Refining the edges of a selection" section, later in this chapter.

FIGURE 8-11:
The Auto Selection tool easily and quickly selects your object.

TIP

If you think the Auto Selection tool is a game changer, you must check out the Background Changer Guided Edit. This edit, found under the Special Edits in Guided mode, lets you change the background in your image and even add a custom background.

Selecting Your Subject

One of the most popular requests that Adobe receives when querying users about its software is "How can I select things more easily and more accurately?" Adobe heard the cries and supplied yet another great way to make a selection.

Here's how to use the Select Subject command:

1. **In either Expert or Quick mode, choose Select ⇨ Subject.**

   You can also click the Select Subject button in the Tool Options of the Quick Selection, Selection Brush, Magic Wand, Refine Selection, and Auto Selection Tool, as shown in Figure 8-12.

2. **If your selection needs some cleanup after Step 1, add to or subtract from your selection using any of the selection tools.**

   Our favorite tool for small cleanups is the Lasso tool, found in the Tool Options of the Auto Selection Tool.

   - **To add to your selection,** press the Shift key while dragging across your desired image areas.

   - **To delete from your selection,** press the Alt key (Option key on the Mac) while dragging across your unwanted image areas.

   You can also select the Add to Selection and Subtract from Selection options in the Tool Options.

3. **If you need to fine-tune your selection further, click the Refine Edge option in the Tool Options and adjust the settings as desired.**

   The settings are explained in detail in the "Refining the edges of a selection" section, later in this chapter.

FIGURE 8-12:
The Select
Subject
command
analyzes and
selects people,
animals, cars,
and other
objects.

Fine-Tuning with the Refine Selection Brush

As we mention in the beginning of this chapter, being able to make selections quickly and accurately is a coveted skill. Luckily, Elements has an additional tool to make this skill easier to obtain. The Refine Selection Brush helps you to add or delete portions of your selection by automatically detecting edges of your desired element.

Here's how to refine your selections with this tool:

1. **Make your selection using the Quick Selection tool, Selection Brush, or any other selection tool, for that matter.**

   Elements doesn't care how you make your initial selection, as long as you have one. Don't worry if it isn't perfect. That's where the Refine Selection Brush comes in.

2. **Select the Refine Selection Brush.**

   This tool shares a tool slot with the Quick Selection tool, Magic Wand, Selection Brush, and Smart Selection tool.

   Your cursor appears as two concentric circles. The outer circle reflects the Tolerance setting to detect an edge. For more on tolerance, see "Talking about Tolerance," earlier in this chapter.

3. **Specify the settings in the Tool Options.**

   Here are descriptions of the options:

   - **Size:** Use the slider to adjust your brush diameter from 1 to 2,500 pixels.

   - **Snap Strength:** Use the slider to adjust your snap strength from 0 to 100 percent. Snap Strength indicates the intensity of the pull.

   - **Selection Edge:** Use the slider to determine how hard or soft you want your edge. If you have an object that has wispier edges, such as hair, fur, or feathers, moving the slider more toward soft may be more effective in getting your desired selection. If you set your mode to Add and press and hold your cursor on your object, the selection within your concentric circles grows. Specifically, the lighter-colored area around your center circle, called the *selection edge,* grows. This area represents your object's edge. Be sure to include your entire edge within this area. Note that you can also "paint" the edge with the Refine Selection Brush tool. Getting the selection you want on a complex object may take a bit of experimentation and refining using the options, but hang in there and you should get the detail you want.

   - **Add/Subtract:** Choose this mode to either add to or subtract from your selection.

   - **Push:** Place your cursor inside the selection to increase your selection within the diameter of the outer circle of your cursor. It will snap to the edge of the element closest to the cursor. Place your cursor outside the selection to decrease your selection within the diameter of the outer circle.

   - **Smooth:** If your selection border looks a little too jagged, use this mode to smooth your selection edge.

   - **View:** Choose an option to view the selection. Options include viewing your selected object against a white or black background. Or you can choose Overlay to view it against a red semi-opaque overlay. Note that with the Overlay option, you can adjust the corresponding opacity of that overlay.

4. **Continue to use the Refine Selection Brush to perfect your selection until you're satisfied. The finished selection is shown in Figure 8-13.**

FIGURE 8-13:
Use the Refine
Selection
Brush to
fine-tune your
selection.

Working with the Cookie Cutter Tool

The Cookie Cutter tool is a cute name for a pretty powerful tool. You can think of it as a Custom Shape tool for images. But, whereas the Custom Shape tool creates a mask and just hides everything outside the shape, the Cookie Cutter tool cuts away everything outside the shape. The preset libraries offer you a large variety of interesting shapes, from talk bubbles to Swiss cheese. (We're not being funny here — check out the food library.)

Here's the lowdown on using the Cookie Cutter:

1. **Select the Cookie Cutter tool from the Tools panel.**

   There's no missing this tool; it looks like a flower. You can also press the C key. The Cookie Cutter shares a space with the Crop and Perspective Crop tools. If you don't see it, press C until you do, or select the Crop tool and then select the Cookie Cutter in the Tool Options.

2. **Specify your options in the Tool Options.**

   Here's the list:

   - **Shape:** Choose a shape from the Custom Shape picker preset library. To load other libraries, click the Shapes pop-up menu and choose one from the submenu.

   - **Geometry Options:** These options let you draw your shape with certain parameters.

     - **Unconstrained:** Enables you to draw freely.

     - **Defined Proportions:** Enables you to keep the height and width proportional.

     - **Defined Size:** Crops the image to the original, fixed size of the shape you choose. You can't make it bigger or smaller.

     - **Fixed Size:** Allows you to enter your desired width and height.

   - **From Center:** Allows you to draw the shape from the center outward.

   - **Feather:** This option creates a soft-edged selection. See the section "Applying Marquee options," earlier in this chapter, for more details.

   - **Crop:** Click this option to crop the image into the shape. The shape fills the image window.

3. **Drag your mouse on the image to create your desired shape, size the shape by dragging one of the handles of the bounding box, and position the shape by placing the mouse cursor inside the box and dragging.**

   You can also perform other types of transformations, such as rotating and skewing. You can use these functions by dragging the box manually or by entering values in the Tool Options. For more on transformations, see Chapter 10.

4. **Click the Commit button on the image or press Enter to finish the cutout.**

   See Figure 8-14 to see the image cut into a leaf shape. If you want to bail out of the bounding box and not cut out, you can always click the Cancel button on the image or press Esc.

© Evgeniya Moroz/Shutterstock Image #86044411

FIGURE 8-14:
Crop your photo into interesting shapes with the Cookie Cutter.

Eliminating with the Eraser Tools

The Eraser tools let you erase areas of your image. Elements has three Eraser tools: the regular Eraser, the Magic Eraser, and the Background Eraser. The Eraser tools look like those pink erasers you used in grade school, so you can't miss them. If you can't locate them, you can always press E to cycle through the three tools.

WARNING

When you erase pixels, those pixels are history — they're gone. So before using the Eraser tools, always have a backup of your image stored somewhere. Think of it as a cheap insurance policy in case things go awry.

The Eraser tool

The Eraser tool enables you to erase areas on your image to either your background color or, if you're working on a layer, a transparent background, as shown in Figure 8-15. For more on layers, check out Chapter 9.

FIGURE 8-15:
Erase either
to your
background
color (left) or to
transparency
(right).

To use this tool, simply select it and drag through the desired area on your image, and you're done. Because it isn't the most accurate tool on the planet, remember to zoom way in and use smaller brush tips to do some accurate erasing.

You have several Eraser options to specify in the Tool Options:

» **Brush Presets Picker:** Click the drop-down list to access the Brush presets. Choose a brush. Again, additional brush libraries are available on the Brush list. (Click the down-pointing arrow in the top-right corner.)

» **Size:** Slide the Size slider and choose a brush size between 1 and 2,500 pixels. You can also use the left and right bracket keys to decrease and increase the brush size, respectively.

» **Opacity:** Specify a percentage of transparency for your erased areas. The lower the Opacity setting, the less it erases. Opacity isn't available in Block mode.

» **Type:** Select Brush, Pencil, or Block. When you select Block, you're stuck with one size (a 16-x-16-pixel tip) and can't select other preset brushes.

The Background Eraser tool

The Background Eraser tool, which is savvier than the Eraser tool, erases the background from an image while being mindful of leaving the foreground untouched. The Background Eraser tool erases to transparency on a layer. If you use this tool on an image with only a background, Elements converts the background into a layer.

The key to using the Background Eraser is to carefully keep the *hot spot*, the cross-hair at the center of the brush, on the background pixels while you drag. The hot spot samples the color of the pixels and deletes that color whenever it falls inside the brush circumference. But if you accidentally touch a foreground pixel with the hot spot, it's erased as well. And the tool isn't even sorry about it! This tool works better with images that have good contrast in color between the background and foreground objects, as shown in Figure 8-16. If your image has very detailed or wispy edges (such as hair or fur) and you're up for a challenge, layer masking can also provide good results. We describe layer masks in Chapter 9.

FIGURE 8-16: The Background Eraser erases similarly colored pixels sampled by the hot spot of your brush cursor.

© webphotographer/Stockphoto Image #5213985

Here's the rundown on the Background Eraser options:

>> **Brush Settings:** Click the Brush Settings button to bring up the settings to customize the Size, Hardness, Spacing, Roundness, and Angle of your brush tip. The Size and Tolerance settings at the bottom are for pressure-sensitive drawing tablets.

>> **Limits:** *Discontiguous* erases all similarly colored pixels wherever they appear in the image. *Contiguous* erases all similarly colored pixels that are adjacent to those under the hot spot.

> » **Tolerance:** The percentage determines how similar the colors have to be to the color under the hot spot before Elements erases them. A higher value picks up more colors, whereas a lower value picks up fewer colors. See the section "Talking about Tolerance," earlier in this chapter, for more details.

The Magic Eraser tool

You can think of the Magic Eraser tool as a combination Eraser and Magic Wand tool. It selects *and* erases similarly colored pixels simultaneously. Unless you're working on a layer with the transparency locked (see Chapter 9 for more on locking layers), the pixels are erased to transparency. If you're working on an image with just a background, Elements converts the background into a layer.

Although the Magic Eraser shares most of the same options with the other erasers, it also offers unique options:

> » **Sample All Layers:** Samples colors using data from all visible layers but erases pixels on the active layer only
>
> » **Contiguous:** Selects and erases all similarly colored pixels that are adjacent to those under the hot spot
>
> » **Anti-aliasing:** Creates a slightly soft edge around the transparent area

Using the Select Menu

In the following sections, we breeze through the Select menu. Along with the methods we describe in the "Modifying Your Selections" section, earlier in this chapter, you can use this menu to further modify selections by expanding, contracting, smoothing, softening, inversing, growing, and grabbing similarly colored pixels. If that doesn't satisfy your selection needs, nothing will.

Selecting all or nothing

The Select All and Deselect commands are no-brainers. To select everything in your image, choose Select ➪ All or press Ctrl+A (⌘ +A on the Mac). To deselect everything, choose Select ➪ Deselect or press Ctrl+D (⌘ +D on the Mac). Remember that you usually don't have to Select All. If you don't have a selection border in your image, Elements assumes that the whole image is fair game for any manipulation.

Reselecting a selection

If you sacrifice that second cup of coffee to steady your hand and take the time to carefully lasso around your desired object, you don't want to lose your selection before you have a chance to perform your next move. But all it takes is an inadvertent click of your mouse while you have an active selection border to obliterate your selection. Fortunately, Elements anticipated such a circumstance and offers a solution: If you choose Select⇨Reselect, Elements retrieves your last selection.

REMEMBER

One caveat: The Reselect command works for only the last selection you made, so don't plan to reselect a selection you made last Tuesday or even just 5 minutes ago if you selected something else after that selection. If you want to reuse a selection for the long term, save it as we explain in the section "Saving and loading selections," later in this chapter.

Inversing a selection

You know the old song lyric: "If you can't be with the one you love, love the one you're with." Well, making selections in Elements is kind of like that. Sometimes it's just easier to select what you don't want rather than what you do want. For example, if you're trying to select your beloved in his senior photo, it's probably easier to just click the studio backdrop with the Magic Wand and then inverse the selection by choosing Select⇨Inverse.

Feathering a selection

In the "Applying Marquee options" section earlier in this chapter, we describe how to feather a selection when using the Lasso and Marquee tools by entering a value in the Feather box in the Tool Options. Remember that this method of feathering requires that you set the Feather value *before* you create your selection. What we didn't tell you is that there's a way to apply a feather *after* you make a selection.

Choose Select⇨Feather and enter your desired amount from 0.2 to 250 pixels. Your selection is subsequently softened around the edges.

TIP

This method is actually a better way to go. Make your selection and fine-tune it by using the methods we describe earlier in this chapter. Then apply your feather. The problem with applying the feather before you make a selection happens when you want to modify your initial selection. When you make a selection with a feather, the marquee outline of the selection adjusts to take into account the amount of the feathering. So the resulting marquee outline doesn't resemble your precise mouse movement, making it harder to modify that selection.

Refining the edges of a selection

The Refine Edge option enables you to fine-tune the edges of your selection. It doesn't matter how you got the selection, just that you have one. You can find the command in the Tool Options of the Magic Wand, Lasso, and Quick Selection tools. And, of course, you can find it on the Select menu. Here's the scoop on each setting for this option, as shown in Figure 8-17:

>> **View Mode:** Choose a mode from the pop-up menu to preview your selection. Hover your cursor over each mode to get a tooltip. For example, Marching Ants shows the selection border. Overlay lets you preview your selection with the edges hidden and a semi-opaque layer of color in your unselected area. On Black and On White show the selection against a black or white background. Show Original shows the image without a selection preview. Show Radius displays the size of the area in which the edge refinement is happening.

>> **Smart Radius:** Select this option to have Elements automatically adjust the radius for hard and soft edges near your selection border. If your border is uniformly hard or soft, you may not want to select this option. This enables you to have more control over the radius setting.

>> **Radius:** Specifies the size of the selection border you will refine. Increase the radius to improve the edge of areas with soft transitions or a lot of detail. Move the slider while looking at your selection to find a good setting.

>> **Smooth:** Reduces jaggedness along your selection edges.

>> **Feather:** Move the slider to the right to create an increasingly softer, more blurred edge.

>> **Contrast:** Removes artifacts while tightening soft edges by increasing the contrast. Try using the Smart Radius option before playing with Contrast.

>> **Shift Edge:** Decreases or increases your selected area. Slightly decreasing your selection border can help to defringe (eliminate undesirable background pixels) your selection edges.

>> **Decontaminate Colors:** Replaces background fringe with the colors of your selected element. Because decontamination changes the colors of some of the pixels, you will have to output to, or create, another layer or document to preserve your current layer. To see the decontamination in action, choose Reveal Layer for your View mode. Chapter 9 explains how to work with layers.

>> **Amount:** Changes the level of decontamination.

>> **Output To:** Choose whether you want to output your refined, decontaminated selection to a selection on your current layer, layer mask, layer, layer with layer mask, new document, or new document with layer mask.

- **Refine Radius tool:** Select the Paintbrush tool on the left and brush around your border to adjust the area you're refining. To understand exactly what area is being included or excluded, change your View mode to Marching Ants. Use the right and left brackets to decrease and increase the brush size.

- **Erase Refinements tool:** Use this tool (which looks like an Eraser), also located on the left, to clean up any unwanted refinements made with the Refine Radius tool.

- **Zoom tool:** Allows you to zoom in to your image to see the effects of your settings.

- **Hand tool:** Enables you to pan around your image window to see the effects of your settings.

FIGURE 8-17:
Fine-tune your selection with Refine Edge.

Using the Modify commands

Although the commands on the Modify submenu definitely won't win any popularity contests, they may occasionally come in handy. Here's the scoop on each command:

- **Border:** Selects the area, from 1 to 200 pixels, around the edge of the selection border. By choosing Edit ⇨ Fill Selection, you can fill the border with color.

- **Smooth:** Rounds off any jagged, raggedy edges. Enter a value from 1 to 100 pixels, and Elements looks at each selected pixel and then includes or deselects the pixels in your selection based on your chosen value. Start with a low number, like 1, 2, or 3 pixels. Otherwise, your selection may be less accurate.

- **Expand:** Enables you to increase the size of your selection by a given number of pixels, from 1 to 100. This command is especially useful if you just barely missed getting the edge of an elliptical selection and need it to be a little larger.

- **Contract:** Decreases your selection border by 1 to 100 pixels. When you're compositing multiple images, you often benefit by slightly contracting your selection if you plan to apply a feather. That way, you avoid picking up a fringe of background pixels around your selection.

Applying the Grow and Similar commands

The Grow and Similar commands are often used in tandem with the Magic Wand tool. If you made an initial selection with the Magic Wand but didn't quite get everything you want, try choosing Select ⇨ Grow. The Grow command increases the size of the selection by including adjacent pixels that fall within the range of tolerance. The Similar command is like Grow except that the pixels don't have to be adjacent to be selected. The command searches throughout the image and picks up pixels within the Tolerance range.

These commands don't have their own Tolerance options. They use whatever Tolerance value is displayed on the Tool Options when the Magic Wand tool is selected. You can adjust that Tolerance setting to include more or fewer colors.

Saving and loading selections

At times, you toil so long over a complex selection that you really want to save it for future use. Saving it is not only possible but highly recommended. It's also a piece of cake. Here's how:

1. **After you perfect your selection, choose Select ⇨ Save Selection.**

2. **In the Save Selection dialog box that appears, leave the Selection option set to New Selection and enter a name for your selection, as shown in Figure 8-18.**

   The operation is automatically set to New Selection.

3. **Click OK.**

4. **When you want to access the selection again, choose Select ⇨ Load Selection and choose a selection from the Selection drop-down list.**

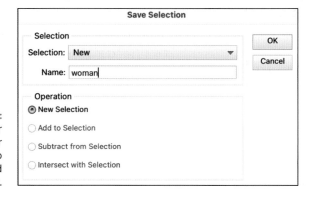

FIGURE 8-18: Save your selection for later use to save time and effort.

IN THIS CHAPTER

» **Using the Layers panel and the Layer menu**

» **Working with the Select menu**

» **Creating new layers**

» **Moving, merging, transforming, and flattening layers**

» **Adding layer masks**

Chapter **9**

Working with Layers

U sing Elements without ever using layers would be like writing a book with a pen and paper pad: Sure, you could do it, but it wouldn't be fun. An even bigger issue would occur when it came time to edit that book and make changes. Correction tape, correction fluid, and erasers would make that task downright tedious, not to mention messy. The benefit of using layers is that you have tremendous flexibility. You can make as many edits as you want for as long as you want, as long as you keep your composite image in layers. Layers make working in Elements a lot more productive. Don't give a darn about productivity? Well, let's just say that layers also make it a breeze for you to bring out your more artsy side.

This chapter explains the tools and techniques you need to start working with layers. After you give layers a try, you'll wonder how you ever lived without them.

Getting to Know Layers

Think of layers as sheets of acetate or clear transparency film. You have drawings or photographs on individual sheets. What you place on each sheet doesn't affect any of the other sheets. Any area on the sheet that doesn't have an image on it is transparent. You can stack these sheets on top of each other to create a combined image, or *composite* (or *collage,* if you prefer). You can reshuffle the order of the sheets, add new sheets, and delete old sheets.

In Elements, *layers* are essentially digital versions of these clear acetate sheets. You can place elements, such as images, text, or shapes, on separate layers and create a composite, as shown in Figure 9-1. You can hide, add, delete, or rearrange layers. Because layers are digital, of course, they have added functionality. You can adjust how opaque or transparent the element on a layer is. You can also add special effects and change how the colors interact between layers.

© homydesign/Shutterstock Image #334170533, mervas/Shutterstock Image #271812446, ArtFamily/Shutterstock Image #25608805, Alex_Rodionov/Shutterstock Image #301316285

FIGURE 9-1:
Layers enable you to easily create composite images.

TIP

To work with layers, you must be in the Photo Editor in Expert mode.

Converting a background to a layer

When you create a new file with background contents of white or a background color, scan an image into Elements, or open a stock photo or a file from a CD or your digital camera, you basically have a file with just a *background.* There are no layers yet.

An image contains at most one background, and you can't do much to it besides paint on it and make basic adjustments. You can't move the background or change its transparency or blend mode. How do you get around all these limitations? Convert your background into a layer by following these easy steps:

1. **Choose Window ⇨ Layers to display the Layers panel.**

   The Layers panel is explained in detail in the following section.

2. **Double-click Background on the Layers panel.**

   Or choose Layer ⇨ New ⇨ Layer From Background.

3. **Name the layer or leave it at the default name of Layer 0.**

   You can also adjust the blend mode and opacity of the layer in the New Layer dialog box. Or you can do it via the Layers panel commands later.

   You can also color-code your layers (but not your Background), which lets you better visually distinguish your layers within the Layers panel. If you decide to do it later, simply right-click (Control-click on the Mac) and choose a color from the contextual menu.

4. **Click OK.**

   Elements converts your background into a layer, known also as an *image layer*.

TIP

   When you create a new image with transparent background contents, the image doesn't contain a background but instead is created with a single layer.

Anatomy of the Layers panel

Elements keeps layers controlled with a panel named, not surprisingly, the *Layers panel*. To display the Layers panel, choose Window ⇨ Layers in the Photo Editor in Expert mode. (Figure 9-2 shows you what you can expect.)

The order of the layers on the Layers panel represents the order in the image. We refer to this concept in the computer graphics world as the *stacking order*. The top layer on the panel is the top layer in your image, and so on. Depending on what you're doing, you can work on a

FIGURE 9-2:
The Layers panel controls layers in your image.

single layer or on multiple layers at one time. Here are some tips for working with the Layers panel:

>> **Select a layer.** Click a layer name or its thumbnail. Elements highlights the *active layer* on the panel.

>> **Select multiple contiguous layers.** Click your first layer and then Shift-click your last layer.

>> **Select multiple noncontiguous layers.** Ctrl-click (⌘ -click on the Mac) your desired layers.

>> **View and hide layers.** To hide a layer, click the eye icon for that layer and the layer disappears. To redisplay the layer, click the blank space in the eye column. You can also hide all the layers except one by selecting your desired layer and Alt-clicking (Option-clicking on the Mac) the eye icon for that layer. Redisplay all layers by Alt-clicking (Option-clicking on the Mac) the eye icon again. Hiding all the layers except the one you want to edit can be helpful in allowing you to focus without the distraction of all the other imagery.

REMEMBER

Only layers that are visible are printed. This can be useful if you want to have several versions of an image (each on a separate layer) for a project within the same file.

>> **Select the actual element (the nontransparent pixels) on the layer.** Ctrl-click (⌘ -click on the Mac) the layer's thumbnail (not the name) on the panel.

>> **Create a new blank layer.** Click the Create a New Layer icon at the top of the panel.

>> **Create a new group.** Elements enables you to better organize your layers by incorporating *layer groups.* Think of a layer group as the digital version of an analog manila folder. Select your desired layers and drag them into a group folder. You can expand or collapse layer groups to see or hide their contents. When collapsed, layer groups are a nice way to avoid endless scrolling in a file with many layers. Layer groups also let you apply opacity settings, blend modes, and layer styles to a group of layers at a time.

>> To create a layer group, click the Create a New Group icon (the stacked layers icon) at the top of the Layers panel. You can also select New Group from the Layers panel pop-up menu or choose Layer ➪ New ➪ Group. The latter two methods prompt you for a group name in addition to a few other options (similar to regular layers). You can color-code your group and specify a blend mode and opacity setting. The default mode is Pass Through, which lets the blend modes applied to the individual layers remain intact (for more on blend modes, see Chapter 12). If you select any other mode, that mode overrides all the layers in the group. After you create your group, drag your layers into the

group folder in the Layers panel. To collapse or expand the group, click the triangle icon to the left of the group icon. As with regular layers, you can select, duplicate, show, hide, lock, and rearrange layer groups.

A couple other tips:

- **You can create a layer group from selected layers.** Select the layers that you want to be in a group, and then select New Group from Layers from the Layers panel pop-up menu or choose Layer ⇨ New ⇨ Group from Layers. Name the group in the dialog box that appears and click OK.

- **Rename your group.** You can rename your group by double-clicking the group name in the Layers panel.

>> **Add a layer mask.** Click the Add Layer Mask icon (rectangle with white circle) at the top of the panel. A layer mask enables you to selectively show and hide elements or adjustments on your layer, as well as creatively blend layers together. For more details, see "Adding Layer Masks," later in this chapter.

>> **Create an Adjustment layer.** Click the Create a New Fill or Adjustment Layer icon at the top of the panel. *Adjustment layers* are special layers that modify contrast and color in your image. You can also add *fill layers* — layers containing color, gradients, or patterns — by using this command. We give you more details on adjustment and fill layers in the section "Working with Different Layer Types," later in this chapter.

>> **Duplicate an existing layer.** Drag the layer to the Create a New Layer icon at the top of the panel.

>> **Rearrange layers.** To move a layer to another position in the stacking order, drag the layer up or down on the Layers panel. While you drag, you see a fist icon. Release the mouse button when a highlighted line appears where you want to insert the layer.

If your image has a background, it always remains the bottommost layer. If you need to move the background, convert it to a layer by double-clicking the name on the Layers panel. Enter a name for the layer and click OK.

>> **Rename a layer.** When you create a new layer, Elements provides default layer names (Layer 1, Layer 2, and so on). If you want to rename a layer, double-click the layer name on the Layers panel and enter the name directly on the Layers panel.

>> **Adjust the interaction between colors on layers and adjust the transparency of layers.** You can use the blend modes and the opacity options at the top of the panel to mix the colors between layers and adjust the transparency of the layers, as shown in Figure 9-3. For more on blend modes, see Chapter 12.

>> **Link layers.** Sometimes you want your layers to stay grouped as a unit to make your editing tasks easier. If so, link your layers by selecting your desired layers in the panel and then clicking the Link/Unlink Layers icon on any one of the selected layers. To remove the link, click the Link/Unlink Layers icon again.

>> **Lock layers.** Select your desired layer or layers and then click one of the two lock icons at the top of the panel. The *checkerboard square icon* locks all transparent areas of your layers. This lock prevents you from painting or editing any transparent areas on the layers. The *lock icon* locks your entire layer and prevents it from being changed in any way, including moving or transforming the elements on the layer. You can, however, still make selections on the layer. To unlock the layer, simply click the icon again to toggle off the lock.

By default, the background is locked and can't be unlocked until you convert it into a layer by choosing Layer ⇨ New ⇨ Layer from Background.

>> **Delete a layer.** Drag it to the Trash icon.

FIGURE 9-3:
We created this effect by using blend modes and opacity options.

© Andrey Nekrasov/ImageBROKER/Corbis #4264117116, Rocksweeper/Shutterstock Image #264273713

Using the Layer and Select menus

As with many features in Elements, you usually have more than one way to do something. This is especially true when it comes to working with layers. Besides the commands on the Layers panel, you have two other menus that are applicable to layers — the Layer menu and the Select menu — both of which you can find on the main menu bar at the top of the application window (top of the screen on the Mac).

The Layer menu

Much of what you can do with the Layers panel icons you can also do by using the Layer menu on the menu bar and the Layers panel menu connected to the Layers panel. (Access the Layers panel menu by clicking the horizontally lined button in the upper-right corner of the Layers panel.) Commands, such as New, Duplicate, Delete, and Rename, are omnipresent throughout. But you find commands that are exclusive to the Layers panel, the main Layer menu, and the Layers panel menu, respectively. So if you can't find what you're looking for in one area, just go to another. Some commands require more explanation and are described in the sections that follow. However, here's a quick description of most of the commands:

>> **Delete Linked Layers and Delete Hidden Layers:** These commands delete only those layers that have been linked or those hidden from display on the Layers panel.

>> **Layer Style:** These commands manage the styles, or special effects, you apply to your layers.

>> **Arrange:** This enables you to shuffle your layer stacking order with options, such as Bring to Front and Send to Back. Reverse switches the order of your layers if you have two or more layers selected.

>> **Create Clipping Mask:** In a clipping mask, the bottommost layer (or *base* layer) acts as a mask for the layers above it. The layers above "clip" to the opaque areas of the base layer and don't show over the transparent areas of the base layer. Clipping masks work well when you want to fill a shape or type with different image layers.

>> **Type:** The commands in the Type submenu control the display of type layers. For more on type, see Chapter 14.

>> **Rename Layer:** This enables you to give a layer a new name. You can also simply double-click the name on the Layers panel.

>> **Simplify Layer:** This converts a type layer, shape layer, or fill layer into a regular image layer. Briefly, a *shape layer* contains a vector object, and a *fill layer* contains a solid color, a gradient, or a pattern.

>> **Merge and Flatten:** The various merge and flatten commands combine multiple layers into a single layer or, in the case of flattening, combine all your layers into a single background.

>> **Panel Options:** You can select display options and choose to use a layer mask on your adjustment layers. Leave this option selected.

The Select menu

Although the Select menu's main duties are to assist you in making and refining your selections, it offers a few handy layer commands. Here's a quick introduction to each command:

» **Select all layers.** Want to quickly get everything in your file? Choose Select ➪ All Layers.

» **Deselect all layers.** If you want to ensure that nothing is selected in your document, simply choose Select ➪ Deselect Layers.

Working with Different Layer Types

Layer life exists beyond just converting an existing background into a layer, which we describe in the section "Getting to Know Layers," earlier in this chapter. In fact, Elements offers five kinds of layers. You'll probably spend most of your time creating image layers, but just so that you're familiar with all types, the following sections describe each one.

Image layers

The *image layer,* usually just referred to as a *layer,* is the type of layer we're referring to when we give the analogy of acetate sheets in the section "Getting to Know Layers," earlier in this chapter. You can create blank layers and add images to them, or you can create layers from images themselves. You can have as many image layers as your computer's memory allows.

REMEMBER

The more layers you have, the larger your file size and the longer it takes to save and open your file.

Each layer in an image can be edited without affecting the other layers. You can move, paint, size, or apply a filter, for example, without disturbing a single pixel on any other layer or on the background, for that matter. And when an element is on a layer, you no longer have to make a selection to select it — just drag the element with the Move tool. If, however, you want only part of that layer, you need to make a selection. (See Chapter 8 for information on selections.)

Adjustment layers

An *Adjustment layer* is a special kind of layer used primarily for modifying color and contrast; Figure 9-4 shows an example. The advantage of using Adjustment layers for your corrections, rather than applying them directly on the image layer, is that you can apply the corrections without permanently affecting the pixels. This means that Adjustment layers are totally nondestructive. And because the correction is on a layer, you can edit, or even delete, the adjustment at any time. Adjustment layers apply the correction only to all the layers below them without affecting any of the layers above them.

FIGURE 9-4:
Adjustment layers correct color and contrast in your image.

TECHNICAL STUFF

Another unique feature of Adjustment layers is that when you create one, you also create a layer mask on that layer at the same time. If you're unfamiliar with layer masks, take a peek at the section "Adding Layer Masks," later in this chapter. The layer mask allows you to selectively and even partially apply the adjustment to the layers below it by applying shades of gray — from white to black — on the mask. By default, the mask is completely white, which allows the adjustment to be fully applied to the layers. If you paint on a layer mask with black, the areas under those black areas don't show the adjustment. If you paint with a shade of gray, those areas partially show the adjustment. *Note:* If you have an active selection border in your image before you add an Adjustment layer, the adjustment is applied only to that area within the selection border.

Elements has eight kinds of Adjustment layers, and you can use as many as you want. These are the same adjustments that you find on the Enhance⇨Adjust Lighting, Enhance⇨Adjust Color, and Filter⇨Adjustments submenus. For specifics on each adjustment, see Chapters 10 and 11. Here's how to create an Adjustment layer:

1. **Open an image that needs a little contrast or color adjustment.**

   You don't need to convert your background into a layer to apply an Adjustment layer.

2. **Click the Create New Fill or Adjustment Layer icon at the top of the Layers panel, and from the drop-down list, choose your desired adjustment.**

   The Adjustment layer icon and a thumbnail appear on the adjustment layer. The thumbnail represents the layer mask. And the dialog box specific to your adjustment appears in the Adjustments panel.

3. **Make the necessary adjustments in the particular Adjustments panel.**

REMEMBER

   To selectively allow only portions of your image to receive the adjustment, you can paint on the layer mask using the Brush or Pencil tool. Another technique is to use the Gradient tool on the mask to create a gradual application of the adjustment. Or you can make a selection and fill that selection with any shade of gray, from white to black, as shown in Figure 9-5, where we hid the original background of the surfer.

FIGURE 9-5: Layer masks control the amount of adjustment applied to your layers.

As with image layers, you can adjust the opacity and blend modes of an Adjustment layer. Reducing the opacity of an adjustment layer reduces the effect of the adjustment on the underlying layers.

Here are a few more tips on using adjustment layers:

>> **To view your image without the adjustment,** click the eye icon in the left column of the Layers panel to hide the Adjustment layer.

>> **To delete the Adjustment layer,** drag it to the Trash icon on the Layers panel.

>> **To edit an Adjustment layer,** simply double-click the Adjustment layer on the Layers panel. In the Adjustments panel, make any desired edits. The only Adjustment layer that you can't edit is the Invert adjustment. It's either on or off.

>> **To use the adjustment panel controls,** click an icon (shown in Figure 9-4 at the bottom of the Hue/Saturation window). From left to right, here's what the icons do:

- **Have the Adjustment layer clip to the layer below.** (It will affect only the layer directly beneath it, not all the underlying layers in the stack.)

- **Toggle the Adjustment layer on and off.**

- **Reset the Adjustment layer settings back to the default.**

Fill layers

A *fill layer* lets you add a layer of solid color, a gradient, or a pattern. Like adjustment layers, fill layers also include layer masks. You can edit, rearrange, duplicate, delete, and merge fill layers similarly to adjustment layers. You can blend fill layers with other layers by using the opacity and blend mode options on the Layers panel. Finally, you can restrict the fill layer to just a portion of your image by either making a selection first or painting on the mask later.

Follow these steps to create a fill layer:

1. **Open an image.**

   Use an image that will look good with a frame or border of some kind. Remember that if you don't have a selection, the fill layer covers your whole image.

2. **Click the Create New Fill or Adjustment Layer icon on the Layers panel. From the drop-down list, choose a fill of a solid color, gradient, or pattern.**

   The dialog box specific to your type of fill appears.

3. **Specify your options, depending on the fill type you chose in Step 2:**

   - **Solid Color:** Choose your desired color from the Color Picker. See Chapter 13 for details on choosing colors and also gradients and patterns.

   - **Gradient:** Click the down-pointing arrow to choose a preset gradient from the drop-down panel, or click the gradient preview to display the Gradient Editor and create your own gradient.

   - **Pattern:** Select a pattern from the drop-down panel. Enter a value to scale your pattern, if you want. Click Snap to Origin to make the origin of the pattern the same as the origin of the document. Select the Link with Layer option to specify that the pattern moves with the fill layer if you move that layer.

4. **Click OK.**

   The fill layer appears on the Layers panel, as shown in Figure 9-6. Notice the layer mask that was created on the fill layer. We filled our entire layer mask with black, with just the exception of the outside edge to create a frame around our image.

Shape layers

If you haven't made your way to Chapter 13 yet, you may be surprised to discover that Elements also lets you draw shapes with seven different drawing tools. These shapes have the bonus of being *vector*-based. This means that the shapes are defined by mathematical equations, which consist of points and paths, instead of pixels. The advantage of vector-based objects is that you can freely resize these objects without causing degradation. In addition, they're always printed with smooth edges, not with the jaggies you're familiar with seeing in pixel-based elements.

To create a shape layer, grab a shape tool from the Tools panel and drag it on your canvas. When you create a shape, it resides on its own, unique shape layer, as shown by the yin-and-yang logo in the bottom-left corner of Figure 9-6. As with other types of layers, you can adjust the blend modes and opacity of a shape layer. You can also edit, move, and transform the actual shapes. However, to apply filters, you must first *simplify* the shape layer by choosing Layer ⇨ Simplify Layer. This process converts the vector paths to pixels.

Type layers

To add words to your images (refer to Figure 9-6), click your canvas with the Type
tool selected and just type. It's really as easy as that. Well, you can specify options,
such as a font family and size, in the Tool Options, but when you click the Commit
button on the image window, you create a type layer. On the Layers panel, the type
layer displays a T icon. For details on working with type, check out Chapter 14.

Tackling Layer Basics

Image layers are the heart and soul of the layering world. You can create multiple
image layers within a single image. Even more fun is creating a composite from
several different images. Add people you like; take out people you don't. Pluck
people out of boring photo studios and put them in exotic locales. The creative
possibilities are endless. In the following sections, we cover all the various ways
to create image layers.

Creating a new layer from scratch

If you're creating a new, blank file, you can select the Transparent option for your background contents. Your new file is created with a transparent layer and is ready to go. If you have an existing file and want to create a new, blank layer, here are the ways to do so:

>> Click the Create a New Layer icon at the top of the Layers panel.

>> Choose New Layer from the Layers panel menu.

>> Choose Layer ➪ New ➪ Layer.

If you create a layer by using either of the menu commands, you're presented with a dialog box with options. In that dialog box, you can name your layer and specify options for creating a clipping mask, color coding, blending, and adjusting opacity. Provide a name for your layer and click OK. You can always adjust the other options directly on the Layers panel later.

TIP

You can also use the Copy and Paste commands without even creating a blank layer first. When you copy and paste a selection without a blank layer, Elements automatically creates a new layer from the pasted selection. A better method of copying and pasting between multiple images, however, is to use the drag-and-drop method, which we describe in the section "Dragging and dropping layers," later in this chapter.

TIP

The Copy Merged command on the Edit menu creates a merged copy of all visible layers within the selection.

After you create your layer, you can put selections or other elements on that layer by doing one or more of the following:

>> **Paint:** Grab a painting tool, such as the Brush or Pencil, and paint on the layer.

>> **Copy a selection:** Make a selection on another layer or on the background within the same document, or from another image entirely, and then choose Edit ➪ Copy. Select your new, blank layer on the Layers panel and then choose Edit ➪ Paste.

>> **Cut a selection:** Make a selection on another layer or on the background within the same document, or from another image, and then choose Edit ➪ Cut. Select your new, blank layer and then choose Edit ➪ Paste. Be aware that this action removes that selection from its original location and leaves a transparent hole, as shown in Figure 9-7.

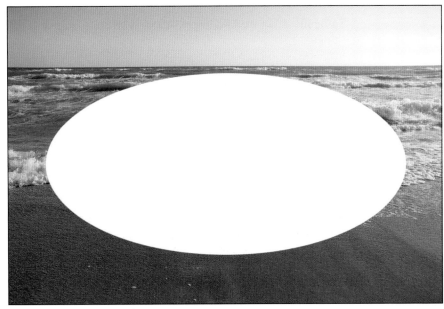

FIGURE 9-7: When you cut a selection from a layer, take note of the resulting hole in the original location.

TIP

If you cut a selection from a Background instead of an image layer, the space isn't a transparent hole; it's filled with the background color.

Using Layer via Copy and Layer via Cut

Another way to create a layer is to use the Layer via Copy and Layer via Cut commands on the Layer menu's New submenu. Make a selection on a layer or background and choose Layer⇨New⇨Layer via Copy or Layer via Cut. Elements automatically creates a new layer and puts the copied or cut selection on the layer. Remember that if you use the Layer via Cut command, your selection is deleted from its original location layer, and you're left with a transparent hole when cutting from an image layer. If you use the background for the source, your background color fills the space. A reminder: You can use these two commands only within the same image. You can't use them among multiple images.

Duplicating layers

Duplicating layers can be helpful if you want to protect your original image while experimenting with a technique. If you don't like the results, you can always delete the duplicate layer. No harm, no foul.

To duplicate an existing layer, select it on the Layers panel and do one of four things:

» Drag the layer to the Create a New Layer icon at the top of the panel. Elements creates a duplicate layer with *Copy* appended to the name of the layer.

» Choose Duplicate Layer from the Layers panel menu.

» Choose Layer ⇨ Duplicate Layer.

» Choose Layer ⇨ New ⇨ Layer via Copy. (Make sure you don't have an active selection when choosing this command.)

If you use the menu methods, with the exception of Layer ⇨ New ⇨ Layer via Copy, a dialog box appears, asking you to name your layer and specify other options. Provide a name for your layer and click OK. You can specify the other options later if you want.

Dragging and dropping layers

The most efficient way to copy and paste layers between multiple images is to use the drag-and-drop method. Why? Because it bypasses your *Clipboard,* which is the temporary storage area on your computer for copied data. Storing data, especially large files, can bog down your system. By keeping your Clipboard clear of data, your system operates more efficiently.

TIP

If you already copied data and it's lounging on your Clipboard, choose Edit ⇨ Clear ⇨ Clipboard Contents to empty your Clipboard.

Here's how to drag and drop layers from one file to another:

1. **In your first (or source) file, select your desired layer in the Layers panel.**

2. **Grab the Move tool (the four-headed arrow) from the Tools panel.**

3. **Drag and drop the layer onto your second (or destination) file.**

   The dropped layer pops in as a new layer above the active layer in the image. You don't need to have a selection border to copy the entire layer. But if you want to copy just a portion of the layer, make your selection before you drag and drop with the Move tool. If you want the selected element to be centered on the destination file, press the Shift key while you drag and drop.

If you have several elements (that aren't touching each other) on one layer and you want to select only one of the elements to drag and drop, use the Lasso tool to make a crude selection around the object without touching any of the other elements. Then press the Ctrl (⌘ on the Mac) key and press the up-arrow key once. The element then becomes perfectly selected. You can now drag and drop with the Move tool.

Using the Paste into Selection command

The Paste into Selection command lets you put an image on a separate layer while also inserting that image into a selection border. For example, in Figure 9-8, we use this command to make it appear as though our surfer is in the water.

You can do the same by following these steps:

1. **Create a new blank layer and then make your desired selection on the layer in your destination image.**

   In our figure, we selected the area in the water where the surfer would be positioned.

2. **Select the image that will fill that selection.**

   We selected a surfer from another image.

3. **Choose Edit ⇨ Copy.**

   Return to the destination image blank layer and choose Edit ⇨ Paste into Selection.

   The pasted selection is visible only inside the selection border.

© Alex_Rodionov/Shutterstock Image #301316285,
homydesign/Shutterstock Image #334170533

FIGURE 9-8:
Use the Paste into Selection command to make one element appear as though it's coming out of another element.

Position your pasted selection as desired and then choose Select ⇨ Deselect. In our example, the surfer shows only inside the selected area. Parts of his feet were positioned outside the selection border to make him appear as if he is really in the water.

Moving a Layer's Content

Moving the content of a layer is a piece of cake: Grab the Move tool from the Tools panel, select your layer on the Layers panel, and drag the element on the canvas to your desired location. You can also move the layer in 1-pixel increments by using the keyboard arrow keys. Press Shift with the arrows to move in 10-pixel increments. *Note:* If you hold down the Alt (Option on the Mac) key while moving your element, you make a duplicate of that element.

TIP

The Auto Select Layer option in the Tool Options enables you to switch to a layer when you click any part of that layer's content with the Move tool. But be careful if you have a lot of overlapping layers because this technique can sometimes be more trouble than it's worth.

The Move tool has additional settings found in Tool Options. Here's the lowdown:

» **Show Bounding Box:** This option surrounds the contents of your layer with a dotted box that has handles, enabling you to easily transform your layer. Find details in the following section.

» **Show Highlight on Rollover:** Hover your mouse anywhere over the canvas to make an outline appear around the element on your layer. Click the highlighted layer to select it and then move it.

» **Arrange submenu:** This menu enables you to change your selected layer's position in the stacking order.

» **Link Layers:** This option, which resides not in the Tool Options, but in the Layers panel, connects the layers to make it easier to move (or transform) multiple layers simultaneously. Select a layer and then Ctrl-click (⌘-click on the Mac) to select more layers. Click the Link Layers icon (chain).

» **Align submenu:** Align your selected layers on the left, center, right, top, middle, and bottom. As with linking, select your first layer and then Shift-click to select more layers. Ctrl-click (⌘-click on the Mac) to select nonconsecutive layers. Choose an alignment option.

» **Distribute submenu:** Use this menu to evenly space your selected layers on the left, center, right, top, middle, and bottom. As with aligning, select your first layer and then Shift-click to select more layers. Ctrl-click (⌘-click on the Mac) to select nonconsecutive layers. Choose your desired distribution option.

Transforming Layers

When working with layers, you may need to scale or rotate some of your images. You can do so easily by applying the Transform and Free Transform commands. The methods to transform layers and selections are identical.

Here's how to transform a layer:

1. **Select your desired layer.**

   You can also apply a transformation to multiple layers simultaneously by linking the layers first.

2. **Choose Image ➪ Transform ➪ Free Transform.**

   A bounding box surrounds the contents of your layer.

3. **Adjust (or transform) the bounding box.**

   - **Size the contents:** Drag a corner handle.

   - **Constrain the proportions:** Press Shift while dragging a corner handle.

   - **Rotate the contents:** Move the mouse cursor just outside a corner handle until it turns into a curved arrow, and then drag. Or choose Image ➪ Rotate and select a rotation option.

   - **Distort, skew, or apply perspective to the contents:** Right-click and choose the desired command from the context menu. You can also click the rotate, scale, and skew icons in the Tool Options, as well as enter your transform values numerically in the fields.

     If you want to apply just a single transformation, you can also choose the individual Distort, Skew, and Perspective commands from the Image ➪ Transform menu.

4. **When your layer is transformed to your liking, double-click inside the bounding box.**

WARNING

Try to perform all your transformations in one execution. Each time you transform pixels, you put your image through the *interpolation process* (analyzing the colors of the original pixels and "manufacturing" new ones). Done to the extreme, this process can degrade the quality of your image. This is why it's prudent to use the Free Transform command rather than individual commands — so that all transformations can be executed in one fell swoop.

TIP

When the Move tool is active, you can transform a layer without choosing a command. Select the Show Bounding Box option in the Tool Options. This option surrounds the layer or selection with a box that has handles. Drag the handles to transform the layer or selection.

Adding Layer Masks

One of the best creative tools Elements has to offer is layer masks. *Masking* is essentially just another way of making a selection. Instead of making a selection with a single selection outline — either it is selected or it isn't — masks enable you to define your selection with up to 256 levels of gray (from white to black). You can therefore have varying levels of a selection.

Here's how it works. First, think of a layer mask as a sheet of acetate that hovers over your layer. To add it to a layer, click the layer mask icon (dark rectangle with a light circle) at the top of the Layers panel. Then, with any of the painting tools (Brush tool, Gradient tool, and others), you apply black, white, or any shade of gray onto the layer mask. Where the mask is white, the image on the underlying layer is selected and shows. Where the mask is black, the image is unselected and is hidden. And where the mask is gray, the image is partially selected; therefore, it partially shows. The lighter the gray, the more the image shows. By default, the mask starts out completely white so that everything is selected and shows.

Here are some things you can do with layer masks:

>> **Creatively blend one layer into another.** If you want one image to gradually dissolve into another, using a layer mask is the way to go. Try using the Gradient tool with the black-to-white gradient selected to create a soft dissolve. You can use layer masks to blend images together in a realistic manner, as shown in Figure 9-9, where we combined a goldfish and a sudsy brew. In the figure, you can see where we painted with black to completely hide the original background of the fish image. We painted with light gray on the fish to make it appear as if it is truly "swimming" in the golden liquid. In other words, some of the liquid of the underlying glass of beer image shows through to the fish layer.

>> **Adjust your layer mask to selectively show and hide the effects of the adjustment layer.** See the earlier section, "Adjustment layers."

TIP

>> **Apply a filter to your layer mask to create an interesting special effect.** One of the best aspects of layer masks is that you can endlessly edit them. Unlike just making a feathered selection, you can keep adjusting how much of your current layer or underlying images show. Or you can adjust how gradually one image blends into another: Simply change the areas of white, black, and gray on the layer mask by painting with any of the painting tools. Just make sure you select the layer mask and not the image. When you select the layer mask thumbnail in the Layers panel, you see the appearance of an outline around the thumbnail.

You can't add a layer mask to a background. You must convert the background into a layer first.

If you're just not up to tackling a layer mask, you'll want to check out the Double Exposure Guided Edit. You'll find it under Guided ➪ Fun Edits ➪ Double Exposure. This great edit enables you to easily merge two photos and also apply various preset effects.

FIGURE 9-9:
Add a layer mask to blend one layer into another.

© Tischenko Irina/Shutterstock Image #58458289, flubydest/Getty Images Image #183341783

Here are some other things to keep in mind when you use layer masks:

>> **To load the mask as a selection outline,** simply Ctrl-click (⌘ -click on the Mac) the layer mask thumbnail in the Layers panel.

>> **To temporarily hide a mask,** Shift-click the layer mask thumbnail in the Layers panel. Repeat to show the mask.

>> **To view the mask without viewing the image,** Alt-click (Option-click on the Mac) the Layer Mask thumbnail in the Layers panel. This trick can be helpful when editing a layer mask.

>> **To unlink a layer from its layer mask,** click the link icon in the Layers panel. Click again to reestablish the link. By default, Elements links a layer mask to the contents of the layer. This link enables them to move together.

>> **To delete a layer mask,** drag its thumbnail to the Trash icon in the Layers panel.

>> **To apply a layer mask,** drag the mask thumbnail to the Trash icon in the Layers panel and be sure to click Apply in the dialog box. When you apply a layer mask, you fuse the mask to the layer so editing is no longer possible.

Note: Many of the preceding commands are also available in the Layer⇨Layer Mask submenu.

Flattening and Merging Layers

Layers are fun and fantastic, but they can quickly chew up your computer's RAM and bloat your file size. And sometimes, to be honest, having too many layers can start to make your file tedious to manage, thereby making you less productive. Whenever possible, you should merge your layers to save memory and space. *Merging* combines visible, linked, or adjacent layers into a single layer (not a Background). The intersection of all transparent areas is retained.

In addition, if you need to import your file into another program, certain programs don't support files with layers. Therefore, you may need to flatten your file before importing it. *Flattening* an image combines all visible layers into a Background, including type, shape, fill, and adjustment layers. You're prompted as to whether you want to discard hidden layers, and any transparent areas are filled with white. We recommend, however, that before you flatten your image, you make a copy of the file with all its layers intact and save it as a native Photoshop file. That way, if you ever need to make any edits, you have the added flexibility of having your layers.

TECHNICAL STUFF

By the way, the only file formats that support layers are native Photoshop (.psd); Tagged Image File Format, or TIFF (.tif); and Portable Document Format, or PDF (.pdf) (called Photoshop PDF in PSE). If you save your file in any other format, Elements automatically flattens your layers into a background. See Chapter 3 for details on these file types.

Flattening layers

To flatten an image, follow these steps:

1. **Make certain that all layers you want to retain are visible.**

   If you have any hidden layers, Elements asks whether you want to discard those hidden layers.

REMEMBER

It's always good insurance to save a copy of an image with layers while flattening another copy. You just never know — you may need to make edits at a later date.

2. **Choose Flatten Image from the Layers panel menu or the Layer menu.**

All your layers are combined into a single background, as shown in Figure 9-10.

TIP

If you mistakenly flatten your image, choose Edit ⇨ Undo or use your Undo History panel. (If you're not familiar with the History panel, see Chapter 1 for details.)

Merging layers

Unlike flattening layers, where all layers get combined into a single Background, you can choose to merge just a few layers. Also, remember, when you do choose to merge all your layers, they combine into a single layer versus a Background.

You can merge your layers in a few ways. Here's how:

>> **Select only those layers you want to merge.** Choose Merge Layers from the Layers panel menu or the Layer menu.

>> **Display only those layers you want to merge.** Click the eye icon on the Layers panel to hide those layers you don't want to merge. Choose Merge Visible from the Layers panel menu or the Layer menu.

>> **Arrange the layers you want to merge so that they're adjacent on the Layers panel.** Select the topmost layer of that group and choose Merge Down from the Layers panel menu or the Layer menu. Merge Down merges your active layer with the layer directly below it.

© homydesign/Shutterstock Image #334170533, mervas/Shutterstock Image #271812446, ArtFamily/Shutterstock Image #25608805, Alex_Rodionov/Shutterstock Image #301316285

FIGURE 9-10:
Flattening combines all your layers into a single background.

Chapter **10**

Simple Image Makeovers

ixing images quickly, without pain or hassle, is probably one of the most desirable features you'll find in Elements and one that we're sure you'll embrace frequently. Whether you're an experienced photographer or an amateur shutterbug, cropping away unwanted background, tweaking the lighting or color of an image, and erasing the minor blemishes of a loved one's face are all editing tasks you'll most likely tackle. With the simple image-makeover tools in Elements, completing these tasks is as easy as clicking a single button or making a few swipes with a brush.

Cropping and Straightening Images

Cropping a photo is probably one of the easiest things you can do to improve its composition. Getting rid of the unnecessary background around your subject creates a better focal point. Another dead giveaway of amateurish photography is crooked horizon lines. Not a problem. Elements gives you several ways to straighten those images after the fact. So after your next photo shoot, launch the Elements Photo Editor and then crop and straighten your images before you show them off.

Cutting away with the Crop tool

The most common way to crop a photo is by using the Crop tool. Simple, quick, and easy, this tool gets the job done. Here's how to use it:

1. **In either Expert or Quick mode, select the Crop tool from the Tools panel.**

   You can also press the C key. The Crop tool looks like two intersecting "L" shapes. For details on the different editing modes, see Chapter 3. For full details on Quick mode, see the section "Editing in Quick Mode," later in this chapter.

2. **(Optional) Choose one of the four cropping suggestions Elements provides for you.**

   Simply hover your mouse over each of the crop suggestion thumbnails to get an idea of how it will frame your image. If you don't like any of the suggestions, proceed to Step 3.

3. **Specify your aspect ratio and resolution options in the Tool Options under the image window.**

   Here are your choices:

   - **No Restriction:** Allows you to freely crop the image at any size.

   - **Use Photo Ratio:** Retains the original aspect ratio of the image when you crop.

   - **Preset Sizes:** Offers a variety of common photographic sizes. When you crop, your image then becomes that specific dimension.

WARNING

   When you crop an image, Elements retains the original resolution of the file (unless you specify otherwise in the resolution option). Therefore, to keep your image at the same image size while simultaneously eliminating portions of your image, Elements must resample the file. Consequently, your image must have sufficient resolution so that the effects of the resampling aren't too noticeable. This is especially true if you're choosing a larger preset size. If all this talk about resolution and resampling is fuzzy, be sure to check out Chapter 3.

   - **Width (W) and Height (H):** Enables you to specify a desired width and height to crop your image.

   - **Resolution:** Specify a desired resolution for your cropped image. Again, try to avoid upsampling your image.

   - **Pixels/in or Pixels/cm:** Specify your desired unit of measurement.

- **Grid Overlay:** Elements gives you an added tool to help you frame your image prior to cropping. Choose from the three options: None, Rule of Thirds, or Grid.

- **Rule of Thirds:** This rule is a longtime photographic principle that encourages placing the most interesting elements, or your intended focal point, at one of four intersecting points in your grid of two vertical and two horizontal lines, as shown in Figure 10-1.

- **Grid:** Displays just that — a grid of intersecting horizontal and vertical lines over the image.

4. **Drag around the portion of the image you want to retain and release the mouse button.**

   When you drag, a crop marquee bounding box appears. Don't worry if your cropping marquee isn't exactly correct. You can adjust it in Step 5.

   The area outside the cropping marquee (called a *shield*) appears darker than the inside in order to better frame your image, as shown in Figure 10-1. If you want to change the color and opacity of the shield, or if you don't want it at all, change your Crop preferences by choosing Edit ⇨ Preferences ⇨ Display & Cursors. (On the Mac, choose Adobe Photoshop Elements 2022 Editor ⇨ Preferences ⇨ Display & Cursors.)

5. **Adjust the cropping marquee by dragging the handles of the crop marquee bounding box.**

   To move the entire marquee, position your mouse inside the marquee until you see a black arrowhead cursor, and then drag.

TIP

   If you move your mouse outside the marquee, your cursor changes to a curved arrow. Drag with this cursor to rotate the marquee. This action allows you to both rotate and crop your image simultaneously — handy for straightening a crooked image. Just be aware that rotation, unless it's in 90-degree increments, also resamples your image.

6. **Double-click inside the cropping marquee.**

   You can also just press Enter or click the green Commit button next to the marquee. Elements then discards the area outside the marquee. To cancel your crop, click the red Cancel button.

TIP

If you're in the Organizer and not the Photo Editor, click the Instant Fix button at the bottom. You can find the Crop tool at the top of the tool panel on the right.

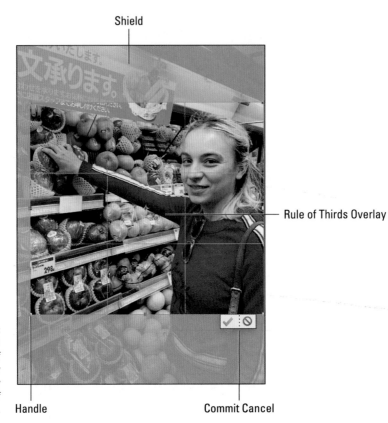

Shield

Rule of Thirds Overlay

Handle

Commit Cancel

FIGURE 10-1:
The shield
and Rule of
Thirds overlay
allow for easy
framing of
your image.

Fixing distortion with the Perspective Crop tool

The Perspective Crop tool allows you to crop an image while also correcting key-stone distortion. For example, if you shoot a tall building from below looking up or a long hallway from an angle, your object may appear trapezoidal rather than square or rectangular. Here's how to crop and correct this at the same time:

1. **In Expert mode, select the Perspective Crop tool from the Tools panel.**

   You can also press the C key until you get the tool, which shares a space with the Crop and Cookie Cutter tools.

2. **Draw a marquee around the distorted image by clicking at each corner, as shown in Figure 10-2.**

3. **Adjust the edges and corners of your marquee as needed.**

   You have some options to choose if desired.

- **Width (W) and Height (H):** Specify a desired width and height to crop your image.

- **Resolution:** Specify a desired resolution for your cropped image. As with the Crop tool, try to avoid upsampling your image.

- **Pixels/in or Pixels/cm:** Specify your desired unit of measurement.

- **Grid:** Toggle the view on or off of a grid of intersecting horizontal and vertical lines over the image.

4. **Double-click inside the cropping marquee.**

You can also just press Enter or click the green Commit button next to the marquee. To cancel your crop, click the red Cancel button. Elements should improve the keystone distortion and crop your image.

If you're not happy with the result, choose Edit ⇨ Undo and tweak the angle of your marquee in Step 3. Admittedly, it took us a couple tries to get the result we wanted, which is shown in Figure 10-2.

FIGURE 10-2: The Perspective Crop tool crops while correcting keystone distortion.

© istockphoto.com/Jeremy Edwards Image #4193924

TIP

If the Perspective Crop doesn't fix the distortion, you may want to try the Correct Camera Distortion filter (see Chapter 12).

Cropping with a selection border

You can alternatively crop an image by choosing Image ⇨ Crop in either Expert or Quick mode. First, make a selection with any of the selection tools and then choose the command. You can use this technique with any selection border shape. That is, your selection doesn't have to be rectangular; it can be round or even freeform. Your cropped image doesn't take on that shape, but Elements crops as close to the boundaries of the selection border as it can. For details about making selections, see Chapter 8.

Straightening images

There may be times when you just didn't quite get that horizon straight when you took a photo of the beach. Or maybe you scanned a photo and it wasn't quite centered in the middle of the scanning bed. It's not a big deal. Elements gives you several ways to straighten an image.

Using the Straighten tool

This tool enables you to specify a new straight edge, and it then rotates the image accordingly. Here's how to use the Straighten tool:

1. **In Expert mode, select the Straighten tool from the Tools panel (or press the P key).**

It looks like an analog level tool.

2. **Specify your desired setting from the Canvas Options in the Tool Options.**

Here are your choices:

- **Grow or Shrink** rotates the image and increases or decreases the size of the canvas to fit the image area.

- **Remove Background** trims the background canvas outside the image area. This choice is helpful if you scan an image and white areas appear around your photo that you want removed.

- **Original Size** rotates your image without trimming any background canvas.

If you select either the Original Size or Remove Background option, you can select the Auto Fill Edges option. When selected, after you straighten the image, the edges that have missing pixels will fill using the content-aware algorithm. *Note:* You can also vertically straighten your image by dragging along a vertical edge.

3. **(Optional) Select Rotate All Layers.**

If you have an image with layers and you want them all rotated, select this option.

4. **Draw a line in your image to represent the new straight edge.**

Your image is then straightened and, if you chose any of the crop options in Step 2, also cropped.

The Straighten Tool is also available in Quick mode. To straighten an image, draw a line with the Straighten tool in your After image to represent the new straight edge. Then choose an option to crop and resize your image. Choose to fill in empty spaces either by maintaining the image size or by maintaining the canvas size. In addition, you can choose the option to fill any empty edges using content-aware algorithms.

Using the Straighten menu commands

In addition to using the Straighten tool, you can straighten your images by using two commands on the Image menu, in either Expert or Quick mode:

» **To automatically straighten an image without cropping,** choose Image ⇨ Rotate ⇨ Straighten Image. This straightening technique leaves the canvas around the image.

» **To automatically straighten and crop the image simultaneously,** choose Image ⇨ Rotate ⇨ Straighten and Crop Image.

Recomposing Images

This great tool actually allows you to resize, or as the name implies, *recompose*, your image without losing any vital content. For example, if you need to have people or animals in your shot closer together because you need the final, cropped image to be more square than rectangular, this tool can help. Here's how it works:

1. **In Expert mode, select the Recompose tool from the Tools panel.**

   You can also press the W key. The tool looks like a square with a gear on it.

2. **In the Tool Options, select the Mark for Protection Brush (the brush with a plus sign icon) and brush over the areas in your image that you want to keep or protect.**

   You can specify your brush size with the Size option slider. You can erase any mistakes by using the Erase Highlights Marked for Protection tool (the eraser with a plus sign icon).

3. **With the Mark for Removal Brush (the brush with a minus sign icon), brush over the areas in your image that you want to remove or aren't vital to your final image, as shown in Figure 10-3.**

   You can specify your brush size with the Size option slider. You can erase any mistakes by using the Erase Highlights Marked for Removal tool (the eraser with a minus sign icon).

4. **Specify any other desired settings in the Tool Options.**

   Here are the other options:

   - **Threshold:** The slider determines how much recomposing appears in your adjustment. Selecting 100% totally recomposes your image. Experiment to get the results you want.

   - **Preset Ratios:** Choose from preset aspect ratios to have your image framed to those dimensions. Or choose No Restriction to have free rein.

   - **Width and Height:** This option resizes your image to your specified dimensions.

   - **Highlight Skin Tones (green man icon):** Select this option to prevent skin tones from distorting when resizing.

5. **Resize, or recompose, your image by dragging the corner or side handles.**

   The kangaroos are now closer together, as shown in Figure 10-4.

6. **Click the Commit button (green check-mark icon) when you have your desired composition.**

   Note that you may have to do a little retouching at the seam. You can see in our image how the horizon line doesn't quite match up. Use the Clone Stamp or Healing Brush to clean up the seam. You can find out more about both tools later in this chapter.

FIGURE 10-3:
Brush over areas you want to protect and remove in your image.

FIGURE 10-4:
Recompose your image to your desired size and aspect ratio without losing vital content.

Employing One-Step Auto Fixes

Elements has a variety of automatic lighting-, contrast-, and color-correction tools that can improve the appearance of your images with just one menu command. These commands are available in either Expert or Quick mode, and they're all on the Enhance menu. For more on Quick mode, see the section "Editing in Quick Mode," later in this chapter.

REMEMBER

The advantage of these one-step correctors is that they're extremely easy to use. You don't need to have one iota of knowledge about color or contrast to use them. The downside to using them is that sometimes the result isn't as good as you could get via a manual color-correction method. And sometimes these correctors may even make your image look worse than before by giving you weird color shifts. But because these correctors are quick and easy, you can try them on an image that needs help. Usually, you don't want to use more than one of the auto fixes. If one doesn't work on your image, undo the fix and try another. If you still don't like the result, move on to one of the manual methods we describe in Chapter 11.

Auto Smart Fix

The Auto Smart Fix tool is an all-in-one command touted to adjust it all. It's designed to improve the details in shadow and highlight areas as well as correct the color balance, as shown in Figure 10-5. The overexposed, overly green image on the left was improved quite nicely with the Auto Smart Fix command.

If the Auto Smart Fix was just too "auto" for you, you can crank it up a notch and try Adjust Smart Fix. This command is similar to Auto Smart Fix but gives you a slider that allows you, not Elements, to control the amount of correction applied to the image.

Auto Smart Tone

The Auto Smart Tone auto fix is designed to adjust the tonal values in your image.

Here are the steps to use this adjustment:

1. **In either Expert or Quick mode, with your image open, choose Enhance ⇨ Auto Smart Tone.**

   Elements automatically applies a default correction.

2. **Moving the controller "joystick" (double circle icon in the center of the image), fine-tune your correction.**

The thumbnail previews in each corner, as shown in Figure 10-6, give you an idea of how the image will look when you move the joystick in that particular direction.

Move the Before and After toggle to see the before-and-after adjustment previews.

3. **Select the Learn from This Correction option (arrow with lines icon) in the lower-left corner of the dialog box to have Elements "learn" from this editing session.**

If you select this option, Elements remembers the corrections you made on this image and positions the joystick on the basis of that correction on the next image you open and correct. The more images that are corrected, the smarter the Auto Smart Tone corrections become. This intelligent algorithm can distinguish between various image types (based on the tonal characteristics) and remembers the adjustment for that particular type of image.

If your adjustments are starting to get out of whack and you need to reset the learning archive, choose Edit ➪ Preferences ➪ General ➪ Reset AutoSmart Tone Learning (on the Mac, Adobe Photoshop Elements Editor ➪ Preferences ➪ General ➪ Reset Auto Smart Tone Learning).

4. **After you're satisfied with the adjustment, click OK.**

If you want to start over, click the Reset button.

FIGURE 10-6:
Apply Auto
Smart Tone to
quickly adjust
the tonal
values in an
image.

Auto Levels

The Auto Levels command adjusts the overall contrast of an image. This command works best on images that have pretty good contrast (an even range of tones and detail in the shadow, highlight, and midtone areas) to begin with and need just a minor amount of adjustment. Auto Levels works by *mapping,* or converting, the lightest and darkest pixels in your image to black and white, thereby making highlights appear lighter and shadows appear darker, as shown in Figure 10-7.

FIGURE 10-7:
Auto Levels
adjusts the
overall contrast
of an image.

Although the Auto Levels command can improve contrast, it may also produce an unwanted *color cast* (a slight trace of color). If this happens, undo the command and try the Auto Contrast command instead. If that still doesn't improve the contrast, it's time to bring out the big guns. Try the Levels command that we describe in Chapter 11.

Auto Contrast

The Auto Contrast command is designed to adjust the overall contrast in an image without adjusting its color. This command may not do as good a job of improving contrast as the Auto Levels command, but it does a better job of retaining the color balance of an image. Auto Contrast usually doesn't cause the funky color casts that can occur when you're using Auto Levels. This command works well on images with a haze, as shown in Figure 10-8.

FIGURE 10-8: The Auto Contrast command adjusts contrast without messing up color.

Auto Haze Removal

Although the Auto Contrast command does a good job of removing haze in images, the Auto Haze Removal command does a great job with this task, as shown in Figure 10-9. But also be sure to check out the Haze Removal command under the Enhance menu in both Expert and Quick modes. Under that command, you have a couple more options to really home in on to add clarity to your image. Find out more about this command in Chapter 11.

Auto Color Correction

The Auto Color Correction command adjusts both the color and contrast of an image, based on the shadows, midtones, and highlights it finds in the image and a default set of values. These values adjust the amount of black and white pixels that Elements removes from the darkest and lightest areas of the image. You usually use this command to remove a color cast or to balance the color in your image, as shown in Figure 10-10. Occasionally, this command can also be useful in correcting oversaturated or undersaturated colors.

Auto Shake Reduction

The Auto Shake Reduction is designed to reduce the blur caused by camera movement; as shown in Figure 10-11, this auto adjustment is pretty effective. You can also find a more robust manual adjustment by using the Enhance ⇨ Shake Reduction command. Get details in Chapter 11.

Auto Sharpen

Photos taken with a digital camera or scanned on a flatbed scanner often suffer from a case of overly soft focus. Sharpening gives the illusion of increased focus by increasing the contrast between pixels. Auto Sharpen attempts to improve the focus, as shown in Figure 10-12, without overdoing it. What happens when you oversharpen? Your images go from soft to grainy and noisy. For more precise sharpening, check out the Unsharp Mask and Adjust Sharpness features that we cover in Chapter 11.

TIP

Always make sharpening your last fix after you make all your other fixes and enhancements.

Auto Red Eye Fix

The Auto Red Eye Fix command is self-explanatory. It automatically detects and fixes red eye in an image. Red eye happens when a person or an animal (where red eye can also be yellow, green, or even blue eye) looks directly into the flash.

FIGURE 10-12:
Use Auto
Sharpen to
improve focus.

TIP

If for some reason the Auto Red Eye Fix doesn't quite do the trick, you can always reach for the Red Eye tool on the Tools panel. Here's how to remove red eye manually:

1. **Select the Red Eye Removal tool from the Tools panel.**

   You can also press Y.

2. **Using the default settings, click the red portion of the eye in your image.**

   This one-click tool darkens the pupil while retaining the tonality and texture of the rest of the eye, as shown in Figure 10-13. Repeat for the other eye.

3. **If you're unhappy with the fix, adjust one or both of these settings in the Tool Options:**

   - **Pupil Radius:** Use the slider to increase or decrease the size of the pupil.

   - **Darken:** Use the slider to darken or lighten the color of the pupil.

TIP

Note that there is also an option for fixing images whose subject has closed their eyes. You will need another image in which their eyes are open. If that isn't available you will have to provide another source image. Find out how this option works in Chapter 11, in the section "Opening closed eyes."

Pets can get white, green, blue, or yellow eyes from the flash. Elements provides a Pet Eye option in Tool Options. If this option still doesn't do it, your best bet is to use the Color Replacement tool. See the section "Replacing one color with another," at the end of this chapter.

Editing in Quick Mode

Quick mode is a pared-down version of Expert mode that conveniently provides basic fixing tools and tosses in a few unique features, such as a before-and-after preview of your image.

Here's a step-by-step workflow that you can follow in Quick mode to repair your photos:

1. **Select one or more photos in the Organizer, click the Editor button at the bottom of the workspace, and then click the Quick button at the top of the workspace.**

   Or, if you're in Expert mode, select your desired image(s) from the Photo Bin and then click the Quick button at the top of the workspace.

   Note: You can also open images by simply clicking the Open button and selecting your desired files.

2. **Specify your preview preference from the View drop-down list at the top of the workspace.**

   You can choose to view just your original image (Before Only), your fixed image (After Only), or both images side by side (Before & After) in either portrait (Vertical) or landscape (Horizontal) orientation, as shown in Figure 10-14.

3. **Use the Zoom and Hand tools to magnify and navigate around your image.**

Click your image with the Zoom tool to zoom in. Press Alt (Option on the Mac) to zoom out. Drag within the image window to move around the image. You can also specify the Zoom percentage by using the Zoom slider in the Tool Options or in the top right of the workspace.

4. **Choose your desired window view by clicking one of the following buttons located in the Tool Options: 1:1 (Actual Pixels), Fit Screen, Fill Screen (which zooms your image to fill your screen), or Print Size.**

You also have another Zoom slider located in the Tool Options.

5. **Crop your image by using the Crop tool on the Tools panel.**

You can also use any of the methods we describe in the "Cropping and Straightening Images" section, earlier in this chapter.

6. **To rotate the image in 90-degree increments, click the Rotate Left or Rotate Right (which is accessed via the arrow next to Rotate Left) button under the Options panel on the bottom left side of the workspace.**

7. **Apply any necessary auto fixes, such as Auto Smart Fix, Auto Levels, Auto Contrast, and Auto Color Correction.**

All these commands are on the Enhance menu or in the Smart Fix, Lighting, and Color sections in the Adjustments pane of the workspace. If the commands aren't visible, click the Adjustments button in the bottom-right corner of the workspace.

Each of these fixes is described in detail in the section "Employing One-Step Auto Fixes," earlier in this chapter. Remember that usually one of the fixes is enough. Don't stack them on top of each other. If one doesn't work, click the Reset button in the top-right corner of the image preview and try another. If you're not happy with the results, go to Step 8. If you are happy, skip to Step 9.

8. **If the auto fixes don't quite cut it, get more control by using the sliders, or by clicking the thumbnails, available for Smart Fix, Exposure, Lighting, Color, and Balance, in the Adjustments panel located on the right side of the workspace.**

TIP

For all adjustments, you can hover your mouse over any of the thumbnails in the pane to get a dynamic preview of that particular adjustment. The slider automatically moves accordingly.

Here's a brief description of each available adjustment, which are available under the Exposure, Lighting, Color, and Balance drop-down menus:

- **Exposure:** Adjusts the brightness or darkness of an image. Move the slider left to darken and right to lighten. The values are in increments of f-stops and range from –4 to 4.

- **Shadows:** When you drag the slider to the right, it lightens the darker areas of your image without adjusting the highlights.

- **Midtones:** Adjusts the contrast of the middle (gray) values and leaves the highlights and shadows as they are.

- **Highlights:** When you drag the slider to the right, it darkens the lighter areas of your image without adjusting the shadows.

- **Saturation:** Adjusts the intensity of the colors.

- **Hue:** Changes all colors in an image. Make a selection first to change the color of just one or more elements. Otherwise, use restraint with this adjustment.

- **Vibrance:** Adjusts the saturation of an image by increasing the saturation of less saturated colors more than those that are already saturated. This option tries to minimize *clipping* (or loss of color) as it increases saturation and preserves skin tones. Move the slider right to increase saturation.

- **Temperature:** Adjusts the colors to make them warmer (red) or cooler (blue). You can use this adjustment to correct skin tones or to correct overly cool images (such as snowy winter photos) or overly warm images (such as photos shot at sunset or sunrise).

- **Tint:** Adjusts the tint after you adjust temperature to make the color more green or magenta.

If you still don't get the results you need, move on to one of the more manual adjustments that we describe in Chapter 11.

TIP

You can also apply fixes to just selected portions of your image. Quick mode offers the Quick Selection tool for your selection tasks. For details on using this tool, see Chapter 8.

9. **Add finishing fixes by using the remaining tools in the Tools panel.**

Here's a description of each tool:

- **Red Eye Removal tool:** Try the Auto Red Eye Fix to remove red eye from people's eyes. But if it doesn't work, try using the Red Eye tool. This method is described in the section "Auto Red Eye Fix," earlier in this chapter.

- **Whiten Teeth:** This fix does what it says — it whitens teeth. Be sure to choose an appropriate brush size from the Size slider in the Tool Options. Click the Brush Settings option to specify Hardness, Spacing, Roundness, and Angle of the brush tip. (For more on brush options, see Chapter 13.) Using a brush diameter that's larger than the area of the teeth also whitens/brightens whatever else it touches — lips, chin, and so on. Click the teeth. (**Note:** This tool makes a selection and whitens simultaneously.) After your initial click, your selection option converts from New Selection to Add to Selection in the Tool Options. If you pick up too much in your dental selection, click the Subtract from Selection option and click the area you want to eliminate. When you're happy with the results of your whitening session, choose Select ⇨ Deselect or press Ctrl+D (⌘ +D on the Mac).

- **Spot Healing Brush/Healing Brush:** These tools are great for fixing flaws, both big (Healing Brush) and small (Spot Healing Brush). For a detailed explanation on using these tools, see the upcoming sections "Retouching with the Healing Brush" and "Zeroing in with the Spot Healing Brush."

10. **(Optional) Add any desired text by clicking your image with the Text tool.**

See Chapter 14 for details on working with text.

Use the Move tool in Quick mode to fine-tune the positioning of your text.

11. **Sharpen your image automatically by clicking the Auto button under Sharpen in the right pane.**

You can also choose Enhance ⇨ Auto Sharpen. If automatically sharpening doesn't do the fix, you can manually drag the Sharpen slider.

As noted earlier in the chapter, this fix should always be the last adjustment you make on your image.

FIGURE 10-14:
Quick mode enables you to view before-and-after previews of your image.

The Quick mode sports additional panels. Click the Effects icon in the bottom-right corner of the workspace to access various effects. Click the Classic tab and you will find effects, such as Toy Camera and Cross Process, that you can apply to your image. Click the Frames icon to apply borders, such as Scrapbook and Comic, to the perimeter of your photo. You can also click the Textures icon to access textures, such as Cracked Paint and Sunburst. Click the Adjustments icon to return to your default panel settings. To apply any effect, texture, or frame, simply click the appropriate thumbnail in the pane.

TIP

The new Artistic tab offers fun new filters. See Chapter 12 to learn more about effects as well as filters and styles.

Fixing Small Imperfections with Tools

Elements provides you with several handy tools to correct minor imperfections in your photos. You can use the Clone Stamp tool to clone parts of your image, heal blemishes with the Healing Brush or Spot Healing Brush tools, lighten or darken small areas with the Dodge and Burn tools, soften or sharpen the focus with the Blur or Sharpen tools, and fix color with the Sponge or Color Replacement tools.

Cloning with the Clone Stamp tool

Elements enables you to clone elements without the hassle of genetically engineering DNA. In fact, the Clone Stamp tool works by just taking sampled pixels from one area and copying, or *cloning,* them onto another area. The advantage of cloning, rather than making a selection and then copying and pasting, is that it's easier to realistically retain soft-edged elements, such as shadows, as shown in Figure 10-15.

The Clone Stamp doesn't stop there. You can also use this tool for fixing flaws, such as scratches, bruises, date/time stamp imprints from cameras, and other minor imperfections. Although the birth of the healing tools (discussed in the following sections) has somewhat pushed the Clone Stamp tool out of the retouching arena, it can still do a good repair job in many instances.

Here's how to use the Clone Stamp tool:

1. **In Expert mode, choose the Clone Stamp tool from the Tools panel.**

   It looks like an analog rubber stamp.

FIGURE 10-15:
The Clone
Stamp tool
enables you
to realistically
duplicate
soft-edged
elements, such
as shadows.

2. **In the Tool Options, choose a brush from the Brush Preset Picker panel and then use the brush as is or adjust its size with the Size slider.**

    Keep in mind that the size of the brush you specify should be appropriate for what you're trying to clone or retouch. If you're cloning a large object, use a large brush. For repairing small flaws, use a small brush. Cloning with a soft-edged brush usually produces more natural results. For details on brushes, see Chapter 13.

3. **Choose your desired Opacity and Blend Mode percentage.**

    For more on blend modes, see Chapter 12. To make your cloned image appear ghosted, use an Opacity percentage of less than 100 percent.

4. **Select or deselect the Aligned option.**

    With Aligned selected, the clone source moves when you move your cursor to a different location. If you want to clone multiple times from the same location, leave the Aligned option deselected.

5. **Select or deselect the Sample All Layers check box.**

    This option enables you to sample pixels from all visible layers for the clone. If this option is deselected, the Clone Stamp tool clones from only the active layer. Check out Chapter 9 for details about working with layers.

6. **Click the Clone Overlay button if you want to display an overlay.**

   Displaying an overlay can be helpful when what you're cloning needs to be in alignment with the underlying image. In the Clone Overlay dialog box, select the Show Overlay check box. Adjust the opacity for your overlay. If you select Auto Hide, when you release your mouse, you see a ghosted preview of how your cloned pixels will appear on the image. While you're cloning, however, the overlay is hidden. Select Clipped to have the overlay contained only within the boundaries of your brush. We think that this makes it easier to more precisely clone what you want. Finally, select Invert Overlay to reverse the colors and tones in your overlay.

7. **Alt-click (Option-click on the Mac) the area of your image that you want to clone to define the source of the clone.**

8. **Click or drag along the area where you want the clone to appear.**

   While you drag, Elements displays a crosshair cursor along with your Clone Stamp cursor. The crosshair is the source you're cloning from, and the Clone Stamp cursor is where the clone is being applied. While you move the mouse, the crosshair also moves, so you have a continuous reference to the area of your image that you're cloning. Watch the crosshair, or else you may clone something you don't want.

9. **Repeat Steps 7 and 8 until you've finished cloning your desired element.**

REMEMBER

If you've selected the Aligned option when cloning an element, try to clone it without lifting your mouse. Also, when you're retouching a flaw, try not to overdo it. One or two clicks on each flaw is usually plenty. If you're heavy-handed with the Clone Stamp, you get a blotchy effect that's a telltale sign something has been retouched.

Retouching with the Healing Brush

The Healing Brush tool is similar to the Clone Stamp tool in that you clone pixels from one area onto another area. But the Healing Brush is superior in that it takes into account the tonality (highlights, midtones, and shadows) of the flawed area. The Healing Brush clones by using the *texture* from the sampled area (the *source*) and then using the *colors* around the brush stroke while you paint over the flawed area (the *destination*). The highlights, midtones, and shadow areas remain intact, giving you a realistic and natural repair that isn't as blotchy or miscolored as the repair you get with the Clone Stamp tool.

Here are the steps to heal a photo:

1. **In Expert mode, open an image in need of a makeover and select the Healing Brush tool from the Tools panel.**

   The tool looks like a bandage. You can also press J to cycle between the Healing Brush and Spot Healing Brush tools. You can also select either of these tools and then choose the other tool from the Tool Options.

   You can also heal between two images, but be sure that they have the same color mode — for example, both RGB (red, green, blue). We chose a couple who are super photogenic but might appreciate a little tune-up, as shown in Figure 10-16.

2. **Specify a size for the Healing brush tool in the Tool Options.**

   You can also adjust the hardness, spacing, angle, and roundness in the Brush Settings. For details on these options, see Chapter 13. Don't be shy. Be sure to adjust the size of your brush as needed. Using the appropriate brush size for the flaw you're retouching is critical to creating a realistic effect.

3. **Choose your desired blend mode.**

   For most retouching jobs, you probably should leave the mode as Normal. Replace mode preserves textures, such as noise or film grain, around the edges of your strokes.

4. **Choose one of these Source options:**

   - **Sampled** uses the pixels from the image. You use this option for the majority of your repairs.

   - **Pattern** uses pixels from a pattern chosen from the Pattern Picker drop-down panel.

5. **Select or deselect the Aligned option.**

   For most retouching tasks, you probably should leave Aligned selected. Here are the details on each option:

   - **With Aligned selected:** When you click or drag with the Healing Brush, Elements displays a crosshair along with the Healing Brush cursor. The crosshair represents the sampling point, also known as the *source*. When you move the Healing Brush tool, the crosshair also moves, providing a constant reference to the area you're sampling.

   - **With Aligned deselected:** Elements applies the source pixels from your initial sampling point, no matter how many times you stop and start dragging.

6. Select the Sample All Layers check box to heal an image by using all visible layers.

If this option is deselected, you heal from only the active layer.

TIP

To ensure maximum editing flexibility later, select the Sample All Layers check box and add a new, blank layer above the image you want to heal. When you heal the image, the pixels appear on the new layer and not on the actual image, which means you can adjust opacity and blend modes and make other adjustments to the healed layer.

7. (Optional) Click the Clone Overlay button.

See the earlier section, "Cloning with the Clone Stamp tool," for details on using an overlay.

8. Establish the sampling point by Alt-clicking (Option-clicking on the Mac).

Make sure to click the area of your image that you want to clone from. In our example, we clicked a smooth area of the forehead when working on each person.

9. Release the Alt (Option on the Mac) key and click or drag over a flawed area of your image.

Keep an eye on the crosshair because that's the area you're healing from. We brushed over the wrinkles under and around the eyes, mouth, and forehead. (Refer to Figure 10-16.) This couple never looked so good, and they endured absolutely no recovery time.

FIGURE 10-16:
Wipe out ten years in two minutes with the Healing Brush tool.

© racorn/Shutterstock Image #152524079

Zeroing in with the Spot Healing Brush

Whereas the Healing Brush is designed to fix larger flawed areas, the Spot Healing Brush is designed for smaller imperfections, with one exception — the Content-Aware option, which we explain in Step 3 in the following steps. The Spot Healing Brush doesn't require you to specify a sampling source. It automatically takes a sample from around the area to be retouched. It's quick, easy, and often effective. But it doesn't give you control over the sampling source, so keep an eye out for less-than-desirable fixes.

Here's how to quickly fix flaws with the Spot Healing Brush tool:

1. **In Expert mode, open your image and grab the Spot Healing Brush tool.**

   The tool looks like a bandage with a dotted oval behind it. You can also press J to cycle between the Healing Brush and Spot Healing Brush tools. You can also select either of these tools and then choose the other tool from the Tool Options.

2. **In the Tool Options, click the Brush Preset Picker and select a brush tip. You can further adjust the diameter by dragging the Size slider. You can also press the left and right brackets to decrease and increase the brush size, respectively.**

   Select a brush that's a little larger than the flawed area you're fixing.

3. **Choose a type in the Tool Options:**

   - **Proximity Match:** This type samples the pixels around the edge of the selection to fix the flawed area.

   - **Create Texture:** This type uses all the pixels in the selection to create a texture to fix the flaw.

   - **Content-Aware:** If you want to eliminate something larger than a mole or freckle, this is the option of choice where actual content from the image is used as a kind of patch for the flawed area. Large objects can be zapped away; Figure 10-17 shows how we eliminated the girl on the swing. ***Note:*** You may have to paint over the offending object a couple of times to get your desired result. Also, a touch-up with the Clone Stamp or other healing tools may be needed.

   Try Proximity Match first, and if it doesn't work, undo it and try Create Texture or Content-Aware.

   For removal of larger areas, you also have the option of using Edit ⇨ Fill Selection and choosing Content-Aware from the Use pop-up menu.

4. **Select the Sample All Layers check box to heal an image by using all visible layers.**

   If you leave this check box deselected, you heal from only the active layer.

5. **Click, drag, or "paint" over the area you want to fix.**

   We painted over the girl on the swing with the Spot Healing Brush and achieved realistic results, as shown in the after image in Figure 10-17.

FIGURE 10-17: Eliminate kids on swings and other objects with the Content-Aware option.

© Don Mason/Blend Images/Getty Images Image #87369347

NEW

If you find that the Healing or Spot Healing Brushes aren't doing the job for you, check out the Object Removal Guided Edit in the Special Edits category in Guided mode. Make your selection using one of the four tools and click Remove Object Touch up any remaining flaws with the Spot Healing Brush or Clone Stamp. Just a note of caution: This edit works best when the object you want to eliminate isn't touching anything you want to remain untouched.

Repositioning with the Content-Aware Move tool

The Content-Aware Move tool enables you to select and move a portion of an image. The best thing, however, is that when you move that portion, the hole left behind is miraculously filled using content-aware technology. In other words, Elements analyzes the area surrounding the selected portion you're moving and then fills the hole with matched content.

Here's how to use this beneficial editing tool:

1. **In Expert mode, open your image and select the Content-Aware Move tool.**

   The tool looks like two arrows. You can also press the Q key.

2. **Choose either Move or Extend mode.**

   - **Move:** Elements moves your selection to a new location and then fills the remaining hole with content-aware pixels. The Move mode works great when you need to move an object, or objects, in your image for a more desirable composition. Keep in mind that this technique works best when the background of the new location of the object is similar to the background from which it was plucked.

   - **Extend:** Elements extends your selected area while maintaining any lines and structural elements and blending them into the existing object. This option works great for expanding or contracting objects such as hair, fur, trees, buildings, and so on.

   For Figure 10-18, we chose the Move mode to move the girl to the right so that we could add some type.

3. **Choose your desired Healing setting.**

   Healing controls the amount of flexibility Elements uses in determining how to shift pixels around and how strictly regions are preserved when determining the content-aware fill. The default setting is smack-dab in the middle, which is what we stuck with.

   You can also select the Sample All Layers check box to use content from all your layers. If you leave this check box deselected, you use only content from the active layer.

4. **Drag around the area of your image that you want to move or extend.**

   If you need to fine-tune your selection, you can use the Path Operations options on the Options bar. Or you can press the Shift key to add to your selected area or press Alt (Option on the Mac) to delete from your selection.

You can also transform — scale or rotate — your selected area by selecting the Transform On Drop option. When you move your selection, the transform box will appear and the Transform options will appear in the Options bar. You can select your options there or manually drag or rotate the handles of your transform box. Click the Commit button (the green check-mark icon) to complete the transformation.

5. **If you did not select the Transform On Drop option in Step 4, move your selection to your desired location. Deselect the selection.**

6. **Touch up any areas that require it.**

You can break out the Healing tools or the Clone Stamp tool to fix any mismatches or remaining flaws. We fixed a few spots along the girl that weren't quite matched up, as shown in Figure 10-18. We also spot-healed the ugly light fixture at the top of the image.

FIGURE 10-18: Recompose your image by using the Content-Aware Move tool.

You also have the option of filling any selected area with a Content-Aware option. Make a selection and choose Edit ➪ Fill. Under Contents, choose Content-Aware from the Use pop-up menu.

Lightening and darkening with Dodge and Burn tools

The techniques of dodging and burning originated in the darkroom, where photographers fixed negatives that had overly dark or light areas by adding or subtracting exposure, using holes and paddles as an enlarger made prints. The Dodge and Burn tools are even better than their analog ancestors because they're more flexible and much more precise. You can specify the size and softness of your tool by simply selecting from one of the many brush tips. You can also limit the correction to various tonal ranges in your image — shadows, midtones, or highlights. Finally, you can adjust the amount of correction that's applied by specifying an exposure percentage.

REMEMBER

Use these tools only on small areas (such as the girl's face shown in Figure 10-19) and in moderation. You can even make a selection prior to dodging and burning to ensure that the adjustment is applied only to your specific area. Also, keep in mind that you can't add detail that isn't there to begin with. If you try to lighten extremely dark shadows that contain little detail, you get gray areas. If you try to darken overly light highlights, you just end up with white blobs.

FIGURE 10-19:
Use the Dodge and Burn tools to lighten and darken small areas.

Follow these steps to dodge or burn an image:

1. **In Expert mode, choose either the Dodge (to lighten) or Burn (to darken) tool from the Tools panel.**

   These tools look like a darkroom paddle and a hand making an *O*, respectively. Press O to cycle through the Dodge and Burn tools. You can also select any of these tools and then choose your desired tool from the Tool Options.

2. **Select a brush from the Brush Preset Picker panel and also adjust the brush size if necessary.**

   Larger, softer brushes spread the dodging or burning effect over a larger area, making blending with the surrounding area easier.

3. **From the Range drop-down list, choose Shadows, Midtones, or Highlights.**

   Choose Shadows to darken or lighten the darker areas of your image. Choose Midtones to adjust the tones of average darkness. Choose Highlights to make the light areas lighter or darker.

   In Figure 10-19, the original image had mostly dark areas, so we dodged the shadows.

4. **Choose the amount of correction you want to apply with each stroke by adjusting the Exposure setting in the Tool Options.**

   Start with a lower percentage to better control the amount of darkening or lightening. Exposure is similar to the opacity setting that you use with the regular Brush tool. We used a setting of 10 percent.

5. **Paint over the areas you want to lighten or darken.**

   If you don't like the results, press Ctrl+Z (⌘ +Z on the Mac) to undo.

Smudging away rough spots

The Smudge tool (see Figure 10-20), one of the focus tools, pushes your pixels around using the color that's under the cursor when you start to drag. Think of it as dragging a brush through wet paint. You can use this tool to create a variety of effects. When it's used to the extreme, you can create a warped effect. When it's used more subtly, you can soften the edges of objects in a more natural fashion than you can with the Blur tool. Or you can create images that take on a painterly effect, as shown in Figure 10-20. Keep an eye on your image while you paint, however, because you can start to eliminate detail and wreak havoc if you're not careful with the Smudge tool.

To use the Smudge tool, follow these steps:

1. **In Expert mode, select the Smudge tool from the Tools panel.**

   The tool looks like a finger. Press R to cycle through the Smudge, Blur, and Sharpen tools. You can also select any of these tools and then choose your desired tool from the Tool Options.

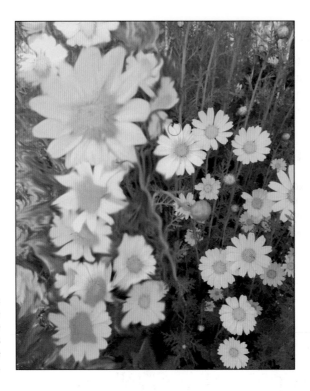

FIGURE 10-20:
The Smudge tool can make your images appear to be painted.

2. **Select a brush from the Brush Preset Picker panel. Use the Size slider to fine-tune your brush diameter.**

Use a small brush for smudging tiny areas, such as edges. Larger brushes produce more extreme effects.

3. **Choose a blending mode from the Mode drop-down list.**

4. **Choose the strength of the smudging effect with the Strength slider or text box.**

The lower the value, the lighter the effect.

5. **If your image doesn't have layers, skip to Step 6. If your image has multiple layers, select the Sample All Layers check box to make Elements use pixels from all the visible layers when it produces the effect.**

The smudge still appears on only the active layer, but the look is a bit different, depending on the colors of the underlying layers.

6. **Use the Finger Painting option to begin the smudge by using the foreground color.**

Rather than use the color under your cursor, this option smears your foreground color at the start of each stroke. If you want the best of both worlds, you can quickly switch into Finger Painting mode by pressing the Alt key while you drag. Release Alt to go back to Normal mode.

7. **Paint over the areas you want to smudge.**

Pay attention to your strokes because this tool can radically change your image. If you don't like the results, press Ctrl+Z (⌘ +Z on the Mac) to undo the changes and then lower the Strength percentage (discussed in Step 4) even more.

Softening with the Blur tool

The Blur tool (looks like a teardrop) can be used to repair images, as well as for more artistic endeavors. You can use the Blur tool to soften a small flaw or part of a rough edge. You can add a little blur to an element to make it appear as though it was moving when photographed. You can also blur portions of your image to emphasize the focal point, as shown in Figure 10-21, where we blurred everything except the girl's face. The Blur tool works by decreasing the contrast among adjacent pixels in the blurred area.

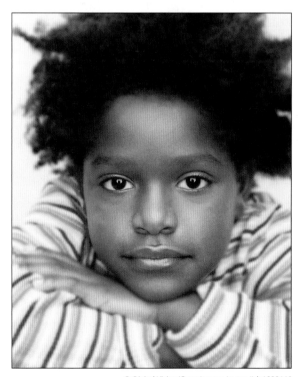

FIGURE 10-21: The Blur tool can be used to emphasize a focal point.

© Digital Vision/Getty Images Image #dv1833110

The mechanics of using the Blur tool and its options are similar to those of the Smudge tool, as we describe in the preceding section. When you use the Blur tool, be sure to use a small brush for smaller areas of blur.

Focusing with the Sharpen tool

If the Blur tool is yin, the Sharpen tool is yang. The Sharpen tool (looks like a triangle) increases the contrast among adjacent pixels to give the illusion that things are sharper. You should use this tool with restraint, however. Sharpen can quickly give way to overly grainy and noisy (random bright and dark pixels) images if you're not cautious.

Use a light hand and keep the areas you sharpen small. Sometimes, the eyes in a soft portrait can benefit from a little sharpening, as shown in Figure 10-22. You can also slightly sharpen an area to emphasize it against a less-than-sharp background.

FIGURE 10-22:
Reserve the Sharpen tool for small areas, such as eyes.

© Dimo Popcev/iStockphoto Image #186853333

To use the Sharpen tool, grab the tool from the Tools panel and follow the steps provided for the Smudge tool in the section "Smudging away rough spots," earlier in this chapter. Here are some additional tips for using the Sharpen tool:

>> Use a low value, around 25 percent or less.

>> Remember that you want to gradually sharpen your element to avoid the nasty, noisy grain that can occur from oversharpening.

>> Because sharpening increases contrast, if you use other contrast adjustments, such as Levels, you boost the contrast of the sharpened area even more.

>> Select the Protect Detail option to enhance the details in the image and minimize artifacts. If you leave this option deselected, your sharpening is more pronounced.

If you need to sharpen your overall image, try choosing either Enhance ⇨ Unsharp Mask or Enhance ⇨ Adjust Sharpness instead. These features offer more options and better control.

Sponging color on and off

The Sponge tool soaks up color or squeezes it out. In more technical terms, this tool reduces or increases the intensity, or *saturation,* of color in both color and grayscale images. Yes, the Sponge tool also works in Grayscale mode by darkening or lightening the brightness value of those pixels.

As with the Blur and Sharpen tools, you can use the Sponge tool to reduce or increase the saturation in selected areas in order to draw attention to or away from those areas.

Follow these steps to sponge color on or off your image:

1. **In Expert mode, choose the Sponge tool from the Tools panel.**

   The tool looks like a sponge. Press O to cycle through the Sponge, Dodge, and Burn tools. You can also select any of these tools and then choose your desired tool from the Tool Options.

2. **Select a brush from the Brush Preset Picker panel. Further adjust the size of the brush tip if needed.**

   Use large, soft brushes to saturate or desaturate a larger area.

3. **Choose either Desaturate or Saturate from the Mode drop-down list to decrease or increase color intensity, respectively.**

4. **Choose a flow rate with the Flow slider or text box.**

   The *flow rate* is the speed with which the saturation or desaturation effect builds while you paint. Start with a lower rate and then adjust as desired.

5. **Paint carefully over the areas you want to saturate or desaturate with color.**

   In the example shown in Figure 10-23, we used saturation to make the pup the focal point and desaturated the humans.

FIGURE 10-23:
The Sponge tool increases or decreases the intensity of the color in your image.

Replacing one color with another

The Color Replacement tool allows you to replace the original color of an image with the foreground color. You can use this tool in a multitude of ways:

» Colorize a grayscale image to create the look of a hand-painted photo.

» Completely change the color of an element, or elements, in your image, as shown in Figure 10-24, where we painted part of the girl with the balloons with the Color Replacement tool using the color black.

» Eliminate red eye (or yellow, green, or otherwise in animals) if other, more automated methods don't work to your satisfaction.

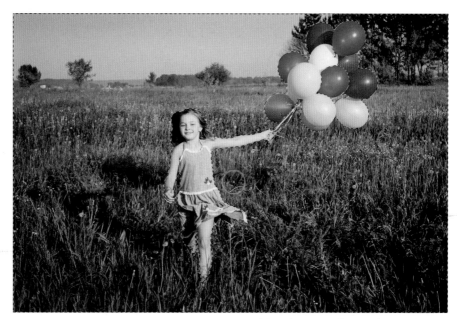

FIGURE 10-24:
The Color Replacement tool replaces the color in your image with the foreground color.

REMEMBER

What we particularly like about the Color Replacement tool is that it preserves all the tones in the image. The color that's applied isn't like the opaque paint that's applied when you paint with the Brush tool. When you're replacing color, the mid-tones, shadows, and highlights are retained. The Color Replacement tool works by first sampling the original colors in the image and then replacing those colors with the foreground color. By specifying different sampling methods, limits, and Tolerance settings, you can control the range of colors that Elements replaces.

Follow these steps to replace existing color with your foreground color:

1. **In Expert mode, select the Color Replacement tool from the Tools panel.**

   The tool looks like a paintbrush with a small blue square next to it. Press B to cycle through the Brush, Impressionist Brush, and Color Replacement tools. You can also select any of these tools and then choose your desired tool from the Tool Options.

2. **In the Tool Options, choose your desired brush tip from the Brush Preset Picker panel. Further adjust your brush size as needed. Then adjust the hardness, spacing, roundness, and angle under Brush Settings.**

3. **Choose your desired blend mode.**

   Here's a brief rundown of each one:

   - **Color:** The default, this mode works well for most jobs. It will change the color without changing the brightness levels, thereby retaining your tonal range. This mode works great for eliminating red eye.

- **Hue:** Similar to color, this mode is less intense and provides a subtler effect.

- **Saturation:** This mode is the one to use to convert the color in your image to grayscale. Set your foreground color to Black on the Tools panel.

- **Luminosity:** This mode, the opposite of Color, doesn't provide much of an effect. It changes the brightness levels, with no regard to color.

4. **Select your Limits mode.**

   You have these options:

   - **Contiguous** replaces the color of adjacent pixels containing the sampled color.

   - **Discontiguous** replaces the color of the pixels containing the sampled color, whether or not they're adjacent.

5. **Set your Tolerance percentage.**

   Tolerance refers to a range of color. The higher the value, the broader the range of color that's sampled, and vice versa.

6. **Set your Sampling method.**

   You have these options:

   - **Continuous** allows you to sample and replace color continuously while you drag your mouse.

   - **Once** replaces color only in areas containing the color that you first sample.

   - **Background Swatch** replaces colors only in areas containing your current Background color.

7. **Select the Anti-aliasing option.**

   Anti-aliasing slightly softens the edges of the sampled areas.

8. **Click or drag your image.**

   The foreground color replaces the original colors of the sampled areas. Back in Figure 10-24, we used a black foreground color to replace the photo's original background colors.

TIP

If you want to be very precise, make a selection before you replace your color. We did this with the girl in Figure 10-24 so that we could avoid coloring outside the lines.

Chapter **11**

Correcting Contrast, Color, and Clarity

I f you've tried the quick and easy automatic fixes on your images and they didn't quite do the job, you've come to the right place. The great thing about Elements is that it offers multiple ways and multiple levels of repairing and enhancing your images. If an auto fix doesn't cut it, move on to a manual fix.

TECHNICAL STUFF

If you're still not happy, you can consider shooting in Camera Raw format, as long as your camera can do so. Elements has wonderful Camera Raw support, enabling you to process your images to your exact specifications. For details on Camera Raw check out Chapter 7, "Editing Camera Raw Images." Chances are good that if you can't find the tools to correct and repair your images in Elements, those images are probably beyond salvaging.

This chapter covers the manual fixes you can make to your photos to correct lighting, contrast, color casts, artifacts, dust, scratches, sharpening, and blurring. We also cover using the Smart Brush tools to selectively apply an image adjustment.

Editing Your Photos Using a Logical Workflow

REMEMBER

With the information in Chapter 10 (where we explain quick fixes) and this chapter at your fingertips, you can develop a logical workflow when you tackle the correction and repair of your images. By performing steps in a particular order, you will be less likely to exacerbate the flaws and more able to accentuate what's good. For example, we use the following workflow when editing photos:

1. **Crop, straighten, and resize your images, if necessary.**

2. **When you have the images in their proper physical state, correct the lighting and establish good tonal range for your shadows, highlights, and midtones to display the greatest detail possible.**

   Often, just correcting the lighting solves minor color problems. If not, move on to adjusting the color balance.

3. **Eliminate any color casts and adjust the saturation, if necessary.**

4. **Grab the retouching tools, such as the healing tools and filters, to retouch any flaws.**

5. **(Optional) Apply any enhancements or special effects.**

6. **Sharpen your image if you feel that it could use a boost in clarity and sharpness.**

By following these steps and allocating a few minutes of your time, you can get all your images in shape to print, post, and share with family and friends.

USING TOUCHSCREEN MONITORS

Elements supports touchscreen capability on both Windows and Mac platforms. Not only can you browse through images in the Organizer by flicking with your fingers, but you can even retouch and enhance your images by using all the tools in your Tools panel with your fingers. Talk about digital finger-painting!

Adjusting Lighting

Elements has several simple, manual tools to use to fix lighting if the Auto tools that we describe in Chapter 10 didn't work or were just too, well, automatic for you. The manual tools offer more control over adjusting overall contrast as well as bringing out details in shadows, midtones, and highlight areas of your images. You can find all lighting adjustments in both Expert and Quick modes.

Fixing lighting with Shadows/Highlights

The Shadows/Highlights command offers a quick and easy method of correcting over- and underexposed areas, as shown on the left in Figure 11-1. This feature works especially well with images shot in bright, overhead light or in light coming from the back *(backlit).* These images usually suffer from having the subject partially or completely covered in shadows.

FIGURE 11-1:
Correct the lighting in your images with the Shadows/ Highlights adjustment.

To use the Shadows/Highlights adjustment, follow these steps:

1. **In Expert or Quick mode, choose Enhance ⇨ Adjust Lighting ⇨ Shadows/Highlights and make sure the Preview check box is selected.**

   When the dialog box appears, the default correction is applied automatically in your preview.

2. **If the default adjustment doesn't quite do the job, move the sliders (or enter a value) to adjust the amount of correction for your shadows (dark areas), highlights (light areas), and midtones (middle-toned areas).**

   Your goal is to reveal more detail in the dark and light areas of your image. If, after you do so, your image still looks like it needs more correction, add or delete contrast in your midtone areas.

   If only part of your image needs correcting, you can select just that portion before applying the adjustment. For more on selections, see Chapter 8.

3. **Click OK to apply the adjustment and close the dialog box.**

   If you want to start over, press the Alt (Option on the Mac) key, and the Cancel button becomes Reset. Click Reset to start again.

Using Brightness/Contrast

Despite its aptly descriptive moniker, the Brightness/Contrast command doesn't do a great job of *brightening* (making an image darker or lighter) or adding or reducing contrast. Initially, users tend to be drawn to this command because of its appropriate name and ease of use. But after users realize its limitations, they move on to better tools with more control, such as Shadows/Highlights and Levels.

The problem with the Brightness/Contrast command is that it applies the adjustment equally to all areas of your image. For example, a photo's highlights may need darkening, but all the midtones and shadows are perfect. The Brightness slider isn't smart enough to recognize that, so when you darken the highlights in your image, the midtones and shadows also become darker. To compensate for the unwanted darkening, you try to adjust the contrast, which doesn't fix the problem.

The moral is, if you want to use the Brightness/Contrast command, select only the areas that need the correction, such as Alcatraz, shown in Figure 11-2. (For more on selections, see Chapter 8.) After you make your selection, choose Enhance ⇨ Adjust Lighting ⇨ Brightness/Contrast.

FIGURE 11-2:
The Brightness/ Contrast adjustment is best reserved for correcting selected areas (left) rather than the entire image (right).

Pinpointing proper contrast with Levels

If you want real horsepower when it comes to correcting the brightness and contrast (and even the color) in your image, look no further than the Levels command. Granted, the dialog box is a tad more complex than what you find with the other lighting and color adjustment commands, but when you understand how the Levels dialog box works, it can be downright user friendly.

You can get a taste of what Levels can do by using Auto Levels, detailed in Chapter 10. The Levels command, its manual cousin, offers much more control. And unlike the primitive Brightness/Contrast control, Levels enables you to darken or lighten 256 different tones. Keep in mind that you can use the Levels command on your entire image, a single layer, or a selected area. You can also apply the Levels command by using an adjustment layer. We describe working with an adjustment layer in Chapter 9.

If you're serious about image editing, the Levels command is one tool you want to know how to use. Here's how Levels works:

1. **In Expert or Quick mode, choose Enhance ⇨ Adjust Lighting ⇨ Levels.**

We recommend using Expert mode for this command, where you'll have access to the Info panel in Step 2. If you're in Quick mode, skip to Step 3.

The Levels dialog box appears, displaying a *histogram,* as shown in Figure 11-3. This graph displays how the pixels of the image are distributed at each of the 256 available brightness levels. Shadows are shown on the left side of the histogram, midtones are in the middle, and highlights are on the right. **Note:** In addition to viewing the histogram of the composite RGB channel (the entire image), you can view the histogram of just the Red, Green, or Blue channel by selecting one of them from the Channel drop-down menu.

FIGURE 11-3:
The Levels
histogram
displays the
distribution
of brightness
levels.

TIP

Although you generally make changes to the entire image by using the RGB channel, you can apply changes to any one of an image's component color channels by selecting the specific channel from the Channel drop-down menu. You can also make adjustments to just selected areas, which can be helpful when one area of your image needs adjusting and others don't.

2. **In Expert mode, choose Window ⇨ Info to open the Info panel.**

3. **In the Levels dialog box, set the white point manually by using the eyedroppers in the dialog box:**

   (a) **Select the White Eyedropper tool and then move the cursor over the image.**

   (b) **Look at the Info panel, try to find the lightest white in the image, and then select that point by clicking it.**

   The lightest white has the highest RGB values.

4. **Repeat Step 3, this time using the Black Eyedropper tool and trying to find the darkest black in the image.**

   The darkest black has the lowest RGB values.

   When you set the pure black and pure white points, the remaining pixels are redistributed between those two points.

   You can also reset the white and black points by moving the position of the white and black triangles on the input sliders (just below the histogram). Or you can enter values in the Input Levels boxes. The three boxes represent the black, gray, and white triangles, respectively. Use the numbers 0 to 255 in the white and black boxes.

5. **Use the Gray Eyedropper tool to remove any color casts by selecting a neutral gray portion of your image, one in which the Info panel shows equal values of red, green, and blue.**

If your image is grayscale, you can't use the Gray Eyedropper tool.

TIP

If you're not sure where there's a neutral gray, you can also remove a color cast by choosing a color channel from the Channel drop-down list and doing one of the following:

- Choose the Red channel and drag the midtone slider to the right to add cyan or to the left to add red.

- Choose the Green channel and drag the midtone slider to the right to add magenta or to the left to add green.

- Choose the Blue channel and drag the midtone slider to the right to add yellow or to the left to add blue.

6. **If your image requires a tweak in reducing contrast, adjust the Output Levels sliders at the bottom of the Levels dialog box.**

Moving the black triangle to the right reduces the contrast in the shadows and lightens the image. Moving the white triangle to the left reduces the contrast in the highlights and darkens the image.

7. **Adjust the midtones (or gamma values) with the gray triangle input slider.**

The default value for gamma is 1.0. Drag the triangle to the left to lighten midtones and drag to the right to darken them. You can also enter a value.

8. **Click OK to apply your settings and close the dialog box.**

Your image should be greatly improved, as shown in Figure 11-4.

FIGURE 11-4:
Improve the contrast of an image with the intelligent Levels command.

If you're not up to the task of manually adjusting your levels, you can opt to click the Auto button in the Levels dialog box. Elements applies the same adjustments as the Auto Levels command, as we explain in Chapter 10. Note the changes and subsequent pixel redistribution made to the histogram after you click this button.

Adjusting Color

Getting the color you want can seem about as attainable as winning the state lottery. Sometimes an unexpected *color cast* (a shift in color) can be avoided at the shooting stage, for example, by using (or not using, in some cases) a flash or lens filter or by setting the camera's white balance for lighting conditions that aren't present. After the fact, you can usually do a pretty good job of correcting the color with one of the many Elements adjustments. Occasionally, you may want to change the color of your image to create a special effect. Conversely, you may want to strip out an image's color altogether to create a vintage feel. Remember that you can apply all these color adjustments to your entire image, a single layer, or just a selection. Whatever your color needs are, they'll no doubt be met in Elements.

You can find all color adjustments in either Expert or Quick mode, except for Defringe Layers, which is reserved for Expert mode only.

If you shoot your photos in the Camera Raw file format, you can open and fix your files in the Camera Raw dialog box. Remember that Camera Raw files haven't been processed by your camera. You're in total control of the color and exposure. For more about editing Camera Raw images, see Chapter 7, "Editing Camera Raw Images."

Removing color casts automatically

If you ever took a photo in an office or classroom and got a funky green tinge in your image, it was probably the result of the overhead fluorescent lighting. To eliminate this green color cast, you can apply the Remove Color Cast command. This feature is designed to adjust the image's overall color and remove the cast.

Follow these short steps to correct your image:

1. **In either Expert or Quick mode, choose Enhance ⇨ Adjust Color ⇨ Remove Color Cast.**

    The Remove Color Cast dialog box appears. Move the dialog box to better view your image.

2. **Click an area in your photo that should be white, black, or neutral gray, as shown in Figure 11-5.**

In our example, we clicked the girl's white T-shirt in the image on the left.

The colors in the image are adjusted according to the color you choose. Which color should you choose? The answer depends on the subject matter of your image. Feel free to experiment. Your adjustment is merely a preview at this point and isn't applied until you click OK. If you goof up, click the Reset button, and your image reverts to its unadjusted state.

3. **Repeat Step 2 if you aren't happy with your image. If you're satisfied with the adjustment, click OK to accept it and close the dialog box.**

FIGURE 11-5:
Get rid of nasty color shifts with the Remove Color Cast command.

TIP

If the Remove Color Cast command doesn't cut it, try applying a photo filter (as we describe in the section "Adjusting color temperature with photo filters," later in this chapter). For example, if your photo has too much green, try applying a magenta filter.

Adjusting with Hue/Saturation

The Hue/Saturation command enables you to adjust the colors in your image based on their hue, saturation, and lightness. *Hue* is the color in your image. *Saturation* is the intensity, or richness, of that color. And *lightness* controls the brightness value.

Follow these steps to adjust color by using the Hue/Saturation command:

1. **In either Expert or Quick mode, choose Enhance ⇨ Adjust Color ⇨ Adjust Hue/Saturation.**

   The Hue/Saturation dialog box appears. Be sure to select the Preview check box so that you can view your adjustments. The Hue/Saturation command is also available in Guided mode.

2. **Choose Master from the Edit drop-down list to adjust all the colors or choose one color to adjust.**

3. **Drag the slider for one or more of the following attributes to adjust the colors as described:**

   - **Hue:** Shifts all the colors clockwise (drag right) or counterclockwise (drag left) around the color wheel.

   - **Saturation:** Increases (drag right) or decreases (drag left) the richness of the colors. *Note:* Dragging all the way to the left gives the photo the appearance of a grayscale image.

   - **Lightness:** Increases the brightness values by adding white (drag right) or decreases the brightness values by adding black (drag left).

   The top color bar at the bottom of the dialog box represents the colors in their order on the color wheel before you make any changes. The lower color bar displays the colors after you make your adjustments.

TIP

When you select an individual color to adjust, sliders appear between the color bars so that you can define the range of color to be adjusted. You can select, add, or subtract colors from the range by choosing one of the Eyedropper tools and clicking in the image.

The Hue/Saturation dialog box also lets you colorize images, a useful option for creating sepia-colored images.

4. **(Optional) Select the Colorize option to change the colors in your image to a new, single color. Drag the Hue slider to change the color to your desired hue.**

   The pure white and black pixels remain unchanged, and the intermediate gray pixels are colorized.

5. **Click OK to apply your adjustments and exit the dialog box.**

TIP

Use the Hue/Saturation command with the Colorize option to create tinted photos, such as the one shown in Figure 11-6. You can also make selections in a grayscale image and apply a different tint to each selection. This can be especially fun with portraits. Tinted images can create a vintage or moody feel, and they can transform even mediocre photos into something special.

FIGURE 11-6:
Adjust the color, intensity, or brightness of your image with the Hue/ Saturation command.

Eliminating color with Remove Color

Despite all the talk in this chapter about color, we realize that there may be times when you don't want *any* color. With the Remove Color command, you can easily eliminate all the color from an image, a layer, or a selection. To use this one-step command, simply choose Enhance ⇨ Adjust Color ⇨ Remove Color.

TIP

Sometimes, stripping away color with this command can leave your image *flat*, or low in contrast. If this is the case, adjust the contrast by using one of Elements' many lighting fixes, such as Auto Levels, Auto Contrast, or Levels.

If you want to convert a selection, a layer, or an entire image to grayscale, you can do that with the Convert to Black and White dialog box, as shown in Figure 11-7. (Choose Enhance ⇨ Convert to Black and White.) But rather than just arbitrarily strip color as the Remove Color command does, the Convert to Black and White command enables you to select a conversion method by first choosing an image style. To further tweak the results, you can add or subtract colors (red, green, or blue) or contrast by moving the Intensity sliders until your grayscale image looks the way you want. *Note:* You aren't really adding color; you're simply altering the amount of data in the color channels. For more information on channels, see Chapter 2.

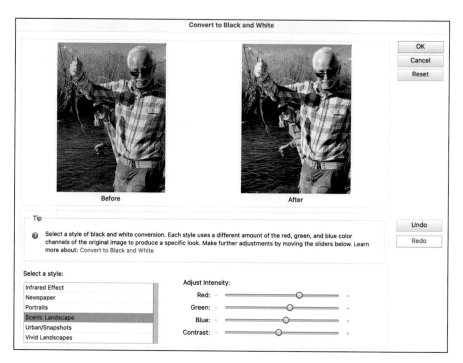

Switching colors with Replace Color

The Replace Color command enables you to replace designated colors in your image with other colors. You first select the colors you want to replace by creating a *mask*, which is a selection made by designating white (selected), black (unselected), and gray (partially selected) areas. See Chapter 9 for more details on masks. You can then adjust the hue and/or saturation of those selected colors.

Follow these steps to get on your way to replacing color:

1. **In Expert or Quick mode, choose Enhance ⇨ Adjust Color ⇨ Replace Color.**

   The Replace Color dialog box appears.

2. **Select the Preview check box and then choose either Selection or Image:**

   - **Selection** shows the mask in the Preview area. The deselected areas are black, partially selected areas are gray, and selected areas are white.

   - **Image** shows the actual image in the Preview area.

3. **With the Eyedropper tool, click the colors you want to select in either the image or the Preview area.**

4. **Shift-click or use the plus sign (+) Eyedropper tool to add more colors.**

5. **Press the Alt (Option on the Mac) key or use the minus sign (–) Eyedropper tool to delete colors.**

6. **To add colors similar to the ones you select, use the Fuzziness slider to fine-tune your selection, adding to or deleting from the selection based on the Fuzziness value.**

    If you can't quite get the selection you want with the Fuzziness slider, try selecting the Localized Color Clusters option. This option enables you to select multiple clusters, or areas, of color and can assist in getting a cleaner, more precise selection, especially when trying to select more than one color.

7. **Move the Hue and/or Saturation sliders to change the color or color richness, respectively. Move the Lightness slider to lighten or darken the image.**

    Be careful to use a light hand (no pun intended) with the Lightness slider. You can reduce the tonal range too much and end up with a mess.

8. **View the result in the image window.**

9. **If you're satisfied, click OK to apply the settings and close the dialog box.**

    Figure 11-8 shows the result of substituting the color of our tulips to change them from red to blue.

Correcting with Color Curves

Elements borrowed a much-used feature from Photoshop named Curves. However, Elements adds the word *Color*, and Color Curves doesn't have all the sophistication of its Photoshop cousin. Nevertheless, the Color Curves adjustment attempts to improve the tonal range in color images by making adjustments to highlights, shadows, and midtones in each color channel. (For more on channels, see Chapter 2.) Try using this command on images in which the foreground elements appear overly dark due to backlighting. Conversely, the adjustment is designed to correct images that appear overexposed and washed out.

Here's how to use this great adjustment on a selection, a layer, or an entire image:

1. **In Expert or Quick mode, choose Enhance ⇨ Adjust Color ⇨ Adjust Color Curves.**

    The Adjust Color Curves dialog box appears.

2. **Select a curve adjustment style from the Select a Style area to make your desired adjustments while viewing your image in the After window.**

FIGURE 11-8:
The Replace Color command enables you to replace one color with another.

3. **(Optional) If you need greater precision, use the highlights, brightness, contrast, and shadows adjustment sliders, as shown in Figure 11-9, and then adjust the sliders as desired.**

The graph in the lower right represents the distribution of tones in your image. When you first access the Color Curves dialog box, the tonal range of your image is represented by a straight line. While you drag the sliders, the straight line is altered, and the tonal range is adjusted accordingly.

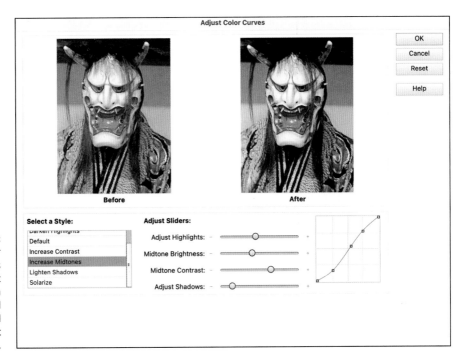

FIGURE 11-9:
The Color
Curves
adjustment
provides both
basic and
advanced
adjustment
controls.

TIP

Note that you can often easily increase the contrast in an image by creating a subtle S-shaped curve. To achieve this, decrease the shadows value and increase the highlights value equally.

To start over, click the Reset button.

4. **Click OK when you've adjusted the image satisfactorily.**

   Check out Figure 11-10 for another before-and-after image.

Adjusting skin tones

Occasionally, you may find that the skin tone of people in your photos has taken on a shade of green, red, or some other tone not natural to them. To rectify that problem, Elements has the Adjust Color for Skin Tone command specifically designed to adjust the overall color in the image and get skin tones back to their natural shades.

Here's how to use this feature:

1. **Open your image in Expert or Quick mode and do one or both of the following:**

   ● **Select the layer that needs to be adjusted.** If you don't have any layers, your entire image is adjusted.

Original

After the Color Curves adjustment

FIGURE 11-10:
Color Curves
improves tonal
range in color
images.

- **Select the areas of skin that need to be adjusted.** Only the selected areas are adjusted. This is a good way to go if you're happy with the color of your other elements and just want to tweak the skin tones. For more on selection techniques, see Chapter 8.

2. **Choose Enhance ➪ Adjust Color ➪ Adjust Color for Skin Tone.**

   The Adjust Color for Skin Tone dialog box appears. This command is also found in Guided mode.

3. **In the image window, click the portion of skin that needs to be corrected.**

   The command adjusts the color of the skin tone, as well as the color in the overall image, layer, or selection, depending on what you selected in Step 1.

4. **If you're not satisfied with the results, click another area or fiddle with the Skin and Ambient Light sliders:**

   - **Tan** adds or removes the amount of brown in the skin.
   - **Blush** adds or removes the amount of red in the skin.
   - **Temperature** adjusts the overall color of the skin, making it warmer (right toward red) or cooler (left toward blue).

   To start anew, click the Reset button. And, of course, to bail out completely, click Cancel.

5. **When you're happy with the correction, click OK to apply the adjustment and close the dialog box.**

   The newly toned skin appears, as shown in Figure 11-11.

Defringing layers

A telltale sign of haphazardly composited images is selections with fringe. We don't mean the cute kind hanging from your leather jacket or upholstery; we mean the unattractive kind that consists of background pixels that surround the edges of your selections, as shown in Figure 11-12.

Fringe   Defringed

Inevitably, when you move or paste a selection, some background pixels are bound to go along for the ride. These pixels are referred to as a *fringe* or *halo.* Luckily, the Defringe command replaces the color of the fringe pixels with the colors of neighboring pixels that don't contain the background color. In our example, we plucked the red flower out of a blue background and placed it on a white background. Some of the background pixels were included in our selection and appear as a blue fringe. When we apply the Defringe command, those blue fringe pixels are changed to colors of nearby pixels, such as red, as shown in Figure 11-12.

Follow these steps to defringe your selection:

1. **In Expert or Quick mode, copy and paste a selection onto a new or existing layer, or drag and drop a selection onto a new document.**

    For more on selections, see Chapter 8.

2. **Choose Enhance ⇨ Adjust Color ⇨ Defringe Layer.**

    The Defringe dialog box appears.

3. **Enter a value for the number of pixels you want to convert.**

    Try entering 1 or 2 first to see whether that does the trick. If not, you may need to enter a slightly higher value.

4. **Click OK to accept the value and close the dialog box.**

Eliminating haze

Elements provides a useful and easy-to-use feature to quickly eliminate haze from your photos. Haze, caused by light hitting particles in the air, dust, dirt, and so on, can be further enhanced by weather and time of day. Sometimes, increasing the contrast and sharpness in your image can help to lessen the effect of haze in your image. But with this feature, eliminating it has never been easier.

Here are the steps to eliminate haze from your images:

1. **Open an image in Expert or Quick mode.**

2. **Choose Enhance ⇨ Haze Removal.**

    The Haze Removal dialog box appears.

3. **Specify your Haze Reduction setting by adjusting the slider.**

    Sliding right will increase the amount of haze that is reduced.

4. **Specify your Sensitivity setting by adjusting the slider.**

Sliding right will increase the threshold of how much haze is detected.

5. **Toggle your Before and After button to check your results and then click OK.**

The results of this great feature are shown in Figure 11-13.

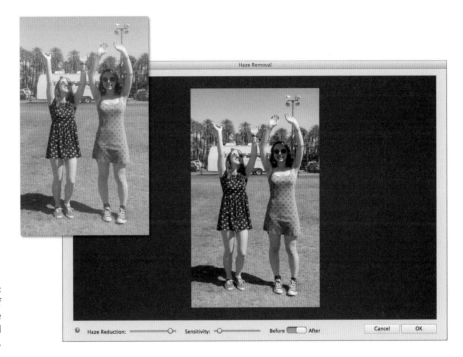

FIGURE 11-13:
Get rid of
haze with the
Haze Removal
command.

Adjusting color temperature with photo filters

Light has its own color temperature. A photo shot in a higher color temperature of light makes the image blue. Conversely, a photo shot in a lower color temperature makes the image yellow. In the old days, photographers placed colored glass filters in front of their camera lenses to adjust the color temperature of the light. They did this to either warm up or cool down photos or to just add a hint of color for subtle special effects. Elements gives you the digital version of these filters with the Photo Filter command.

To apply the Photo Filter adjustment, follow these steps:

1. **In Expert or Quick mode, choose Filter ⇨ Adjustments ⇨ Photo Filter.**

The Photo Filter dialog box appears.

TIP

You can also apply the photo filter to an individual layer by creating a photo-filter adjustment layer. For details, see Chapter 9.

2. **In the dialog box, select Filter to choose a preset filter from the drop-down list, or select Color to choose your own filter color from the Color Picker.**

Here's a brief description of each of the preset filters:

- **Warming Filter (85), (81), and (LBA):** These adjust the white balance in an image to make the colors warmer, or more yellow. Filter (81) is like (85) and (LBA), but it's best used for minor adjustments.

- **Cooling Filter (80), (82), and (LBB):** These also adjust the white balance that's shown, but instead of making the colors warmer, they make the colors cooler, or bluer. Filter (82) is like (80) and (LBB), but it's designed for slight adjustments.

- **Red, Orange, Yellow, and so on:** The various color filters adjust the hue, or color, of a photo. Choose a color filter to try to eliminate a color cast or to apply a special effect.

3. **Adjust the Density option to specify the amount of color applied to your image.**

4. **Select the Preserve Luminosity option to prevent the photo filter from darkening your image.**

5. **Click OK to apply your filter and close the dialog box.**

TIP

One way to minimize the need for color adjustments is to be sure you set your camera's white balance for your existing lighting conditions before shooting your photo.

Mapping your colors

Elements provides color mapper commands that change the colors in your image by mapping them to other values. You find the color mappers on the Filter ⇨ Adjustments submenu. Figure 11-14 shows an example of each command, and we explain all in the following list:

>> **Equalize:** This mapper first locates the lightest and darkest pixels in the image and assigns them values of white and black. It then redistributes all the

remaining pixels among the grayscale values. The exact effect depends on your individual image.

>> **Gradient Map:** This command maps the tonal range of an image to the colors of your chosen gradient. For example, colors (such as orange, green, and purple) are mapped to the shadow, highlight, and midtone areas.

>> **Invert:** This command reverses all the colors in your image, creating a kind of negative. Black reverses to white, and colors convert to their complementary hues. Complementary colors (which are opposite each other on the color wheel), when combined in the proper proportions, produce white, gray, or black. So blue goes to yellow, red goes to cyan, and so on.

>> **Posterize:** This command reduces the number of brightness levels in your image. Choose a value between 2 and 255 levels. Lower values create an illustrative, poster-like look, and higher values produce a more photo-realistic image.

>> **Threshold:** Threshold makes your image black and white, with all pixels that are brighter than a value you specify represented as white and all pixels that are darker than that value as black. You can change the threshold level to achieve different high-contrast effects.

| Equalize | Gradient Map | Invert | Posterize | Threshold |

FIGURE 11-14:
Change the colors in your image by remapping them to other values.

© Vetta/iStockphoto Image #2847462

Adjusting Clarity

After your image has the right contrast and color, and you fix any flaws (as we describe in Chapter 10), you're ready to work on the overall clarity of that image. Although you may have fixed the nitpicky blemishes with the healing tools, if your image suffers from an overall problem, such as dust, scratches, or *artifacts* (blocky pixels or halos), you may need to employ the help of a filter. After you totally clean up your image, your last chore is to give it a good sharpening. Why wait until the bitter end to do so? Sometimes, while you're improving the contrast and color and getting rid of flaws, you can reduce the clarity and sharpness of an image. So you want to be sure that your image is as soft as it's going to get before you tackle your sharpening tasks.

REMEMBER

Sharpening increases contrast, so depending on how much of your image you're sharpening, you may need to go back and fine-tune it by using the lighting adjustments described in the section "Adjusting Lighting," earlier in this chapter.

Finally, with all this talk about sharpening, we know that you may find it strange when we say that you may also need to occasionally blur your image. You can use blurring to eliminate unpleasant patterns that occur during scanning, to soften distracting backgrounds to give a better focal point, or even to create the illusion of motion.

Removing noise, artifacts, dust, and scratches

Surprisingly, the tools you want to use to eliminate junk from your images are found on the Filter ➪ Noise submenu in Expert or Quick mode. With the exception of the Add Noise filter, the others help to hide noise, dust, scratches, and artifacts. Here's the list of junk removers:

>> **Despeckle:** Decreases the contrast, without affecting the edges, to make the dust in your image less pronounced. You may notice a slight blurring of your image (that's what's hiding the junk), but hopefully the edges are still sharp.

>> **Dust & Scratches:** Hides dust and scratches by blurring those areas of your image that contain the nastiness. (It looks for harsh transitions in tone.) Specify your desired Radius value, which is the size of the area to be blurred. Also, specify the Threshold value, which determines how much contrast between pixels must be present before they're blurred.

WARNING

Use this filter with restraint because it can obliterate detail and make your image go from bad to worse.

>> **Median:** Reduces contrast around dust spots. The process the filter goes through is rather technical, so suffice it to say that the light spots darken, the dark spots lighten, and the rest of the image isn't changed. Specify your desired radius, which is the size of the area to be adjusted.

>> **Reduce Noise:** Designed to remove luminance noise and artifacts from your images. *Luminance noise* is grayscale noise that makes images look overly grainy. Specify these options to reduce the noise in your image:

- **Strength:** Specify the amount of noise reduction.

- **Preserve Details:** A higher percentage preserves edges and details but reduces the amount of noise that's removed.

- **Reduce Color Noise:** Remove random colored pixels.

- **Remove JPEG Artifact:** Remove the blocks and halos that can occur from low-quality JPEG compression.

Blurring when you need to

It may sound odd that anyone would intentionally want to blur an image. But, if your photo is overly grainy or suffers from a nasty *moiré* (wavy) pattern (as described in the following list), you may need to blur the image to correct the problem. Often, you may even want to blur the background of an image to de-emphasize distractions or to make the foreground elements appear sharper and provide a better focal point.

All the blurring commands are found on the Filter ⇨ Blur menu in Expert or Quick mode, with the exception of the Blur tool itself, found in the Tools panel (explained in Chapter 10):

>> **Average:** This one-step filter calculates the average value of the image or selection and fills the area with that average value. You can use it for smoothing overly noisy areas in your image.

>> **Blur:** Another one-step filter, this one applies a fixed amount of blurring to the whole image.

>> **Blur More:** This one-step blur filter gives the same effect as Blur, but more intensely.

>> **Gaussian Blur:** This blur filter is probably the one you'll use most often. It offers a Radius setting to let you adjust the amount of blurring you desire.

TIP

Use the Gaussian Blur filter to camouflage moiré patterns on scanned images. A *moiré pattern* is caused when you scan halftone images. A *halftone* is created when a continuous-tone image, such as a photo, is digitized and converted into a screen pattern of repeating lines (usually between 85 and 150 lines per inch) and then printed. When you then scan that halftone, a second pattern results and is overlaid on the original pattern. These two different patterns bump heads and create a nasty moiré pattern. The Gaussian Blur filter doesn't eliminate the moiré — it simply merges the dots and reduces the appearance of the pattern. Play with the Radius slider until you get an acceptable trade-off between less moiré and less focus. If you happen to have a descreen filter (which attempts to remove the moiré pattern on scanned halftones) built into your scanning software, you can use that as well during the scanning of the halftone image.

>> **Motion Blur:** This filter mimics the blur given off by moving objects. Specify the angle of motion and the distance of the blur. Make sure to select the Preview check box to see the effect while you enter your values.

>> **Radial Blur:** Need to simulate a moving Ferris wheel or some other round object? This filter produces a circular blur effect. Specify the amount of blur you want. Choose the Spin method to blur along concentric circular lines, as shown in the thumbnail. Or choose Zoom to blur along radial lines and mimic the effect of zooming in to your image. Specify your desired Quality level. Because the Radial Blur filter is notoriously slow, Elements gives you the option of Draft (fast but grainy), Good, or Best (slow but smooth). The difference between Good and Best is evident only on large, high-resolution images. Finally, indicate where you want to place the center of your blur by moving the blur diagram thumbnail.

>> **Smart Blur:** This filter provides several options to enable you to specify how the blur is applied. Specify a value for the radius and threshold, both defined in the following section. Start with a lower value for both and adjust from there. Choose a quality setting from the drop-down list. Choose a mode setting:

- **Normal** blurs the entire image or selection.

- **Edge Only** blurs only the edges of your elements and uses black and white in the blurred pixels.

- **Overlay Edge** also blurs just the edges, but it applies only white to the blurred pixels.

>> **Surface Blur:** This filter blurs the surface or interior of the image instead of the edges. If you want to retain your edge details but blur everything else, use this filter.

If you've ever experimented with the aperture settings on a camera, you know that you can set how shallow or deep your depth of field is. Depth of field relates to the *plane of focus* (the areas in a photo that are in front of or behind the focal point and that remain in focus) or how in focus the foreground elements are when you compare them with the background elements. The Lens Blur filter, as shown in Figure 11-15, enables you to give the effect of a shallower depth of field after you've already captured your image, thereby enabling you to take a fully focused image and create this selective focus.

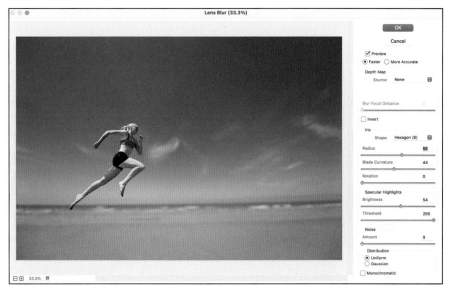

FIGURE 11-15:
Use the
Lens Blur filter
to create a
shallow depth-
of-field effect.

© Extreme Sports Photo/Alamy Stock Photo Image #C5R820

Here's how to use the Lens Blur filter:

1. Choose Filter ⇨ Blur ⇨ Lens Blur.

The Lens Blur Filter dialog box appears.

2. Select your Preview mode.

The Faster option gives you a quick preview, whereas More Accurate shows you the final rendered image.

3. Choose a Source from the drop-down list for your depth map, if you have one.

You can choose between a layer mask and a transparency. The filter uses a depth map to determine how the blur works.

A good way to create an image with this shallow depth-of-field effect is to create a layer mask on your image layer and fill it with a white-to-black gradient — black where you want the most focus, and white where you want the least focus or most blur. Choose Transparency to make an image blurrier and more transparent.

4. Drag the Blur Focal Distance slider to specify how blurry or in focus an area of the image is. Or click the crosshair cursor on the part of the image that you want to be in full focus.

Dragging the slider enables you to specify a value. You can also select Invert to invert, or reverse, the depth map source.

5. **Choose an Iris shape, such as triangle or octagon, from the Shape drop-down list.**

   The Iris settings are meant to simulate the aperture blades of a camera lens. Specify the shape of the lens, as well as the radius (size of the iris), blade curvature (the smoothness of the iris's edges), and rotation of that shape.

6. **Set the Brightness and Threshold values in the Specular Highlights area.**

   The Lens Blur filter averages the highlights of an image, which, if left uncorrected, cause some highlights to appear grayish. The Specular Highlights controls help to retain Specular Highlights, or those highlights that should appear very white. Set the Threshold value to specify which highlights should be *specular* (remain white). Set a Brightness value to specify how much to relighten any blurred areas.

7. **Drag the Amount slider in the Noise area to add noise back into your image. Choose Monochromatic to add noise without affecting the color.**

   Blurring obliterates any noise (or *film grain*) that an image may have. This absence of noise can cause the image to appear inconsistent or unrealistic, in many cases.

8. **Click OK to apply the Lens Blur and exit the dialog box.**

Sharpening for better focus

Of course, if your images don't need any contrast, color, and flaw fixing, feel free to jump right into sharpening. Sometimes, images captured by a scanner or a digital camera are a little soft, and it's not due to any tonal adjustments. Occasionally, you may even want to sharpen a selected area in your image just so that it stands out more.

REMEMBER

You can't really improve the focus of an image after it's captured. But you can do a pretty good job of faking it.

All sharpening tools work by increasing the contrast between adjacent pixels. This increased contrast causes the edges to appear more distinct, thereby giving the illusion that the focus is improved, as shown in Figure 11-16. Remember that you can also use the Sharpen tool for small areas, as described in Chapter 10. Here's a description of the two sharpening commands:

» **Unsharp Mask:** Found on the Enhance menu in Expert or Quick mode, Unsharp Mask (which gets its odd name from a darkroom technique) is the sharpening tool of choice. It gives you several options that enable you to control the amount of sharpening and the width of the areas to be sharpened. Use them to pinpoint your desired sharpening:

- **Amount:** Specify an amount (from 1 to 500 percent) of edge sharpening. The higher the value, the more contrast between pixels around the edges. Start with a value of 100 percent (or less), which usually gives good contrast without appearing overly grainy.

- **Radius:** Specify the width (from 0.1 to 250 pixels) of the edges that the filter will sharpen. The higher the value, the wider the edge. The value you use is largely based on the resolution of your image. Low-resolution images require a smaller radius value. High-resolution images require a higher value.

  Be warned that specifying a value that's too high overemphasizes the edges of your image and makes it appear too "contrasty" or even "goopy" around the edges.

TIP

  A good guideline in selecting a starting radius value is to divide your image's resolution by 150. For example, if you have a 300 ppi image, set the radius at 2 and then use your eye to adjust from there.

- **Threshold:** Specify the difference in brightness (from 0 to 255) that must be present between adjacent pixels before the edge is sharpened. A lower value sharpens edges with very little contrast difference. Higher values sharpen only when adjacent pixels are very different in contrast. We recommend leaving Threshold set at 0 unless your image is very grainy. Setting the value too high can cause unnatural transitions between sharpened and unsharpened areas.

TIP

  Occasionally, the values you enter for Amount and Radius may sharpen the image effectively but in turn create excess *grain,* or noise, in your image. You can sometimes reduce this noise by increasing the Threshold value.

FIGURE 11-16:
Sharpening mimics an increase in focus by increasing contrast between adjacent pixels.

» **Adjust Sharpness:** When you're looking for precision in your image sharpening, Unsharp Mask is one option. The Adjust Sharpness command, as shown in Figure 11-17, is the other. This feature enables you to control the amount of sharpening applied to shadow and highlight areas. It also allows you to select from various sharpening algorithms.

Here are the various options you can specify:

- **Amount and Radius:** These work similar to the Unsharp Mask command; see the previous bullet.

- **Preset:** You can save your sharpening settings as a preset that you can load and use later.

- **Remove:** Choose your sharpening algorithm. Gaussian Blur is the algorithm used for the Unsharp Mask command. Lens Blur detects detail in the image and attempts to respect the details while reducing the nasty halos that can occur with sharpening. Motion Blur tries to sharpen the blurring that occurs when you move the camera (or if your subject doesn't sit still).

- **Angle:** Specify the direction of motion for the Motion Blur algorithm, described in the preceding bullet.

FIGURE 11-17:
The Adjust Sharpness dialog box.

- **Shadows/Highlights:** You can control the amount of sharpening in the Shadow and Highlight areas of your image. Determine the amount of sharpening with the Fade Amount setting. For the Tonal Width option, specify the range of tones you want to sharpen. Move the slider to the right to sharpen only the darker of the shadow areas and the lighter of the highlight areas. Finally, for the Radius setting, specify the amount of space around a pixel that's used to determine whether a pixel is in the shadow or the highlight area. Move the slider right to specify a greater area.

Opening closed eyes

It's hard to get everyone in your photo to have great smiles and open eyes at the exact same instant. Luckily, now you have a tool to at least fix the eye problem. The Open Closed Eyes feature lets you use another photo of the same person(s) in which their eyes were open and merge the two images into a nice hero shot.

Here's what you do:

1. **Open an image in Expert or Quick mode.**

   You can open a photo from your computer, the Organizer, or the Photo Bin.

2. **Choose Enhance ⇨ Open Closed Eyes or click the Eye tool in the Tools panel and then click the Open Close Eyes button in the tool options.**

   The Open Closed Eyes dialog box appears, as shown in Figure 11-18.

   In the dialog box, a circle surrounds the area that will be affected by the adjustments.

3. **Choose a photo as your eye source image.**

4. **Click the source image to apply it.**

   Elements automatically applies the eyes from the source image and replaces the closed eyes.

Colorizing a photo

This enhancement enables you to either add color to black and white images, or edit the color in colored images. Yes, you can also colorize images in Elements a couple different ways — using Hue/Saturation (described earlier in this chapter) or using the Brush tool with a Color blend mode applied — but this technique can give your image more of a vintage, hand–painted look.

FIGURE 11-18:
Fix images
with the Open
Closed Eyes
feature.

Follow these steps to colorize a photo:

1. **Open an image in Expert or Quick mode.**

2. **Choose Enhance ⇨ Colorize Photo.**

   The Colorize Photo dialog box appears.

3. **Choose either Auto or Manual mode.**

4. **If you choose Auto mode, choose one of four presets in Basic mode.**

   Each one creates a more contrasty image.

5. **If you want a little more customization, choose Manual mode and follow these steps:**

   (a) **Use either the Quick Selection or Lasso tool and select an area where you want more color.**

   If you are using the Quick Selection tool you can make the tool's diameter larger or smaller by adjusting the Size slider.

   (b) **With either tool, use the Add to or Subtract From buttons to further define your desired area (you can also press the Shift key to add and the Option/Alt key to subtract).**

(c) Select the Droplet Tool and then click inside your selected area to mark the area to be colorized.

(d) Click your desired color swatch from the Color Palette or from the All Applicable Colors panel.

If you want to see your image without the Droplet icons (see Figure 11-19, where the Droplet icons are visible), toggle off the Show Droplets option at the bottom.

(e) Repeat the steps as desired.

6. If you're happy with the results, click OK. If you want to start over, click the Reset button.

See Figure 11-19 for two colorized variations using Manual mode.

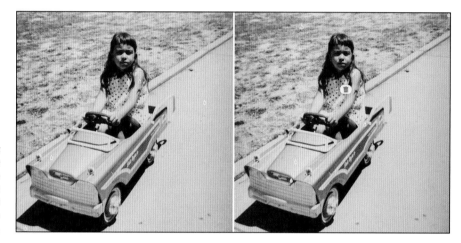

FIGURE 11-19: Use the Colorize Photo feature to bring life to black-and-white images.

Smoothing skin

Elements gives you yet another feature to make people look better in the digital world than they do in real life. Luckily, the new Smooth Skin feature doesn't allow you to go crazy and eliminate all traces of having lived life, but instead just softens and refreshes lines and blemishes.

Here's how to use the Smooth Skin feature:

1. Open an image in Expert or Quick mode.

2. Choose Enhance ➪ Smooth Skin.

The Smooth Skin dialog box appears.

In the dialog box, a circle surrounds the area that will be affected by the adjustments.

3. **Use the Smoothness slider to apply the amount of smoothing desired, as shown in Figure 11-20.**

4. **Toggle your Before and After button to view your results.**

5. **If you like the results, click OK. If not, click Reset or Cancel.**

FIGURE 11-20:
The Smooth Skin feature quickly softens wrinkles and blemishes.

If you feel that your subject needs a little more "work," check out the Perfect Portrait feature in the Special Edits category in Guided Edit mode. The Smooth Skin feature is part of that edit, along with the abilities to whiten teeth, darken eyebrows, brighten eyes, and perform other enhancements.

Adjusting facial features

The Adjust Facial Features command is a light, automated version of the infamous Liquify feature, the power tool used to retouch many a magazine photo. Adjust Facial Features doesn't allow for much manual manipulation, but the effect is pretty dramatic, not to mention seamless and easy to use. Get ready for retouching requests from friends and family!

Here's how to use this feature:

1. **Open an image in Expert or Quick mode.**

2. **Choose Enhance ⇨ Adjust Facial Features.**

   The Adjust Facial Features dialog box appears.

   In the dialog box, a circle surrounds the area that will be affected by the adjustments. Note that Elements first analyzes whether it's truly a face. We tried it with an image of a cat. No dice.

3. **Use the sliders to modify facial features such as eyes, nose, lips, chin, and face, as shown in Figure 11-21.**

   The Face Tilt feature enables you to adjust the various angles of the face.

4. **Toggle your Before and After button to view your results.**

5. **Satisfied? Click OK. Not satisfied? Start over by clicking Reset.**

   Figure 11-21 shows the seamless adjustment of the model's features.

FIGURE 11-21: The Adjust Facial Features command easily modifies facial characteristics.

© Compassionate Eye Foundation/Getty Images Image #173974707

Choose Preferences ⇨ Performance and verify that the Use Graphic Processor option is selected to ensure better and smoother performance when using features like Adjust Facial Features and the Lens Blur and Liquify filters.

Reducing shake

By far one of best recent features added to Elements is the Shake Reduction command. Although cellphones have revolutionized the ease and convenience in snapping quick pics of life's best moments, many of those images suffer from either poor lighting or blur caused by moving the phone and, therefore, the camera. The Shake Reduction command does an amazingly good job of correcting that blur.

Here's how to use it:

1. **Open an image in Expert or Quick mode.**

2. **Choose Enhance ⇨ Shake Reduction.**

   The Shake Reduction dialog box appears.

   In the Shake Reduction dialog box, a bounding box surrounds the area that is used for sampling shake detection. This is referred to as a shake region.

3. **Resize the bounding box as needed by dragging a handle.**

4. **Specify your Sensitivity setting by adjusting the slider.**

   If your image is very blurry, sliding right will increase the extent of the blur that is fixed.

5. **To add additional shake region for sampling, click the bounding box icon to the left of the Zoom tool (magnifying glass icon) and drag around your desired area on your image.**

   Use Zoom to zoom in and out of your image. To delete a shake region, click the center "pin" and then click the delete icon in the top-right corner of the bounding box.

6. **Toggle your Before and After button to check your results and then click OK.**

   Figure 11-22 shows how the slightly blurry image of Japan's crazy plastic food was improved.

Moving Overlays

The previous release of Elements gave us the cool Moving Photos feature. This release gives us another fun animated feature, Moving Overlays. You can now add moving content from three different categories to your static photos.

FIGURE 11-22:
Fix blur caused
by camera
movement
with Shake
Reduction.

Follow these steps to add moving overlays:

1. **Open an image in Expert or Quick mode.**

2. **Choose Enhance ⇨ Moving Overlays.**

   The Moving Overlays dialog box appears.

3. **On the right side of the dialog box, select either Overlays, Graphics, or Frames from the drop-down menu.**

4. **Double-click the motion overlay that you want to apply to your image.**

   Note that if you are choosing a frame or graphic, you can size it by dragging a handle of the accompanying transform box.

   Elements takes a minute or two to generate a preview.

5. **(Optional) Select the Protect Subject option to put your motion content behind your static image.**

   You can also adjust the Opacity slider to make your motion content less opaque.

6. **(Optional) Click the Refine Overlay button to Subtract content if you want. Note the you can adjust your brush size and opacity using the sliders.**

   If you change your mind, you can always use the Add button to bring it back in.

7. **Click the Play/Stop button under your image.**

   The motion effect is added to your photo, as you can see in Figure 11-23.

8. **When you're pleased with the results, click the Export button at the bottom of the dialog box.**

   Your file can be exported either as an animated GIF or, in Elements 2022, an MP4 file. You can then use your file on websites, Facebook, Twitter, and in iPhone messages.

FIGURE 11-23:
Add animated content to your static images with the Moving Overlays enhancement.

Tischenko Irina/Shutterstock Image #58458289

TIP

Although the content available in Moving Overlays is limited right now, Adobe promises to provide more fun overlays in the near future.

Moving Photos

Introduced in Elements 2021, the Moving Photos enhancement enables you to take your still images and give them a little motion. It's so surprisingly easy that you'll wonder how in the heck those Adobe programmers hid all the technical machinations behind the curtain.

Here's how to use it:

1. **Open an image in Expert or Quick mode.**

2. **Choose Enhance ⇨ Moving Photos.**

   The simple Moving Photos dialog box appears.

3. **On the right side of the dialog box, double-click the motion effect that you want to apply to your image.**

   Give Elements a few moments to generate a preview.

4. **Click the Play/Stop button under your image.**

   Amazingly the motion effect is applied to your photo, as you sadly can't see in Figure 11-24!

5. **By default, the 3D Effect is applied, thereby giving your image more depth. Toggle it off to see it without the 3D Effect.**

6. **When you're happy with the file, click the Export button at the bottom of the dialog box.**

   Your moving image can be exported either as an animated GIF or MP4 file. Show it off on social media sites or in your iPhone messages.

FIGURE 11-24:
Create animated GIFs or MP4 files easily with the Moving Photos enhancement.

Working Intelligently with the Smart Brush Tools

The Smart Brush and Detail Smart Brush tools enable you to selectively apply an image adjustment or special effect that appears on all or part of your image. What's even more exciting is that these adjustments and effects are applied via an adjustment layer, meaning that they hover over your layers and don't permanently alter the pixels in your image. It also means that you can flexibly edit or delete adjustments, if so desired.

Follow these steps to use the Smart Brush tool:

1. **In Expert mode, select the Smart Brush tool from the toolbar.**

   The tool icon looks like a house paintbrush. You can also press F, or Shift+F, if the Detail Smart Brush tool is visible.

2. **Select an adjustment category and then your particular preset adjustment from the Preset Picker drop-down list in the Tool Options.**

   In the Preset menu, you can find adjustments ranging from Photographic effects, such as a vintage Yellowed Photo, to Nature effects, such as Create a Sunset (which gives a warm, orange glow to your image).

   The Textures category has 13 presets, such as Broken Glass and Old Paper. Use these textures with your smart brushes to jazz up backgrounds and other elements in your images. For example, if that white wall in your shot is less than exciting, give it a Brick wall texture. If the drop cloth behind your portrait to reduce background clutter is a tad boring, give it a satin ripple.

3. **Choose your desired brush attributes, such as size, as shown in Figure 11-25. Or adjust attributes such as hardness, spacing, roundness, and angle from the Brush Settings drop-down panel.**

   For more on working with brushes, see Chapter 13.

4. **Paint an adjustment on the desired layer in your image.**

   While you paint, the Smart Brush tool attempts to detect edges in your image and snaps to those edges. In addition, while you brush, a selection border appears.

   A new adjustment layer is created automatically with your first paint stroke. The accompanying layer mask also appears on that adjustment layer. For more on adjustment layers, see Chapter 9.

5. **Using the Add and Subtract Smart Brush modes in the Tool Options, fine-tune your adjusted area by adding to and subtracting from it.**

   When you add to and subtract from your adjusted area, you're essentially modifying your layer mask. Adding to your adjusted area adds white to your layer mask, and subtracting from your adjusted area adds black to your layer mask. For more on layer masks, see Chapter 9.

6. **Make your necessary adjustments in the dialog box:**

   - **Refine your selected area.** Select the Refine Edge option in the Tool Options. For more on the Refine Edge option, see Chapter 8.

   - **Apply the adjustment to your unselected area.** Select the Inverse option in the Tool Options.

FIGURE 11-25:
The Smart Brush enables you to paint on adjustments.

- **Modify your adjustment.** Double-click the Adjustment Layer pin on your image. The pin is annotated by a small, square, black-and-red gear icon. After you double-click the pin, the dialog box corresponding to your particular adjustment appears. For example, if you double-click the Shoebox photo adjustment (under Photographic), you access the Hue/Saturation dialog box.

TIP

You can also right-click and choose Change Adjustment Settings. Or you can choose Delete Adjustment and Hide Selection from the same menu.

7. **Click OK.**

8. **After you finish, simply deselect your selection by choosing Select ⇨ Deselect.**

TIP

You can add multiple Smart Brush adjustments. After you apply one effect, reset the Smart Brush tool and apply additional adjustments.

Follow these steps to work with the Detail Smart Brush tool:

1. **In Expert mode, select the Detail Smart Brush tool in the toolbar.**

   This tool shares the flyout menu with the Smart Brush tool. The tool icon looks like an art paintbrush. You can also press F, or Shift+F, if the Smart Brush tool is visible.

2. **Select your desired adjustment category and then your particular preset adjustment from the Preset Picker drop-down list in the Tool Options.**

3. **Choose a brush tip from the Brush Preset Picker drop-down list. Also choose your desired brush size.**

   Feel free to change your brush tip and size as needed for your desired effect. You can also choose other brush preset libraries from the Brush drop-down list in the Brush tip preset menu. For more on working with brushes, see Chapter 13.

   Several of the Special Effect adjustments are shown in Figure 11-26.

4. **Paint an adjustment on the desired portion of your image.**

   A new adjustment layer is created automatically with your first paint stroke, along with an accompanying layer mask. For details on adjustment layers and layer masks, see Chapter 9.

5. **Follow Steps 5 through 8 in the preceding list for the Smart Brush tool.**

FIGURE 11-26:
The Detail Smart Brush lets you paint on a variety of special effects.

4
Exploring Your Inner Artist

Use tools to draw and paint on existing photos. Or create new, blank documents and create your own drawings.

Apply different artistic effects by using many tools and customizing them for your own use.

Discover tips for applying filters and styles to create dazzling images.

Explore how to work with text — from setting headline type to creating special type effects.

IN THIS CHAPTER

» **Fooling with filters and exploring the Filter Gallery**

» **Fixing camera distortion and enhancing with effects**

» **Changing colors with blend modes**

» **Compositing images with Photomerge**

Chapter **12**

Playing with Filters, Effects, Styles, and More

After giving your images a makeover — edges cropped, color corrected, flaws repaired, focus sharpened — you may want to get them all gussied up for a night out on the town. You can do just that with filters, effects, layer styles, and blend modes. These features enable you to add that touch of emphasis, drama, whimsy, or just plain goofy fun. We're the first to admit that often the simplest art (and that includes photographs) is the best. That gorgeous landscape or the portrait that perfectly captures the expression on a child's happy face is something you may want to leave unembellished. But for the times when a little artistic experimentation is in order, turn to this chapter as your guide.

Having Fun with Filters

Filters have been around since the early days of digital imaging, when Photoshop was just a little bitty program. *Filters,* also dubbed *plug-ins* because they can be installed or removed independently, change the look of your image in a variety of ways, as shown in Figure 12-1. They can correct less-than-perfect images by making them appear sharper or by covering up flaws, as we describe in Chapter 11.

Or they can enhance your images by making them appear as though they're painted, tiled, photocopied, or lit by spotlights. The following sections give you the basics on how to apply a filter, as well as a few filtering tips.

FIGURE 12-1:
Use filters to correct image imperfections or to completely transform images.

| Original | Unsharp Mask Filter | Cutout Filter |

TECHNICAL STUFF

You can't apply filters to images that are in Bitmap or Indexed Color mode. And some filters don't work on images in Grayscale mode. For a refresher on color modes, see Chapter 2.

Applying filters

You can apply a filter in three ways:

» **The Filter menu:** In either Expert or Quick mode, from the Filter menu, choose your desired filter category and then select a specific filter.

» **The Filters panel:** In Expert mode, open the panel by choosing Window ⇨ Filters or by clicking the Filters icon in the bottom right of the workspace. Choose your filter category from the drop-down list at the top of the panel. Click the thumbnail of your desired filter.

Filters have sliders, which appear for most filters when you click them. You can then adjust the various settings for that particular filter. Some filters also have an Advance Options button. Click to go to the dialog box with additional filter settings. Note that some filters, however, are still one-click filters (for example, Blur). Of these filters, some have an Apply More button, which does just that when clicked. Click the Revert button (the curved arrow icon) at the top of the panel to start back at square one.

>> **The Filter Gallery:** In either Expert or Quick mode, choose Filter ⇨ Filter Gallery to apply one or more filters in a flexible editing environment. The Filter Gallery is described in the section "Working in the Filter Gallery," later in this chapter.

WARNING

When you're using the Filter Gallery, make a backup copy of your image (or at least create a duplicate layer) before you apply filters. Filters change the pixels of an image permanently, and when you exit the Filter Gallery, the filters you apply can't be removed, except for using the Undo command or History panel. But when those options are exhausted, you're stuck with the image as is.

Corrective or destructive filters

Although there are no hard-and-fast rules, most digital-imaging folks classify filters into two basic categories:

>> **Corrective filters** usually fix some kind of image problem. They adjust color, improve focus, remove dust or artifacts, and so on. Don't get us wrong — pixels are still modified. It's just that the basic appearance of the image remains the same, albeit modified, we hope, for the better. Two of the most popular corrective filters, Sharpen and Blur, are covered in Chapter 11.

>> **Destructive filters** are used to create some kind of special effect. Pixels are also modified, but the image may look quite different from its original. These kinds of filters create effects, such as textures, brush strokes, mosaics, lights, and clouds. They can also distort an image with waves, spheres, and ripples.

One-step or multistep filters

All corrective and destructive filters are one or the other:

>> **One-step filters** have no options and no dialog boxes; select the filter and watch the magic happen.

>> **Multistep filters** act almost like mini-applications. When you choose a multistep filter, you specify options in a dialog box. The options vary widely depending on the filter, but most come equipped with at least one option to control the intensity of the filter. A multistep filter appears on the menu with an ellipsis following its name, indicating that a dialog box opens when you choose the command.

Fading a filter

Sometimes you don't want the full effect of a filter applied to your image. Fading a filter a bit softens the effect and can make it look less "computerish." Here's what you can do:

1. **Choose Layer ⇨ Duplicate Layer.**

   The Duplicate Layer dialog box appears.

2. **Click OK.**

3. **Apply your desired filter to the duplicate layer.**

   Applying your filter to a duplicate layer enables you to blend the filtered layer with the unfiltered and gives you much more control over the result (see Step 4). See the earlier "Applying filters" section for details.

4. **Use the blend modes and opacity settings located on the Layers panel to merge the filtered layer with the original unfiltered image.**

5. **(Optional) With the Eraser tool, selectively erase portions of your filtered image to enable the unfiltered image to show through.**

   For example, if you applied a Gaussian Blur filter to soften a harshly lit portrait, try erasing the blurred portion that covers the subject's eyes to let the unblurred eyes of the layer below show through. The sharply focused eyes provide a natural focal point.

Instead of erasing, you can also apply a layer mask to selectively show and hide portions of your filtered image. For details on layer masks, see Chapter 9.

Selectively applying a filter

Up to this point in the book, we refer to applying filters to your *images.* But we use this word loosely. You don't necessarily have to apply filters to your entire image. You can apply filters to individual layers or even to selections. You can often get better effects when you apply a filter just to a portion of an image or layer. For example, you can blur a distracting background so that the person in your image gets due attention. Or, as shown in Figure 12-2, you can apply an Ocean Ripple or Wave filter to the ocean, leaving your surfer unfiltered to avoid that "overly Photoshopped" effect.

Exercising a little restraint in applying filters usually produces a more attractive image.

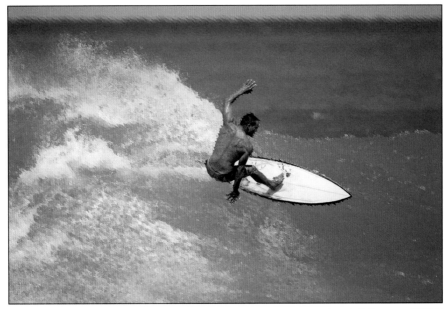

FIGURE 12-2:
Selectively
applying a filter
can prevent
an image from
looking overly
manipulated.

Working in the Filter Gallery

When you apply a filter, don't be surprised if you're presented with a gargantuan dialog box. This *editing window*, as it's officially called, is the Filter Gallery. You can also access it by choosing Filter ⇨ Filter Gallery. In the flexible Filter Gallery, you can apply multiple filters, tweak their order, and edit them *ad nauseam*.

Follow these steps to work in the Filter Gallery:

1. In either Expert or Quick mode, choose Filter ⇨ Filter Gallery.

The Filter Gallery editing window appears, as shown in Figure 12-3.

2. In the center of the editing window, click your desired filter category folder.

The folder expands and shows the filters in that category. A thumbnail displays each filter's effect.

3. Select your desired filter.

You get a large, dynamic preview of your image on the left side of the dialog box. To preview a different filter, just select it. Use the magnification controls to zoom in and out of the preview. To hide the Filter menu and get a larger preview box, click the arrow to the left of OK.

4. **Specify any settings associated with the filter.**

   The preview is updated accordingly.

5. **When you're happy with the results, click OK to apply the filter and close the editing window.**

6. **(Optional) If you want to apply another filter, click the New Effect Layer button at the bottom of the editing window.**

   This step duplicates the existing filter.

7. **Choose your desired new filter, which then replaces the duplicate in the Applied Filters area of the dialog box.**

   Each filter you apply is displayed in the lower-right area of the Filter Gallery dialog box.

   You can make these changes to your filter:

   - **Delete a filter.** Select it and click the Delete Effect Layer button.

   - **Edit a filter's settings.** Select the filter from the list and make any changes. Keep in mind that when you edit a filter's settings, the edit may affect the look of any subsequent filters you've applied.

   - **Rearrange the order of the applied filters.** Drag one of the filters above or below the other(s). Doing so changes the overall effect, however.

8. **When you're completely done, click OK to apply the filters and close the editing window.**

FIGURE 12-3:
Apply and edit multiple filters in the Filter Gallery.

© Gorilla/Fotolia Image #41932096

Distorting with the Liquify filter

The Liquify filter is really much more than a filter. It's a distortion that allows you to manipulate an image as though it were warm taffy. You can interactively twist, pull, twirl, pinch, and bloat parts of your image. You can even put your image on a diet, as we did in Figure 12-4. In fact, most ads and magazine covers feature models and celebrities whose photos have "visited" the Liquify filter once or twice. You can apply this distortion filter on the entire image, on a layer, or on a selection. This *überfilter* comes equipped with a mega–dialog box that has its own set of tools and options, as shown in Figure 12-4.

Tools   Options

Before Nip/Tuck   After Nip/Tuck

FIGURE 12-4: The Liquify filter enables you to interactively distort your image.

© Ratchapol Yinkresuk/Shutterstock Image #152063705

Follow these steps to turn your image into a melted Dalí-esque wannabe:

1. **In either Expert or Quick mode, choose Filter ⇨ Distort ⇨ Liquify.**

Your image appears in the preview area.

2. **Choose your distortion weapon of choice.**

You also have a number of tools to help zoom and navigate around your image window.

Here's a description of each tool to help you decide which to use. (The letter in parentheses is the keyboard shortcut.)

- **Warp (W):** This tool pushes pixels forward while you drag, creating a stretched effect. Use short strokes or long pushes.

- **Twirl Clockwise (R) and Twirl Counterclockwise (L):** These options rotate pixels either clockwise or counterclockwise. Place the cursor in one spot, hold down the mouse button, and watch the pixels under your brush rotate; or drag the cursor to create a moving twirl effect.

- **Pucker (P):** Click and hold or drag to pinch your pixels toward the center of the area covered by the brush. To reverse the pucker direction *(bloat),* press the Alt (Option on the Mac) key while you hold or drag.

- **Bloat (B):** Click and hold or drag to push pixels toward the edge of the brush area. To reverse the bloat direction *(pucker),* press the Alt (Option on the Mac) key while you hold or drag.

- **Shift Pixels (S):** This tool moves pixels to the left when you drag the tool straight up. Drag down to move pixels to the right. Drag clockwise to increase the size of the object being distorted. Drag counterclockwise to decrease the size. To reverse any direction, press the Alt (Option on the Mac) key while you hold or drag.

- **Reconstruct (E):** See Step 4 for an explanation of this tool's function.

- **Zoom (Z):** This tool, which works like the Zoom tool on the Elements Tools panel, zooms the focus in and out so that you can better see your distortions.

   You can zoom out by holding down the Alt (Option on the Mac) key when you press Z. You can also zoom by selecting a magnification percentage from the pop-up menu in the lower-left corner of the dialog box.

- **Hand (H):** This tool works like the Hand tool on the Elements Tools panel. Drag with the Hand tool to move the image around the preview window.

3. **Specify your options in the Tool Options:**

   - **Brush Size:** Drag the pop-up slider or enter a value from 1 to 15,000 pixels to specify the width of your brush.

   - **Brush Pressure:** Drag the pop-up slider or enter a value from 1 to 100 to change the pressure. The higher the pressure, the faster the distortion effect is applied.

   - **Stylus Pressure:** If you're lucky enough to have a graphics tablet and stylus, click this option to select the pressure of your stylus.

4. **(Optional) If you get a little carried away, select the Reconstruct tool and then hold down or drag the mouse on the distorted portion of the image that you want to reverse or reconstruct.**

   Reconstructing enables you to undo portions of your distorted image back to a less distorted or original state. (The reconstruction occurs faster at the center of the brush's diameter.) To partially reconstruct your image, set a low brush pressure and watch closely while your mouse drags across the distorted areas.

5. **Click OK to apply the distortions and close the dialog box.**

   If you mucked things up and want to start again, click the Revert button to get your original, unaltered image back. This action also resets the tools to their previous settings.

Correcting Camera Distortion

If you've ever tried to capture a looming skyscraper or cathedral in the lens of your camera, you know that it often involves tilting your camera and putting your neck in an unnatural position. And then, after all that, what you end up with is a distorted view of what was an impressive building in real life, as shown with the before image on the left in Figure 12-5. Fortunately, that's not a problem with Elements. The Correct Camera Distortion filter fixes the distorted perspective created by both vertical and horizontal tilting of the camera. As a bonus, this filter also corrects other kinds of distortions caused by lens snafus.

FIGURE 12-5:
The Correct Camera Distortion filter fixes distortions caused by camera tilt and lens flaws.

© Bernd Wittelsback/Getty Images Image #471177309

Here's how to fix it all:

1. **In either Expert or Quick mode, choose Filter ⇨ Correct Camera Distortion.**

2. **In the Correct Camera Distortion dialog box that appears, select the Preview option.**

3. **Specify your correction options:**

   - **Remove Distortion:** Corrects *lens barrel,* which causes your images to appear spherized or bloated. This distortion can occur when you're using wide-angle lenses. It also corrects *pincushion* distortion, which creates images that appear to be pinched in at the center, a flaw that's found when using telephoto or zoom lenses. Move the slider while keeping an eye on the preview. Use the handy grid as your guide for proper alignment.

   - **Vignette Amount:** Adjusts the amount of lightening or darkening around the edges of your photo that you can get sometimes from incorrect lens shading. Change the width of the adjustment by specifying a midpoint value. A lower midpoint value affects more of the image. Then move the Amount slider while viewing the preview.

- **Vertical Perspective:** Corrects the distorted perspective created by tilting the camera up or down. Again, use the grid to assist in your correction. We used the vertical perspective to correct Westminster Abbey, as shown in Figure 12-5. It was a nice shot as is, but it could use a little tweaking.

- **Horizontal Perspective:** Also corrects the distorted perspective. Use the grid to make horizontal lines (real and implied) in your image parallel. For better results, set the angle of movement under the Angle option.

- **Angle:** Enables you to rotate the image to compensate for tilting the camera. You may also need to tweak the angle slightly after correcting the vertical or horizontal perspective.

- **Edge Extension Scale:** When you correct the perspective on your image, you may be left with blank areas on your canvas. You can scale your image up or down to crop into the image and eliminate these holes. Scaling up results in interpolating your image up to its original pixel dimensions. Basically, *interpolation* means Elements analyzes the colors of the original pixels in your image and creates new ones, which are then added to the existing ones. This often results in less than optimum quality. Therefore, if you do this, be sure to start with an image that has a high-enough pixel dimension, or *resolution,* to avoid severe degradation. For more on resolution, see Chapter 2.

- **Show Grid:** Shows and hides the grid, as needed. You can also choose the color of your grid lines by clicking on the Color option.

- **Zoom Tool:** Zooms in and out for your desired view. You can also use plus (+) and minus (–) icons and the Magnification pop-up menu in the bottom-left corner of the window.

- **Hand Tool:** Moves you around the image window when you're zoomed in.

4. **Click OK to apply the correction and close the dialog box.**

Exploring Elements' Unique Filters

Elements has a set of its very own filters. Prior to Elements 11, all the filters were hand-me-downs from Photoshop. You can find the three unique filters under the Filter ⇨ Sketch submenu. To really get a feel for the cool effects these filters can create, we invite you to open a couple of your favorite images and play with the various presets and settings.

Here are the general steps to apply any of these filters:

1. **In either Expert or Quick mode, choose Filter ⇨ Sketch ⇨ *Your Specific Filter.***

   For example, if you want to use the Comic filter, choose Filter ⇨ Sketch ⇨ Comic.

2. **In the filter dialog box, choose from four presets.**

3. **Adjust any default settings.**

   You can find details about each filter's settings in the following sections outlining each filter.

TIP

   If you want to reset your sliders back to the default values for the preset, hold down the Alt (Option on the Mac) key, and the Cancel button in the dialog box changes to a Reset button.

4. **Adjust your view as needed by using the following controls:**

   - **Zoom:** Zoom in and out for your desired view. You can also use the 1:1 view (recommended) or Fit in Window view.

   - **Hand:** Moves you around the image window when you're zoomed in.

5. **Click OK to apply the filter and close the dialog box.**

Creating a comic

The Comic filter takes your image and creates an effect that mimics a hand-drawn comic book illustration. In the Comic filter dialog box, you can choose from four presets, as shown in Figure 12-6:

>> **Comic:** The default setting creates a basic comic book illustrative effect.

>> **Grayscale:** Like comic, but converts all colors to grayscale.

>> **Sunny Day:** Makes a high contrast, vivid effect.

>> **Old Print:** Creates a more desaturated, old-newspaper effect.

Using the sliders, you can adjust the default settings for the Color and Outline areas of the filtered image:

>> **Soften:** Creates rounder or rougher areas of colors.

>> **Shades:** A higher value adds more tonal levels.

FIGURE 12-6: The Comic filter turns a photo into an illustration.

>> **Steepness:** A higher value makes the colored areas more defined and contrasty.

>> **Vibrance:** Brightens the overall color of the image.

>> **Thickness:** Affects the thickness and blackness of the outlined strokes.

>> **Smoothness:** Fine-tunes your edges and enhances the overall filter effect.

Getting graphic

The Graphic Novel filter might take a bit of experimentation to create the effect you want — at least it did for us. But after you get your settings established, the look is pretty fun and the result is like an illustration sketched for a graphic novel. *Note:* All the colors in your images convert to grayscale when you use this filter.

In the Graphic Novel filter dialog box, choose from four presets, as shown in Figure 12-7:

>> **Painted Gray:** Creates an effect with a lot of midtone grays

>> **Fine Detail:** Results in an image with more white areas and an emphasis on retaining detail

>> **Hard Edges:** Like Fine Detail, but the overall look is more contrasty and the edges are more "sketchy" and less finely rendered

>> **Twisted Plot:** Creates a harsher effect with more dark areas

FIGURE 12-7:
Create an image worthy of a graphic novel.

Then, using the sliders, you can adjust the default settings for the filtered image:

>> **Darkness:** A higher value creates more areas of lightness.

>> **Clean Look:** A higher value makes smoother, more refined strokes.

>> **Contrast:** The higher the value, the more contrasty — and, overall, darker — an image appears. A lower value produces a lower-contrast, light-gray image.

>> **Thickness:** Affects the thickness and blackness of the outlined strokes. A higher value produces a "goopier" stroke appearance.

>> **Smoothness:** Fine-tunes your edges and enhances the overall filter effect.

Using the Pen and Ink filter

The Pen and Ink filter creates an effect that looks like a hand-drawn pen-and-ink sketch.

In the Pen and Ink filter dialog box, choose from four presets, as shown in Figure 12-8. Each preset colors the image blue, purple, gray, or green, respectively.

FIGURE 12-8:
Create a cartoon-like image with the Pen and Ink filter.

Then you can adjust the default setting of the sliders for the various settings for the Pen and Ink areas of the filtered image:

>> **Detail:** A higher value creates finer, crisper edges.

>> **Width:** A higher value creates thicker, goopier strokes, and a lower value creates crisper strokes.

>> **Darkness:** A higher value creates more areas of darkness.

>> **Contrast:** The higher the value, the more contrasty the image and the more dark ink strokes are applied.

>> **Hue:** Adjust the slider to select your desired color along the color ramp.

>> **Contrast:** A higher value adds more contrast, darkness, and colored areas.

>> **Fill:** Fills the image with more areas of color and less white.

Dressing Up with Photo and Text Effects

In addition to the multitude of filters at your disposal, Elements provides a lot of effects that you can apply to enhance your photos, such as the Fluorescent Chalk effect we applied in Figure 12-9. *Note:* Some effects automatically create a duplicate of the selected layer, whereas other effects can work only on flattened images. (See Chapter 9 for details on layers.)

NEW

Elements 2022 has added some new artistic effects that mimic art styles such as Post Impressionistic and Traditional Oil.

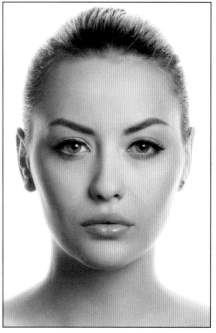

FIGURE 12-9:
Enhance your images by adding effects.

© Anton Zabielskyi/Shutterstock Image #30450358

REMEMBER

Unlike with filters, you can't preview how an effect will look on your image or type, nor do you have any options to specify.

Here are the steps to follow to apply an effect:

1. **In Expert mode, select your desired image layer in the Layers panel.**

Or, if you're applying the effect to just a selection, make the selection before applying the effect.

2. **Choose Window ⇨ Effects or click the Effects icon in the bottom right of the workspace.**

3. **Under the Classic tab, choose your desired category of effects from the drop-down list at the top of the panel.**

- **Faded Photo, Monotone Color, and Vintage:** This group of effects makes your image fade from color to grayscale, appear as a single color, or look like an old pencil sketch or a photo on old paper.

CHAPTER 12 **Playing with Filters, Effects, Styles, and More** **303**

- **Glow:** This group adds a soft focus, a white glow, or both to your images.

- **Painting:** Makes your images look like paintings or chalk illustrations.

- **Panels:** These effects divide your image into paneled sections.

- **Seasons:** Includes effects to make your image appear snowy, rainy, sunny (bright and yellow), or wintery (white and overexposed).

- **Textures:** Gives your images a lizard skin or rubber stamped appearance.

Elements 2022 has added some new artistic effects that mimic art styles such as Post Impressionistic and Traditional Oil. You can find these under the Artistic tab.

4. **On the Effects panel, click your desired effect or drag the effect onto the image.**

   You can view your styles and effects as just thumbnails or as thumbnails with the name of the style or effect. Click the down-pointing arrow in the upper-right corner of the panel to access the menu commands.

Quick mode sports its very own Effects panel. Be sure to check it out — you'll find effects not found in Expert mode, such as Toy Camera and Cross Process. Click the Effects icon in the bottom-right corner of the workspace. To apply an effect, double-click it or drag it onto your image.

You may also want to check out the interesting effects found in Guided mode. Guided mode is nicely organized into categories of effects with corresponding interactive thumbnail images.

One of the best edits is Double Exposure under Fun Edits, as shown in Figure 12-10. All the effects in Guided mode are very user friendly (hence, the name). Simply click your desired effect and follow the detailed steps delineated in the panel on the right of the workspace.

© anneberg/Shutterstock Image #329376446

FIGURE 12-10:
The Double Exposure edit enables you to creatively merge two photos.

TIP

You can also apply an effect to type. Select your type layer and follow Steps 2 through 4 in the preceding list. A dialog box alerts you that the type layer must be simplified before the effect can be applied. Simplifying that layer, of course, means you lose the ability to edit the text. Chapter 14 covers working with type in detail.

Adding Shadows, Glows, and More

Styles, also known as Layer Styles, go hand in hand with filters and photo effects. Also designed to enhance your image and type layers, styles range from simple shadows and bevels to the more complex styles, such as buttons and patterns.

REMEMBER

The wonderful thing about styles is that they're completely nondestructive. Unlike filters, styles don't change your pixel data. You can edit them or even delete them if you're unhappy with the results.

Here are some important facts about styles:

>> **Styles can be applied only to layers.** If your image is just a background, convert it to a layer first.

>> **Styles are dynamically linked to the contents of a layer.** If you move or edit the contents of the layers, the results are updated.

>> **When you apply a style to a layer, an fx symbol appears next to the layer's name on the Layers panel.** Double-click the fx icon to bring up the Style Settings dialog box and perform any editing that's necessary to get the look you want.

Applying styles

Styles are stored in a few different libraries. You can add shadows, glows, beveled and embossed edges, and more complex styles, such as neon, plastic, chrome, and various other image effects. Figure 12-11 shows a sampling of styles.

Here are the steps to apply a style and a description of each style library:

1. **Select your desired image, shape, or type layer in the Layers panel.**

   You can apply styles to type layers, and the type layer doesn't need to be simplified.

Drop Shadow	Inner Shadow	Bevel

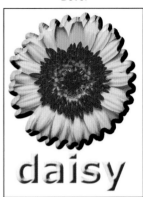

FIGURE 12-11:
Add dimension by applying shadows and bevels to your object or type.

2. **Choose Window ⇨ Styles or click the Styles icon in the bottom-right corner of the workspace.**

3. **Select your desired library of styles from the drop-down list at the top of the panel:**

   - **Bevels:** Bevels add a three-dimensional edge on the outside or inside edges of the contents of a layer, giving the element some dimension. Emboss styles make elements appear as though they're raised off or punched into the page. You can change the appearance of these styles, depending on the type of bevel chosen. Adjust parameters, such as the lighting angle, distance (how close the shadow is to the layer contents), size, bevel direction, and opacity.

   - **Drop and Inner Shadows:** Add a soft drop or an inner shadow to a layer. Choose from the garden-variety shadow or one that includes noise, neon, or outlines. You can adjust the lighting angle, distance, size, and opacity as desired.

   - **Outer and Inner Glows:** Add a soft halo that appears on the outside or inside edges of your layer contents. Adjust the appearance of the glow by changing the lighting angle, size, and opacity of the glow.

   - **Strokes:** Add a stroke of varying width (size), opacity, and color to your selection or layer. You can position the stroke on the inside, center, or outside of your selection marquee.

   - **Visibility:** Click Show, Hide, or Ghosted to display, hide, or partially show the layer contents. The layer style remains fully displayed.

- **Complex and others:** The remaining layer styles are a cornucopia of different effects ranging from simple Glass Buttons to the more exotic effects, such as Groovy and Rose Impressions (under Complex). You can customize all these layer styles to a certain extent by adjusting the various settings, which are similar to those for other styles in this list.

4. **On the Styles panel, click your desired effect or drag the effect onto the image.**

   The style, with its default settings, is applied to the layer. Styles are cumulative. You can apply multiple styles — specifically, one style from each library — to a single layer.

Working with styles

Here are a few last tips for working with styles:

>> **Edit the style's settings.** Do one of the following: Double-click the fx icon on the Layers panel; choose Layer Layer Style Style Settings; or click the gear icon located just below the Styles tab.

   Not all styles are editable. Editing is limited to drop shadows, glows, bevels, and strokes only.

REMEMBER

>> **Delete a layer style or styles.** Choose Layer ➪ Layer Style ➪ Clear Layer Style, or drag the fx icon on the Layers panel to the Trash icon.

>> **Copy and paste layer styles onto other layers.** Select the layer containing the layer style and choose Layer ➪ Layer Style ➪ Copy Layer Style. Select the layer(s) on which you want to apply the effect and choose Layer ➪ Layer Style ➪ Paste Layer Style. If it's easier, you can also just drag and drop an effect from one layer to another while holding down the Alt (Option on the Mac) key.

>> **Hide or show layer styles.** Choose Layer ➪ Layer Style ➪ Hide All Effects or Show All Effects.

>> **Scale a layer style.** Choose Layer ➪ Layer Style ➪ Scale Effects. Select the Preview option and enter a value between 1 and 1,000 percent. This action allows you to scale the style without scaling the element.

TIP

If by chance you apply a layer style and nothing seems to happen, choose **Layer** ➪ **Layer Style** ➪ **Show All Effects.**

Using the Graphics panel

If you're looking for an interesting graphic, frame, background, shape, or text to go along with your photographic composition, don't bother with searching and downloading a stock image. Look no further than the Graphics panel (shown in Figure 12-12). This panel is a cinch to use. Here's how:

1. **In Expert mode, choose Window ⇨ Graphics or click the Graphics icon in the bottom right of the workspace.**

2. **Choose your desired category of graphics from the left drop-down list at the top of the panel.**

   For example, choose by color, event, seasons, and so on. Depending on your selection, choose a more specific category from the right drop-down list. For example, if you choose Event, you may choose Birthday or Wedding.

3. **Choose your desired type of art — Backgrounds, Frames, Graphics, Shapes, or Text — from the lower-left drop-down list.**

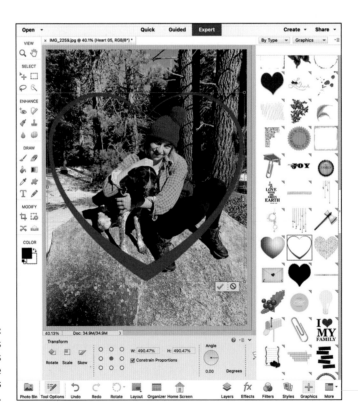

FIGURE 12-12: The Graphics panel provides an abundance of backgrounds and frames.

4. **On the Graphics panel, click your desired effect or drag the effect onto the image.**

   Be sure to convert your image into a layer before you select a Background graphic. Otherwise, the Background graphic will essentially replace your image.

   If you have a layered file and you choose Frame, you'll get a message in the frame to "Click here to add photo or drag photo here." If your image is not a layer, Elements will automatically fill the frame opening with your image.

5. **In your Layers panel, select your graphic layer(s) and choose Image ⇨ Transform ⇨ Free Transform to scale and rotate your graphic.**

The previous version of Elements added more than 50 new backgrounds and frames. The newest ones are easy to find. They're at the top of the panel.

Mixing It Up with Blend Modes

Elements sports a whopping 25 blend modes. *Blend modes* affect how colors interact between layers as well as how colors interact when you apply paint to a layer. Not only do blend modes create interesting effects, but you can also easily apply, edit, or remove blend modes without touching your image pixels.

The various blend modes are located on a drop-down list at the top of your Layers panel in Expert mode. The best way to get a feel for the effect of blend modes is not to memorize the descriptions we give you in the following sections. Instead, grab an image with some layers and apply each of the blend modes to one or more of the layers to see what happens. The exact result varies, depending on the colors in your image layers.

General blend modes

The Normal blend mode needs no introduction. It's the one you probably use the most. Dissolve is the next one on the list and, ironically, is probably the one you use the least.

Figure 12-13 shows both blend modes:

» **Normal:** The default mode displays each pixel unadjusted. You can't see the underlying layer at all with the Normal blend mode.

» **Dissolve:** This mode can be seen only on a layer with an opacity setting of less than 100 percent. It allows some pixels from lower layers, which are randomized, to show through the target (selected) layer.

Normal	Dissolve

FIGURE 12-13:
The Dissolve blend mode allows pixels from one layer to peek randomly through another.

© Maria teijeiro/Getty Images Image #200364729-001, kwanchai.c/Shutterstock Image #180304241

Darken blend modes

These blend modes produce effects that darken your image in various ways, as shown in Figure 12-14:

- » **Darken:** Turns lighter pixels transparent if the pixels on the target layer are lighter than those below. If the pixels are darker, they're unchanged.

- » **Multiply:** Burns the target layer onto the layers underneath, thereby darkening all colors where they mix. When you're painting with the Brush or Pencil tool, each stroke creates a darker color, as though you're drawing with markers.

- » **Color Burn:** Darkens the layers underneath the target layer and burns them with color, creating a contrast effect, like applying a dark dye to your image.

- » **Linear Burn:** Darkens the layers underneath the target layer by decreasing the brightness. This effect is similar to Multiply but often makes parts of your image black.

- » **Darker Color:** When blending two layers, the darker color of the two colors is visible.

Lighten blend modes

The lighten blend modes are the opposite of the darken blend modes. All these blend modes create lightening effects on your image, as shown in Figure 12-15:

- » **Lighten:** Turns darker pixels transparent if the pixels on the target layer are darker than those below. If the pixels are lighter, they're unchanged. This effect is the opposite of Darken.

- » **Screen:** Lightens the target layer where it mixes with the layers underneath. This effect is the opposite of Multiply.

Darken

Multiply

Color Burn

Linear Burn

Darker Color

FIGURE 12-14: These blend modes darken your image layers.

>> **Color Dodge:** Lightens the pixels in the layers underneath the target layer and infuses them with colors from the top layer. This effect is similar to applying bleach to your image.

>> **Linear Dodge (Add):** Lightens the layers underneath the target layer by increasing the brightness. This effect is similar to Screen but often makes parts of your image white.

>> **Lighter Color:** When blending two layers, the lighter color of the two colors is visible.

Lighten	Screen

Color Dodge | Linear Dodge

Lighter Color

FIGURE 12-15:
These blend modes lighten your image layers.

Lighting blend modes

This group of blend modes plays with the lighting in your layers, as shown in Figure 12-16:

>> **Overlay:** Overlay multiplies the dark pixels in the target layer and screens the light pixels in the underlying layers. It also enhances the contrast and saturation of colors.

>> **Soft Light:** This mode darkens the dark (greater than 50-percent gray) pixels and lightens the light (less than 50-percent gray) pixels. The effect is like shining a soft spotlight on the image.

>> **Hard Light:** This mode multiplies the dark (greater than 50-percent gray) pixels and screens the light (less than 50-percent gray) pixels. The effect is similar to shining a bright, hard spotlight on the image.

>> **Vivid Light:** If the pixels on the top layer are darker than 50-percent gray, this mode darkens the colors by increasing the contrast. If the pixels on the top layer are lighter than 50-percent gray, the mode lightens the colors by decreasing the contrast.

>> **Linear Light:** If the pixels on the top layer are darker than 50-percent gray, the mode darkens the colors by decreasing the brightness. If the pixels on the top layer are lighter than 50-percent gray, the mode lightens the colors by increasing the brightness.

>> **Pin Light:** If the pixels on the top layer are darker than 50-percent gray, the mode replaces pixels darker than those on the top layer and doesn't change lighter pixels. If the pixels on the top layer are lighter than 50-percent gray, the mode replaces the pixels lighter than those on the top layer and doesn't change pixels that are darker. The mode is usually reserved for special effects.

>> **Hard Mix:** This mode is similar to Vivid Light but reduces the colors to a total of eight: cyan, magenta, yellow, black, red, green, blue, and white. This mode creates a posterized effect.

Inverter blend modes

The inverter blend modes invert your colors and tend to produce some radical effects, as shown in Figure 12-17:

>> **Difference:** Produces a negative effect according to the brightness values on the top layers. If the pixels on the top layer are black, no change occurs in the underlying layers. If the pixels on the top layer are white, the mode inverts the colors of the underlying layers.

>> **Exclusion:** Like Difference, but with less contrast and saturation. If the pixels on the top layer are black, no change occurs in the underlying layers. If the pixels on the top layer are white, this mode inverts the colors of the underlying layers. Medium colors blend to create shades of gray.

FIGURE 12-16: Some blend modes adjust the lighting between your image layers.

© Maria teijeiro/Getty Images Image #200364729-001, kwanchai.c/Shutterstock Image #180304241

Difference

Exclusion

FIGURE 12-17:
Difference and Exclusion blend modes invert colors.

HSL blend modes

These blend modes use the HSL (hue, saturation, lightness) color model to mix colors, as shown in Figure 12-18:

» **Hue:** Blends the *luminance* (brightness) and *saturation* (intensity of the color) of the underlying layers with the *hue* (color) of the top layer.

Hue

Saturation

Color

Luminosity

FIGURE 12-18:
Some blend modes mix colors based on the actual hue, richness, and brightness of color.

>> **Saturation:** Blends the luminance and hue of the underlying layers with the saturation of the top layer.

>> **Color:** Blends the luminance of the underlying layers with the saturation and hue of the top layer. This mode enables you to paint color while preserving the shadows, highlights, and details of the underlying layers.

>> **Luminosity:** The opposite of Color, this mode blends the hue and saturation of the underlying layers with the luminance of the top layer. This mode also preserves the shadows, highlights, and details from the top layer and mixes them with the colors of the underlying layers.

Using Photomerge

The awesome Photomerge features help you to create fabulous composites from multiple images. Whether it's creating the perfect shot of a group of friends or of your favorite vacation spot (without the passing cars and people), the Photomerge feature is the go-to tool to get it done. The following sections tell you how the Photomerge commands help to create the special type of composite image you need.

REMEMBER

All Photomerge commands have been migrated over to Guided mode only.

Photomerge Panorama

The Photomerge Panorama command enables you to combine multiple images into a single panoramic image. From skylines to mountain ranges, you can take several overlapping shots and stitch them together into one.

TIP

The following tips can help you start with good source files that will help you successfully merge photos into a panorama:

>> Make sure that when you shoot your photos, you overlap your individual images by 15 to 40 percent, but no more than 50 percent.

>> Avoid using distortion lenses (such as fish-eye) as well as your camera's zoom setting. 50mm is a good focal length to use for panoramas.

>> Try to keep the same exposure settings for even lighting.

>> Try to stay in the same position and keep your camera at the same level for each photo. If possible, using a tripod and moving both the tripod and camera along a level surface, taking the photos from the same distance and angle, is

the best approach. However, if conditions don't allow for this, using a tripod and just rotating the head is the next best method. Be aware, however, that it can be harder to keep the lighting even, depending on the angle of your light source relative to the camera. You can also run into perspective-distortion issues with your shots.

Follow these steps to create a Photomerge Panorama image:

1. **Select your desired photos in the Photo Bin.**

2. **In Guided mode, click the Photomerge tab at the top of the Guided window. Choose the Photomerge Panorama option.**

   The Photomerge Panorama window opens, as shown on Figure 12-19.

3. **Choose your desired mode under Panorama Settings.**

   Here's a brief description of each mode:

   - **Auto Panorama:** Elements analyzes your images.

   - **Perspective:** If you shot your images with perspective or at extreme angles, this is your mode. Try this mode if you shot your images with a tripod and rotating head.

   - **Cylindrical:** If you shot your images with a wide-angle lens or you have those 360-degree, full-panoramic shots, this is a good mode.

   - **Spherical:** This projection method aligns images by rotating, positioning, and uniformly scaling each image. It may be the best choice for true panoramas, but you can also find it useful for stitching images together using common features.

   - **Collage:** This mode is handy when stitching together a 360-degree panorama, in which you have a wide field of view, both horizontally and vertically. Use this option for shots taken with a wide-angle lens.

   - **Reposition:** Elements doesn't take any distortion into account; it simply scans the images and positions them as best it can.

4. **Select from the following Settings:**

   - **Blend Images Together:** Corrects the color differences that can occur from blending images with different exposures

   - **Vignette Removal:** Corrects exposure problems caused by lens *vignetting* (when light at the edges of images is reduced and the edges are darkened)

   - **Geometric Distortion Correction:** Corrects lens problems such as radial distortions — for instance, barrel distortion (bulging out) and pincushion distortion (pinching in)

FIGURE 12-19:
Combine
multiple
images
into a single
panorama with
Photomerge
Panorama.

© FilippoBacci/Getty Images Image #514138599

- **Content Aware Fill Transparent Areas:** Intelligently fills in transparent areas that may be created during the stitching of the images by analyzing adjacent pixels

TIP

5. **Click Create Panorama.**

   Elements automatically assembles the source files to stitch together the composite panorama in a new file. Note that Elements may ask if you want to fill in the edges of the image. Click Yes.

6. **After the images are stitched, Elements will ask what you want to do next: Save the image or continue editing in either Quick or Expert mode. You can also click Done to return to the Photomerge Guided window.**

TIP

   Elements creates your merged image in layers. You'll also notice that a layer mask has been added to each layer to better blend your panoramic image. You can edit your layer masks or move your layers to fine-tune the stitching of the images. For more on layer masks, see Chapter 9.

   Note that Elements alerts you if it can't composite your source files. If that happens, you may have to composite your images manually by creating a large canvas and then dragging and dropping your images onto that canvas.

Photomerge Group Shot

We're sure you know how hard it is to get a group of people to all look great in one shot. Well, Photomerge Group Shot lets you take multiple group photos and merge the best of them to get that perfect shot.

Here are the steps to create a Photomerge Group Shot image:

1. **In Guided Mode, select two or more photos from your Photo Bin.**

2. **Click the Photomerge tab and choose the Photomerge Group Shot option.**

3. **Take your best overall group shot and drag it from the Photo Bin onto the Final window.**

4. **Select the Source window and click one of your photos in the Photo Bin to use as your source image.**

5. **With the Pencil tool, draw a line around the portions of the source photo you want to merge into your final photo, as shown in Figure 12-20.**

   You can choose to show your pencil strokes and/or show your regions, which will be highlighted with an overlay.

6. **Repeat Steps 4 and 5 with any remaining photos.**

   If your photos aren't aligned, you can use the Alignment Tool under the Advanced Options.

7. **With the Alignment Tool, click your source image and position the three target markers on three key locations. Do the same on the final image and choose similar locations.**

8. **Click the Align Photos button.**

   As with Photomerge Panorama, the more alike in framing, size, and so on that your source and final images are, the better the merged result.

TIP

9. **(Optional) If you see any noticeable seams on your final image around the copied area, click the Pixel Blending button to help smooth over those flaws.**

10. **When you're satisfied with the result, click Next.**

    Elements creates a new file.

11. **Choose to either save the image or continue editing in either Quick or Expert mode. You can also click Done to return to the Photomerge Guided window.**

PHOTOMERGE FACES

Photomerge Faces, a more-fun-than-useful tool, lets you blend features from multiple faces to get a kind of hybrid face. To create a hybrid human by using the Photomerge Faces feature, select two or more photos from your Photo Bin and choose the Photomerge Faces option in the Photomerge category in Guided mode. Use the Alignment and Pencil tools to choose how you want to merge the photos, similar to the steps described in the nearby section "Photomerge Group Shot."

FIGURE 12-20:
Get the perfect group shot from several images.

Photomerge Scene Cleaner

Photomerge Scene Cleaner sounds like a tool you might see in an episode of *CSI* to mop up a crime scene, but it isn't quite that gory. This member of the Photomerge commands family enables you to create the optimum image by allowing you to eliminate annoying distractions, such as cars, passersby, and so on.

TIP

To get the best source images for a clean scene, take multiple shots of your scene from the same angle and distance. It also works best when the elements you want to eliminate are moving.

Follow these steps to create a Photomerge Scene Cleaner composite:

1. **In Guided mode, select two or more photos from your Photo Bin.**

2. **Click the Photomerge tab and choose the Photomerge Scene Cleaner option.**

3. **Take your best overall shot of the scene and drag it from the Photo Bin onto the Final window.**

4. **Select the Source window and click one of your other photos in the Photo Bin to use as your source image.**

5. **With the Pencil tool, draw an outline around the area on the source photo that you want copied into the final photo.**

   We drew around the section by the back tire where the young man is walking in the final image, as shown in Figure 12-21 (see small image with yellow rectangle).

6. **Repeat Steps 4 and 5 with the remaining shots of the scene.**

   If your photos aren't aligned, you can use the Alignment tool under the Advanced Options.

7. **With the Alignment tool, click your source image and position the three target markers on three key locations. Do the same on the final image, choosing similar locations.**

8. **Click the Align Photos button in the Advanced Options section.**

   Again, as with the other Photomerge commands, the more similar your starting source images are (framing, angle), the better the merged result.

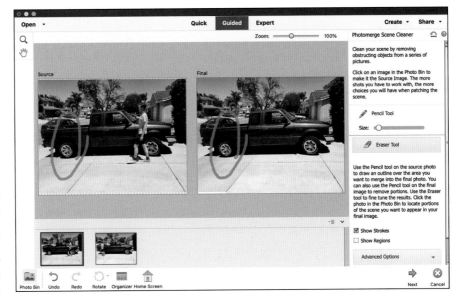

FIGURE 12-21: Eliminate annoying distractions with Photomerge Scene Cleaner to get the perfect shot.

9. **(Optional) If you see any noticeable seams on your final image around the copied area, click the Pixel Blending button to help smooth over those flaws.**

   Elements creates the cleaned image.

10. **Click Next and choose whether to save the image or continue editing in either Quick or Expert mode.**

    You can also click Done to return to the Photomerge Guided window.

Photomerge Exposure

Sometimes you need to capture a shot that poses an exposure challenge — your foreground and background require different exposure settings. This dilemma often occurs in shots that are backlit. For example, suppose you have a person in front of an indoor window in the day or someone in front of a lit nighttime cityscape. With Photomerge Exposure, you can take shots with two different exposure settings and let the command blend them together for the perfect shot.

You can shoot your initial images using *exposure bracketing* (shooting at consecutive exposure camera settings) or with a flash and then without. Elements can detect all these camera settings. Many cameras offer exposure bracketing as a menu option. Avoid shooting any of your bracketed images at a slow shutter speed or they will be blurry. If you don't have a fairly steady hand, we recommend that you use a tripod, if possible, to keep your shots aligned. The added stability helps the blending algorithm do its job. Also, if your camera supports a timer, use it. That way, you don't accidentally bump the camera when pressing the shutter button.

Here's how to use this great command:

1. **In Guided mode, select two or more photos from your Photo Bin.**

2. **Click the Photomerge tab and choose the Photomerge Exposure option.**

3. **Choose either Automatic or Manual mode.**

   If you've done a good job keeping your shots aligned, leave the mode on Automatic and go to Step 4.

   If you feel the need for even more control, click the Manual tab and go to Step 5.

4. Select an option in Automatic mode and then skip to Step 11:

- **Simple Blending:** Elements automatically blends the two images.

- **Smart Blending:** Access sliders to adjust the Highlights, Shadows, and Saturation settings for finer tuning of the resulting images.

If you muck things up, click the Reset button.

5. In Manual mode (as shown in Figure 12-22), choose your first shot from the Photo Bin and drag it to the Final window. If your other image isn't already the source image, select the Source window and click your image in the Photo Bin.

6. With the Pencil tool, draw over the well-exposed areas you want to retain in the source image.

As you draw, your final image shows the incorporation of those drawn areas, as shown in Figure 12-22.

7. If you mistakenly draw over something you don't want, grab the Eraser tool and erase the Pencil tool marks.

Choose the appropriate option to have your preview show strokes or regions.

8. Control the blending by dragging the Transparency slider.

Dragging to the right blends less of the source areas into the final image. Select the Edge Blending option to get an even better blend of the two images.

9. If your photos aren't aligning correctly, grab the Alignment tool under Advanced Options.

With the Alignment tool, click your source image and position the three target markers on three key locations.

Do the same on the final image, choosing similar locations.

10. Click the Align Photos button.

As with the other Photomerge commands, the more similar your starting source images are (framing, angle), the better the merged result.

11. Click Next and choose whether to save the image or continue editing in either Quick or Expert mode. You can also click Done to return to the Photomerge Guided window.

Elements creates a new, layered file. The blended image appears on Layer 1. The background is your starting final image. You can either flatten the layered file, which keeps the appearance of Layer 1, or you can double-click your background to convert it to a layer and then delete it by dragging it to the Trash icon in the Layers panel.

FIGURE 12-22:
Combine images shot with two different exposures into a hero shot.

Photomerge Compose

Although there are several methods to select and extract portions of images in Elements, the Photomerge Compose feature enables you to more easily extract one image and composite it into another.

Here's how to extract an element from one image and composite it into another:

1. **In Guided mode, select two photos in the Photo Bin.**

   We chose the images of the kid eating ice cream and the beach, as shown in Figure 12-23.

2. **In any of the edit modes, choose Enhance ➪ Photomerge ➪ Photomerge Compose.**

3. **From the Photo Bin, drag the image from which you want to extract an element onto the canvas.**

4. **Choose a Selection tool:**

   - **Quick Select:** Brush over to select your desired element. This tool works exactly like the regular Quick Selection tool described in Chapter 8. Choose your selection mode — a new selection, or you can add or subtract from an existing selection. You can also adjust the size of the diameter of your brush.

© wundervisuals/Getty Images Image #467030453 and Alex_Rodionov Image #301316285

- **Outline Select:** Trace around your desired element. After your initial trace, release your mouse. A red overlay appears over the unselected areas. Add or subtract from the red overlay, and then adjust the size of the diameter of your brush as needed.

5. **Further refine your selection using the Refine Selection Brush tool.**

Click inside or outside of your selection to add or subtract from the selected area. In addition to the options found with the tools earlier, you can specify these additional settings:

- **Snap:** Use the slider to adjust your snap strength from 0 to 100%. *Snap* is the intensity of the pull.

- **Push:** Place your cursor inside the selection to increase your selection within the diameter of the outer circle of your cursor. It will snap to the edge of the element closest to the cursor. Place your cursor outside the selection to decrease your selection within the diameter of the outer circle.

- **Smooth:** If your selection border looks a little too jagged, use this option to smooth your selection edge.

6. **Click Advance Edge Refinement.**

You can choose to set the background — in other words, the unselected portion of your current image — to Source Image (which leaves your image as is) or have it fill with transparency, black, white, or a red overlay.

You can also access the Refine Edge feature, which is described in detail in Chapter 8.

7. **Click Next.**

Your extracted image appears on your second image, its new background.

8. **You can Move and Resize the extracted image by dragging within the bounding box or dragging on a corner of the bounding box, respectively.**

You can further refine your selection by using the Hide and Reveal tools to either add to, or delete from, your selection. You can adjust the size, opacity, and hardness of your brush to better fine-tune your extracted image.

9. Click Next.

10. Click the Auto Match Color Tone to have Elements try to blend your extracted image with the new background image.

You can make further adjustments by adjusting the Luminance, Contrast, Temperature, and Saturation sliders.

If you're not happy with the results, click the Reset button.

11. Click Next and choose whether to save the image or continue editing in either Quick or Expert mode. You can also Click Done to return to the Photomerge Guided window.

Your final extracted image is composited into your second image, as shown in Figure 12-24.

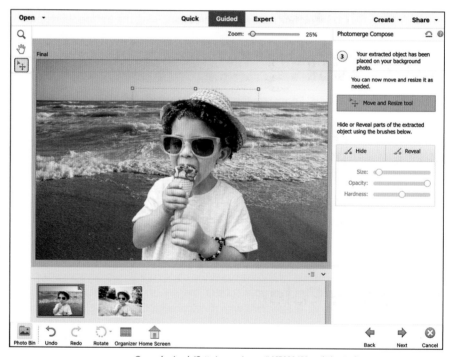

FIGURE 12-24:
Composite two images seamlessly with Photomerge Compose.

Chapter **13**

Drawing and Painting

lements is such a deluxe, full-service image-editing program that it doesn't stop at giving you tools to select, repair, organize, and share your images. It figures that you may need to add a swash of color, either freeform with a brush or pencil, or in the form of a geometric or organic shape. Don't worry: This drawing and painting business isn't just for those with innate artistic talent. In fact, Elements gives you plenty of preset brushes and shapes to choose from. If you can pick a tool and drag your mouse, you can draw and paint.

Choosing Color

Before you start drawing or painting, you may want to change your color to something other than the default color of black. If you read the earlier chapters in this book, you may have checked out the Elements Tools panel and noticed the two overlapping color swatches at the bottom of the panel. These two swatches represent two categories of color: *foreground* and *background.*

Here's a quick look at how they work with different tools:

>> **Foreground:** When you add type, paint with the Brush tool, or create a shape, you're using the foreground color.

>> **Background:** On the background layer of an image, when you use the Eraser tool, or when you increase the size of your canvas, you're revealing the background color.

>> **Foreground and background:** When you drag with the Gradient tool, as long as your gradient is set to the default, you're laying down a blend of color from the foreground to the background.

Elements gives you three ways to choose your foreground and background colors: the Color Picker, the color swatches, and the Eyedropper tool, which samples color in an image. In the following sections, we explore each one.

Working with the Color Picker

By default, Elements uses a black foreground color and a white background color. If you're experimenting with color and want to go back to the default colors, press the D key. If you want to swap between foreground and background colors, press the X key. If you want any color other than black and white, click your desired swatch (either foreground or background) at the bottom of the Tools panel. This action transports you to the Color Picker, as shown in Figure 13-1.

Here are the steps to choose your color via the Color Picker:

1. **Click either the foreground or background color swatch on the Tools panel.**

The Color Picker appears.

2. **Drag the color slider (the white double-arrow icon) or click the color bar to get close to the general color you desire.**

3. **Choose the exact color you want by clicking in the large square, or** *color field,* **on the left.**

The circle cursor targets your selected color. The two swatches in the upper-right corner of the dialog box represent your newly selected color and the original foreground or background color.

The numeric values on the right side of the dialog box also change according to the color you selected. If you happen to know the values of your desired color, you can enter them in the text boxes. RGB (red, green, blue) values are based on brightness levels from 0 (black) to 255 (white). You can also enter HSB (hue, saturation, brightness) values or the hexadecimal formula for web colors.

New color   Current color   HSB values

Color Picker (Foreground Color)

? Learn more about: Choosing Colors   new   OK

                                                          Cancel

                                              current

                                        ⊙ H: 0   °
                                        ○ S: 86   %
                                        ○ B: 84   %

                                        ○ R: 214
                                        ○ G: 30
                                        ○ B: 30

                                        # d61e1e

☐ Only Web Colors

FIGURE 13-1:
Choose your
desired color
from the Color
Picker.

Color field   Color slider   RGB values

Hexadecimal value

If a 3-D cube icon appears when choosing your color, it means your color is not web safe. Web-safe colors appear consistently in all browsers on all platforms. To get the closest web-safe color match, click the small swatch directly below the 3-D cube icon.

4. **When you're happy with your color, click OK.**

If you want to save your color for later use, do so by using the Color Swatches panel, described in the following section.

Dipping into the Color Swatches panel

Elements enables you to select a foreground or background color by selecting a color on the Color Swatches panel. The Color Swatches panel is a digital version of the artist's paint palette. In addition to preset colors, you can mix and store your own colors for use now and later. You can have palettes for certain types of projects or images. For example, you may want a palette of skin tones for retouching portraits. Choose Window ➪ Color Swatches to bring up the panel, as shown in Figure 13-2.

To grab a color from the Color Swatches panel, click the color swatch you want. By the way, it doesn't matter which tool you have. As soon as you move the tool over the panel, it temporarily converts to an eyedropper that samples the color and makes it your new foreground or background color.

TIP

Although the Color Swatches panel is a breeze to use, here are a few tips to help you along:

» **Change the background color.** Either first click the background swatch on the Tools panel or Ctrl-click (⌘ -click on the Mac) a swatch in the Color Swatches panel.

» **Use preset colors.** To load a particular preset swatch library, choose it from the drop-down list at the top of the Color Swatches panel. Elements offers libraries specific to web graphics, photo filters, and Windows and macOS systems.

» **Add a color to the Color Swatches panel.** Choose New Swatch from the panel menu. You can also simply click an empty portion of the panel. Name your swatch and click OK. Remember, it doesn't matter whether you created the color by using the Color Picker or by sampling with the Eyedropper tool — adding the color for later use is done the same way.

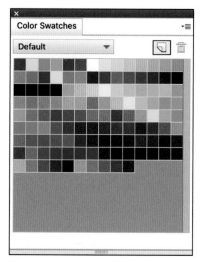

FIGURE 13-2:
Choose and store colors in the Color Swatches panel.

» **Save swatches.** Choose Save Swatches from the panel menu in the upper-right corner of the panel. We recommend saving the swatch library in the default Color Swatches folder in the Presets folder. If by chance this folder doesn't come up by default, just navigate to the Color Swatches folder by following this partial path: `Program Files\Adobe\Photoshop Elements 2022\Presets\Color Swatches` (Windows) or `Applications\ Adobe Photoshop Elements 2022/Support Files/Presets/color swatches` (Mac).

» **Save swatches for Exchange.** Choose this command from the panel menu to save your swatches for use in another Adobe program. Name the swatch set and save it in the same folder listed in the preceding bullet point.

» **Load swatches.** If you want to load a custom library created by you or someone else, choose Load Swatches from the panel menu. In the dialog box, select your desired library from the Color Swatches folder. The new library is added to your current library.

You can also work with swatches by using the Preset Manager. For more on the Preset Manager, see Chapter 3.

» **Delete swatches.** To delete a swatch, drag it to the Trash icon at the top of the panel or Alt-click (Option-click on the Mac) the swatch.

- » **Change the panel's appearance.** Click the panel menu in the upper-right corner to choose Small or Large Thumbnail (swatch squares) or Small or Large List (swatch squares with a name).

- » **Replace your current swatch library with a different library.** Choose Replace Swatches from the panel menu. Choose a library from the Color Swatches folder.

Sampling with the Eyedropper tool

Another way that Elements enables you to choose color is via the Eyedropper tool. The Eyedropper tool comes in handy when you want to sample an existing color in an image and use it for another element. For example, you may want your text to be the same color as the green background in the image shown in Figure 13-3. Grab the Eyedropper tool (or press I) and click a shade of green in the background. The tool samples the color and makes it your new foreground color. You can then create the type with your new foreground color.

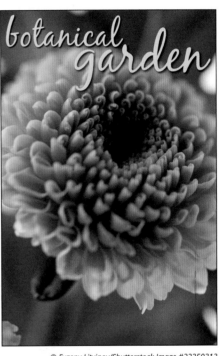

© Evgeny Litvinov/Shutterstock Image #22350313

FIGURE 13-3:
The Eyedropper tool enables you to sample color from your image to use with other elements, such as type.

REMEMBER

Here are a few things to remember when you're using the Eyedropper tool:

- » **Sample a new foreground or background color.** Obviously, you can select either the foreground or the background swatch on the Tools panel before you sample a color. But if the foreground color swatch is active, holding down the Alt (Option on the Mac) key samples a new background color, and vice versa.

- » **Choose a color from any open image.** If you have multiple images open, you can even sample a color from an image that you're not working on!

- **Choose your sample size in the Tool Options.** You can select the color of just the single pixel you click (Point Sample), or Elements can average the colors of the pixels in a 3-x-3- or 5-x-5-pixel area.

- **Specify web colors.** If you right-click your image to bring up the contextual menu, you have a hidden option: Copy Color as HTML. This option provides the web hexadecimal color formula for that sampled color and copies it to the Clipboard. You can then paste that formula into an HTML file or grab the Type tool and choose Edit ⇨ Paste to view the formula in your image.

- **Choose to sample All Layers or just the Current Layer.** If you have multiple layers in your image, you can choose to sample from all those layers or just your currently active layer.

- **Toggle between the Eyedropper and other tools.** Elements, multitasker that it is, enables you to temporarily access the Eyedropper tool when you're using the Brush, Pencil, Color Replacement, Gradient, Paint Bucket, Cookie Cutter, or Shape tool. Simply press the Alt (Option on the Mac) key to access the Eyedropper tool. Release the Alt (Option on the Mac) key to go back to your original tool.

Getting Artsy with the Pencil and Brush Tools

If you want to find out how to paint and draw with a color you've chosen, you've come to the right place. The Pencil and Brush tools give you the power to put your creative abilities to work, and the following sections show you how.

TIP

When you use these two tools, you benefit immensely from the use of a pressure-sensitive digital drawing tablet. The awkwardness of trying to draw or paint with a mouse or trackpad disappears and leaves you with tools that behave much closer to their analog ancestors.

Drawing with the Pencil tool

Drawing with the Pencil tool creates hard edges. You can't get the soft, feathery edges that you can with the Brush tool. In fact, the edges of a pencil stroke can't even be *anti-aliased.* (For more on anti-aliasing, see the following section.) Keep in mind that if you draw anything other than vertical or horizontal lines, your lines will have some jaggies when they're viewed up close. But hey, don't diss the Pencil just yet. Those hard-edged strokes can be perfect for web graphics. What's more, the Pencil tool can erase itself, and it's great for digital sketches, as shown in Figure 13-4.

Follow these steps to become familiar with the Pencil tool:

1. **Select the Pencil tool from the Tools panel.**

   You can also press the N key. By default, the Pencil tool's brush tip is the 1-pixel brush. Yes, even though the Pencil tip is hard-edged, we still refer to it as a brush. In the next few steps, you customize the brush by setting various options.

Illustration by Chris Blair

FIGURE 13-4:
You can use the Pencil tool for digital drawings.

2. **In the Options panel, click the arrow and select your desired brush from the Brush Preset Picker drop-down panel.**

3. **(Optional) To load another preset library, click the Brushes menu at the top of the panel.**

TIP

   You aren't limited to the standard old brushes. Check out the Assorted and Special Effects brushes found in the Brush drop-down list at the top of the Brush Preset Picker panel, as shown in Figure 13-5. You'll be surprised by the interesting brushes lurking on these panels. Use them to create stand-alone images or to enhance your photographic creations.

   Access the menu on the Brush Preset Picker panel to save, rename, or delete individual brushes and also save, load, and reset brush libraries. For more on these operations, see the following section.

4. **Choose your brush size, and optionally, if you want to change the size of that brush tip, drag the Size slider.**

5. **(Optional) If you want the background to show through your strokes, adjust the opacity by dragging the slider or entering an opacity percentage less than 100 percent.**

   The lower the percentage, the more the background images show through.

REMEMBER

   Your strokes must be on a separate layer above your images for you to be able to adjust the opacity and blend modes after you draw them. For more on layers, see Chapter 9.

6. **Select a blend mode.**

   Blend modes alter the way the color you're applying interacts with the color on your canvas. You can find more about blend modes in Chapter 12.

7. **(Optional) Select Auto Erase if you want to remove portions of your pencil strokes.**

For example, say that your foreground color is black and your background color is white, and you apply some black strokes. With Auto Erase enabled, you apply white if you drag back over the black strokes. If you drag over the white background, you apply black.

8. **Click and drag with the mouse to create your freeform lines.**

To draw straight lines, click at a starting point, release the mouse button, and then Shift-click at a second point.

If you like the organic look of a pencil sketch, be sure to check out the Partial Sketch feature under Fun Edits in Guided mode. This edit allows you to selectively brush in a hand-sketched effect on your photo.

Painting with the Brush tool

The Brush tool creates soft-edged strokes. How soft those strokes are depends on which brush you use. By default, even the hardest brush has a slightly soft edge because it's antialiased. *Anti-aliasing* creates a single row of partially filled pixels along the edges to produce the illusion of a smooth edge. You can also get even softer brushes, which use feathering. For details on feathering, see Chapter 8.

The Brush tool shares most of the options found in the Pencil tool, except that the Auto Erase feature isn't available. Here's the lowdown on the unique Brush options:

>> **Airbrush:** Click the Airbrush button in the Options panel to apply the Airbrush mode. In this mode, the longer you hold down the mouse button, the more paint the Brush pumps out and the wider the airbrush effect spreads.

>> **Tablet Settings:** If you're using a pressure-sensitive digital drawing tablet, check the settings you want the tablet to control, including size, scatter, opacity, roundness, and hue jitter. The harder you press with the stylus, the greater the effect of these options.

>> **Brush Settings:** These options, referred to as brush *dynamics*, change while you apply your stroke. See Figure 13-6 for an example of each one. These options include the following:

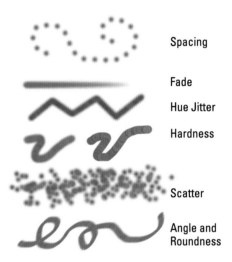

Spacing

Fade

Hue Jitter

Hardness

Scatter

Angle and Roundness

FIGURE 13-6:
Change brush options to create a custom brush.

- **Fade:** The lower the value, the more quickly the stroke fades. However, 0 creates no fade.

- **Hue Jitter:** Vary the stroke between the foreground and background colors. The higher the value, the more frequent the variation.

- **Scatter:** The higher the value, the higher the number of brush marks and the farther apart they are.

- **Spacing:** The higher the number, the more space between marks.

- **Hardness:** The higher the value, the harder the brush.

- **Roundness:** A setting of 100 percent is totally circular. The lower the percentage, the more elliptical your brush becomes.

- **Angle:** If you create an oval brush by adjusting the roundness, this option controls the angle of that oval brush stroke. It's so much easier to drag the points and the arrow on the diagram than to guesstimate values in the text boxes.

TIP

You can lock in these brush dynamics by selecting the Set This as a Default check box; this ensures that every brush you select adopts these settings.

As with the Pencil tool, you can load additional Brush libraries from the Brush drop-down list at the top of the Brush Preset Picker panel. Additional features for the Brush tool also appear in the menu on the Brush Preset Picker panel. Here's a quick description of each:

>> **Save Brush:** Allows you to save a custom brush as a preset. See the following section for details.

>> **Rename Brush:** Don't like your brush's moniker? Change it with this option.

>> **Delete Brush:** Don't like your entire brush? Eliminate it with this option.

>> **The display options:** Not a single command, but a set of commands that enable you to change the way your brush tips are displayed. The default view is Stroke Thumbnail, which displays the appearance of the stroke. These commands include Text Only, Small and Large Thumbnail, and Small and Large List.

>> **Reset Brushes:** Reverts your current brush library to the default.

>> **Save Brushes:** Saves custom brushes in a separate library.

>> **Load Brushes:** Loads a preset or custom brush library.

You can also manage brush-tip libraries by using the Preset Manager. See Chapter 3 for information on using the Preset Manager.

Using the Impressionist Brush

The Impressionist Brush is designed to paint over your photos in a way that makes them look like fine art paintings. You can set various options that change the style of the brush strokes.

Here's how to use this artistic brush:

1. **Select the Impressionist Brush from the Tools panel.**

    It looks like a brush with a curlicue next to it. You can also press B to cycle through the brushes.

2. **Set your brush options.**

    The Brushes presets (Size, Opacity, and Mode options) are identical to those found with the Brush tool, described in the section "Painting with the Brush tool," earlier in this chapter. You can also find some unique options on the Advanced drop-down panel in the Tool Options:

    - **Style:** This drop-down list contains various brush stroke styles, such as Dab and Tight Curl.

    - **Area:** Controls the size of your brush stroke. The larger the value, the larger the area covered.

- **Tolerance:** Controls how similar color pixels have to be before they're changed by the brush stroke.

3. **Drag on your image and paint with your brush strokes, as shown in Figure 13-7.**

   The best way to get a feel for what this tool does is to open your favorite image, grab the tool, and take it for a test drive.

TIP

For the remaining brush tool, the Color Replacement tool, see the section about replacing one color with another in Chapter 10.

FIGURE 13-7:
The Impressionist Brush turns your photo into a painting.

© monticello/Getty Images Image #452591071

Creating your own brush

If you customize any brush to the point that you've created your own special Franken-brush that you'd love to use again, feel free to save it as a preset that you can access in the future. To do so:

1. **Choose Save Brush from the panel menu on the Brush Preset Picker panel.**

2. **Name the brush and click OK.**

   Your new custom brush shows up at the bottom of the Brush Preset Picker drop-down panel.

There's one additional way to create a brush. Elements allows you to create a brush from all or part of your image. The image can be a photograph or something you've painted or drawn.

Here's how to create a brush from your image:

1. **Select part of your image with any of the selection tools.**

   If you want to use the entire image or entire layer, deselect everything.

   For more on selections, see Chapter 8.

2. **Choose Edit ➪ Define Brush or Edit ➪ Define Brush from Selection.**

   You see one command or the other, depending on what you do in Step 1.

3. **Name the brush and click OK.**

   The new brush shows up at the bottom of your Brush Preset Picker drop-down panel. ***Note:*** Your brush is only a grayscale version of your image. When you use the brush, it automatically applies the color you've selected as your foreground color, as shown in Figure 13-8.

FIGURE 13-8:
Create a custom brush from a portion of your image.

© TinnaPong/Shutterstock Image #302479208

Be sure to check out the Pattern Brush feature under Fun Edits in Guided mode. What's great about this edit is that when you check the Protect Subject option, your subject remains unscathed as you drag your brush freely around the photo, as shown in Figure 13-9.

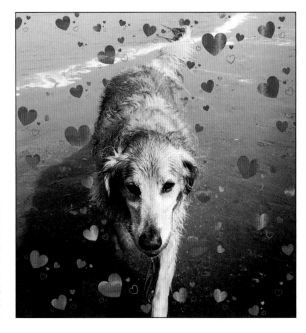

FIGURE 13-9: The Pattern Brush enables you to brush graphics onto your image while keeping your subject pattern free.

Filling and Outlining Selections

At times, you may want to create an element on your canvas that can't quite be created with a brush or pencil stroke. Maybe it's a perfect circle or a five-point star. If you have a selection, you can fill or stroke that selection to create that element, rather than draw or paint it on. The Fill command adds a color or a pattern to the entire selection, whereas the Stroke command applies the color to only the edge of the selection border.

Fill 'er up

You won't find a Fill tool on the Tools panel. Elements decided to avoid the over-populated panel and placed the Fill and Stroke commands on the Edit menu.

Here are the simple steps to fill a selection:

1. **Grab the selection tool of your choice and create your selection on a new layer.**

WARNING

Although you don't have to create a new layer to make a selection to fill, we recommend doing so. That way, if you don't like the filled selection, you can delete the layer, and your image or background below it remains safe. See Chapter 8 for more on selections and Chapter 9 for details on working with layers.

2. **Select either the foreground or background color and then choose a fill color.**

See the section "Choosing Color," earlier in this chapter, if you need a refresher.

3. **Choose Edit ⇨ Fill Selection.**

The Fill Layer dialog box, shown in Figure 13-10, appears.

TIP

If you want to bypass the Fill Layer dialog box (and the rest of these steps), you can use these handy keyboard shortcuts instead:

FIGURE 13-10:
Fill your selection or layer with color or a pattern.

- **To fill the selection with the foreground color,** press Alt+Backspace (Option+Delete on the Mac).

- **To fill the selection with the background color,** press Ctrl+Backspace (⌘ +Delete on the Mac).

4. **Choose your desired fill from the Use drop-down list.**

You can select whether to fill with the foreground or background color. You also can select Color, Pattern, Black, 50% Gray, or White. If you select Color, you're transported to the Color Picker. If you choose Pattern, you must then choose a pattern from the Custom Pattern drop-down panel. For more on patterns, see the section "Working with Patterns," later in this chapter.

If you don't have an active selection border in your image, the command says Fill Layer and your entire layer is filled with your color or pattern.

You can also fill your selection using the Content-Aware option, which will fill your selection with pixels sampled from content nearby.

5. **In the Blending area, specify whether to preserve transparency, which enables you to fill only the portions of the selection that contain pixels (the nontransparent areas).**

TIP

Although you can also choose a *blend mode* (how the fill color interacts with colors below it) and opacity percentage, we urge you not to adjust your blend mode and opacity in the Fill Layer dialog box. Make those adjustments on your layer later by using the Layers panel commands, which give you more flexibility for editing.

6. **Click OK.**

The color or pattern fills the selection.

Outlining with the Stroke command

Stroking a selection enables you to create colored outlines, or *borders*, of selections or layers. You can put this border inside, outside, or centered on the selection border. Here are the steps to stroke a selection:

1. **Choose a foreground color and create a selection.**

2. **Choose Edit ⇨ Stroke (Outline) Selection.**

The Stroke dialog box opens.

3. **Select your desired settings.**

Many settings are the same as those found in the Fill Layer dialog box, as we explain in the preceding section. Here's a brief rundown of the options that are unique to strokes:

- **Width:** Enter a width of 1 to 250 pixels for the stroke.

- **Location:** Specify how Elements should apply the stroke: outside the selection, inside the selection, or centered on the selection border.

4. **Click OK to apply the stroke.**

We gave a 30-pixel centered stroke to our selection, as shown in Figure 13-11.

FIGURE 13-11:
Stroke a selection to create a colored border.

Splashing on Color with the Paint Bucket Tool

The Paint Bucket tool is a longtime occupant of the Tools panel. This tool, whose icon looks just like a bucket, behaves like a combination of the Fill command and the Magic Wand tool. (See Chapter 8.) The Paint Bucket tool makes a selection based on similarly colored pixels and then immediately fills that selection with color or a pattern. Like the Magic Wand tool, this tool is most successful when you have a limited number of colors, as shown in Figure 13-12.

FIGURE 13-12: The Paint Bucket tool makes a selection and fills it at the same time.

To use the Paint Bucket tool, simply click inside the selection you want to fill. Before you click, however, specify your settings in the Tool options:

- » **Color:** Choose between Paint (a fill of the foreground color) or a Pattern fill.

- » **Pattern:** If you select Pattern, choose a preset pattern from the Pattern picker drop-down panel. For more details on patterns, see the section "Working with Patterns," later in this chapter.

- » **Opacity:** Adjust the opacity to make your fill more or less transparent.

- » **Tolerance:** Choose a tolerance level that specifies how similar in color a pixel must be before it's selected and then filled. The lower the value, the more similar the color must be. For more on tolerance, see the section on the Magic Wand in Chapter 8.

- » **Mode:** Select a blending mode to change how your fill color interacts with the color below it.

- » **All Layers:** This option selects and fills pixels within the selection in all layers that are within your tolerance level.

- » **Contiguous:** If selected, this option selects and fills only pixels that are touching within your selection. If the option is deselected, pixels are selected and filled wherever they lie within your selection.

- » **Anti-aliasing:** Choose this option to smooth the edges between the filled and unfilled areas.

Working with Multicolored Gradients

If one color isn't enough for you, you'll be pleased to know that Elements enables you to fill a selection or layer with a gradient. A *gradient* is a blend of two or more colors that gradually dissolve from one to another. Elements provides a whole slew of preset gradients, but creating your own custom gradient is also fun and easy.

Applying a preset gradient

Similar to colors, patterns, and brushes, gradients have a whole group of presets that you can apply to your selection and layers. You can also load other libraries of gradients from the Gradient panel menu.

Here's how to apply a preset gradient:

WARNING

1. **Make the selection you want to fill with a gradient.**

   We recommend making the selection on a new layer so that you can edit the gradient later without harming the underlying image.

   If you don't make a selection, the gradient is applied to the entire layer or background.

2. **Select the Gradient tool from the Tools panel or press the G key.**

   It looks like a rectangle that goes from black on the left to white on the right.

3. **In the Tool Options, click the down-pointing arrow on the Gradient Picker swatch.**

The Gradient Picker drop-down panel appears.

4. **Choose a preset gradient.**

Remember that you can choose other preset libraries from the Gradient panel menu. Libraries, such as Color Harmonies and Metals, contain interesting presets.

5. **Choose your desired gradient type by clicking one of the icons.**

See Figure 13-13 for an example of each type.

6. **Choose from the following options in the Tool Options:**

- **Mode:** Select a blending mode to change how the color of the gradient interacts with the colors below it.

- **Opacity:** Specify how opaque or transparent the gradient is.

- **Reverse:** Reverse the order in which the colors are applied.

- **Transparency:** Deselect this option to make Elements ignore any transparent areas in the gradient, making them opaque instead.

- **Dither:** Add *noise,* or random information, to produce a smoother gradient that prints with less *banding* (weird stripes caused by printing limitations).

7. **Position your gradient cursor at your desired starting point within your selection or layer.**

8. **Drag in any direction to your desired end point for the gradient.**

Longer drags result in a subtler transition between colors, whereas shorter drags result in a more abrupt transition. Hold down the Shift key to restrain the direction of the gradient to multiples of a 45-degree angle.

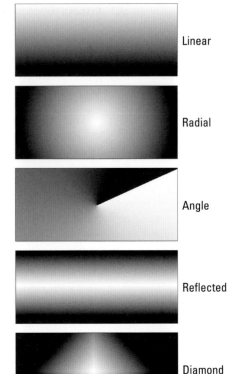

Linear

Radial

Angle

Reflected

Diamond

FIGURE 13-13:
Choose one of five gradient types.

TIP

9. **Release the mouse button to apply the gradient.**

   We applied an Orange, Yellow radial gradient from the Color Harmonies 2 preset library to a selection of a sun in Figure 13-14. We selected the Reverse option and dragged from the center of the sun to the tip of the top ray.

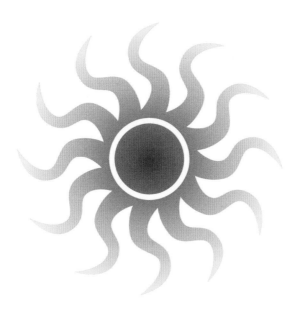

FIGURE 13-14:
We filled our sun selection with a radial Orange, Yellow gradient.

Customizing gradients

If you can't find the exact gradient you need, you can easily create your own. The Gradient Editor lets you create your own custom gradient using as many colors as you want. After you create a custom gradient, you can save it as a preset to reuse in the future.

Follow these steps to create a custom gradient:

1. **Select the Gradient tool from the Tools panel.**

2. **Click the Edit button in the Tool Options.**

   The Gradient Editor dialog box opens, as shown in Figure 13-15.

3. **Pick an existing preset to use as the basis for your new gradient.**

   If you want to choose a gradient from a different preset library, choose that library from the Preset drop-down list.

4. **Choose your gradient type, either Solid or Noise, from the Type drop-down list.**

A Noise gradient contains random colors. Interestingly, each time you create a Noise gradient, the result is different.

As soon as you start to edit the existing gradient, the name of the gradient changes to Custom.

5. **Choose your options for either a Solid or Noise gradient, depending on what you chose in Step 4:**

- **If you chose Solid,** adjust the Smoothness percentage to determine how smoothly one color blends into another.

- **If you chose Noise,** you can choose which Color Model to use to set the color range. You can also adjust the Roughness, which affects how smoothly or abruptly the color transitions from one to another. Click Restrict Colors to avoid oversaturated colors. The Add Transparency option adds transparency to random colors. Click the Randomize button to randomly generate a new gradient. You can then skip to Step 13 to finish the gradient-making process.

6. **If you're creating a solid gradient, choose the first color of your gradient by double-clicking the left color stop under the gradient bar. (Refer to Figure 13-15.)**

The triangle on top of the stop turns black to indicate that you're working with the starting point of the gradient, and the Color Picker appears so that you can then choose your desired color.

In the Stops area, you can also single-click the left color stop and then click the Color swatch to access the Color Picker. If you click the Color down-pointing arrow, you access the Color Swatches drop-down list, where you can choose from various preset Swatch libraries from the top of the panel.

7. **Select the ending color by double-clicking the right color stop. Repeat the process in Step 6 to define the color.**

8. **Change the percentage of one color versus the other by moving the starting or ending point's color stop to the left or right. Drag the midpoint slider (a diamond icon) to where the colors mix equally, 50/50.**

You can also change the position of the midpoint by typing a value in the Location box.

9. **To add another color, click below the gradient bar at the position you want to add the color. Define a color in the same way you did in Steps 6 to 8.**

10. **Repeat Step 9 to add colors.**

11. **To add transparency to your gradient, select an opacity stop (refer to Figure 13-15) and adjust the Opacity slider to specify the amount of transparency you desire.**

By default, a gradient has colors that are 100-percent opaque. You can fade a gradient to transparency so that the portion of the image under the gradient shows through.

You can also add opacity stops in the same way you add color stops.

12. **Adjust your color and opacity stops and their midpoint sliders to vary the percentages of each color.**

You can also redefine any of the colors. To delete a color stop, drag it up or down off the gradient bar.

13. **When you're done, name your gradient and click the Add To Preset/ Create a new gradient preset button.**

Your gradient is added to the Presets menu.

Opacity stop

Color stop   Midpoint slider

FIGURE 13-15:
Use the
Gradient Editor
to edit and
customize
gradients.

TIP

After all that work, you may want to consider saving your gradients for later use. To save a gradient, click the Save button in the Gradient Editor dialog box. Save the current presets, with your new gradient, under the current library's name or a new name altogether. You can later load that preset library. You can also manage your gradient presets with the Preset Manager, as we explain in Chapter 3.

Working with Patterns

If you've ever seen someone wearing leopard-print pants with an argyle sweater and a plaid blazer, you're familiar with patterns. You can use patterns to occasionally fill selections or layers. (Don't go overboard, though — patterns aren't always pretty when used without restraint.) You can also stamp your image by using the Pattern Stamp tool. You can even retouch by using a pattern with the Healing Brush tool. Elements offers a lot of preset patterns to keep you happy. If you're not happy with Elements' selection, you can create your own, of course.

Applying a preset pattern

Although you can apply patterns by using many different tools, this chapter sticks with applying patterns as fills. To fill a layer or selection with a preset pattern, follow these steps:

TIP

1. **Choose the layer or selection you want to fill with a pattern.**

   Again, we recommend making your selection on a new layer above your image for more flexible editing later on.

2. **Choose Edit ⇨ Fill Selection or Fill Layer and choose Pattern from the Use drop-down list.**

3. **Click the down-pointing arrow and choose a pattern from the Custom Pattern drop-down panel, as shown in Figure 13-16.**

   If you don't see a pattern to your liking, click the panel pop-up menu at the bottom of the submenu and choose another preset library.

FIGURE 13-16:
Fill your selection with one of the many Elements preset patterns.

4. **Choose any other fill options you want to apply, such as Mode, Opacity, or Preserve Transparency.**

   For details on these options, see the section "Filling and Outlining Selections," earlier in this chapter.

5. **Click OK to fill the layer or selection with the chosen pattern.**

Creating a new pattern

You may someday want to create your own pattern. Patterns can be easily created from any existing photo or painting you create in Elements. You can even scan your signature or logo, define it as a pattern, and use it with the Pattern Stamp tool to sign all your work.

To create your own pattern, follow these steps:

1. **Open the photographic, painted, or scanned image that contains the area you want to use as a pattern.**

2. **Use the Rectangular Marquee tool to select the area you want to convert into a pattern.**

   Make sure that your Feather option is set to 0, or the pattern command won't be available.

   If you don't make a selection, Elements uses your entire layer as a basis for the pattern.

3. **Choose Edit ⇨ Define Pattern from Selection or Edit ⇨ Define Pattern, if you haven't created a selection.**

   The Pattern Name dialog box appears.

4. **Enter a name for your pattern.**

   Your new pattern now appears in every Pattern panel, wherever it may lurk in Elements.

REMEMBER

In addition to filling your selection with a pattern, you can stamp on a pattern with the Pattern Stamp tool. Press S to select the Pattern Stamp tool. If you get the Clone Stamp tool, press S again. Choose your desired pattern from the Pattern Picker drop-down list and your desired brush tip from the Brush Preset Picker drop-down list. Select your brush size, opacity, and mode and then brush your pattern on your image. You can also select the Impressionist option to have your pattern appear more "painterly."

Creating Shapes of All Sorts

In this section, we leave the land of pixels and head into uncharted territory — Vectorville. Before we discuss the ins and outs of creating shapes, here's a little overview that explains the difference between pixels and vectors:

>> **Pixel images describe a shape in terms of a grid of pixels.** When you increase the size of a pixel-based image, it loses quality and begins to look

blocky, mushy, and otherwise nasty. For more details on resizing pixel-based images and the ramifications of doing so, see Chapter 2.

>> **Vectors describe a shape mathematically.** The shapes comprise paths made up of lines, curves, and anchor points. Because vector shapes are math-based, you can resize them without any loss of quality whatsoever.

In Figure 13-17, you can see both types of images.

When you create a shape in Elements, you're creating a vector-based element. Shapes reside on a special kind of layer called, not surprisingly, a *shape layer.* Use shapes to create simple logos, web buttons, and other small spot illustrations.

Drawing a shape

Elements offers an assortment of shape tools for you to choose from. Follow these steps to draw a shape in your document:

FIGURE 13-17:
Elements images can be vector-based (top) or pixel-based (bottom).

1. **Choose your desired shape tool from the Tools panel.**

   You can also press U to cycle through the shape tools. All the following tools have associated Geometry options, which are described in the section "Specifying Geometry options," later in this chapter. Here are the available tools:

   - **Rectangle and Ellipse:** As with their Marquee counterparts, you can hold down the Shift key while dragging to produce a square or circle; select the From Center option to draw the shape from the center outward.

   - **Rounded Rectangle:** This tool works like the regular Rectangle but with the addition of a radius value used to round off the corners of the rectangle.

   - **Polygon:** This tool creates a polygon with a specified number of sides, from 3 to 100.

- **Star:** This tool creates a polygon or star with a specified number of sides/vertices, from 3 to 100.

- **Line:** This tool draws a line with a width from 1 to 1,000 pixels. You can also add arrowheads at either end.

- **Custom:** Custom is the most varied shape tool. You have numerous preset custom shapes to choose from. As with any shape, hold down Shift to constrain proportions or select the From Center option to draw the shape from the center outward.

2. **In the Tool Options, click the down-pointing arrow to access Geometry options.**

   By default, the option is set to Unconstrained. For detailed explanations on the various Geometry options, see the upcoming sections.

3. **If you chose the Custom Shape tool in Step 1, click the Custom Shapes Preset picker down-pointing arrow to access the pop-up Shapes panel and choose your desired shape.**

   You can access more preset shape libraries via the pop-up menu at the top of the panel.

4. **Choose your desired color from the Color drop-down list.**

   Click the color-wheel icon in the bottom-right corner to access the Color Picker for additional color choices.

5. **Choose a style from the Style picker drop-down panel.**

   To jazz up the shape with bevels and other fancy edges, choose a style from the panel. For more on styles, see Chapter 12.

6. **Drag in the document to draw the shape you defined.**

   The shape appears in the image window on its own shape layer. Check out the Layers panel to see this phenomenon. Figure 13-18 shows our shape, a Japanese hairstyle, from the Dressup preset library, which we add to in the following section.

FIGURE 13-18:
Custom shapes run the gamut from the ordinary to the exotic, such as this hairstyle.

Drawing multiple shapes

After you create a shape layer, you can draw additional shapes on that layer. You can add, subtract, overlap, and intersect shapes in exactly the same way you do with selections. (See Chapter 8.) Just follow these steps:

1. **Select your desired state button in the Tool Options.**

   You can choose from the following options:

   - **Create New Shape Layer:** Creates your initial shape layer

   - **Add to Shape Area:** Combines and joins two or more shapes

   - **Subtract from Shape Area:** Subtracts one shape from another shape

   - **Intersect Shape Areas:** Creates a shape from only the areas that overlap

   - **Exclude Overlapping Shape Areas:** Creates a shape from only the areas that don't overlap

2. **Choose your desired shape tool and draw the next shape.**

   We completed the shape by adding the face, as shown in Figure 13-19.

FIGURE 13-19:
Add to your shape layer.

Specifying Geometry options

Geometry options help define how your shapes look. Click the down-pointing arrow in the Tool Options to access the Geometry options described in the sections that follow.

Rectangle and Rounded Rectangle Geometry options

Here are the Geometry options for the Rectangle and Rounded Rectangle shapes:

>> **Unconstrained:** Enables you to have free rein to draw a rectangle at any size or proportion.

>> **Square:** Constrains the shape to a perfect square.

>> **Fixed Size:** Lets you draw rectangles in fixed sizes, as specified by your width and height values.

>> **Proportional:** Allows you to define a proportion for the rectangle. For example, specifying 2W and 1H makes a rectangle twice as wide as it is high.

>> **From Center:** Enables you to draw from the center out.

>> **Snap:** Aligns the shape to the pixels on your screen.

TIP

>> **Radius:** For Rounded Rectangles, applies the radius of a circle used to round off the corners. This option is found in the Tool Options itself, not in the Geometry Options pop-up menu.

Ellipse geometry options

The Ellipse shape has the same options that are available for rectangles, except for the Snap option. The only difference is that, instead of being able to create a perfect square, you can create a perfect circle with the Circle option.

Polygon Geometry options

The Geometry options for the Polygon shape are as follows:

>> **Sides:** Specify the number of sides for your polygon.

>> **Smooth: Corners:** Round off the corners.

Star Geometry options

The Geometry options for the Star shape are as follows:

>> **Sides:** Specify the number of points for your star.

>> **Smooth: Corners:** Round off the inner corners of indented sides or round off the corners.

>> **Smooth: Indents:** Determine the amount that the sides indent inward.

Line Geometry options

The line's Geometry settings include whether to put arrowheads at the start or end of the line. You can also adjust the width, length, and concavity settings to change the arrowhead shapes.

Custom Shape Geometry options

The Custom Shape options are similar to those you find for the other shapes, but with a couple unique options:

>> **Defined Proportions:** Draws a shape based on the original proportions you used when you created it

>> **Defined Size:** Draws a shape based on its original size when you created it

Editing shapes

You can edit shapes that you create by using a variety of tools and techniques. Here's a list of the things you can do to modify your shapes:

>> **Select:** Choose the Shape Selection tool to select one or more shapes in their layers. You can find this tool in the Tool Options along with the shapes tools.

>> **Move:** Choose the Move tool (press V) to move the entire contents of the shape layer.

>> **Delete:** Select a shape with the Shape Selection tool and press Delete to remove it.

>> **Transform Shape:** Choose the Shape Selection tool and select your shape. Choose Image ⇨ Transform Shape and choose your desired transformation.

>> **Change the color:** Double-click the thumbnail of the shape layer on the Layers panel. This action transports you to the Color Picker, where you can choose a new color.

>> **Clone a shape:** Hold down the Alt (Option on the Mac) key and move the shape with the Move tool.

TIP

To convert your vector-based shape into a pixel-based shape, click the Simplify button in the Tool Options or choose Layer ⇨ Simplify Layer. You can't edit a shape after you simplify it except to modify the pixels. But you can now apply filters to the layer. See Chapter 12 for more on fun with filters.

IN THIS CHAPTER

» **Understanding type basics**

» **Creating point, paragraph, and path type**

» **Setting type options**

» **Editing and simplifying (rasterizing) type**

» **Masking with type**

» **Stylizing and warping type**

Chapter **14**

Working with Type

Although we spout on in this book about how a picture says a thousand words, we'd be terribly negligent if we didn't at least give a nod to the power of the written word as well. You may find that you never need to go near the type tools. That's fine. We won't be offended if you skip right past this chapter.

Then again, you may have an occasional need to add a caption, a headline, or maybe even a short paragraph to an image. Although it's by no means a word-processing or even page-layout program, Elements does give you ample tools for creating, editing, stylizing, and even distorting type.

Understanding Type Basics

Elements has seven type tools. Two of them are for entering horizontally oriented type, and two are for entering vertically oriented type. Don't worry about the vertical type tools. Although you can use them, they're really designed for the Asian market so that users can enter Chinese and Japanese characters. The remaining three tools are for creating type on a selection, shape, or *path* (which is a line, curved or straight, that doesn't appear in your actual image but that your text follows).

Tools

The horizontal and vertical type tools are identical in their attributes, so we cover just the two horizontal type tools here. For the sake of simplicity, we call them the Type and Type Mask tools:

TIP

>> **Type:** Use this tool to enter type. This type is created on its own type layer except when used in Bitmap mode or Index Color mode, neither of which supports layers.

We refer to layers a lot in this chapter, so if your layer knowledge is rusty, check out Chapter 9.

>> **Type Mask:** This tool doesn't create actual type; instead, it creates a selection border in the shape of the type you want to enter. The selection border is added to the active layer. You can do anything with a type selection that you can do with any other selection. (Chapter 8 is your one-stop guide to selections.)

The remaining three type tools all create type on a path in different ways:

>> **Text On Selection:** This tool enables you to draw on your image to create a selection, similar to the Quick Selection tool. The selection converts into a path. When you add text, it follows the shape of the path.

>> **Text On Shape:** This tool enables you to draw any chosen shape from your shapes menu. When you add text, it follows the shape.

>> **Text On Custom Path:** This tool lets you draw any custom path that you desire on your image. Enter text on that custom path, and it adheres to that path.

The three path type tools all create a type layer. Find out how to use these tools in the upcoming section "Creating Path Type."

TECHNICAL STUFF

A path has three components: anchor points, straight segments, and curved segments. The path essentially hovers above the image in its own "space," thereby not altering or marking the image in any way. The path in this context is merely a track upon which the text can flow. You can alter the path to your liking by using the Refine Path option.

Modes

You can enter text in Elements in three different modes: point, paragraph, and path. Both the Type and Type Mask tools can enter either point or paragraph mode. Here's a brief description of each mode (for the step-by-step process of creating the text, see the following sections):

REMEMBER

>> **Point:** Use this mode if you want to enter only a few words. Select the Type tool, click in your image, and, well, type. The text appears while you type and continues to grow. In fact, it even continues past the boundary of your image!

Point type never wraps around to a new line. To wrap to the next line, you must press Enter (Return on a Mac).

>> **Paragraph:** Use this mode to enter longer chunks (or constrained blocks) of text on an image. Click and drag your type tool to create a text bounding box and then type. All the text is entered in this resizable bounding box. If a line of text is too long, Elements automatically wraps it around to the next line.

>> **Path:** Elements also offers the capability of placing text along a path via three unique type tools. Double-click the path and type; the text appears, adhering to the shape of the path.

Formats

Elements can display and print type in two formats. Each format has its pros and cons, and which format you use depends on your needs. Here's the lowdown on both of them:

>> **Vector:** All text in Elements is initially created as vector type. *Vector* type provides scalable outlines that you can resize without producing jaggy edges in the diagonal strokes. Vector type remains fully editable and always prints with optimum quality, appearing crisp and clean. Vector type is the default type format in Elements, except for images in Bitmap or Index Color mode.

>> **Raster:** When Elements converts vector type into pixels, the text is *rasterized.* Elements refers to this rasterization process as simplifying. When text is *simplified,* it's no longer editable as text but is converted into a raster image. You usually simplify your vector type when you want to apply filters to the type to produce a special effect or when you want to merge the type with the image. You can't resize simplified type without losing some quality or risking jagged edges. For more details, see the section "Simplifying Type," later in this chapter.

Creating Point Type

The majority of your type entry will most likely be in *point type mode.* Point type is useful for short chunks of text, such as headlines, labels, logos, and headings for web pages.

Point type is so called because it contains a single *anchor point,* which marks the starting point of the line of type. Remember that point–type lines don't wrap automatically, as you can see in Figure 14-1.

FIGURE 14-1:
Point type
doesn't wrap
automatically,
but instead
can run off
your image
into a type
Neverland.

Point type doesn't wra

Follow these steps to create point type:

1. **Open the Photo Editor and choose Expert mode.**

2. **Open an image or create a new, blank Elements file by choosing File ⇨ New ⇨ Blank File and clicking OK.**

3. **Select the Horizontal Type tool from the Tools panel.**

   You can also press T to cycle through the various type tools. Additionally, you can also select the Horizontal Type tool from the Tool Options. It looks like a capital letter *T.*

4. **On the image, click where you want to insert your text.**

   Your cursor is called an *I-beam.* When you click, you make an insertion point.

   A small, horizontal line about one-third of the way up the I-beam shows the *baseline* (the line on which the text sits) for horizontal type.

5. **Specify your type options from the Tool Options.**

   All the options are described in detail in the section "Specifying Type Options," later in this chapter.

6. **Type your text and press Enter (Return on a Mac) to begin a new line.**

   When you press Enter (or Return), you insert a hard return that doesn't move.

7. **When you finish entering the text, click the Commit button (the green check-mark icon) near your text.**

If you want to bail out, click the Cancel button (the red No icon).

You can also commit the type by pressing Enter on the numeric keypad or by clicking any other tool on the Tools panel. A new type layer with your text is created. Type layers appear on your Layers panel and are indicated by the T icon.

Creating Paragraph Type

If you have larger chunks of text, it's usually more practical to enter the text as paragraph type. Entering paragraph type is similar to entering text in a word-processing or page-layout program, except that the text is contained inside a bounding box. When you type and come to the end of the bounding box, Elements automatically wraps the text to the next line.

To enter paragraph type, follow these steps:

1. **Open the Photo Editor and choose Expert mode.**

2. **Open an image or create a new, blank Elements file by choosing File ⇨ New ⇨ Blank File and clicking OK.**

3. **Select the Horizontal Type tool from the Tools panel or press T to cycle through the various type tools.**

   You can also select the Horizontal Type tool from the Tool Options.

4. **On the image, insert and size the bounding box by using one of two methods:**

   - **Drag to create a bounding box close to your desired size.** After you release the mouse button, you can drag any of the handles at the corners and sides of the box to resize it.

   - **Hold down the Alt (Option on the Mac) key and click the image.** The Paragraph Text Size dialog box appears. Enter the exact dimensions of your desired bounding box. When you click OK, your specified box appears, complete with handles for resizing later.

5. **Specify your type options from the Tool Options.**

   Options are described in detail in the following section.

6. **Enter your text; to start a new paragraph, press Enter (Return on a Mac).**

    Each line wraps around to fit inside the bounding box, as shown in Figure 14-2.

TIP

    If you type more text than can squeeze into the text box, an overflow icon (a box with a plus sign inside) appears. Resize the text box by dragging a bounding box handle.

7. **Click the Commit button (the green check-mark icon) next to the text box or press Enter on the numeric keypad.**

    If you're not happy with the text, you can click the Cancel button (the red No icon) and start over.

    After you click Commit, Elements creates a new type layer.

Paragraph type wraps automatically without your assistance, so there's no need to enter a hard return as you type.

FIGURE 14-2:
Paragraph type automatically wraps to fit within your bounding box.

Creating Path Type

If you want your type to flow in a circle, wave, stair step, or any other shape, you're in luck. Elements provides three type tools that enable you to do just that. The great things are that path type is easy to create and is totally editable, and the type resides on its very own layer.

Using the Text On Selection tool

You can create path type by first creating a selection of your image, which is similar to the way you create a selection with the Quick Selection tool. Here's how:

1. **Open the Photo Editor and choose Expert mode.**

2. **Open an image or create a new, blank Elements file by choosing File ⇨ New ⇨ Blank File and clicking OK.**

3. **Select the Text On Selection tool from the Tools panel or press T to cycle through the various type tools.**

   You can also select the Text On Selection tool from the Tool Options. It looks like a capital letter *T* with a dotted square around it.

4. **On the image, "paint" (drag) over your desired selection.**

5. **Refine your selection by adding or subtracting from it in one of four ways:**

   - Press the Shift key and drag around the additional area that you want to include in your selection.

   - Press the Alt (Option on the Mac) key and drag around the area that you want to subtract from your selection.

   - Select the Add to Selection or Subtract from Selection button in the Tool Options and drag around your desired areas.

   - In the Tool Options, drag the Offset slider right to expand, or left to contract, your selection.

   You can specify additional options, which are common to all the type tools; these are described in detail in the later section, "Specifying Type Options."

6. **When your selection is complete, click the Commit button (the green check-mark icon) to convert your selection to a path.**

   If you want to start over, click the red Cancel (a slashed circle) icon to do so.

7. **Position your mouse pointer over the path and, when the cursor icon changes to an I-beam (a capital letter *I* with a crooked line crossing over), click the path and type your text.**

   The text wraps along the path. If you type more text than can fit on the path, an overflow icon appears. Resize the selection until all your text appears.

8. **When you're done entering your text, click the Commit button (the green check-mark icon).**

   Elements creates a new type layer. You can edit any attributes, such as font and size, just as you can with point or paragraph text. See the upcoming section "Editing Text" for details.

Using the Text On Shape tool

The Text On Shape tool enables you to create type that flows along the perimeter of any shape. To do so, follow these steps:

1. **Open the Photo Editor and choose Expert mode.**

2. **Open an image or create a new, blank Elements file by choosing File ⇨ New ⇨ Blank File and clicking OK.**

3. **Select the Text On Shape tool from the Tools panel or press T to cycle through the various type tools.**

   You can also select the Text on Shape tool from the Tool Options. It looks like a capital letter *T* with a wavy box around it.

4. **Select your desired shape from the shape options in the Tool Options.**

5. **Drag your tool over the image to create the shape.**

   - **To constrain your proportions,** hold down the Shift key while dragging.

   - **To draw from the center outward,** hold down the Alt (Option on the Mac) key while dragging.

6. **Position your mouse pointer over the path and, when the cursor icon changes to an I-beam (a capital letter *I* with a crooked line crossing over), click the path and type your text.**

   The text wraps along the shape's path, as shown in Figure 14-3.

   If you type more text than can fit on the path, an overflow icon appears. Adjust the path until all your text appears. You can also specify type options, which are common to all the type tools; these are described in detail in the upcoming section "Specifying Type Options."

7. **When you're done entering your text, click the Commit button (the green check-mark icon).**

   If you want to start over, click the red Cancel icon.

   Elements creates a new type layer. You can edit any attributes, such as font and size, just as you can with point or paragraph text. See the section "Editing Text" for details.

   You can also transform your shape by choosing Image ⇨ Transform Shape and choosing your desired transformation. For details on transformations, see Chapter 9.

You can also refine your shape path by using the Modify tool, which appears in the Tool Options when the Text On Custom Path tool is selected. Just be sure that your type layer is selected in the Layers panel before working with this option.

TIP

Using the Text On Custom Path tool

If you want to create your own path or shape as the basis for your type, the Text On Custom Path tool is for you. Here's how:

1. **Open the Photo Editor and choose Expert mode.**

2. **Open an image or create a new, blank Elements file by choosing File ⇨ New ⇨ Blank File and clicking OK.**

3. **Select the Text On Custom Path tool from the Tools panel or press T to cycle through the various type tools.**

    You can also select the Text On Custom Path tool from the Tool Options. It looks like a capital letter *T* on a line.

4. **Drag your tool over the image to create the custom path of your choice.**

5. **Refine your path by selecting the Modify tool (Arrow icon) in the Tool Options. Drag the anchor points or path segments with the tool to get your desired shape.**

6. **Position your mouse pointer over the path and, when the cursor icon changes to an I-beam (a capital letter *I* with a crooked line crossing over), click the path and type your text.**

The text wraps along the shape's path.

If you type more text than can fit on the path, an overflow icon appears. Adjust the path as needed so that all the text appears. Note that you can also refine the path after you've entered your type. Choose Image ➪ Transform Shape and select a command, like Free Transform Shape, from the submenu. For details on transformations, see Chapter 9.

7. **When you're done entering your text, click the Commit button (the green check-mark icon) or click the red Cancel icon to start again.**

   Elements creates a new type layer. You can edit any attributes, such as font and size, just as you can with point or paragraph text. See the section "Editing Text" for details.

8. **To create a new custom path, select the background layer in the Layers panel and repeat Steps 3–7.**

Specifying Type Options

When you're using a Type tool, the Tool Options box (found at the bottom of the workspace) includes several character and paragraph type settings, as shown in Figure 14-4. These options enable you to specify your type to your liking and pair it with your images.

Here's an explanation of each available option in the Tool Options:

TECHNICAL
STUFF

>> **Font Family:** Select the font you want from the drop-down list. Elements provides a WYSIWYG (What You See Is What You Get) font menu. After each font name, the word *Sample* is rendered in the actual font — no more selecting a font without knowing what it really looks like.

   You also find one of these abbreviations before each font name to let you know what type of font it is:

- **a:** Adobe Type 1 (PostScript) fonts
- **TT:** TrueType fonts
- **O:** OpenType fonts

Fonts with no abbreviation are bitmapped fonts, where several dots comprise the character and scaling can be iffy. Use PostScript, TrueType, or OpenType fonts whenever possible. Note that if you are an Adobe Creative Cloud subscriber, you may also see a Tk abbreviation, which stands for Typekit (now known as Adobe Fonts), a free font library that you can access online.

>> **Font Style:** Some font families have additional styles, such as light or condensed. Only the styles available for a particular font appear in the list. This is also a WYSIWYG menu.

>> **Font Size:** Choose your type size from the drop-down list or just type a size in the text box. Type size is most commonly measured in points (in which 72 points equals about 1 inch at a resolution of 72 ppi). You can switch to millimeters or pixels by choosing Edit ➪ Preferences ➪ Units & Rulers (on the Mac, choose Adobe Photoshop Elements Editor ➪ Preferences ➪ Units & Rulers).

>> **Leading:** Leading (pronounced *LED-ding*) is the amount of space between the baselines of lines of type. A *baseline* is the imaginary line on which a line of type sits. You can choose Auto Leading or specify the amount of leading to apply. When you choose Auto Leading, Elements uses a value of 120 percent of your type point size. Therefore 10-point type gets 12 points of leading. Elements adds that extra 20 percent so that the bottoms of the lowest letters don't crash into the tops of the tallest letters on the next line.

>> **Tracking:** This new setting adjusts the spacing between a group of letters. Negative amounts bring the letters closer together, whereas positive amounts space them farther apart.

>> **Color:** Click the color swatch to select a color for your type from the Color Picker. You can also choose a color from the Swatches panel.

>> **Faux Bold:** Use this option to create a fake bold style when a real bold style (which you'd choose under Font Style) doesn't exist. Be warned that, although the sky won't fall, applying faux styles can distort the proportions of a font. You should use fonts with real styles, and if they don't exist, oh, well.

>> **Faux Italic:** This option creates a phony oblique style and carries the same warning as the Faux Bold option.

>> **Underline:** This setting (obviously) underlines your type, like <u>this</u>.

>> **Strikethrough:** Choose this option to apply a strikethrough style to your text.

>> **Text Alignment:** These three options align your horizontal text on the left or right or in the center. If you happen to have vertical text, these options rotate 90 degrees clockwise and change into top, bottom, and center vertical settings.

>> **Style:** Click this option to access a drop-down panel of preset layer styles that you can apply to your type. This option is accessible after you have committed your type. For more on this option and the Create Warped Text option (described in an upcoming bullet), see the section "Stylizing and Warping Type," later in this chapter.

>> **Change the Text Orientation:** Select your type layer and then click this option to switch between vertical and horizontal type orientations.

>> **Create Warped Text:** This fun option lets you distort type in more than a dozen ways.

>> **Anti-aliasing:** Select this option to slightly smooth out the edges of your text. The Anti-aliasing option softens that edge by 1 pixel, as shown in Figure 14-5. For the most part, you want to keep this option turned on. The one occasion on which you may want it turned off is when you're creating small type to be displayed onscreen, such as on web pages. The soft edges can sometimes be tough to read.

You can apply type settings either before or after you enter your text.

Anti-aliased   Not anti-aliased

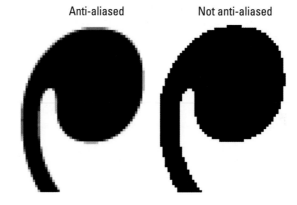

The Anti-aliasing option softens the edges of your type.

Editing Text

To correct typos, add and delete type, or change any of the type options, simply follow these steps:

1. **Select the Type tool from the Tools panel.**

2. **Double-click within the text to automatically select the type layer.**

3. **Make any changes to your text:**

   - **Change the font family, size, color, or other type option.** If you want to change all the text, simply select that type layer on the Layers panel. To select only portions of the text, highlight the text by dragging across it with the I-beam of the Type tool. Then select your changes in the Tool Options; see the preceding section "Specifying Type Options" for details about your options for the Type tool.

   - **Delete text.** Highlight the text by dragging across it with the I-beam of the Type tool. Then press the Backspace key (Delete on the Mac).

   - **Add text.** Make an insertion point by clicking your I-beam within the line of text. Then type your new text.

   Note: These editing steps apply to all types of text — point, paragraph, and path.

4. **When you're done editing your text, click the Commit button (the green check-mark icon).**

TIP

You may also occasionally need to transform your text. To do so, make sure that the type layer is selected on the Layers panel. Then choose Image ⇨ Transform ⇨ Free Transform. Grab a handle on the bounding box and drag to rotate or scale. Press Ctrl (⌘ on the Mac) and drag a handle to distort. When you're done, double-click inside the bounding box to commit the transformation, or click the Commit button (the green check-mark icon). For more details on transformations, see Chapter 9.

Simplifying Type

As we explain in the section "Understanding Type Basics," earlier in this chapter, Elements can display and print type in two different formats: vector and raster.

REMEMBER

As long as you keep type in a vector format on a type layer, you can edit and resize that type all day long.

Occasionally, however, you may need to *simplify* your type — to convert your type into pixels. After it's simplified, you can apply filters, paint on the type, and apply gradients and patterns. If you're working with layers and *flatten* your image (merge your layers into a single background image), your type layer is also simplified and merged with the other pixels in your image. By the way, if you try to apply a filter to a type layer, Elements barks at you that the type layer must be simplified before proceeding and gives you the opportunity to click OK (if you want to simplify) or Cancel.

To simplify your type, select the type layer on the Layers panel and choose Layer ⇨ Simplify Layer. Your type layer is then converted (the T icon disappears) into a regular layer on which your type is now displayed as pixels against a transparent background, as shown in Figure 14-6.

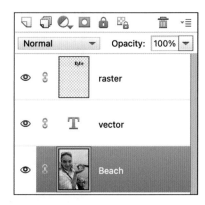

FIGURE 14-6:
Simplifying your type layer converts vector type into pixels.

WARNING

To avoid having to re-create your type from scratch, make all necessary edits before simplifying. This includes sizing your text. After you simplify your type, you can't resize your text without risking the dreaded jaggies. The other downside to remember about simplified type is that although it looks identical to vector type onscreen, it never prints as crisply and cleanly as vector type. Even at higher-resolution settings, a slight jagged edge always appears on simplified type. So, if you're experimenting with painting or filters on your type, just make a duplicate of your type layer before simplifying it and then hide that layer.

Masking with Type

Using the Type Mask tool epitomizes the combination of type and image. Unlike the Type tool, the Type Mask tool doesn't create a new layer. Instead, it creates a selection on the active layer. Type Mask is the tool of choice for filling text with an image or cutting text out of an image so that the background shows through, as shown in Figure 14-7.

REMEMBER

A selection is a selection no matter how it was created. So, even though type mask selections look like letters, they act like selections. You can move, modify, and save them.

Here are the steps to create a type mask:

1. **In the Photo Editor in Expert mode, open the image of your choice.**

We selected a stone texture.

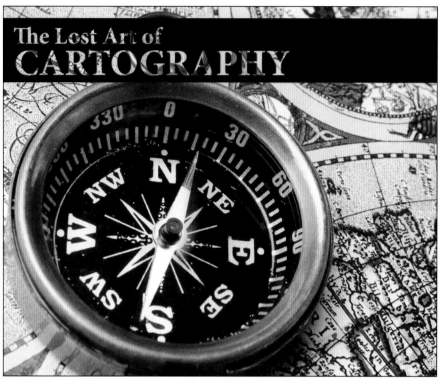

FIGURE 14-7:
The Type Mask tool enables you to cut type out of solid color or image layers.

2. **Convert your background into a layer by double-clicking the word** *Background* **on the Layers panel, and then click OK.**

   This step enables you to jazz up the type with styles later.

3. **Choose the Horizontal Type Mask tool from the Tools panel.**

4. **Specify your type options (such as Font Family, Style, and Size) in the Tool Options.**

5. **Click the image and type your desired text. When you're done, click the Commit button (the green check-mark icon).**

   A selection border in the shape of your type appears on your image.

6. **Choose Select ⇨ Inverse, which deselects your letter selections and selects everything else.**

7. **Press the Backspace (Delete on a Mac) key to delete everything outside your selection border.**

   Your type is now filled with your image.

8. **Choose Select ⇨ Deselect.**

9. **Experiment with applying layer styles to your type.**

(a) **Choose Window ⇨ Styles or click the Styles button at the bottom of the workspace (assuming you're in Basic Workspace).**

If you need to get back to the Basic Workspace, click the arrow on the More button in the bottom-right corner of the workspace and choose Basic Workspace from the submenu.

(b) **Choose the type of layer styles you desire from the drop-down list at the top of the panel, such as Drop Shadows or Bevels.**

(c) **Click the exact style you want.**

We used a drop shadow and a simple inner bevel in Figure 14-8. See Chapter 12 for more about layer styles.

TIP

If you want to admire your type against a solid background, as we did, create a new layer, choose Edit ⇨ Fill Layer, and then choose your desired color from the Use drop-down list.

FIGURE 14-8:
Fill type with imagery by using the Type Mask tool.

© Mike Charles/Shutterstock Image #410887357

A Guided Edit called Photo Text, shown in Figure 14-9, makes creating masked type even easier than following the preceding steps. Go into Guided Edit mode, click the Fun Edits tab, and follow the few simple steps provided. You can also easily add a bevel, stroke, or shadow using this edit.

And if just having one photo inside of your text isn't enough, be sure to check out the Multi-Photo Text Guided Edit (also under Fun Edits), where you can put a different photo inside each letter of your text!

FIGURE 14-9:
The Photo
Text Guided
Edit creates
masked type in
a few steps.

Stylizing and Warping Type

If you've tried your hand at creating a type mask, you know that Elements is capable of much more than just throwing a few black letters at the bottom of your image. And with a few clicks here and there, you can also warp, distort, enhance, and stylize your type. If you're not careful, your creative typography can outshine your image.

Adjusting type opacity

If you checked out Chapter 9 before reading this chapter, you know that *layers* are a digital version of the old analog transparency sheets. You can change element opacity on layers to let the underlying layer show through in varying degrees. This is also possible on a type layer. Figure 14-10 shows how varying the opacity percentage of your type layer makes more of the underlying layer show through. In Figure 14-10, the underlying layer is an image of water.

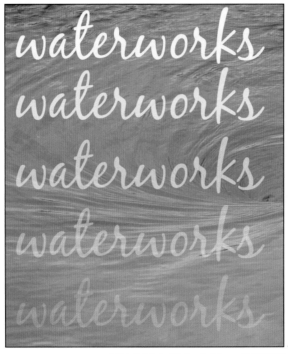

FIGURE 14-10:
You can vary
the opacity
of type layers
to allow the
underlying
layer to peek
through.

© Valeriy Lebedev/Shutterstock Image #127191773

To change the opacity of a type layer, simply select the layer on the Layers panel, click the arrow to the right of the Opacity percentage, and drag the slider. You can also enter a value in the Opacity field. The lower the percentage, the less opaque the type (and the more the underlying layer shows through).

Applying filters to your type

One of the most interesting things you can do with type in Elements that you can't do in a word-processing or page-layout program is apply special effects, such as filters. You can make type look like it's on fire, underwater, or on the move — as shown in Figure 14-11, in which we applied a motion blur.

REMEMBER

The only caveat is that type has to be simplified before a filter can be applied. Be sure to do all your text editing before you move to the filtering stage.

Applying the filter is as easy as selecting the simplified type layer on the Layers panel and choosing a filter from the Filter menu. For more on filters, see Chapter 12.

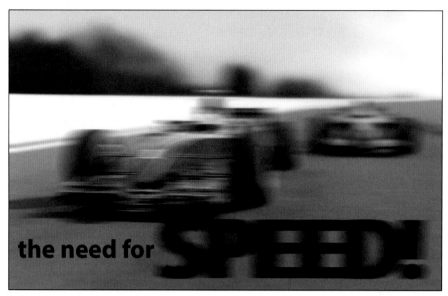

FIGURE 14-11:
Applying a motion blur to type can make it appear as fast as the car.

Painting your type with color and gradients

FIGURE 14-12:
Bring your type to life with color (top) or a gradient (bottom).

Changing the color of text is as easy as highlighting it and selecting a color from the Color Picker. But what if you want to do something a little less conventional, such as apply random brush strokes of paint across the type, as we did in the top image shown in Figure 14-12? It's really easier than it looks. Again, as with applying filters to text, the only criterion is that the type has to be simplified first. After that's done, select a color, grab the Brush tool with settings of your choice, and paint. In our example, we used the Granite Flow brush, found in the Special Effect Brushes presets. We used a diameter of 39, 15, and 6 pixels and just swiped our type a few times.

You can also apply a gradient to your type. Here are the steps to follow after simplifying your type:

1. **Select the text by either Ctrl-clicking (⌘-clicking on a Mac) the layer containing the text or locking the layer's transparency on the Layers panel.**

2. **Select the Gradient tool from the Tools panel.**

3. **In the Tool Options, click the down-pointing arrow next to the Gradient Picker to access the Gradient Picker panel.**

4. **Choose your desired gradient.**

   If you want to create a custom gradient, find out how in Chapter 13.

5. **Position your gradient cursor on the text where you want your gradient to start; drag to where you want your gradient to end.**

REMEMBER

Don't like the results? Drag again until you get the look you want. You can drag at any angle and to any length, even outside your type. In the bottom image shown in Figure 14-12, we used the copper gradient and just dragged from the top of the letters to the bottom. We also locked the transparent pixels on the layer to confine the gradient to just the type area.

Warping your type

If horizontal or vertical text is just way too regimented for you, try the Warp feature. The best part about the distortions you apply is that the text remains fully editable. This feature is fun and easy to use. Click the Create Warped Text button at the far right of the Tool Options. (It's the T with a curved line below it.) This action opens the Warp Text dialog box, where you find a vast array of distortions on the Style drop-down list with descriptive names such as Bulge, Inflate, and Squeeze.

After selecting a warp style, you can adjust the orientation, amount of bend, and degree of distortion by dragging the sliders. The Bend setting affects the amount of warp, and the Horizontal and Vertical Distortions apply perspective to that warp. Luckily, you can also view the results while you adjust. We could give you technical explanations of these adjustments, but the best way to see what they do is to just play with them. See Figure 14-13 to get a quick look at a few warp styles. The names speak for themselves.

FIGURE 14-13:
Text remains
fully editable
after you apply
distortions
with the Warp
command.

joan of arc   grandoldflag

squeezeme

twistedsister

battle of the bulge   overinflate

TIP

You can also use the Transform command, such as scale and skew, to manipulate text. See Chapter 9 for details on transforming.

5
Printing, Creating, and Sharing

Manage color, use color profiles, and get your output to closely match what you see onscreen.

Print your pictures either at home or through an online service.

Share your pictures with family and friends on social media and online sharing services.

Display your photos in photo books, greeting cards, and slideshows.

Chapter **15**

Getting It on Paper

Perhaps the greatest challenge when using programs such as Photoshop Elements (and even the professionals who use its granddaddy, Adobe Photoshop) is getting what you see on your monitor to render a reasonable facsimile on a printed page. You can find all sorts of books on color printing — how to get color right, how to calibrate your equipment, and how to create and use color profiles — all for the purpose of getting a good match among your computer monitor, your printer, and the paper used to print your output. It's downright discouraging to spend a lot of time tweaking an image so that all the brilliant blue colors jump out on your computer monitor, only to find that all those blues turn to murky purples when the photo is printed.

In this chapter, we talk about options — many options — for setting print attributes for printing to your own color printer. If you need to, reread this chapter a few times just to be certain that you understand the process for printing good-quality images. A little time spent here will, we hope, save you some headaches down the road.

Getting Pictures Ready for Printing

The first step toward getting your photos to your desktop printer is to prepare each image for optimum output. You have several considerations when you're preparing files, including the ones in this list:

>> **Set resolution and size.** In years past, better performance was obtained by downsampling images for desired print resolutions. Print drivers for just about all newer printers do a great job handling sampling for your output. As long as you have sufficient resolution for a quality print, leave the sampling to the print driver.

>> **Make all brightness and color corrections before printing.** Make sure that your pictures appear their best before sending them to your printer. If you have your monitor properly calibrated, you should see a fair representation of what your pictures will look like before you print them. Chapters 10 and 11 cover corrections.

>> **Decide how color will be managed before you print.** You can color-manage output to your printer in three ways, as we discuss in the following section. Know your printer's profiles and how to use them before you start to print your files. (See the next section, "Working with Color Printer Profiles," for more on understanding profiles.)

>> **Get your printer ready.** When printing to desktop color printers, always be certain that your ink cartridges have ink and the nozzles are clean. Make sure you use the proper settings for paper and ink when you send a file to your printer. Be sure to review the manual that came with your printer so that you know how to perform all the steps required to make a quality print.

TIP

If you haven't used your printer for some time and the nozzles appear to be clogged, use the printer's utility over and over again and keep cleaning the nozzles. You may be able to resurrect a printer by running the cleaning operation 20 or more times. If you aren't successful, it's time to buy a new printer. Many of the newer printers today support ink tanks and have moved away from cartridges. If you have an old printer that uses ink cartridges, look at buying a new printer. Printers are relatively cheap, and those with ink tanks will cost you much less when it comes time to replace the inks.

WARNING

Using any inks other than manufacturer-recommended inks can produce color problems. Each developer provides printer profiles specific for its recommended inks. With third-party inks, you don't have the advantage of using color profiles that have been tested by a printer manufacturer. If getting the most accurate color on your prints is important to you, use only those inks and papers recommended by your printer manufacturer.

Also, different papers require using different profiles. Use appropriate color profiles supplied by your printer developer for a given paper type. Use papers specifically recommended for your printer.

Working with Color Printer Profiles

The final leg in a color-managed workflow is to convert color from your color workspace profile to your printer's color profile. Basically, this conversion means that the colors you see on your monitor in your current workspace are accurately converted to the color that your printer can reproduce. To print accurate color, a color profile designed for your printer and the paper you use needs to be installed on your computer.

You can manage color in Photoshop Elements in three ways when it comes time to print your files:

>> **Printer Manages Colors:** This method permits your desktop color printer to decide which profile to use when you print your photo. Your printer makes this decision according to the paper you select. If you choose Epson Premium Glossy Photo Paper, for example, your Epson printer chooses the profile that goes along with that particular paper. If you choose another paper, your printer chooses a different color profile. This method is all automatic, and color profile selection is made when you print your file.

Printers manage color quite well. If you're confused about what options to choose, let your printer manage the color and be done with it. More often than not, this choice produces good results.

>> **Photoshop Elements Manages Colors:** When you make this choice, color management is taken out of the hands of your printer and is controlled by Elements. You must choose the color profile. If color profiles are installed by your printer, you can choose a color profile from the list of profiles that match your printer and the paper source.

TIP

If you choose to let Elements manage color and you don't have a color profile for your printer or the paper, choose sRGB for the profile. With desktop color printers, this profile works well as a default.

>> **No Color Management:** You use this choice if you have a color profile embedded in one of your pictures. You'll probably rarely use this option. Unless you know how to embed profiles or receive files with embedded profiles from other users, don't make this choice in the Print dialog box. Because very few Elements users work with files with embedded profiles, we skip covering this method of printing your files.

Each of these three options requires you to decide how color is managed. You make choices (as we discuss later in this chapter when we walk you through the steps for printing) about whether to color-manage your output. These selections are unique to the Print dialog box and, more specifically, to the More Options dialog box for your individual printer.

PRINTER COLOR PROFILES

Color profiling has been developed quite well by the three top desktop color printer developers (Epson, HP, and Canon). You can find a wealth of information on the Internet for using color profiles with each of these printers. A lot of information is devoted to much earlier versions of Photoshop Elements, but the way profiles are used with desktop color printers hasn't changed much, so the information is still valid. For starters, take a look at the following URLs for more information about printing using color profiles and downloading profiles for your printer:

- **Epson Printers and Photoshop Elements (Windows):** `https://www.redrivercatalog.com/profiles/how-to-use-icc-color-profiles-photoshop-elements-10-windows.html`

- **Epson Printers and Photoshop Elements (Macintosh):** `https://www.redrivercatalog.com/profiles/how-to-use-icc-color-printer-profiles-photoshop-elements-epson-mac.html`

- **HP Printers and Photoshop Elements (Windows):** `https://www.redrivercatalog.com/profiles/how-to-use-icc-color-profiles-photoshop-elements-11-12-windows-hp-video.html`

- **HP Printers and Photoshop Elements (Mac):** `https://www.redrivercatalog.com/profiles/how-to-use-icc-color-printer-profiles-photoshop-elements-hp-mac.html`

- **Canon Printers and Photoshop Elements (Windows):** `https://www.redrivercatalog.com/profiles/how-to-use-icc-color-printer-profiles-photoshop-elements-canon-pc.html`

- **Canon Printers and Photoshop Elements (Macintosh):** `https://www.redrivercatalog.com/profiles/how-to-use-icc-color-printer-profiles-photoshop-elements-canon-mac.html`

- **Brother, Canon, Epson, & HP Profiles:** `https://colorway.com/icc`

    On the ColorWay site, you can find profiles for many different Brother, Canon, Epson, and HP printers. Some of the descriptions on these websites show some legacy versions of Photoshop Elements; however, most of the information is relative to the current Elements update.

Color profiles are also dependent on the ink being used, and refilling cartridges with generic ink can (in some cases) result in colors shifting. Similarly, if the nozzles aren't clean and delivering ink consistently, you may see strange results.

Printing a photo with the printer managing color

Without going into all the settings you have to choose from in the Print and More Options dialog boxes, for now we look at printing a photo and letting the printer manage color. We explain more available print options later in this chapter, in the section "Creating transfers, borders, and more with More Options."

Unless you want to print Picture Packages or Contact Sheets (Windows), use the Print dialog box from the Photo Editor. Color Management options offer you much better choices for managing color.

For the following example, we use an Epson printer. If you have a different printer, some of the dialog boxes and terms may be different. With a little careful examination of the Print dialog box, you can apply the following steps for any printer:

1. **With a photo open in the Photo Editor, choose File ⇨ Print or press Ctrl+P (⌘ +P on the Mac).**

   The Print dialog box that opens contains all the settings you need to print a file, as shown in Figure 15-1.

2. **Click Page Setup.**

   Many different printers are available, and they all have different printer drivers. For this series of instructions, we use an Epson L1300 printer. Your settings may vary between the description and screens you see here and the settings for your printer.

   Try to follow the process for selecting page attributes and color management to print photos to your printer.

3. **In the Page Setup dialog box on Windows and the Print dialog box on the Mac, you make choices for orientation, paper type, paper size, and print quality, as shown in Figure 15-1 for Windows and Figure 15-2 for the Mac.**

   Figure 15-1 shows options for an Epson L1300 printer on Windows. Your printer Page Setup dialog box may differ significantly.

   The Print dialog box on the Mac is the same for many different printers. Figure 15-2 shows the Print dialog box after you open the Layout drop-list in the Print dialog box and choose Print Settings.

FIGURE 15-1:
The Page Setup
dialog box
(Windows).

FIGURE 15-2:
The Print
dialog
box (Mac).

4. **Click OK after making appropriate choices in the Page Setup dialog box (Windows). On the Mac, click Cancel if you opened the Print dialog box.**

On the Mac, you first make choices for color management and then go to the Print dialog box, where you make your choices for orientation, paper type, and size and print quality.

5. **On Windows, you return to the Print dialog box. On the Mac, click Print again to open the Elements Print dialog box.**

6. **Click More Options at the bottom of the Elements Print dialog box.**

7. Click Color Management in the More Options dialog box, as shown in Figure 15-3.

8. Choose your color management option.

This is where you can choose to let either your printer or Elements manage color. In many cases, unless you have special art papers or different paper types, you can choose to let the printer driver manage color.

9. Choose Printer Manages Color and click OK.

10. On the Mac, make your choices for the print attributes in the Print dialog box before printing.

When you click Print in the Elements Print dialog box, you arrive at the OSX Print dialog box. Where you see Layout, open the drop-down list and choose Print Settings. Here, you make choices for the paper type and quality.

11. Click Print.

The file prints with settings you make in the Page Setup dialog box (Windows) or Print Dialog Box (Mac).

FIGURE 15-3:
The More Options dialog box (Windows and Mac).

Printing a photo with Elements managing color

If you want Elements to manage color, follow the same steps as you do for letting the printer manage color. When you arrive at the More Options and click Color Management, choose Photoshop Elements Manages Color. Then open the Printer Profile drop-down list and choose the profile recommended for your printer and the paper.

Printing a picture package or contact sheet

Elements offers two additional printing options that are available in different places on Windows and the Mac:

>> **Picture Package:** This option enables you to arrange one or more images on a page and print those images from a selection of standard-size prints.

>> **Contact Sheet II:** Choose this option to print samples of several images. (Before digital photography, the contact sheet format was how photographers initially evaluated their shots.)

If you want to print a picture package or a contact sheet, you must print from the Organizer (Windows) or choose a command (Picture Package or Contact Sheet) from the File menu in the Photo Editor on the Mac, where these options are available.

All the steps for printing are basically the same, as outlined in the earlier section "Printing a photo with the printer managing color." The key difference is the Color Management options you see. The Color Management options are limited to choosing a Print Space (such as sRGB or Adobe RGB).

On a Windows computer, the Photo Editor offers better Color Management options. Always print your files from the Photo Editor unless you want to print a special print, such as a Picture Package, that requires you to print from the Organizer. Printing from the Photo Editor enables you to make use of all the Color Management options available in the More Options dialog box.

Getting Familiar with the Print Dialog Box

Because the Print dialog box options are identical in the Organizer and the Photo Editor in Windows (with the exception of color profile management), you find the same menus and buttons when you choose File ⇨ Print from either the Organizer or Photo Editor. On the Mac, inasmuch as you can choose File ⇨ Print in the Organizer, when you choose Print in the Organizer you are redirected to the Photo Editor where the printing occurs.

Using the Prints options

The following are the individual items you find in either dialog box (see Figure 15-4):

(A) **Image Thumbnails:** When you select multiple images in the Organizer, all the selected images appear in a scrollable window on the left side of the dialog box

(B) **Select Printer:** Choose a target printer from the drop-down list.

(C) **Printer Settings (Windows only):** Click this button to open properties unique to the selected printer.

(D) **Select Paper Size:** Choose from print sizes that your printer supports. This list may change when you choose a different printer from the Select Printer drop-down list.

(E) **Select Type of Print:** In Windows, you have three print options available — Individual Prints, Contact Sheets, and Picture Packages. On the Mac, these options appear as separate menu commands in the File menu in Expert mode. For more information on contact sheets and picture packages, see the section "Printing a picture package or contact sheet," earlier in this chapter.

(F) **Select a Layout:** Choose from the menu how many images you want on each page.

(G) **Select a Frame:** If you want a frame on each print, choose from one of the many options in the drop-down list.

(H) **Crop to Fit:** Select this check box to crop an image to fit the selected paper size.

(I) **Print __ Copies of Each Image:** By default, one copy is printed. You can choose to print multiple copies by entering the number you want in the text box.

(J) **Add/Remove:** Click + (plus sign) to add more files to the Picture Package and click – (minus sign) to remove photos.

(K) **Help:** Click Help to open online help.

(L) **Page Setup:** Click this button to open the Page Setup dialog box.

(M) **Rotate:** Click the rotate icons to rotate clockwise and counterclockwise. Only a single image can be rotated at a time.

(N) **More Options:** Click More Options to open another dialog box that allows you to choose additional options. (See the section "Creating transfers, borders, and more with More Options," later in this chapter.)

(O) **Scroll Print Preview:** Click the arrows to go through a print preview for all images in the list. Move the slider to zoom photos in the Print Preview.

(P) **Zoom:** Move the slider to zoom in and out of a given image.

(Q) **Print:** Click Print after making all adjustments in the Print dialog box.

(R) **Cancel:** Clicking Cancel dismisses the dialog box without sending a photo to the printer.

FIGURE 15-4:
The Prints dialog box gives you plenty of options.

Creating transfers, borders, and more with More Options

If you want to add special features to your print, check out the More Options dialog box (shown in Figure 15-5) after clicking the More Options button in the Prints dialog box. We explain the Color Management options you find here in the earlier section "Working with Color Printer Profiles." This section is about the fun stuff, available on the Printing Choices pane of the More Options dialog box. Here's a quick tour of what you find:

» **Photo Details:** Select the check boxes for the detail items you want printed as labels on your output.

» **Iron-On Transfer:** This option is used for heat-transfer material such as Mylar, LexJet, and other substrates that require *e-down* printing (*emulsion-down* printing, in which the negative and the image are flipped).

TIP

If you're looking for a border that's fancier than a basic line, check out these other options elsewhere in Elements:

- The Picture Package options offer frames, such as antique ovals and more on Windows only. See "Printing a picture package or contact sheet," earlier in this chapter, for details.

- You can fine-tune how a basic border appears with a fill layer, as we explain in Chapter 9.

- Quick mode offers graphical frames. Chapter 10 has the details.

- Picture Effects (which we cover in Chapter 12) enable you to choose from a range of frames, too.

≫ **Trim Guidelines:** Select the Print Crop Marks check box to print crop marks.

FIGURE 15-5:
Click More
Options in the
Print dialog
box to access
the Printing
Choices
dialog box.

Outsourcing Printing

Previous versions of Elements had links from within the program to online printers. All those links have disappeared because it was difficult for Adobe to keep up with the best sources available to you.

When it comes to online printing services, you have many choices. There are some great printing establishments that offer high-quality prints at affordable prices. There are also many services that don't measure up to offering you quality professional printing.

You may find that it can be even cheaper to use an online service than printing to your desktop printer. If you're a critical artist and you want to match color and contrast in your prints to what you see on your monitor, you may be printing several test shots before you actually produce the final print. The cost of paper and inks is high for all desktop printers.

Online printers offer you many options that you don't typically have when using your desktop printer. For example, papers come in a wide variety with printing services. You can print to wood, plastic, canvas, ultra-thick paper, archival giclée fine-art prints, velvet, smooth matte, photo rag baryta, and more. Choices are abundant with printing sevices. You can also print books, albums, and an assortment of different card types.

A huge assortment of services is available to you. If you want economy prints, you can stop by your local Walmart or Costco. But if you want some good-quality professional prints, we recommend the following three services

>> **WHCC:** https://www.whcc.com

>> **ProDpi:** https://www.prodpi.com

>> **Mpix:** https://www.mpix.com

Rather than provide any description for each service here, browse the providers' web sites and check out their services and prices. Most providers ship directly to you within two days of your order.

IN THIS CHAPTER

» **Understanding packaging and sharing options**

» **Working with video**

» **Sending email attachments**

» **Sharing Facebook cover and profile images**

» **Creating files for web viewing**

Chapter **16**

Sharing Your Work

E lements is a great packaging tool that can deploy your photos and projects for screen viewing — and not just on your computer monitor. You can edit photos or assemble creations that are exported for web viewing, and you can even prepare files to show on your television.

In Chapter 15, we cover the output requirements for printing files, which are much different from what you use for screen viewing.

In this chapter, we cover the options for web and screen viewing that get you started with the basics, including saving images for the web (or for screen viewing), as online slideshows, and sharing files on social networks such as Facebook.

Getting Familiar with the Elements Sharing Options

TIP

Before you delve into making creations for screen viewing in Chapter 17, you should be familiar with your available options for not only screen images but also sharing — particularly online sharing services. You also need to be familiar with the acceptable standards for online hosts, where you eventually expect to send your creations, and the kinds of devices people are likely to use to view your creations.

Planning ahead

Before you choose a sharing activity and ultimately begin work on a creation, you need to ask a few questions:

>> **What device(s) are going to display my creations?** When it comes to viewing photos and movies, you have choices that include computers (including desktop, notebooks, and netbooks), handheld devices such as cellphones and tablets (such as the Apple iPad and Samsung Galaxy), and TVs. If you want your creations to be viewable on all devices, you need to use different Elements tools and file formats than you would use for showing creations exclusively on a TV or on a computer.

Note that hosts vary greatly in terms of space allocated for storing content. If you want to share large video files, be certain that the storage host you choose allocates enough storage space to permit you to upload your files.

>> **What storage hosts are the most popular?** From within Photoshop Elements, you can export photos directly to Facebook, Flickr, and Twitter. For videos, you have direct support for YouTube and Vimeo. For other social media sites — such as Tumblr, Snapchat, WhatsApp, and so on — you need to prepare your images in Elements and upload them according to the developer's specifications.

>> **What types of creations can I share?** Obviously, you can upload individual photos to any one of the online services. More often than not, you need to convert your photos to JPEG format. (For more on the JPEG format, see Chapter 2.)

You can use the Share panel and choose to share directly to Flickr, Facebook, Twitter, YouTube, and Vimeo. In addition to uploading single photos to a service, some of the creations you might want to share include the following:

- **Albums:** You can create photo albums and share the albums on many different sites.

- **Slideshows:** In Windows, you can create a slideshow and choose to export the slideshow as a movie file (.wmv) or a PDF. On the Mac, you can export a Memories file to a video, but you then have to exit Elements and upload the file through another way. Ultimately, you can view exported videos in a number of different online hosts. If you use Facebook, all devices show your creations. Slideshows have the additional benefit of supporting audio files. You can add audio to the creations, and the audio plays on all devices if you upload them to Facebook.

- **Videos:** If you want to host videos on your own website and make the videos available to iPhone/iPod/iPad users as well as computer users, you need a little help from Adobe Premiere Elements. In Premiere Elements, you can export video for mobile devices, and the resultant file can be viewed on an iPhone/iPod/iPad as well as a computer.

Understanding photo sharing in Elements

Not all sharing providers are directly linked to Photoshop Elements. Many more social media sharing providers exist than those you find in the Elements Share panel. You can always make creations and manually upload creations, photos, and videos to many other services. A list of the more popular websites is shown in Table 16-1.

TABLE 16-1   **Photo Sharing Providers**

Source	URL	Description
Behance	www.behance.net	A place to show off your artwork and see examples of excellent design and photography.
dotPhoto	www.dotphoto.com	Requires a club membership fee.
Facebook	www.facebook.com	Free unlimited photo and video uploads. Figure 16-1 shows a video shared on Facebook.
Flickr	www.flickr.com	Allows 1,000 free photo uploads.
Instagram	www.instagram.com	Upload photos/videos from phones or acquire a third-party app to upload from your computer. Number of uploads is unlimited.
Photobucket	http://photobucket.com	Up to 25GB photo and video uploads per month at a cost of $4.99/month; unlimited plan is $11.99/month.
Shutterfly	www.shutterfly.com	Concentrates on photo products — calendars, iPhone cases, cards, cushion covers, and so on — rather than photo storage.
SlickPic	www.slickpic.com	Unlimited uploads for the free account with a maximum file size of 10MB.
SmugMug	www.smugmug.com	Paid service for photo storage. Minimum account is $55/year.
Twitter	www.twitter.com	Allows photo uploads of a maximum of 15MB each.
Vimeo	www.vimeo.com	Free video uploads of 500MB per week. Maximum is 5GB per week with no storage limit.
YouTube	www.youtube.com	Free unlimited video uploads of up to a maximum upload file size of 128GB or 12 hours.

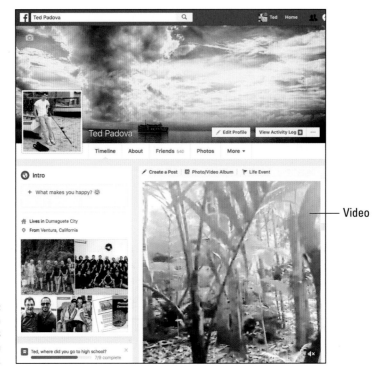

Video

FIGURE 16-1:
Video on
Facebook is
shown on an
Apple iPad.

Using the Share Panel

You choose an option in the Share panel by clicking one of the buttons, and then one of two interfaces appears:

>> Some options lead you to more specific choices in the Share panel.

>> Other choices open a window where you log in to an account for sharing photos. The choices for sharing photos with other services open windows for logging in to your account and proceeding through steps to prepare and upload images.

Figure 16-2 shows the Share panel as it appears in the Organizer (left) on Windows and in the Photo Editor (right). The Photo Editor Share panel has a more abbreviated set of options. On the Mac, the panels are identical, with one exception: The Share panel in the Organizer doesn't have a menu option for Burn Video DVD.

FIGURE 16-2:
The Share
panel as it
appears in the
Organizer (left)
and Photo
Editor (right).

Options available in the Share panel are identical on both platforms. If you're familiar with earlier versions of Photoshop Elements, you'll notice that Elements 2022 provides many fewer share options. This is because some developers have stopped supporting sharing from desktop applications.

In the sections ahead, we explore using the Share panel in the Organizer and making choices for preparing photos for sharing.

Emailing photos

Rather than save your file from Elements and then open your email client (such as Outlook or Apple Mail) and select the photo to attach to an email, you can use Elements to easily share photos via email with one click.

When you want to email a photo or a creation like some of those we talk about in Chapter 17, follow these steps:

1. In the Organizer, select the photos you want to email to a friend.

2. Open the Share panel and select Email Attachments.

The first time you try to email photos, Elements opens the Organizer Preferences panel and requires you to configure your email account. If your email account is already configured, you won't see the Preferences panel appear. Fill in the text boxes and click OK.

3. Check Convert Photos to JPEGs, choose a quality setting for the attachment, and click Next.

Drag the Quality slider and observe the file size noted at the bottom of the panel where you see Estimated Size, as shown in Figure 16-3. If the file is large, you may need to resize it in the Image Size dialog box before emailing the photo. Chapter 2 explains how to resize images.

4. (Optional) Add recipients.

The next panel provides settings for adding a message and adding recipients from an Address Book, as shown in Figure 16-4.

You can bypass adding recipients from your Address Book. If no recipients are listed in the Select Recipients panel, you can add recipient email addresses in the new message window in your email client. On the Mac, depending on the email client you use, you may have to manually add recipient addresses.

5. Click Next.

The photo(s) are first sampled to the output size. Wait a few minutes until Elements completes the sampling; then the photos are attached to a new email message in your default email client.

REMEMBER

Elements attaches the media to a new email message. You need to toggle to your email client in order to see the message and send the mail.

6. Review the To, Subject, and Attach fields to be certain the information is correct. Then click the Send button.

TIP

By default, Elements uses your primary email client application, which may or may not be the email program you use. You can change the default email client by pressing Ctrl+K (⌘ +K on the Mac) to open the Preferences dialog box when you're in the Organizer and then clicking Email in the left pane. From a drop-down list in the Sharing preferences, choose the email client application that you want Elements to use.

Elements supports using web-based email clients. If you use Yahoo!, Gmail, or even another account, you can send your photos using your existing mail client. If you choose Other in the Email Preferences, you need to supply your SMTP Server and the Port number. If you need help with setting up the mail for other accounts not listed in the Email Preferences, contact your Internet Service Provider (ISP) for assistance.

FIGURE 16-3: Set the Quality slider to a medium setting for faster uploads to your mail server.

Working with Adobe Premiere Elements

Several options in the Share and Create panels require that you use Adobe Premiere Elements. The items denoted as Burn Video DVD/BluRay, Online Video Sharing, and Mobile Phones and Players all require Adobe Premiere Elements.

If any of these items interest you, you can download a free trial of Adobe Premiere Elements and work with it for 30 days. If Premiere Elements is a tool you find worthwhile, you can purchase it from the Adobe Store. If you're perusing this book and have not yet purchased Elements 2022, you can purchase the Adobe Photoshop Elements 2022 and Adobe Premiere Elements 2022 bundle. Buying the bundle is much less expensive than buying the products separately.

For Adobe Premiere Elements trial versions, just click one of the options for video sharing in the Share panel, and you're prompted to download a trial version of Premiere Elements.

FIGURE 16-4:
Add recipients from your Address Book.

Sharing your photos on social networks

You have a variety of options for sharing photos and placing orders on a number of service networks. We don't have enough space in this book to cover every service that Elements supports, so we walk through the more popular services (Flickr, Facebook, and Twitter) as examples for connecting with a service provider. If other services interest you, poke around and explore options for the services you use.

Experienced users of Elements will immediately notice that services such as Flickr and Facebook have been promoted from options nested in the More Options dropdown list found in earlier versions of Elements to buttons shown in the Share panel.

Sharing photos on Facebook and Twitter

Elements supports a direct connection to Twitter. In the Share panel, you can choose Twitter. Elements opens your default web browser and takes you to Twitter's site. You need to authenticate your account by providing your login and password.

After your account is authenticated, you return to Elements, where you can type your tweet and click the Tweet button, as shown in Figure 16-5, to add the tweet to your account.

FIGURE 16-5:
Type a message and click Tweet to add to your Twitter account.

Unfortunately, Elements has stopped supporting direct uploads to Facebook. This happened because Facebook keeps external applications from uploading to its site. You need to prepare your photo in Elements and then use Facebook to upload the file by clicking a photo icon in a new Facebook Post. In Figure 16-6, you can see a photo uploaded to Facebook externally after it has been edited in Elements.

After a photo is uploaded, you see the photo on your Timeline (as shown in Figure 16-6) or in a photo collection.

Using other online services

After you become familiar with uploading photos to a service, you can easily follow similar steps to upload photos to any of the services that are supported by Elements. You first encounter the window to authorize an account, such as when using Facebook, Flickr, and Twitter. When setting up a new account, you can log in to the service and create the new account.

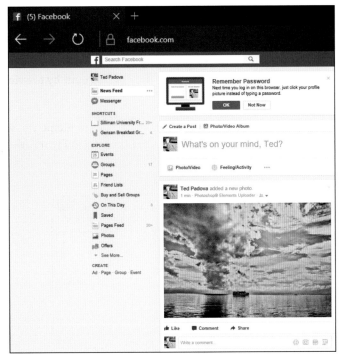

FIGURE 16-6:
A photo
uploaded to
a Facebook
account.

Photo: Ted Padova

When you enter a site for sharing photos, printing photos, or creating items such as photo frames, follow the easy online steps that each service provides.

Chapter **17**

Making Creations

A dobe Photoshop Elements offers you a number of creation tasks that you can share onscreen or in print. From both the Create and Share panels in the Panel Bin in the Organizer and Photo Editor, you have a number of menu choices for making creations designed for sharing.

In this chapter, we talk about creations designed for print and sharing. It's all here in Photoshop Elements, for both Windows and Mac users. If you're looking for how to create files for screen and web viewing, flip back to Chapter 16.

Checking Out the Create Panel

To see the creations available on the Create panel, as shown in Figure 17-1, click the Create tab above the Panel Bin. Like the Share panel we introduce in Chapter 16, the Create panel is available from either the Organizer or the Photo Editor. The Photo Editor doesn't support video creations; therefore, the Organizer offers you three additional items not available in the Photo Editor: Instant Movie, Video Story, and Video Collage.

The Create panel offers identical options in Windows and the Mac. You find options for creating photo prints, photo books, greeting cards, photo calendars, photo collages, an assortment of choices for DVD labels and jackets, and three options for use with Adobe Premiere Elements (Instant Movie, Video Story, and Video Collage). Keep in mind that you need to acquire the bundle of Photoshop Elements and Premiere Elements in order to use the video creation options.

The Video Collage creation offers you a means for creating a collage of video clips and still images to assemble your most memorable events. As with other video creations, you need to install Adobe Premiere Elements.

Note: When you open the Create panel in the Photo Editor, you won't see the options for video creations.

Create ▾	Shar
Slideshow	
Photo Collage	
Quote Graphic	
Photo Prints	
Photo Book	
Greeting Card	
Photo Calendar	
Instant Movie	
Video Story	
Video Collage	
CD Jacket	
DVD Jacket	
CD/DVD Label	

FIGURE 17-1:
The Create panel from the Organizer.

Grasping Creation-Assembly Basics

Creations such as photo books, greeting cards, photo calendars, and photo collages that you assemble from the Create panel (refer to Figure 17-1) are intended for output to either print or screen sharing.

Many creation options follow a similar set of steps to produce a file that is shared with other users or sent to an online printing service. In the Panel Bin, you can find all you need to make a new project by choosing layouts and producing a creation. Here are the common steps to follow when making a choice from the Create panel:

1. **Select photos.**

   In the Organizer or in the Photo Bin in the Photo Editor, select the photos you want to use for your creation. Sort photos or use keyword tags (as we explain in Chapters 5 and 6) to simplify finding and selecting photos you want to use for a creation.

   TIP

   If you want to use photos from different folders, or when the images are spread around your hard drive, create an album, as we explain in Chapter 5. If you want to use the photos once for a creation, you can delete the album. Or you can keep the album around and use the same photos with several different creations.

2. **Click the Create tab.**

   The Create panel opens in the Panel Bin. The minute you click a creation, you're switched automatically to the Photo Editor.

3. **Click an option for the type of creation you want.**

   You can click Photo Book, Photo Calendar, Greeting Card, Photo Collage, and so on.

   After you select the kind of creation you want to make, a wizard opens, and you choose the options you want.

REMEMBER

   When you create a calendar, select 13 images. One image is used for the calendar cover, and the remaining 12 images are used for each month.

4. **Select a size for the output in the left column.**

   In Figure 17-2, we selected to make a photo book, and the sizes are displayed in the left column.

5. **Select a theme/layout.**

   Many of the creation options enable you to select a template. When you click a creation option on the Create panel, the panel changes to display choices for various themes, backgrounds, and borders. You make choices by clicking the theme or background. In Figure 17-2, you can see the Themes column for a photo book creation.

REMEMBER

   Most assets, such as themes, are not installed with your Photoshop Elements installation. When you select an asset such as a theme, it's downloaded from Adobe's website. A message window informs you that a download is in progress. Be patient and wait for the download to complete before moving on.

   Elements automatically creates the number of pages to accommodate the number of photos you selected in the Organizer or Photo Bin.

6. **Select your options in the Create panel. Click OK.**

   The Create panel changes to a wizard and displays three icons at the bottom of the panel, as shown in Figure 17-3:

   - **Pages:** Add or delete pages.

   - **Layouts:** Choose a layout, as shown in Figure 17-4. You can click different layouts and view the results in the wizard.

   - **Graphics:** Add artwork and text with the Graphics panel. Explore each item and choose options available for editing your creation.

TIP

When you make a creation, you can determine the number of pages at the time you first choose a creation. Often, you forget about creating enough pages, or you find that you need more pages than originally anticipated. It can be downright frustrating if you need more pages but don't know how to add the number you need. If you look closely at the top of the Pages panel, you find a Page icon. Click this icon to add more pages. To insert a page between two existing pages, click the first page in the sequence. Click the Page icon in the Pages panel, and the new pages are inserted after the selected page. To delete a page, select the page and click the Trash icon at the top of the Pages panel.

7. **(Optional) Select options in the creation's Advanced mode.**

Up to this point, you couldn't make any changes to your photos (other than sizing and rotating) because the wizard interface is separate from the Organizer and Photo Editor.

Click the Advanced Mode button in the upper-left corner of the wizard, and you have access to the Photo Editor Tools panel. You can now make edits on any photos in the creation, as shown in Figure 17-5.

FIGURE 17-3:
The Pages panel.

When you click Advanced Mode, the button name changes to Basic Mode. Click the Basic Mode button to return to the Create panel.

8. **Click the output option at the bottom of the wizard:**

- **Save:** Save the file as a Photoshop Elements Project. You can return to the project and edit it at a later time.

- **Print:** Before the output is generated, look over the preview of your creation. If you're using Advanced mode, click the Basic button at the top of the window and scroll through the pages to preview the creation.

Whether you want to create a photo book, a calendar, or any one of the other first five options in the Create panel, you follow the same steps.

When you make a creation that will ultimately be shared with other users or sent to an online service for printing, you *must* first select the photos you want in your creation. For example, when you create a photo book by clicking the Photo Book button on the Create panel, you first need to select photos.

FIGURE 17-4:
The Layouts panel offers choices for many layouts.

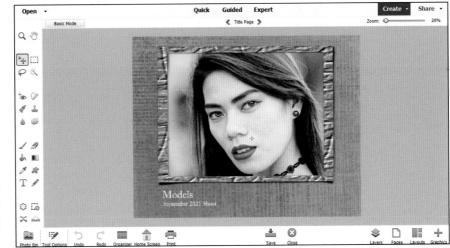

FIGURE 17-5:
Advanced mode provides you with the Photo Editor tools to edit photos in your creation before saving or printing.

Photo: Ted Padova

The reason you must first select photos — in either the Organizer or Photo Bin — is that the creation process involves using a wizard to set the attributes for your creation. Elements must first know what photos you intend to use before it can open a wizard to walk you through the creation process.

Creating a Quote Graphic

You begin with a photo open in the Photo Editor, select a photo in the Organizer, or start from scratch without selecting a photo. In the Create drop-down list that you open from either the Organizer or the Photo Editor, choose Quote Graphic.

The first panel opens, showing you the templates you can choose from. One option lets you start from scratch without using a template, as shown in Figure 17-6.

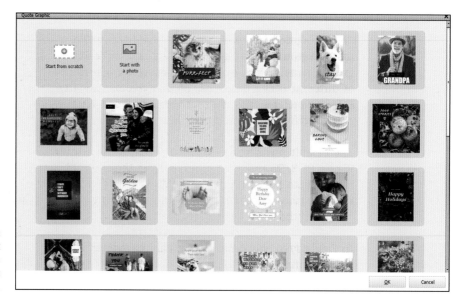

FIGURE 17-6: The first panel for the Quote Graphic creation.

Click the template you want to use. The panel immediately changes to an assortment of fixed sizes and sharing destinations. For example, you can make an Instagram post, a Facebook Cover, a Twitter, or a Pinterest post. If you don't want to post to a social media site, you can choose from a number of different fixed sizes that you can open in the Photo Editor, as shown in Figure 17-7.

Quote Graphic

Instagram Post   Instagram Story   Facebook Cover   Facebook Event   Facebook Post   Pinterest Post   Twitter Post   Letter-Portrait

Letter-Landscape   A4-Portrait   A4-Landscape   A3-Portrait   A3-Landscape   6x6 In   8x8 In   12x12 In

4x6 In   6x4 In   5x7 In   7x5 In   8x10 In   10x8 In

OK   Cancel

FIGURE 17-7:
Choose from a variety of social media and common photo and document sizes.

Click an option in the second panel, and you arrive at the Background/Effects panel. The default is the Background panel, where you can choose from a number of different background designs and colors. Click the Effects panel, and you can choose from a huge assortment of different kinds of effects.

The default photo appears in the panel, as shown in Figure 17-8. To replace the photo, open the Photo Bin in the Photo Editor and drag a photo to the document. When finished, click the Save button that appears at the bottom of the Background/Effects panels.

In Figure 17-9, you can see our final image after using the Beautiful Moments template.

FIGURE 17-8:
The Background/Effects panel.

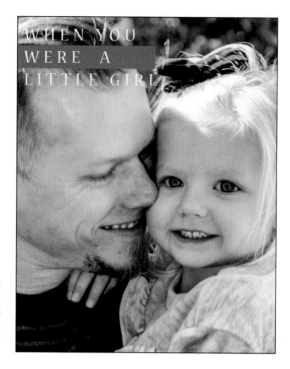

FIGURE 17-9:
Final edited
photo using
the Quote
Graphic
creation.

Creating a Memories Video

When you click the Slideshow button, you can create a video referred to as Memories. Select an album, photos in the Media Browser, or some Smart Picks and then click Slideshow in the Create panel or click the Slideshow button at the bottom of the Organizer window. The Memories Wizard opens. In this window, you find three buttons in the upper-left corner. Click the first button, and you see all the photos that will be included in the video. Click the + (plus sign) icon, and you can add more images. Click the Show Text check box, and you can add captions to the images.

The second button displays several different Themes you can use with a video, as shown in Figure 17-10. Click a Theme to use it with your video export.

The last button enables you to choose an audio track. You can choose from audio files loaded in the Organizer or click the + (plus sign) icon to add an audio file from your hard drive.

FIGURE 17-10:
Click a Theme
to apply to the
video.

When finished making the choices for your images, Theme, and audio track, click the Export button in the upper-right corner of the window. You can export directly to your Facebook account, export to Vimeo, export to YouTube, or save the video file to your hard drive.

To double-check your work, try to export the file to your hard drive and view it on your monitor before uploading the file to a social media site.

Creating a PDF Slideshow

In the Share panel, you have the PDF Slideshow option. When you select photos in the Organizer and choose this option, the Share panel opens and provides the same options as you find when using email (as described in Chapter 16). The only difference between this option and choosing to email your photos is that the selected images are saved as a PDF and then emailed to the recipients you select in the Share panel.

Making Additional Creations

Unfortunately, we don't have room in this book to cover each creation. Fortunately, many of the other creation types are intuitive and easy to master. To create instant videos, you need Adobe Premiere Elements. Other readily available items include photo books, greeting cards, photo stamps, calendars, and CD/DVDs that you burn (Windows only). For each creation type, Elements provides you with many editing options. Explore each of the creations available to you and consult the online Help file for steps you can follow.

6

The Part of Tens

IN THIS CHAPTER

» **Correcting skin tones**

» **Removing objects**

» **Replacing backgrounds**

» **Improving contrast**

» **Resizing images**

Chapter **18**

The Ten Best Guided Edits

With each release of Photoshop Elements, Adobe adds to the library of Guided Edits, which enable you to do complex tasks easily by following a series of steps. Some of the edits are pure fun and whimsy, and you may use them every now and then. Others are more practical and designed to really help improve your photos. These are the ones that will become part of your regular toolkit to get your images looking their best. Here are ten of our favorites.

Correct Skin Tone

Occasionally, certain kinds of lighting can make the people in your portraits look a little green, yellow, magenta, or other color not normally associated with skin. The Correct Skin Tone Guided Edit easily fixes that problem. If you need more information on correcting skin tones, see the section "Adjusting skin tones," in Chapter 11.

Here are the steps to use this edit:

1. **In Guided mode, choose File ➪ Open and select your image.**

2. **Under Basic Edits, choose Correct Skin Tone.**

3. **Specify your view to be Before & After – Horizontal or Before & After - Vertical.**

   This view gives you a side-by-side comparison of your image while editing.

4. **Using the Skin Tone Selection eyedropper tool, click the person's skin in the After image.**

5. **If you feel that you need to refine your results further, use the Tan, Blush, and Light sliders, as shown in Figure 18-1.**

   Note that the Light slider is pretty intense, so we recommend going easy on this adjustment.

6. **After you're satisfied with the edit, click Next.**

7. **Elements now asks what you would like to do next. Select from:**

   - **Save:** This option simply saves over your original image in the same location on your computer.

   - **Save As:** With this option, you now have the choice of saving your image to the cloud or to your computer. Click Continue, name the file, and click Save.

FIGURE 18-1:
The Correct Skin Tone edit removes color casts from your people's skin.

© Blend Images/Shutterstock Image #220912063

- **Continue Editing: In Quick or In Expert:** You can choose to continue editing the image in either Quick or Expert mode.

- **Print:** This option transports you to the Fujifilm Print & Gifts website and enables you to order prints, cards, and merchandise.

- **Share:** Share your image to the Flickr or Twitter websites.

8. **Click Done.**

Sharpen

If you find that your image is a little soft or slightly blurry, you can apply a sharpening adjustment, which will increase the contrast between the pixels, giving the appearance that the focus is better. If you want more details on sharpening, be sure to check out the section "Sharpening for better focus," in Chapter 11.

Here are the steps to use this edit:

1. **In Guided mode, choose File ⇨ Open and choose your photo.**

2. **Under Basic Edits, choose Sharpen.**

3. **Specify your View to Before & After – Horizontal or Before & After - Vertical.**

   This view gives you a side-by-side comparison of your image while editing.

4. **Either click the Auto Fix button to have Elements analyze the image and automatically make the adjustment, or use the Sharpen slider to manually apply the edit.**

   Note that if your image is fairly soft to start with (ours was, as shown in Figure 18-2), you may have to apply quite a bit of sharpening to see a noticeable result. The drawback to doing this sharpening is that the image may start to look a bit grainy.

5. **After you're happy with the edit, click Next.**

6. **Elements now asks what you would like to do next. Select from:**

- **Save:** This option simply saves over your original image in the same location on your computer.

- **Save As:** With this option, you now have the choice of saving your image to the cloud or to your computer. Click Continue, name the file, and click Save.

- **Continue Editing: In Quick or In Expert:** You can choose to continue editing the image in either Quick or Expert mode.

- **Print:** This option transports you to the Fujifilm Print & Gifts website and enables you to order prints, cards, and merchandise.

- **Share:** Share your image to the Flickr or Twitter websites.

7. **Click Done.**

FIGURE 18-2: Sharpening your image can help your image look less soft and blurry.

Object Removal

Sometimes you don't always have control over what you capture in your frame when taking a photo. Or maybe you're given a photo and asked to eliminate something from the image. The Object Removal Guided Edit is what you need to accomplish this task easily.

Follow these steps to remove an object:

1. **In Guided mode, choose File ⇨ Open and select your image.**

2. **Under Basic Edits, choose Object Removal.**

3. **Specify your View to Before & After – Horizontal or Before & After - Vertical.**

   This view gives you a side-by-side comparison of your image while editing.

4. **In the After image, choose your desired selection tool to choose the object you want to eliminate. For more on each of these tools, check out Chapter 8, "Making and Modifying Selections."**

   We chose the Brush tool, adjusted our Brush size to a medium-size diameter, and brushed over the brown horse.

5. **If you need to add or subtract to fine-tune your selection, click the Add or Subtract buttons and brush over your desired areas.**

6. **After you have adequately selected your object, click the Remove Object button.**

7. **If you see any visible seams, smudges, or other imperfections, use either the Spot Healing Brush or Clone Stamp Tool to fix these.**

   We started with the Clone Stamp tool to repair a couple of seams and then followed up with the Spot Healing Brush to fix a few smudges. For further details on these two tools, see the Chapter 10 sections "Cloning with the Clone Stamp Tool" and "Zeroing in with the Spot Healing Brush." As you can see in Figure 18-3, the brown horse is gone. It isn't perfect, and we would choose to edit it a bit more in Expert mode, but it is a good start. Depending on your particular image and object, the Guided Edit could be all you need.

8. **When you're happy with the removal, click Next.**

9. **Elements now asks what you would like to do next. Select from:**

   - **Save:** This option simply saves over your original image in the same location on your computer.

   - **Save As:** With this option, you now have the choice of saving your image to the cloud or to your computer. Click Continue, name the file, and click Save.

   - **Continue Editing: In Quick or In Expert:** You can choose to continue editing the image in either Quick or Expert mode.

   - **Print:** This option transports you to the Fujifilm Print & Gifts website and enables you to order prints, cards, and merchandise.

   - **Share:** Share your image to the Flickr or Twitter websites.

10. **Click Done.**

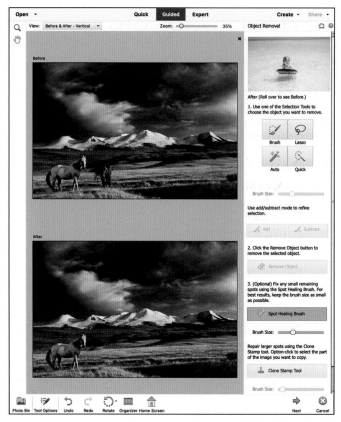

FIGURE 18-3:
Remove objects for your desired composition.

Perfect Portrait

The Perfect Portrait Guided Edit is a kind of one-stop shop for enhancing your portraits. You can do most of these enhancements using the tools and techniques in Expert mode, and if you want more control over the results, that may be where you will end up. But for those who want their enhancing to be quick and easy, Perfect Portrait is the place to be.

Follow these steps to remove an object:

1. **In Guided mode, choose File ⇨ Open and choose your image.**

2. **Under Special Edits, choose Perfect Portrait.**

3. **Specify your View to Before & After – Horizontal or Before & After – Vertical.**

   This view gives you a side-by-side comparison of your image while editing.

4. **Click the Smooth Skin button. Elements applies a smoothing effect. If the effect is too strong, dial it back with the Strength ramp.**

5. **Click the Increase Contrast button to do just that (increase the contrast).**

   We recommend avoiding this edit because it does not give you enough control as to how you want to increase the contrast, plus it's a little heavy handed. If your portrait needs a contrast adjustment, you are better off doing it in Quick or Expert mode and using the Levels or Color Curves adjustment.

6. **Fine-tune your portrait's face by applying the following.**

   - **Remove Blemishes:** This option uses the Spot Healing Brush to eliminate blemishes, wrinkles, and so on. Click areas of the face that need healing. We skipped this option on our girl in Figure 18-4. For more info the Spot Healing Brush, see the section "Zeroing in with the Spot Healing Brush," in Chapter 10.

   If you want to increase the diameter of your brush for this tool and the others, click the right bracket key. To decrease the diameter, click the left bracket key.

   - **Whiten Teeth:** Click or brush over any teeth that need whitening. We skipped this option because our girl has a closed smile.

   - **Brighten Eyes:** Click or brush over the eyes to brighten them. We clicked both the whites and irises of the eyes.

   - **Darken Eyebrows:** Brush over the eyebrows to darken them. We gave our girl one swipe.

7. **Click Add Glow if you want to add a glow effect to the portrait.**

   Clicking on this option transports you into another window, the Filter Gallery, and into the Diffuse Glow filter settings. Specify your options and click OK. We applied a very distinct glow effect to give our girl an other-wordly look, as shown in Figure 18-4.

8. **If you want to slim down your subject, click the Slim down option.**

   Unfortunately, this option really doesn't give you any settings to control how slim you want your subject. We recommend skipping this option and using the Liquify filter in Quick or Expert mode instead. For more on using Liquify, see "Distorting with the Liquify filter," in Chapter 12.

9. **After you're happy with the removal, click Next.**

10. **Elements now asks what you would like to do next. Select from:**

    - **Save:** This option simply saves over your original image in the same location on your computer.

- **Save As:** With this option, you now have the choice of saving your image to the cloud or to your computer. Click Continue, name the file, and click Save.

- **Continue Editing: In Quick or In Expert:** You can choose to continue editing the image in either Quick or Expert mode.

- **Print:** This option transports you to the Fujifilm Print & Gifts website and enables you to order prints, cards, and merchandise.

- **Share:** Share your image to the Flickr or Twitter websites.

11. **Click Done.**

FIGURE 18-4:
Give your image a radiant glow with the Perfect Portrait Guided Edit.

NEW

In this release of PhotoShop Elements, your pet can now also receive a makeover with the new Perfect Pet Guided Edit. With this edit, you can remove dirt, spots, and even a collar and leash! Fix the lighting and color, add an effect, and your pet is ready for showing off on social media.

Replace Background

Sometimes you want to pluck your subject out and put it into another scene. Other times, you want to leave your subject where it is and bring a different scene into the background. This Guided Edit enables you to do the latter.

Follow these steps to remove an object:

1. **In Guided mode, choose File ⇨ Open and select your photo.**

2. **Under Special Edits, choose Replace Background.**

3. **Specify your View to Before & After – Horizontal or Before & After – Vertical.**

   This view gives you a side- by-side comparison of your image while editing.

4. **Click the Select Subject button (Elements automatically detects and selects your subject) or use the Auto Selection, Quick Selection, or Brush tools. To add to or delete from your initial selection, use the Refine Selection Brush tool.**

   For details on these selection tools, see Chapter 8.

   We chose the Select Subject button because we had good contrast between our subject and the background. If you don't get good results with this automatic selection method, try one of the other selection tools.

5. **Choose a new background by**

   - **Importing a photo:** We wanted a nicer-looking body of water, so we imported another image.

   - **Choosing a Preset:** Click your choice from a set of preset backgrounds.

   - **Choosing None:** This option deletes the background and leaves a transparent background.

   - **Choosing Color:** Click within the color field or color ramp in the Color Picker and click OK.

6. **Use the Move tool to position your subject.**

7. **If you have too much of the original background around the edges of your subject, use the Refine Edge Brush (Subtract) to brush it away. If you have inadvertently deleted part of your subject, use the same tool (Add) to brush it back in.**

8. **If your subject and its new background don't really match well in terms of lighting and looks a tad fake, click the Auto Match Color Tone option.**

   Our swan (see Figure 18-5, top) was a bit too bright, but when we clicked the Auto Match Color Tone option, it made our swan too dark, so we chose Edit ⇨ Undo to undo the adjustment.

9. **If you like your composite, click Next.**

10. **Elements now asks what you would like to do next. Select from:**

- **Save:** This option simply saves over your original image in the same location on your computer.

- **Save As:** With this option, you now have the choice of saving your image to the cloud or to your computer. Click Continue, name the file, and click Save.

- **Continue Editing: In Quick or In Expert:** You can choose to continue editing the image in either Quick or Expert mode. Because the Auto Match Color Tone option didn't work for us, we took our swan into Expert mode and darkened it a bit using the Levels adjustment. You can see the final result in Figure 18-5 (bottom).

FIGURE 18-5: Swap out your original background with a new one.

© Denis Kuvaev/Shutterstock Image #98052245,
© S. Hermann and F. Richter/Pixabay Image lake-2063957-1920

- **Print:** This option transports you to the Fujifilm Print & Gifts website and enables you to order prints, cards, and merchandise.

- **Share:** Share your image to the Flickr or Twitter websites.

11. **Click Done.**

Remove a Color Cast

If your image has too much green, magenta, or other color, it's probably suffering from what is referred to as a color cast. Sometimes it is caused by the lighting; other times it can be an old photo whose green or magenta ink has faded. You can remove this unwanted color by using the Remove a Color Cast Guided Edit.

Here's how to use this edit:

1. **In Guided mode, choose File ⇨ Open and choose your image.**

2. **Under Color Edits, choose Remove A Color Cast.**

3. **Specify your View to Before & After – Horizontal or Before & After – Vertical.**

   This view gives you a side-by-side comparison of your image while editing.

4. **Click the Color Cast Selection button.**

   With the eyedropper, click a portion of the image that should be the "truest" gray, black, or white. A word of warning: Selecting this portion may take several attempts. We had to click around several times before we got the results we wanted (see Figure 18-6). We were successful by clicking the center of the left tree trunk in front of our tea house.

5. **Click Next.**

6. **Elements now asks what you would like to do next. Select from:**

   - **Save:** This option simply saves over your original image in the same location on your computer.

   - **Save As:** With this option, you now have the choice of saving your image to the cloud or to your computer. Click Continue, name the file, and click Save.

- **Continue Editing: In Quick or In Expert:** You can choose to continue editing the image in either Quick or Expert mode.

- **Print:** This option transports you to the Fujifilm Print & Gifts website and enables you to order prints, cards, and merchandise.

- **Share:** Share your image to the Flickr or Twitter websites.

7. **Click Done.**

FIGURE 18-6:
Eliminate color casts from your images.

Levels

Adjusting the contrast in your image is a fix that you will find yourself doing quite often. Although you have several ways to make this fix, one of the best is to use Levels. It is a bit more complex than some of the automatic ways of contrast adjustment in Elements, but this Guided Edit walks you through the process. For more details on levels, see "Pinpointing proper contrast with Levels," in Chapter 11.

Here's the lowdown on using the Levels Guided Edit:

1. **In Guided mode, choose File ⇨ Open and select your photo.**

2. **Under Basic Edits, choose Levels.**

3. **Specify your View to Before & After – Horizontal or Before & After – Vertical.**

   This view gives you a side-by-side comparison of your image while editing.

4. **Click the Create Levels Adjustment button.**

   The New Layer dialog box appears. Name your layer and click OK.

5. **In the Levels dialog box that appears, adjust your shadows (black slider), midtones (gray slider), and highlights (white slider).**

   The easiest way to get started with the adjustment is to drag your shadows slider to the right, to the beginning of the histogram (the graph that represents your tonal range). Then drag your highlights slider to the left, to the beginning of the histogram, as shown in Figure 18-7. If you feel that your midtones also need an adjustment, drag the midtone slider to the right to make the midtones darker and to the left to make them brighter. It isn't uncommon to not have to adjust the midtones after the shadows and highlights have been adjusted. Our Taipei shop cat looks so much better.

6. **Click OK.**

7. **Click Next.**

8. **Elements now asks you what you would like to do next. Select from:**

   - **Save:** This option simply saves over your original image in the same location on your computer.

   - **Save As:** With this option, you now have the choice of saving your image to the cloud or to your computer. Click Continue, name the file, and click Save.

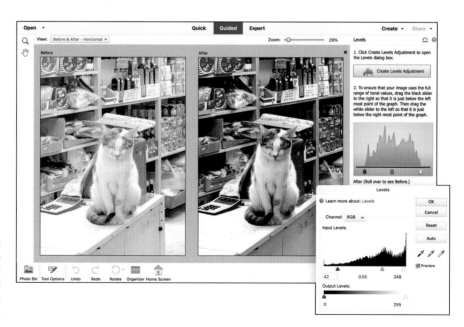

FIGURE 18-7:
Adjust the contrast in your images with the Levels Guided Edit.

- **Continue Editing: In Quick or In Expert:** You can choose to continue editing the image in either Quick or Expert mode.

- **Print:** This option transports you to the Fujifilm Print & Gifts website and enables you to order prints, cards, and merchandise.

- **Share:** Share your image to the Flickr or Twitter websites.

9. **Click Done.**

Resize Your Photo

We realize that resizing your photo may not be the most interesting edit you want to make, but it is a very important. Here's why, in a nutshell. Images need to be sized for their specific purpose. Preparing an image for a screen (a website or social media post) or print will require different pixel dimensions for them to display or print properly and with good quality. For more details on sizing, see "Grappling with the Ubiquitous Pixels" and "The Art of Resampling" in Chapter 2.

Here are the steps to resize your image:

1. **In Guided mode, choose File ⇨ Open and select your image.**

2. **Under Basic Edits, choose Resize Your Photo.**

3. **Specify your View to Before & After – Horizontal or Before & After – Vertical.**

   This view gives you a side-by-side comparison of your image while editing.

4. **Select an output option: either Web or Print.**

5. **Select a size option.**

   For the Web output option, choose from Long Edge, Short Edge, Width & Height, or File Size. For Long Edge or Short Edge options, the height or width is automatically adjusted to keep the aspect ratio. We wanted to resize our image for a Facebook poster, so it is recommended to use 1200 x 630 pixels, as shown in Figure 18-8. For the Print output option, choose from Long Edge, Short Edge, Width & Height, or standard print dimensions in inches.

6. **Depending on the size you specified, you will be asked to Apply or to Preview and adjust the crop window as needed.**

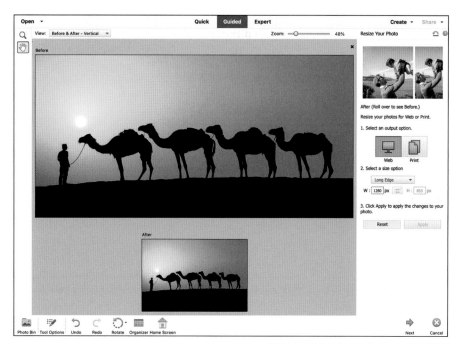

FIGURE 18-8:
Size your images properly for web or print.

© Mariia Savoskula/Shutterstock Image #112835215

7. **Click the green check mark after you're satisfied with your image.**

8. **Click Next.**

9. **Elements now asks you what you would like to do next. Select from:**

   - **Save:** This option simply saves over your original image in the same location on your computer.

   - **Save As:** With this option, you now have the choice of saving your image to the cloud or to your computer. Click Continue, name the file, and click Save.

   - **Continue Editing: In Quick or In Expert:** You can choose to continue editing the image in either Quick or Expert mode.

   - **Print:** This option transports you to the Fujifilm Print & Gifts website and enables you to order prints cards and merchandise.

   - **Share:** Share your image to the Flickr or Twitter websites.

10. **Click Done.**

Recompose

If you're like us, you may have sometimes wished that you would have taken a vertical or square photo instead of a horizontal one. Cropping it wouldn't work because you would be slicing off an important part of the image. This particular Guided Edit can be a lifesaver in that instance. The Recompose Guided Edit enables you to resize your image without sacrificing your vital content.

Here are the steps to recomposing your photo:

1. **In Guided mode, choose File ⇨ Open and choose your photo.**

2. **Under Special Edits, choose Recompose.**

3. **Specify your View to Before & After – Horizontal or Before & After – Vertical.**

    This view gives you a side-by-side comparison of your image while editing.

4. **You can start with the Recompose-Simple option. In the After image, drag the handles on the sides or corners to resize your image.**

    Make sure to pay attention to both your main subjects and especially to the space between the subjects. If all is okay, you are good to go and can go to Step 6. If your results are less than desirable, go to Step 5 to Recompose with finer details.

5. **If Step 4 didn't work, take the Protect brush and brush over any vital content that you want to keep or protect, as shown in Figure 18-9. You can then brush over any content you want to remove with the Remove brush. In the After image, drag the handles on the sides or corners to resize your image.**

    Note that if you need to clean up your protected or removed areas, use the appropriate Eraser brush. You can adjust Brush Size diameter with the slider.

6. **If you want to use a preset size to resize your image, select it from the Preset drop-down menu.**

7. **Click the green check mark when you're satisfied with your image.**

8. **Click Next.**

9. **Elements now asks you what you would like to do next. Select from:**

    - **Save:** This option simply saves over your original image in the same location on your computer.

    - **Save As:** With this option, you now have the choice of saving your image to the cloud or to your computer. Click Continue, name the file, and click Save.

FIGURE 18-9:
Resize
your image
without losing
important
content.

© Kate Trifo/pexels.com Image #4019406

- **Continue Editing: In Quick or In Expert:** You can choose to continue editing the image in either Quick or Expert mode.

- **Print:** This option transports you to the Fujifilm Print & Gifts website and enables you to order prints, cards, and merchandise.

- **Share:** Share your image to the Flickr or Twitter websites.

10. **Click Done.**

TIP

Depending on how much you resize your image you may have to do some retouching, especially in between your subjects. We had to do just that with our final image as shown in Figure 18-9. Use the Clone Stamp tool and Spot Healing Brush tool to eliminate these imperfections. For further details on these two tools, see these sections in Chapter 10: "Cloning with the Clone Stamp Tool" and "Zeroing in with the Spot Healing Brush."

Move & Scale Object

Occasionally you wish that the subject of your photo were bigger, smaller, or in a different location within the frame (see Figure 18-10). Although seamlessly changing any of those aspects sounds difficult, with the Move & Scale Object Guided Edit, each one is amazingly easy.

Here are the steps to resize as well as move (if you want) your image:

1. **In Guided mode, choose File ⇨ Open and choose your photo.**

2. **Under Basic Edits, choose Move & Scale Object.**

3. **Specify your View to Before & After – Horizontal or Before & After – Vertical.**

   This view gives you a side-by-side comparison of your image while editing.

4. **Select your subject with either the Auto Selection or Quick Selection tools. If you choose the Quick Selection tool, you can adjust the Brush Size diameter.**

5. **If you need to add or subtract to fine-tune your selection, click the Add or Subtract buttons and brush over your desired areas.**

   Note that the Brush Size diameter slider works for this tool as well.

6. **Move or duplicate your selected subject by dragging it to your desired location. If you want to also scale your subject, drag a corner handle.**

7. **Click the green check mark after you're satisfied with your image.**

8. **Retouch any seams or flaws around your subject, if needed, using the Spot Healing Brush (smaller flaws) or the Clone Stamp Tool (larger flaws) — and you can use both. You can adjust the Brush Size diameter to better eliminate the flaw.**

   For further details on these two tools, see the Chapter 10 sections "Cloning with the Clone Stamp Tool" and "Zeroing in with the Spot Healing Brush."

9. **Click Next.**

10. **Elements now asks you what you would like to do next. Select from:**

    - **Save:** This option simply saves over your original image in the same location on your computer.

    - **Save As:** With this option, you now have the choice of saving your image to the cloud or to your computer. Click Continue, name the file, and click Save.

- **Continue Editing: In Quick or In Expert:** You can choose to continue editing the image in either Quick or Expert mode.

- **Print:** This option transports you to the Fujifilm Print & Gifts website and enables you to order prints, cards, and merchandise.

- **Share:** Share your image to the Flickr or Twitter websites.

11. **Click Done.**

TIP

Two more of our favorite guided edits are covered in detail in Chapter 12, in the section "Using Photomerge." Photomerge Scene Cleaner enables you to eliminate objects like cars and passersby from multiple shots to get a "clean" image. Photomerge Compose lets you easily extract one image and composite it into another.

FIGURE 18-10: Move and scale your subject seamlessly.

© Abassaka/iStockphoto Image #5525490

Chapter **19**

Ten (or So) More Project Ideas

E ven though Elements already gives you a wide array of creations to make — from photo books to greeting cards to slideshows — you can easily do even more with the program. In this chapter, you find ideas for using your inventory of digital images to make your life more productive, more organized, and more fun. This chapter just scratches the surface. Before you know it, your photos will be a part of every aspect of your life, from your clothing to the art on your walls.

Screen Savers

If you have two or more photos you want to use, you can create a screen saver in Windows or macOS. Follow these steps in Windows 10:

1. **Copy the photos you want to see in your screen saver to a new folder.**

2. **Right-click anywhere on the desktop and select Personalize.**

3. **Click Lock Screen in the Setting window and scroll down to the Screen Saver Settings.**

4. **In the Screen Saver Settings window, select Photos in the drop-down menu.**

5. **Click Settings.**

6. **Click Browse and navigate to the folder you created in Step 1 and select the photo.**

7. **Select a slideshow speed from the drop-down menu.**

   Optionally, check Shuffle to randomize the photo order.

8. **Click Save.**

9. **Click the Preview button to test your screen saver.**

10. **Click the arrows to specify the amount of time before your screen saver displays.**

11. **Click OK.**

Mac users can create custom screen savers even more easily:

>> **Choose System Preferences from the Apple menu.**

>> **Click Desktop & Screen Saver and then click the Screen Saver tab.**

>> **Choose a style from the left, and then, on the right, click the Source drop-down menu and select Choose Folder. Select your desired folder and click Choose.**

>> **Specify the options for your screen saver.**

   For example, have it display after a selected amount of time or Show with clock.

>> **Click the Close button in the top-left corner.**

Flyers, Ads, and Online Auctions

Whether you're selling puppies or advertising an open house, adding a photo to an ad or flyer really helps to drive home your message. Here are the abbreviated steps to quickly create an ad or a flyer:

1. **In Expert mode, choose File ⇨ New ⇨ Blank File.**

2. **In the New dialog box, enter your specs and then click OK.**

REMEMBER

   Enter the final dimensions and resolution for your desired output. If you want to print your ad or flyer on your desktop printer or at a service bureau, a good guideline for resolution is 300 pixels per inch (ppi). Leave the color mode as RGB and the Background Contents as White.

   To fill your background with color, as shown in Figure 19-1, choose Edit ⇨ Fill Layer and then choose Color from the Use pop-up menu. Choose your desired color in the Color Picker and then click OK.

3. **Open your photos and then drag and drop them onto your new canvas with the Move tool.**

   Each image is on a separate layer.

TIP

   Choose Window ⇨ Images ⇨ Cascade or Tile to view all your canvases at the same time.

4. **Select the Type tool, click the canvas, add your desired text, and then position your type with the Move tool.**

   Figure 19-1 shows a bevel and drop shadow on the type. If you want to add either or both as well, select your Type layer and, in the Styles panel (choose Window ⇨ Styles or click the Styles icon in the bottom-right corner), choose Drop Shadows or Bevels from the Styles drop-down menu at the top of the panel. Double-click the shadow or bevel of your choice. We chose a Simple Inner bevel and a Soft Edge shadow.

5. **When you're done, choose File ⇨ Save.**

   Choose whether to save your image to the Cloud or on your computer and click Continue.

6. **Name your file, choose Photoshop (.psd) from the Format drop-down list, and make sure that the Layers and ICC Profile (Embed Color Profile on the Mac) check boxes are selected.**

REMEMBER

   If you're taking your document to a copy shop, save your document as a Photoshop PDF (.pdf) file.

7. **(Optional) To save a copy of your ad or flyer in the Organizer, select the Include in the Elements Organizer check box. In addition, select the Layers, ICC Profile (Embed Color Profile on the Mac), and Use Lower Case Extension (Windows only) options.**

8. **Click Save.**

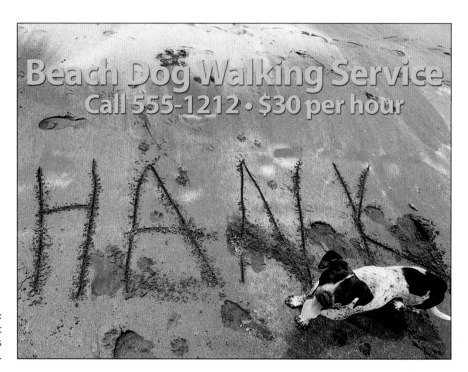

FIGURE 19-1:
Quickly put
together ads
and flyers.

Clothes, Hats, and More

Buy plain, colored T-shirts at your local discount store or plain aprons and
tote bags at a craft or fabric store. Then buy special transfer paper at your office
supply, big-box, or computer store. Print your photos on the transfer paper
(be sure to flip the images horizontally first) and iron the print onto the fabric.
When you're done, you have a personalized gift for very little cash, as shown in
Figure 19-2.

FIGURE 19-2:
Jazz up a plain
T-shirt with art.

Posters

You can get posters and large prints at many copy shops and even your local Costco. Call and talk to a knowledgeable rep so that you know exactly how to pre-pare your file. Here are a few questions to ask:

>> What file format and resolution should the file be?

>> What print sizes do you offer?

>> Do you provide mounting and lamination services?

TIP

Note that online companies such as Shutterfly and CafePress will print your image on everything from cellphone cases to drinkware to beach towels.

Household and Business Inventories

Shoot pictures of your items. In the Organizer, select the image and choose Edit ⇨ Add Caption to include makes, models, purchase dates, and dollar values of each piece. Then create a single PDF document from those multiple files by creating a slide show. Chapter 17 explains how to create the slideshow PDF. After the PDF is finished, you can upload it to cloud storage site or save it to an external drive that's stored somewhere else (in a safe deposit box or other secure location).

Project Documentation

If you're taking a class or workshop, take your camera to class (if the instructor doesn't mind). Documenting the positions or steps of that new yoga, pottery, or gardening class can help you practice or re-create it on your own. Import your desired photos into the Organizer and create notes on each step of the project in the caption area. When you're done, output the images to a PDF slideshow. For details on creating PDF slideshows, see Chapter 17.

School Reports and Projects

Have to write a paper on the habits of the lemurs of Madagascar? Trek down to your local zoo and have a photo shoot. Create a simple collage of lemurs eating, sleeping, and doing the other things that lemurs do. You can use the Photo Collage command on the Create panel, or create a custom collage by making selections (see Chapter 8) and dragging and dropping them onto a blank canvas.

Blogs

Creating a simple blog is a great way to share not only your latest and greatest photos but also recent news about family and friends. Some of the most popular free blogging platforms are `www.blogger.com`, `www.squarespace.com`, `www.wix.com` (all website creators with blogging capabilities), `www.wordpress.com`, `www.tumblr.com`, and `www.medium.com`.

TIP

For info on how to share to social media sites like Twitter and Facebook, see Chapter 16.

Wait — There's More

Before you start taking your photos to the next dimension, consider a few extra ideas: Make fun place cards for dinner party guests; create your own business cards or letterhead; design your own bookmarks, bookplates, and notepads; or label storage boxes with photos of their contents. Check out `www.pinterest.com` and other sites for a slew of projects to do with photos.

Index

Numbers

3D Effect, 283

A

ACR. *See* Camera Raw Editor
Actions, 49–50, 52
active layer, 188
adding to selections, 164
Adjust Facial Features command, 278–280
Adjust Sharpness command, 274
Adjust Smart Fix, 218
adjustment layers, 189, 193–195, 283–286
Adobe Camera Raw. *See* Camera Raw Editor
Adobe Camera Raw profiles, 140–141
Adobe Color profile, 141
Adobe Creative Cloud, 365
Adobe Landscape profile, 141
Adobe Monochrome profile, 141
Adobe Portrait profile, 141
Adobe Premiere Elements, 397
Adobe RGB, 35
Adobe Standard profile, 141
Adobe Vivid profile, 141
ads, 434–436
Airbrush option, 335
albums, 94–97
    creating, 94–96
    editing, 96–97
    sharing, 392
    for temporary work, 96
Aligned option, 230, 232
alignment, text, 366
anchor point, 358
Angle gradient, 344
Angle option, 335
angles, 129, 298
animated content, 282

anti-aliasing, 153, 162, 179, 246
    with Brush tool, 334
    Pencil tool and, 332
    text, 366
aperture, 270
artifacts
    defined, 267
    removing, 268–269
aspect ratio, 210
Aspect settings, 153
auctions, online, 434–436
Auto adjustments, 133
Auto Color Correction command, 221–222
Auto Contrast command, 221
Auto Creation feature, 91–92
Auto Curator, 83
Auto Haze Removal command, 221
Auto Levels command, 220–221
Auto Red Eye Fix command, 223–225
Auto Selection tool, 169–171
Auto Shake Reduction, 222–223
Auto Sharpen, 223
Auto Smart Fix, 218
Auto Smart Tone, 218–220
Auto-Enhance option, 168
automated features, 91–92
    adding new events, 92
    Auto Creation feature, 91–92
Average blur filter, 269–270

B

backgrounds, 327–328
    Background Eraser tool, 177–179
    Background Swatch option, 246
    converting to layers, 186–187
    cutting selections from, 199
    Graphics panel, 308–309
    masking and, 205
    rearranging layers, 189

Remove Background option, 214
Replace Background Guided Edit, 421–423
backing up
    catalogs, 106–107
    photos and files, 107–108
backlit images, 249–250
banding, 344
baseline, 358, 365
Basic panel, 132–135
Behance website, 393
bevels, 306
bit depths, 126
Bitmap mode, 290
black and white adjustments, 133, 257–258
Black Eyedropper tool, 252
blacks, 134
blemishes, 419
blend modes, 309–316, 333
    on Adjustment layers, 195
    darken, 310
    with Fill tool, 341
    HSL (hue, saturation, lightness), 315–316
    inverter, 313–315
    lighten, 310–312
    lighting, 312–313
    overview, 309–310
Bloat tool, 296
blogs, 438
blue color temperature, 265
Blur tool, 241–242
blurring commands, 269–272
Blush slider, 262
bounding box, 202
bracketing, exposure, 322
Brighten Eyes tool, 419
Brightness command, 250–251
Broken Glass texture, 284
Brother printers, 382
bruises, 229–231

Brush tool, 194, 334–336

business inventories, 437

C

calibrating monitor, 33–34

Calibration panel, 138

Camera Connection Kit, 78

Camera Raw Editor, 123–147, 254

  changing image defaults, 143

  file format attributes, 126–127

  filmstrips, 138–140

  launching, 124–125

  opening images in, 127, 143

  panels, 132–138

    Basic panel, 132–135

    Calibration panel, 138

    Detail panel, 135–138

  preferences, 144–147

    changing program defaults, 144–146

    save options, 146

    sidecar files, 146–147

  profiles, 140–142

    Adobe Camera Raw profiles, 140–141

    Favorites list, 142

    managing, 141–142

  tools, 128–131

cameras, 68–70

Canon printers, 382

captions, 113–114

casts, color, 221, 254

catalogs, 103–108

  backing up, 106–108

  Catalog Manager, 104–105

  working with, 105–106

categories, 88

cellphones

  dynamic ranges, 126

  images from, 77–78

  shake and blur from, 280

channels, color, 31–32, 253

cheat sheet, for this book, 3

checkerboard square icon, 190

circular selections, 165

clarity, 134, 267–283

  Adjust Facial Features command, 278–280

  blurring commands, 269–272

  Colorize Photo feature, 275–277

  Moving Overlays enhancement, 280–282

  Moving Photos enhancement, 282–283

  Open Closed Eyes feature, 275

  removing noise, artifacts, dust, and scratches, 268–269

  Shake Reduction command, 280

  sharpening commands, 272–275

  Smooth Skin feature, 277–278

Clipboard, 15, 200

clipping, 129

  masks, 191

  saturation and, 227

Clone Stamp tool, 229–231, 417

close button, 42

clothes, 436–437

color, 31–35

  Auto Color Correction command, 221–222

  calibrating monitor, 33–34

  color cast, 221

  editing, 254–267

    Color Curves, 259–261

    Defringe command, 263–264

    Haze Removal command, 264–265

    Hue/Saturation command, 255–257

    mapping, 266–267

    Photo Filter command, 265–266

    Remove Color Cast command, 254–255

    Remove Color command, 257–258

    Replace Color command, 258–259

    Skin Tone command, Adjust Color, 261–263

  noise reduction, 138

  overview, 31–32

  painting, 327–332

    Color Picker, 328–329

    Color Swatches panel, 329–331

    Eyedropper tool, 331–332

  printing conversions for, 381–386

    Elements managing color, 385

    picture package or contact sheet, 386

    printer managing color, 383–385

  profiles, 35

    saving files with, 19

    stylizing type with, 373–374

    workspace, 34–35

Color Burn blend mode, 310

Color Curves, 259–261

Color Dodge blend mode, 311

Color Picker, 328–329

Color profile, 141

Color Replacement tool, 244–246

Color Swatches panel, 329–331

Colorize Photo feature, 275–277

Comic filter, 299–300

Compose, Photomerge, 324–326

compressed files, 127, 143, 269

contact sheet, 386

Content-Aware Move tool, 236–237

Content-Aware option, 234

context menus, 2, 45

contiguous erasing, 178, 179

Contiguous option, 162, 246

contrast, 134, 137

  Auto Contrast command, 221

  Contrast command, 250–251

Convert to Black and White command, 257–258

Cookie Cutter Tool, 174–176

Cooling Filter, 266

Copy command, 198

Copy Merged command, 198

Correct Camera Distortion filter, 297–298

Correct Skin Tone Guided Edits, 413–415

corrective filters, 291

corrupted catalogs, 105

Create Panel, 50, 401–402

Create Texture option, 234

creations, 401–410

  assembly steps, 402–406

  Create Panel, 401–402

  Memories videos, 408–409

  PDF Slideshow, 409

Quote Graphic, 406–408

cropping, 209–214

    Crop tool, 11, 129, 210–212

    Perspective Crop tool, 212–214

    with selection border, 214

    straightening images and, 215

Cross Process effect, 304

Custom Path tool, 363–364

custom tags, 88–89

D

Darken blend modes, 310

Darken Eyebrows tool, 419

Datacolor Spyder (SpyderX), 34

date/time stamp, 229–231

decontaminating colors, 181

defaults

    changing Camera Raw Editor, 144–146

    changing image, 143

    tags, 89–90

    toggling between current settings and, 131

Defringe command, 263–264

depth of field, 270

desktop printers, 23, 28, 382

Despeckle tool, 268

destructive filters, 291

Detail panel, 135–138

    adjusting noise, 137–138

    sharpening images, 135–137

detail slider, 136

Detail Smart Brush tool, 285–286

Diamond gradient, 344

Difference blend mode, 313

digital drawing tablets, 155, 332

Digital Negative (DNG) format, 125, 145

discontiguous erasing, 178

Discontiguous option, 246

display

    preferences, 57

    resolution, 23–24

Dissolve blend mode, 309

distortions

    correcting camera, 297–298

    Liquify filter, 295

DNG (Digital Negative) format, 125, 145

docked images, 39

documentation, project, 438

Dodge and Burn tools, 238–239

dotPhoto website, 393

Double Exposure Guided Edit, 205, 304

downloading images, 68–70

downsampling, 25

dragging and dropping layers, 200–201

drawing shapes, 350–352

drop shadows, 306

duplicates

    creating layer, 199–200

    searching for, 116

dust, 268–269

dynamic range, 126

E

Edge Extension Scale, 298

editing

    albums, 96–97

    blend modes, 309–316

        darken, 310

        HSL (hue, saturation, lightness), 315–316

        inverter, 313–315

        lighten, 310–312

        lighting, 312–313

        overview, 309–310

    Camera Raw Editor, 123–147

        changing image defaults, 143

        file format attributes, 126–127

        filmstrips, 138–140

        launching, 124–125

        opening images in, 127

        opening non-raw images in, 143

        panels, 132–138

        preferences, 144–147

        profiles, 140–142

        tools, 128–131

    clarity, 267–283

        Adjust Facial Features command, 278–280

        blurring commands, 269–272

        Colorize Photo feature, 275–277

        Moving Overlays enhancement, 280–282

        Moving Photos enhancement, 282–283

        Open Closed Eyes feature, 275

        removing noise, artifacts, dust, and scratches, 268–269

        Shake Reduction command, 280

        sharpening commands, 272–275

        Smooth Skin feature, 277–278

    color, 254–267

        Color Curves, 259–261

        Defringe command, 263–264

        Haze Removal command, 264–265

        Hue/Saturation command, 255–257

        mapping, 266–267

        Photo Filter command, 265–266

        Remove Color Cast command, 254–255

        Remove Color command, 257–258

        Replace Color command, 258–259

        Skin Tone command, Adjust Color, 261–263

    creating versions, 119–120

    cropping, 209–214

        Crop tool, 210–212

        Perspective Crop tool, 212–214

        with selection border, 214

    effects, photo and text, 302–305

    filters

        applying, 290–291

        Correct Camera Distortion filter, 297–298

        corrective or destructive, 291

        fading, 292

        Filter Gallery, 293–294

        Liquify filter, 295–296

        one-step or multistep, 291

        selectively applying, 292–293

        Sketch submenu, 298–302

    layers, 185–207

        converting background to, 186–187

        creating from scratch, 198–199

        dragging and dropping, 200–201

        duplicating, 199–200

        flattening and merging, 206–207

        Layer menu, 191

        Layer via Copy and Layer via Cut commands, 199

        Layers panel, 187–190

editing *(continued)*

  masking, 204–206

  moving content of, 202

  Paste into Selection command, 201

  Select menu, 192

  transforming, 203

  types of, 192–197

lighting, 249–254

  Brightness/Contrast command, 250–251

  Levels command, 251–254

  Shadows/Highlights command, 249–250

minor imperfections, 229–246

  Blur tool, 241–242

  Clone Stamp tool, 229–231

  Color Replacement tool, 244–246

  Content-Aware Move tool, 236–237

  Dodge and Burn tools, 238–239

  Healing Brush tool, 231–233

  Sharpen tool, 242–243

  Smudge tool, 239–241

  Sponge tool, 243–244

  Spot Healing Brush, 234–235

one-step correctors, 218–225

  Auto Color Correction command, 221–222

  Auto Contrast command, 221

  Auto Haze Removal command, 221

  Auto Levels command, 220–221

  Auto Red Eye Fix command, 223–225

  Auto Shake Reduction, 222–223

  Auto Sharpen, 223

  Auto Smart Fix, 218

  Auto Smart Tone, 218–220

Photomerge, 316–326

  Photomerge Compose, 324–326

  Photomerge Exposure, 322–324

  Photomerge Group Shot, 319–320

  Photomerge Panorama command, 316–318

  Photomerge Scene Cleaner, 320–322

Quick Mode, 225–229

recomposing, 215–217

selections, 149–183

  Auto Selection Tool, 169–171

  Cookie Cutter Tool, 174–176

defined, 149–150

Eraser tools, 176–179

Lasso Tools, 154–160

Magic Wand tool, 160–163

modifying, 164–165

Quick Selection Tool, 167–169

rectangular and elliptical, 150–154

Refine Selection Brush, 172–174

Select Menu, 179–183

Select Subject command, 171–172

Selection Brush, 165–167

shapes, 354

Smart Brush Tools, 283–286

straightening, 214–215

  Straighten menu commands, 215

  Straighten tool, 214–215

styles, 305–309

  applying, 305–307

  Graphics panel, 308–309

  working with, 307

text, 366–367

workflow, 248

editing window. *See* Filter Gallery

effects

  Effects panel, 48

  photo and text, 302–305

Elements downloader, 68–70

ellipses

  Geometry options, 353

  selections, 150–154

    Marquee options, 152–154

    perfecting, 151–152

emailing photos, 395–396

emulsion-down printing, 388

Enhance menu, 54–55

Epson printers, 382

Equalize command, 266–267

Eraser tools, 176–179

  Background Eraser tool, 177–179

  Eraser tool, 176–177

  fading filters with, 292

  Magic Eraser tool, 179

events

  adding new, 92

  assigning photos to, 101–102

Exclusion blend mode, 313

Expert mode, 14, 251–254

exposure, 134, 226, 238–239

  bracketing, 322

  Photomerge Exposure, 322–324

Extend mode, 236

eXtensible Markup Language (XML), 88, 144–147

Eyedropper tool, 133, 331–332

eyes, opening closed, 224, 275

F

Face Tilt feature, 279

Facebook, 8, 12–14, 393, 398

Faces feature, Photomerge, 320

Fade option, 335

fading, 292

fastening points, 159

faux styles, 365

Favorites list, 142

feathering selections, 153, 180

files

  creating versions, 119–120

  filenames, 18

    in image windows, 42

    Photo Bin, 52

  flattening layers, 206–207

  formats, 18, 29–31

    Camera Raw, 125

    in Camera Raw Editor, 126–127

    JPEG (Joint Photographic Experts Group), 29–30

    PNG (Portable Network Graphics), 30

    TIFF (Tagged Image File Format), 30–31

  hidden files, 108, 117

  stacking, 118–119

  XML files and preferences, 88, 144–147

    sidecar files, 146–147

    using save options, 146

fill layers, 189, 191, 195–196

filling selections, 339–341

film grain. *See* noise

Film Strip button, 110–111

filmstrips, 138–140

Filter command, Photo, 265–266

Filter Gallery, 293–294

filters, 289–302

applying, 290–291

Correct Camera Distortion filter, 297–298

corrective or destructive, 291

fading, 292

Filter Gallery, 293–294

Liquify filter, 295–296

one-step or multistep, 291

selectively applying, 292–293

Sketch submenu, 298–302

Comic filter, 299–300

Graphic Novel filter, 300–301

Pen and Ink filter, 301–302

stylizing type, 372–373

Finger Painting option, 240

flat images, 257

flattening layers, 206–207

flaws, 229–231

Flickr, 393

floating windows, 39

flow rate, 244

Fluorescent Chalk effect, 302–303

fluorescent lighting, 254

flyers, 434–436

folders

adding images from, 66–68

importing images, 70–71

fonts, 364–365

foreground, 327–328

Free Transform command, 203

fringe, 263–264

f-stops, 126

Full Screen view, 110

Fun Edits, 334, 339

G

gamma, 33, 253

Gaussian Blur filter, 269–270, 274, 292

Geometry options, 350–351, 352–354

custom shapes, 354

Ellipse, 353

Line, 353

Polygon, 353

Rectangle and Rounded Rectangle, 352–353

Star, 353

GIFs, 282–283

glows, 306, 419–420

gradients, 343–347

applying preset, 343–345

customizing, 345–347

with fill layers, 195–196

Gradient Map command, 267

Gradient tool, 194, 204

stylizing type with, 373–374

grain. *See* noise

Granite Flow brush, 373

Graphic Novel filter, 300–301

Graphics panel, 49, 308–309

Gray Eyedropper tool, 253

grayscale images, 73, 244, 253, 256, 300–301

Grayscale mode, 243, 290

Grayscale preset, 299–300

green color cast, 254–255

grid overlay

for cropping, 211

preferences, 57

Group Shot, Photomerge, 319–320

groups, layer, 188–189

Grow command, 183

Grow option, 214

Guided Edits, 8, 413–431

Correct Skin Tone, 413–415

Levels, 424–426

Move & Scale Object, 430–431

Object Removal, 416–418

overview, 53–54

Perfect Portrait, 418–420

Photo Text, 371–372

Photomerge commands, 316–326

Photomerge Compose, 324–326

Photomerge Exposure, 322–324

Photomerge Group Shot, 319–320

Photomerge Panorama command, 316–318

Photomerge Scene Cleaner, 320–322

recomposing, 428–429

Remove Color Cast, 423–424

Replace Background, 421–423

resizing, 426–427

sharpening, 415–416

guideline preferences, 57

H

halftone, 269

halo, 264

Hand tool, 296

hard drive, 44, 64–65

Hard Light blend mode, 313

Hard Mix blend mode, 313

hardware profiling system, 34

hats, 436–437

Haze Removal command, 264–265

Haze Removal command, Auto, 221

Healing Brush tool, 228, 231–233

Healing setting, 236

help resources, 8, 16–17

hidden files, 108, 117

highlights, 134, 202, 227

Auto Smart Fix, 218

Highlight clipping warning, 129

Highlight Skin Tones option, 215–217

Highlights command, 249–250

histogram, 128, 132–133, 251–252

History panel, 14–15, 114

Home Screen, 7–8

horizontal flip, 129

hot spot, 178

household inventories, 437

HP printers, 382

HSL (hue, saturation, lightness) blend modes, 315–316

hue, 227, 246

Hue Jitter option, 335

Hue/Saturation command, 255–257

I

I-beam, 358

ICC (International Color Consortium) Profile, 19

icons

adding to tags, 87–88

Camera Raw Editor, 128–131

Media Browser window, 111–112

in Photo Editor workspace, 37–41

Tools panel, 47

used in this book, 2–3

Image Capture (Mac), 75
Image Size dialog box, 26–27
image window, 41–44
images
 adding to Organizer, 66–71
  downloading camera images with
   Elements downloader, 68–70
  from folders and removable media,
   66–68
  importing additional photos from
   folders, 70–71
 from cellphones and tablets, 77–78
 dimensions, 25
 layers, 187, 192, 197–201
  creating new, 198–199
  dragging and dropping, 200–201
  duplicating layers, 199–200
  Layer via Copy and Layer via Cut
   commands, 199
  Paste into Selection command, 201
 organizing on hard drive, 64–65
 requirements for scanners, 73
importing images, 70–71
Impressionist Brush, 336–337
Indexed Color mode, 290
information box, 43
inkjet printers, 23, 28
inks, 380, 383
inner glows, 306
inner shadows, 306
Instagram, 8, 393
Instant Fix, 84
International Color Consortium (ICC)
 Profile, 19
interpolation process, 203, 298
intersecting selections, 164
inversing selections, 180
Invert command, 267
inverter blend modes, 313–315
Iris settings, 272
Iron-On Transfer option, 388–389
iTunes, 78

J

JPEG (Joint Photographic Experts
 Group), 13, 29–30, 31,
 126–127, 269

K

keyboards
 avoiding key collisions, 165
 keystrokes, 46
keystone distortion, 212–213
keyword tags, 88–89

L

labeling people, 97–99
Landscape profile, 141
Lasso Tools, 154–160
 dragging and dropping layers, 201
 Magnetic Lasso tool, 157–160
 Polygonal Lasso tool, 157
 selecting with, 155–156
Layer menu, 191
Layer Styles. See styles
Layer via Copy and Layer via Cut
 commands, 199
layers, 185–207
 converting background to,
  186–187
 creating from scratch, 198–199
 dragging and dropping, 200–201
 duplicating, 199–200
 Fill tool, 339–341
 filters on, 292–293
 flattening and merging, 206–207
 Layer menu, 191
 Layer via Copy and Layer via Cut
  commands, 199
 Layers panel, 187–190
 masking, 193, 204–206
 moving content of, 202
 Paste into Selection command, 201
 Sample All Layers option, 162
 saving files with, 19
 Select menu, 192
 transforming, 203
 types of, 192–197
  adjustment layers, 193–195
  fill layers, 195–196
  image layers, 192
  shape layers, 196–197
  type layers, 197

Layers panel, 48, 187–190
Layout menu, 40
LCD/LED monitors, 34
leading, 365
lens barrel distortion, 297
Lens Blur filter, 270–272, 274
Levels command, 251–254
Levels Guided Edits, 424–426
libraries, preset, 59–60, 174–176
lighten blend modes, 310–312
lighting, 249–254
 blend modes, 312–313
 Brightness/Contrast command,
  250–251
 Levels command, 251–254
 Shadows/Highlights command,
  249–250
lightness, 255–256
Lightning Adapter, 78
Linear Burn blend mode, 310
Linear Dodge blend mode, 311
Linear gradient, 344
Linear Light blend mode, 313
lines
 art, 73
 geometry option, 353
linking
 layers, 190, 202
 media to Organizer, 103–104
Liquify filter, 278, 295–296
List view, 72
loading
 selections, 183
 swatches, 330
locations, 84, 99–101
locking layers, 190
lossy compression, 127, 143
luminance noise, 268
Luminosity blend mode, 316
LZW compression, 31

M

Mac computers
 backing up to CDs or DVDs, 108
 downloading photos, 66
 resolution on, 23

scanners with, 75

scroll preferences, 42

Magic Eraser tool, 179

Magic Wand tool, 160–163

selecting with, 161–163

tolerance, 161

magnification box, 42

mapping color, 220, 266–267

maps, 99–101

Marching Ants mode, 181

Marquee tools. *See* selections

masking, 136

layers, 189, 204–206

painting with Selection Brush, 166–167

replacing colors with, 258–259

with type, 368–371

Media Browser, 71–72

media cards, 68

Median tool, 268

Memories videos, 84, 408–409

menu command, 2

merging layers, 206–207

metadata, 114–115

midtones, 227, 253

modes, type, 357

Modify commands, 182

moiré pattern, 269

monitors, touchscreen, 72, 248

Monochrome profile, 141

Motion Blur filter, 270, 274, 373

Move & Scale Object Guided Edits, 430–431

Move mode, 236

Move tool, 202

Moving Overlays enhancement, 54–55, 280–282

Moving Photos enhancement, 54–55, 282–283

MP4 files, 282–283

Mpix website, 390

Multiply blend mode, 310

multistep filters, 291

N

Nature effects, 284

noise, 137–138, 242–243, 268–269, 344

non-destructive editing, 126

non-raw images, 143

Normal blend mode, 309

notes, 113–114

O

O (OpenType) font, 365

Object Removal Guided Edits, 416–418

objects, 116–117

Ocean Ripple filter, 292–293

Old Paper texture, 284

Old Print preset, 299–300

On Black and On White mode, 181

one-step correctors, 218–225

Auto Color Correction command, 221–222

Auto Contrast command, 221

Auto Haze Removal command, 221

Auto Levels command, 220–221

Auto Red Eye Fix command, 223–225

Auto Shake Reduction, 222–223

Auto Sharpen, 223

Auto Smart Fix, 218

Auto Smart Tone, 218–220

one-step filters, 291

online auctions, 434–436

online references

Adobe, 16

blogging platforms, 438

cheat sheet for this book, 3

color profiles for printers, 382

DNG converter, 125

photo sharing providers, 393

professional prints, 390

online services, 398–399

onscreen

images, 23

resolution for, 28

opacity

on Adjustment layers, 195

for erased areas, 177

opacity, type, 371–372

Open Closed Eyes feature, 275

Open menu, 38

OpenType (O) font, 365

Organizer, 63–79, 81–102

adding images to, 66–71

downloading camera images with Elements downloader, 68–70

from folders and removable media, 66–68

importing additional photos from folders, 70–71

albums, 94–97

creating, 94–96

editing, 96–97

for temporary work, 96

assigning to events, 101–102

automated features, 91–92

adding new events, 92

Auto Creation feature, 91–92

catalogs, 103–108

backing up, 106–107

backing up photos and files, 107–108

Catalog Manager, 104–105

working with, 105–106

labeling people, 97–99

Media Browser, 71–72

organizing photos and media on hard drive, 64–65

overview, 9, 81–84

photos from cellphones and tablets, 77–78

placing pictures on maps, 99–101

preferences, 79

rating images, 93–94

searching for photos, 111–117

captions and notes, 113–114

by history, 114

metadata, 114–115

similarities, 116–117

untagged items, 113

using Search, 111–113

slideshows, 109–111

tags, 84–89

adding icons to, 87–88

creating and viewing, 85–87

custom tags, 88–89

default tags, 89–90

sorting photos according to, 91

sub-categories, 90

using scanners, 73–77

image requirements, 73

with Mac, 75

for mulitple images, 76–77

plug-ins for Windows, 74–75

viewing options, 108–109

outer glows, 306

outlining, 341

outsourcing printing, 389–390

overexposure, 259

overlays, 166

  Moving Overlays feature, 280–282

  Overlay blend mode, 312

P

Paint Bucket tool, 342–343

painting, 327–354

  choosing color, 327–332

    Color Picker, 328–329

    Color Swatches panel, 329–331

    Eyedropper tool, 331–332

  gradients, 343–347

    applying preset, 343–345

    customizing, 345–347

  Paint Bucket tool, 342–343

  patterns, 348–349

    applying, 348

    creating, 349

  selections, 339–341

    filling, 339–341

    outlining with Stroke command, 341

  shapes, 349–354

    drawing, 350–351

    editing, 354

    Geometry options, 352–354

    multiple, 352

  tools, 332–339

    Brush tool, 334–336

    creating brushes, 337–339

    Impressionist Brush, 336–337

    Pencil tool, 332–334

panels

  Camera Raw Editor, 132–138

    Basic panel, 132–135

    Calibration panel, 138

    Detail panel, 135–138

  Photo Editor, 48–50

Panorama command, Photomerge, 316–318

paper, 381

paragraph type mode, 359–360

Partial Sketch feature, 334

Paste command, 198

Paste into Selection command, 201

path type mode, 360–364

  defined, 356

  using text on Custom Path tool, 363–364

  using text on Selection tool, 360–361

  using text on Shape tool, 362–363

patterns, 232, 348–349

  applying, 348

  creating, 349

  with fill layers, 195–196

  Pattern Brush, 339

PDFs

  files, 206

  slideshow option, 409

Pen and Ink filter, 301–302

Pencil tool, 194, 332–334

people, labeling, 97–99

Perfect Portrait Guided Edits, 278, 418–420

Perspective Crop tool, 212–214

Pet Eye option, 224

Photo Bin, 51–52

  creating different views of image, 51

  Photo Bin Actions menu, 52

  viewing filenames, 52

Photo Editor, 37–60

  creative features, 52–55

    Guided mode, 53–54

    Moving Objects and Moving Photos, 54–55

  features, 37–50

    contextual menus, 45

    creative, 52–55

    image window, 41–44

    panels, 48–50

    selecting tools, 45–48

    selecting tools, Tool Options box, 48

  launching, 9–10

  Photo Bin, 51–52

    creating different views of image, 51

    Photo Bin Actions menu, 52

    viewing filenames, 52

  Preferences dialog box, 55–60

    launching and navigating, 55–56

    panes, 57–58

    preset libraries, 59–60

Photo Filter command, 265–266

Photo Text Guided Edit, 371–372

Photobucket, 393

Photographic effects, 284

Photomerge, 316–326

  Photomerge Compose, 324–326

  Photomerge Exposure, 322–324

  Photomerge Group Shot, 319–320

  Photomerge Panorama command, 316–318

  Photomerge Scene Cleaner, 320–322, 431

Photoshop (PSD) files, 206

Photoshop Elements, 7–20

  concepts, 21–35

    color, 31–35

    file formats, 29–31

    pixels, 22–25

    resampling, 25–28

    resolution for print or onscreen, 28

  help resources on, 16–17

  Home Screen, 7–8

  launching Photo Editor, 9–10

  Photo Editor, 37–60

    features, 37–50, 52–55

    Photo Bin, 51–52

    Preferences dialog box, 55–60

  Quick mode, 10–12

  saving files, 17–20

    Save for Web command, 19–20

    Save/Save As dialog box, 17–19

  sharing options, 391–394

    planning ahead, 392–393

    providers linked with, 393–394

  sharing photos, 12–14

  undo, ways to, 14–16

    History panel, 14–15

    reverting to last save, 15–16

Photoshope PDF, 206

picture package, 386

Pin Light blend mode, 313

pincushion distortion, 297

Pinterest ideas, 438

pixels, 22–25, 349–350

  color pixels, 31

  defringing layers, 263–264

  image dimensions, 25

  Magic Eraser tool, 179

resolution, 22–25
Shift Pixels tool, 296
soft edges and, 153
tolerance and, 161
transforming layers and, 203
plane of focus, 270
plug-ins. *See also* filters
  preferences, 58
  for scanners, 74–75
PNG (Portable Network Graphics), 30
point type mode, 357, 358–359
Polygon shapes, 353
Portrait profile, 141
Post Impressionistic effect, 303
Posterize command, 267
posters, 437
PostScript font, 365
preferences
  Camera Raw Editor, 144–147
    changing program defaults, 144–146
    save options, 146
    sidecar files, 146–147
  dialog box on Photo Editor, 55–60
    launching and navigating, 55–56
    panes, 57–58
    preset libraries, 59–60
  Organizer, 79
presets
  brushes, 166, 177
  colors, 330
  Comic filter, 299–300
  Graphic Novel filter, 300–301
  libraries, 59–60, 174
  sizes for cropping, 210
Print Dialog Box, 386–389
  options, 386–388
  special features, 388–389
printing, 379–390
  color conversions for, 381–386
    Elements managing color, 385
    picture package or contact sheet, 386
    printer managing color, 383–385
  layers, 188
  outsourcing, 389–390
  preparing images for, 380–381

Print Dialog Box, 386–389
  options, 386–388
  special features, 388–389
  resolution for, 23, 28
ProDpi website, 390
profiles
  Camera Raw Editor, 140–142
    Adobe Camera Raw profiles, 140–141
    Favorites list, 142
    managing, 141–142
    overview, 133
  color, 35
projects, 433–438
  blogs, 438
  clothes and hats, 436–437
  flyers, ads, and online auctions, 434–436
  household and business inventories, 437
  Pinterest ideas for, 438
  posters, 437
  project documentation, 438
  school reports and projects, 438
  screen savers, 433–434
Proximity Match option, 234
PSD (Photoshop) files, 206
Pucker tool, 296

Q

Quick mode, 10–12, 215, 225–229, 304
Quick Selection Tool, 167–169
Quote Graphic, 406–408

R

Radial Blur filter, 270
Radial gradient, 344
radius, 136, 181, 273
RAM (random-access memory), 44, 206
raster
  images, 22
  type format, 357
ratings, 83, 93–94
recomposing, 215–217, 428–429
Reconstruct tool, 296

rectangles
  Geometry options, 352–353
  selections, 150–154
    Marquee options, 152–154
    perfecting, 151–152
Red Eye Fix, Auto, 223–225
Red Eye Removal tool, 130, 227
Refine Selection Brush, 172–174, 325
refining edges, 154, 162, 181–182
Reflected gradient, 344
removable media, 66–68
Remove Color Cast command, 254–255
Remove Color Cast Guided Edits, 423–424
Remove Color command, 257–258
Replace Background Guided Edits, 421–423
Replace Color command, 258–259
resampling, 25–28
reselecting selections, 180
resizing
  Guided Edits, 426–427
  Recompose tool, 215–217
resolution, 13
  with cropping, 210
  pixels, 22–25
  for print or onscreen, 28
reverting to last save, 15–16
RGB (red, green, blue) color, 31, 251–252
rotating images, 40, 84, 129, 211
Rounded Rectangle shapes, 352–353
Roundness option, 335
Rule of Thirds, 211
ruler preferences, 57

S

saturation, 227, 243, 246
  in Basics panel, 135
  Saturation command, 255–257
saving, 17–20
  Camera Raw Editor options, 146
  preferences, setting, 57
  Save for Web command, 19–20
  Save/Save As dialog box, 17–19
  selections, 183

Scale Object Guided Edits, 430–431

scanners, 73–77

  image requirements, 73

  with Mac, 75

  for mulitple images, 76–77

  plug-ins for Windows, 74–75

Scatter option, 335

Scene Cleaner, Photomerge, 320–322

school reports and projects, 438

scratch disks, 44, 57, 58

scratches

  removing, 229–231, 268–269

  sizes, 44

Screen blend mode, 310

screen savers, 433–434

scroll bars, 42

searching for photos, 111–117

  captions and notes, 113–114

  by history, 114

  metadata, 114–115

  Search option, 8

  similarities, 116–117

    duplicates, 116

    objects, 116–117

    visually similar photos, 116

  untagged items, 113

  using Search, 111–113

Select Menu, 179–183

  feathering selections, 180

  Grow and Similar commands, 183

  inversing selections, 180

  on layers, 192

  Modify commands, 182

  refining edges of selections, 181–182

  reselecting selections, 180

  saving and loading selections, 183

  selecting all or nothing, 179

Select Subject command, 171–172

Selection Brush, 165–167

Selection tool, 360–361

selections, 149–183

  Auto Selection Tool, 169–171

  Cookie Cutter Tool, 174–176

  cropping with selection border, 214

  defined, 149–150

Eraser tools, 176–179

  Background Eraser tool, 177–179

  Eraser tool, 176–177

  Magic Eraser tool, 179

Fill tool, 339–341

Lasso Tools, 154–160

  Magnetic Lasso tool, 157–160

  Polygonal Lasso tool, 157

  selecting with, 155–156

Magic Wand tool, 160–163

  selecting with, 161–163

  tolerance, 161

modifying, 164–165

  adding to, subtracting from, and intersecting, 164

  avoiding key collisions, 165

painting, 339–341

  filling, 339–341

  outlining with Stroke command, 341

Quick Selection Tool, 167–169

rectangular and elliptical, 150–154

  Marquee options, 152–154

  perfecting, 151–152

Refine Selection Brush, 172–174

Select Menu, 179–183

  feathering selections, 180

  Grow and Similar commands, 183

  inversing selections, 180

  Modify commands, 182

  refining edges of selections, 181–182

  reselecting selections, 180

  saving and loading selections, 183

  selecting all or nothing, 179

Select Subject command, 171–172

Selection Brush, 165–167

shadows, 134, 227

  Auto Smart Fix, 218

  drop and inner, 306

  Shadow clipping warning, 129

  Shadows/Highlights command, 249–250

Shake Reduction command, 280

Shake Reduction command, Auto, 222–223

Shape tool, 362–363

shapes, 349–354

  drawing, 350–351

  editing, 354

  Geometry options, 352–354

    custom shapes, 354

    Ellipse, 353

    Line, 353

    Polygon, 353

    Rectangle and Rounded Rectangle, 352–353

    Star, 353

  layers, 191, 196–197, 350

  multiple, 352

  with path type mode, 360–364

    using text on Custom Path tool, 363–364

    using text on Selection tool, 360–361

    using text on Shape tool, 362–363

Share Panel, 50, 394–399

  Adobe Premiere Elements, 397

  emailing photos, 395–396

  social networks, 397–399

    Facebook and Twitter, 398

    online services, 398–399

sharing photos, 12–14, 391–399

  Elements sharing options, 391–394

    planning ahead, 392–393

    providers linked with, 393–394

  Share Panel, 394–399

    Adobe Premiere Elements, 397

    emailing photos, 395–396

    social networks, 397–399

sharpening

  Auto Sharpen, 223

  commands, 272–275

  in editing workflow, 267–268

  Guided Edits, 415–416

  images, 135–137

  Sharpen tool, 242–243

shield area, 211

Shift Pixels tool, 296

Shrink option, 214

Shutterfly, 393

sidecar files, 146–147

Similar command, 183
similarities, 116–117
  duplicates, 116
  objects, 116–117
  visually similar photos, 116
simplifying
  layers, 196
  type, 357, 367–368
sizes, preset, 210
Sketch submenu, 298–302
  Comic filter, 299–300
  Graphic Novel filter, 300–301
  Pen and Ink filter, 301–302
skin
  Correct Skin Tone Guided Edits,
    413–415
  Skin Tone command, Adjust Color,
    261–263
  Smooth Skin feature, 277–278
SlickPic website, 393
slideshows, 109–111, 392, 409
Smart Blur filter, 270
Smart Brush Tools, 283–286
Smart Fix, 10–11
Smart Radius option, 181
smartphones
  dynamic ranges, 126
  images from, 77–78
  shake and blur from, 280
smoothness, 138
Smudge tool, 239–241
SmugMug website, 393
snap strength, 173
social networks, 397–399
  Facebook and Twitter, sharing photos
    on, 398
  online services, 398–399
Soft Light blend mode, 313
soft-edged selections, 150, 153
Spacing option, 335
Special Effect adjustments, 286
specular highlights, 272
Sponge tool, 243–244
Spot Healing Brush tool, 228,
    234–235, 417
SpyderX (Datacolor Spyder), 34
square selection, 165

sRGB color, 34–35
stacking
  images, 118–119
  order, 187, 189
Stamp tool, Pattern, 349
Standard profile, 141
Star shapes, 353
stock images, 308
straightening, 214–215
  with Polygonal Lasso tool, 157
  Straighten menu commands, 215
  Straighten tool, 214–215
strikethrough, 365
Stroke command, 341
strokes, 306, 333
styles, 49, 305–309
  applying, 305–307
  Graphics panel, 308–309
  resampling, 27
  for type, 366
  type, 371–375
    applying filters, 372–373
    color and gradients, 373–374
    opacity, 371–372
    warping, 374–375
  working with, 307
styluses, 155, 159, 335
sub-categories, 88, 90
Subject command, Select, 171–172
subtracting from selections, 164
Sunny Day preset, 299–300
Surface Blur filter, 270

T

tablets
  images from, 77–78
  Pencil and Brush tools, 332, 335
  stylus pressure, 159
Tagged Image File Format (TIFF),
    30–31, 206
tags, 84–89
  adding icons to, 87–88
  creating and viewing, 85–87
  custom tags, 88–89
  default tags, 89–90

searching for untagged items, 113
sorting photos according to, 91
sub-categories, 90
Tan slider, 262
telephoto lenses, 297
temperature slider, 134, 227, 262
temporary work albums, 96
texture, 231, 284
themes, 403, 408–409
3D Effect, 283
Threshold command, 267
thumbnails, 19
TIFF (Tagged Image File Format),
    30–31, 206
time stamp, 229–231
timelines, 108–109
tint, 134, 227, 256
Tk (Typekit) font, 365
tolerance, 246
  erasing and, 179
  Magic Wand tool, 161–163
  overview, 161
Tone, Auto Smart, 218–220
tools
  Camera Raw Editor, 128–131
  cursor settings, 57
  painting, 332–339
    Brush tool, 334–336
    creating brushes, 337–339
    Impressionist Brush, 336–337
    Pencil tool, 332–334
  Photo Editor toolbox, 39
  selecting, 45–48
  Tool Options box, 48
  type, 356
tooltips, 17
touchscreen monitors, 72, 248
Toy Camera effect, 304
Traditional Oil effect, 303
transforming layers, 203
transparency
  Magic Eraser tool, 179
  preferences, 57
Tree view, 72
TT (TrueType) font, 365
Twirl Clockwise tool, 295

Twirl Counterclockwise tool, 295

Twitter, 8, 393, 398

type, 355–375

  editing text, 366–367

  formats, 357

  layers, 197

  masking with, 368–371

  modes, 357

  options, 364–366

  paragraph type, 359–360

  path type, 360–364

    using text on Custom Path tool, 363–364

    using text on Selection tool, 360–361

    using text on Shape tool, 362–363

  point type, 358–359

  preferences, 58

  simplifying, 367–368

  stylizing, 371–375

    applying filters, 372–373

    color and gradients, 373–374

    opacity, 371–372

    warping, 374–375

  tools, 356

Typekit (Tk) font, 365

U

underlining, 365

undo, 14–16, 40

  History panel, 14–15

  reconstructing, 296

  reverting to last save, 15–16

undocked images, 39

unit preferences, 57

unlinking layers, 190, 205

unlocking layers, 190

Unsharp Mask command, 272–273

unstacking images, 118–119

updates, 58

uploading images, 78

upsampling, 25

V

vectors

  defined, 350

  images, 22

  shapes based on, 196

  type format, 357

Version Set, 19

versions, 119–120

vertical flip, 129

vibrance, 134, 227

videos, Memories, 393, 408–409

views

  creating different image, 51

  switching on Organizer, 108–109

vignette, 297–298

Vimeo website, 393

visibility, 306

Vivid Light blend mode, 313

Vivid profile, 141

W

Warming Filter, 266

warping

  effects, 239

  type, 366, 374–375

  Warp tool, 295

waves

pattern, 269

  Wave filter, 292–293

web

  graphics, 19–20, 28, 126

  hexadecimal color formula, 332

  web-safe colors, 329

WHCC website, 390

white balance, 133, 266

White Eyedropper tool, 252

Whiten Teeth tool, 227–228, 419

whites, 134

wide-angle lenses, 297

Windows

  downloading photos, 66

  plug-ins for scanners, 74–75

  resolution on, 23

  saving files with thumbnails, 19

workspace colors, 34–35

wrapping text, 359–360

X

XML (eXtensible Markup Language), 88, 144–147

XMP files, 146–147

Y

yellow color temperature, 265

Yellowed Photo effects, 284

YouTube, 393

Z

ZIP compression, 31

zoom lenses, 297

zoom levels, 23–24, 42, 130

Zoom tool, 296

About the Authors

Barbara Obermeier: Barbara is the principal of Obermeier Design, a graphic design studio in Ventura, California. She is the author of the *Photoshop All-in-One For Dummies* series and has contributed as author or co-author on more than 30 books on Adobe Photoshop, Adobe Photoshop Elements, Adobe Illustrator, Microsoft PowerPoint, and digital photography for John Wiley & Sons, Inc., Peachpit Press, and Adobe Press. She is currently a Lecturer in the Visual Arts Department at California Lutheran University in Thousand Oaks, California.

Ted Padova: Ted is semi-retired; he still writes and teaches some photo classes. He has written more than 65 computer books on subjects such as Adobe Photoshop, Adobe Photoshop Elements, Adobe Acrobat, Adobe Illustrator, and Adobe InDesign.

Authors' Acknowledgments

We would like to thank our excellent project editor, Susan Christophersen, who kept us on track throughout the development of this work; Steve Hayes, our executive editor; Doug Sahlin, technical editing wizard, who made what we wrote sound better; and all the dedicated production staff at Wiley.

Barbara Obermeier: A special thanks to Ted Padova, my co-author and friend, who always reminds me there is still a 1 in 53 million chance that we can win the lottery.

Ted Padova: First and foremost, I'd like to thank Barbara Obermeier for asking me to join her in this journey on exploring Photoshop Elements —now in our 17th collaboration on this project. Also, special thanks to Bernadette Baro, Dina Lopez, Camille Sedar, and Cindy De Vera for modeling. A very special thank you to my lovely niece Courtany Jensen for her photo contribution.

Publisher's Acknowledgments

Executive Editor: Steven Hayes

Project and Copy Editor: Susan Christophersen

Production Editor: Tamilmani Varadharaj

Cover Image: © Composite image provided by Barbara Obermeier